Walking with God

Walking
with God

Prayers and Promises from the Bible
for Each Day of the Year

Mike Beaumont and
Martin Manser

eagle

Eagle Publishing, Atworth, Wiltshire

Typeset by Eagle Publishing Ltd
Printed by Mackays of Chatham
ISBN No: 0 86347 596 5 (Hardback)
ISBN No: 0 86347 627 9 (Paperback)

CONTENTS

Introduction

'Good morning, ladies and gentlemen. This is your Captain, Mark Rogers, speaking. My co-pilot today is First Officer, Bob Johnson. We'll be flying at a height of 35,000 feet and our expected time of arrival in Frankfurt is 1300 hours. The weather there is mild, but cloudy. In the meantime, sit back, enjoy the flight, and the cabin crew will be happy to look after you.'

Many of us are used to being welcomed aboard a flight by such words. And in a similar sort of way, we both want to welcome you as you join us in this daily devotional guide. May we introduce ourselves: your pilot Mike Beaumont (pastor) and co-pilot Martin Manser (reference-book editor). We've written this book together to help you in your journey with God.

Just as a plane journey sometimes has its turbulent moments, so we know that life too can have its ups and downs. We've written this book out of an absolute conviction that God is with us in such times. God doesn't want us to separate our spiritual lives from the rest of our life, but to take him with us in those times of illness, hardship, bereavement or difficulty – and, of course, to do just the same in life's joys!

This book covers, for each of day of the year, prayers and promises from the Bible, though we have developed those promises and prayers to cover wider themes too. Our aim is quite simple: to help you meet with God! He is the God of the promises. He is the God who inspires our praying. He is the One we can turn to in every situation in life: when we are puzzled, when we find it difficult to carry on, when we need guidance and help, and when we are just simply grateful. Each day's reading begins with an opening verse from the Bible which we then consider in the main body of the text, closing with a final Bible verse. Sometimes other Bible extracts are also quoted, and every book in the Bible is drawn from over the year. We suggest that if possible you find a quiet place where you can let go of the busyness of life for a few moments and quieten your spirit to be still, to listen and to talk to God, as you think over and pray about what is in the day's reading.

The readings are based on our two Eagle handbooks: *The Eagle Handbook of Bible Promises* and *The Eagle Handbook of Bible Prayers*, but we have elaborated on these and the readings are not simple cut-and-paste extracts.

Sometimes we are asked how we work together. On Bible Promises, Martin was the pilot (he wrote the main text) and Mike was the co-pilot (he edited and expanded the text); on Bible Prayers it was the other way round, with Mike piloting (writing) and Martin as co-pilot (editing). On this particular title, Mike is pilot and wrote most of the readings and Martin has been co-pilot (writer of a few readings and editor). We always discuss any points where we may differ slightly in understanding and we both agree on the final texts. This is important to us as we have different temperaments and slightly different outlooks. We both dislike the use of labels to define our Christian stance and perspective, but we are both firmly evangelical. Mike is more outgoing and 'charismatic'; Martin is quieter (usually!) and more cautious. We also sometimes refer to our own experiences. This is not meant to 'blow our own trumpet' in any way, as we are each very aware of how limited and weak we are in ourselves. But we have chosen to open up to you something of our own personalities and outlooks and some of our life experiences, in the hope that these might be helpful in bringing the Bible alive.

It is our prayer that this book will help you in your life with God to give you light, strength and inspiration each day of the year. So, please, sit back, enjoy the flight, and the God of the Bible will be happy to look after you!

Mike Beaumont
Martin Manser

All things have become new

*If anyone is in Christ, he is a new creation; old things have
passed away; behold, all things have become new.*
(2 CORINTHIANS 5:17, NKJV)

There are probably few of us who don't find the birth of a baby a moving
event. Grown adults suddenly become cooing and gurgling idiots and our
faces contort into all sorts of expressions before the presence of new life.
Perhaps it's the baby's freshness, or helplessness; or the fact that
everything just seems so perfect. Little wonder, then, that there are times
when we say, 'If only I could start again.' 'If only my mistakes could be
wiped out; if only the messes could be undone; if only I could have
another chance at life.' Jesus says, 'You can!' When we put our trust in
him, a whole new life begins for us; the past really is over and done with,
and we have a fresh, new start. We truly become 'a new creation' (2
Corinthians 5:17).

These new beginnings do not happen by self-effort or self-
improvement, however, but by new birth (John 3:3); and then we
continue to enjoy that 'new birth' life by being constantly 'filled with the
Spirit' (Ephesians 5:18). No matter what a mess we may have made of our
lives so far, no matter how many times we might have 'got it wrong', God
can always give us a new beginning. If you have put your trust in Christ,
you really are 'a new creation' and do not need to listen to the accusations
of your heart or the lies of the devil.

The psalmist says, 'He put a new song in my mouth, a hymn of praise
to our God' (Psalm 40:3). Last year probably had its difficult moments in
your life; but, like the psalmist, let a new song of worship and adoration
to the Lord well up within your spirit as you launch out into this new year
with him; for what *has been* does not have to shape what *will be*!

At the outset of this New Year, how wonderful it is to know we can
always make a fresh start with our God!

*And He who sits on the throne said,
'Behold, I am making all things new.'*
(REVELATION 21:5, NASB)

The God who speaks

I will listen to what God the LORD will say.
(PSALM 85:8)

As inheritors of Greek thinking, westerners tend to keep the 'spiritual' separate from the 'secular'. God and religion are in one box; 'real life' is in the other. Because of this, western Christianity has often had little expectation of God reaching out of his 'box' into everyday life, and faith has often become entirely 'otherworldly'. But this isn't the God of the Bible! For there God is revealed as fully involved in his world, speaking and acting. Our God is the God who speaks! The challenge is: are we listening?

God has promised, 'Call to me and I will answer you and tell you great and unsearchable things you do not know' (Jeremiah 33:3). This truth that God wants to speak to us is amazing, as Moses expressed when he said, 'The LORD our God has shown us his glory and his majesty, and we have heard his voice from the fire. Today we have seen that a man can live even if God speaks with him' (Deuteronomy 5:24). To heighten this fact that God speaks, he is often contrasted with dumb idols which 'have mouths, but cannot speak, eyes, but they cannot see; they have ears, but cannot hear, noses, but they cannot smell; they have hands, but cannot feel, feet, but they cannot walk; nor can they utter a sound with their throats' (Psalm 115:5–7).

But not only does God speak; he speaks 'in many and various ways' (Hebrews 1:1), through things like audible voices (e.g. 1 Samuel 3:1–10; Matthew 3:16–17), visions (e.g. Genesis 15:1; Acts 9:10–16), dreams (e.g. Genesis 28:10–17; Matthew 2:19–23), pictures (e.g. Jeremiah 1:11–17; Amos 8:1–2), angels (e.g. Judges 6:11–22; Luke 1:26–38), circumstances (e.g. 2 Chronicles 36:22–23; Acts 16:6–10), revelation (e.g. 2 Samuel 7:17; Revelation 1:1), the Scriptures (e.g. 2 Kings 22:11–13; 2 Timothy 3:16–17).

What does all this tell us? That, in contrast to dumb idols, God really does wants to speak to people – and that includes you today! He is speaking! Are you listening?

'Of what value is an idol, since a man has carved it? … It is covered with gold and silver; there is no breath in it. But the LORD is in his holy temple; let all the earth be silent before him.'
(HABAKKUK 2:18–20)

January 3

The eternal God

Now to the King eternal, immortal, invisible, the only God, be honour and glory for ever and ever. Amen.
(1 TIMOTHY 1:17)

We live in a rapidly changing world where things move on and get out of date so quickly. Look, for example, at any pre-packed foodstuff and you'll find it has a 'sell-by' date. This is the final date by which the product must be sold to ensure its freshness; and after this date, the shop must take it off the shelf and discard it. Often the product will also have a 'best before' date too, to ensure that you eat it while it's still at its best. (They don't want you coming back complaining that it's 'gone off'!)

Or consider the world of technology, where 'the latest model' replaces the previous one almost before it's off the shelf. In fact, things change so rapidly these days that it's hardly worth worrying about whether you're getting the best deal, for you can be sure that by tomorrow there will be another 'best deal'!

In the light of this, how wonderfully reassuring it is to remember that our God is 'the eternal God' (Genesis 21:33). He has no 'sell-by' date, after which he is unmarketable; no 'best before' date, after which you can't be sure if he's at his best; no replacement model to surpass him. He is eternal! Not only does this mean that he is without beginning and without end (for that in itself might be rather boring); it means that he is unchanging and dependable, yet up-to-date and ever new.

It is because he is eternal that everything about him is eternal. He shows 'eternal love' (1 Kings 10:9) and gives 'eternal blessings' (Psalm 21:6); his kingdom is 'an eternal kingdom' (Daniel 4:3) and his gift to men and women is 'eternal life' (John 3:16); he is 'from all eternity' (Psalm 93:2) and provides for us 'an eternal home' (Ecclesiastes 12:5).

Remembering that God is eternal makes a difference to life. So don't be small-minded or short-term in your thinking; your God is eternal - and so are his purposes for you. And today, he wants to carry you further into those purposes with him.

The eternal God is our hiding place; he carries us in his arms.
(DEUTERONOMY 33:27, CEV)

JANUARY 4

Praying from promises

The 'yes' to all of God's promises is in Christ.
(2 CORINTHIANS 1:20, NCV)

'I promise to pay the bearer on demand the sum of (ten) pounds,' Bank of England notes proclaim. That promise, backed by the signature of the Bank's Governor (and a host of anti-fraud designs and devices!), is what guarantees that our piece of paper is worth something. And that's exactly what the promises of God are like. They are God's promises with Jesus' signature – Jesus' 'Yes!' – on them; and that's what makes them so valuable when it comes to prayer. When we pray on the basis of these promises, we can be sure we are on firm ground.

It starts with being sure of the *God of the promises*. All effective prayer goes hand in hand with discovering more about him. The best place to start is the Bible, for it is here like nowhere else that God reveals to us what he is like, how he acts, and what his plans are. As we become more sure of the God of the promises, the more sure we become of *the promises of God*. It is because God is so truthful, faithful and dependable that we can trust the promises he makes. God has made plain in his word that when he makes a promise, it is there to be claimed; when he speaks a word, it will surely come to pass and that 'it will not return to me empty, but will accomplish what I desire and achieve the purpose for which I sent it (Isaiah 55:11).

Again and again people in the Bible appealed to God's promises. They said, 'Oh God, I'm reminding you of what you said … And because you are a faithful God, I'm calling on you to fulfil that promise right now.' Such prayers were daring; but they were also on solid ground, for it was to God's own promises that they were appealing. This was not arrogance, but confidence!

Such confidence is not just for people of Bible times; it can be ours also. Whenever we pray like they did, calling on the God of the promises to fulfil the promises of God, we can be sure that our prayers will be effective and powerful.

Let us hold unswervingly to the hope we profess,
for he who promised is faithful.
(HEBREWS 10:23)

Think about that!

*May the words of my mouth and the meditation of my heart be
pleasing in your sight, O LORD, my Rock and my Redeemer.*
(PSALM 19:14)

Life is so busy these days that most of us rarely take time to stop and
think. We know we ought to and need to; but the demands of each day,
whether in the family or at work, just seem to press in and crowd out the
space to truly stop and think. But stopping and thinking is exactly what
the Bible encourages us to do!

The Bible invites us to stop and think through 'meditation' (or
'contemplation', as some Christian writers have described it). Meditation
is about reflecting on something in depth and at length. It's about
deliberately focusing on 'one thing' (Luke 10:42) in order to shut the
door to everything else that would crowd into our thoughts. The Bible
suggests three things we can meditate upon: first, God's word: 'on his law
he meditates day and night' (Psalm 1:2); second, God's love: 'we meditate
on your unfailing love' (Psalm 48:9); third, God's works: 'I will meditate
on all your works and consider all your mighty deeds' (Psalm 77:12). We
can do this through perhaps focusing on just one verse of Scripture or one
aspect of God's nature or even one object.

Meditation seeks to draw close to God to 'contemplate' him and be
drawn deeper into his love, understanding that it is not a 'technique' but
an expression of relationship, and that only in that relationship can our
deepest longings be satisfied. Meditation sees God as a deep ocean to be
explored rather than a divine 'Father Christmas' to be used. As Catherine
of Siena, a 14th-century Dominican Sister, expressed it: 'O eternal
Trinity! O Godhead! You are a deep sea, into which the deeper I enter the
more I find, and the more I find the more I seek.'

OK, so your life is busy. But why not take a few minutes today to stop
and meditate? Your God is wonderful; think about that!

*'Do not let this Book of the Law depart from your mouth; meditate on it
day and night, so that you may be careful to do everything written in it.
Then you will be prosperous and successful.'*
(JOSHUA 1:8)

JANUARY 6

Doing it right

God opposes the proud but gives grace to the humble.
(JAMES 4:6)

It started early one Saturday when Mike needed to repair a toilet cistern. Of course, the easiest way would have been to hire a plumber; but plumbers don't come cheap! So Mike went and bought the required part and started the job. As the morning unfolded, various fittings proved not to fit, one new part led to the need for another, and one joint obstinately refused to seal (witness the wet bathroom floor). Nine hours later (!) Mike swallowed his pride and phoned one of his church members (who was rather better at D-I-Y!) who promptly rushed to the rescue. Twenty minutes later, the job was done!

Doing things right is always so much easier, isn't it? And prayer is no different. By that we don't mean that prayer must be done in a particular way. Prayer is about *a relationship* with God, and so it has many different expressions and no one way is 'right'. Nevertheless, there are certain 'tools' that help to get the job done.

The first tool is knowing that *the heart is more important than the words*. It doesn't matter if we can't get the right words out; as long as our heart is in it, God loves our prayer! words, as the parable of the Pharisee and the tax collector reminds us (Luke 18:9–14), are nowhere near as important as the heart. The second tool is knowing that *the content is more important than the format*. God really isn't interested in the beauty or structure of the language, but in the content of what we say. He wants us to talk to him in our own words and in our own way, no matter how simple that might be. The third tool is knowing that *growing is more important than getting*. So often, we come to God because we want to 'get' something; but God is far more interested in our spiritual growth than in simply giving us all we ask for.

Thankfully, prayer isn't a job where we need an expert to do it for us. God has put the necessary tools into all our hands. If we use them, then we are well on the way to 'getting the job done'. Better get started then…

Be clear minded and self-controlled so that you can pray.
(1 PETER 4:7)

JANUARY 7

Knowing Christ

All I want is Christ.
(PHILIPPIANS 3:8, CEV)

In these early days of January, after the excitement of Christmas and New Year is over, the days can sometimes seem difficult; and if you're in the northern hemisphere, then they can be cold and dark as well. At the time of writing, Martin's daughter has just booked a visit to Australia for three months to escape the winter; but changing hemisphere isn't normally a possibility for most of us!

So what can we focus on at such times? In a word, Christ! Paul's deepest longing was to know Christ. When he wrote these words, he was imprisoned. If we'd been him, we would have wanted to escape from prison so we could then 'get our act together' for Christ. But no, Paul stayed where he was, prison and all, confident that Christ was right there with him. Wherever he was, his focus was Christ.

So here are two tips to help us focus on Christ too. First, do you remember the days of slide projectors when we had to adjust the picture to get it clearly focused? We need to do the same with our spiritual life. All the time, things get thrown at us in life; and they tend to make our spiritual perception fuzzy and out of focus, so that our vision of Christ all too easily becomes faint. This is where the great value of a personal daily devotional time and of weekly corporate worship come in: they help keep our vision of Christ clear, sharp and focused.

Secondly, we need to keep alive our devotion to Christ. Books on marriage remind us of the need for romance in the marriage relationship – and that means doing things that keep the relationship alive. The same is true spiritually. Martin finds that reading hymns helps keep alive his love for the Lord; Mike enjoys singing along to worship tapes. Others find watching Christian TV or reading Christian books or walking in the wonders of God's creation helpful. Do whatever you need to do, whatever suits your personality and temperament; but keep the fire of your love for Christ burning fervently and constantly.

Today, let Christ be your focus, let him be your passion.

'We would like to see Jesus.'
(JOHN 12:21)

January 8

The promised presence

*Even though I walk through the valley of the shadow of death,
I will fear no evil, for you are with me, your rod and your staff,
they comfort me.*
(Psalm 23:4)

Let's face it, none of us likes going through hard times – and given the choice, we would certainly rather have a smooth and comfortable journey through life. Yet if there is one thing that we can all be fairly sure of encountering, it is 'hard times' – and if we don't, then we shall have been very fortunate indeed! But for most of us, we can be reasonably certain that, at some point or other, we will face illness, or pain, or bereavement, or redundancy, or marital or financial problems, or family strains … the list could go on. And, whether we face those things or not, the one thing that all of us can be certain of facing one day is death.

But in the face of all these challenges of life God makes a promise. It is a promise to always *be there*, to always be *with us* in every situation we face. In fact, the Bible is full of promises that God will encourage us in times of difficulty, comfort us in times of sorrow, strengthen us in times of weakness, help us in time of need. This is what people in the Bible discovered time and again. David went through some dreadful experiences on his journey to fulfil his call to be king; but he found God's promised presence in them all and discovered that, 'Even though I walk through the valley of the shadow of death, I will fear no evil, for you are with me' (Psalm 23:4). Paul faced all sorts of hardships on his journey to fulfil his call to be an apostle; but he too found God's promised presence in them all, discovering for himself that 'my grace is sufficient for you, for my power is made perfect in weakness' (2 Corinthians 12:9).

Today, whatever situations we may be facing – in health, or relationships, or circumstances – the promised presence of the Lord can be found. We only need to ask him to keep that promise!

The following night the Lord stood near Paul . . .
(Acts 23:11)

Change indeed

'Today salvation has come to this house, because this man, too, is a son of Abraham. For the Son of Man came to seek and to save what was lost.'
(LUKE 19:9–10)

The 'tax man' in New Testament Times was hated even more than today, for the tax system was open to blatant abuse. A rich man bought the right to gather taxes for a particular area in exchange for a fixed payment to Rome. For Rome, this had the advantage of getting taxes 'up front'; for the tax collector, of having Rome and its soldiers now support his tax demands on others – including the surcharge added for his profit. This is how Zacchaeus had spent his life and had become very rich through it.

But when Jesus called him from the tree that he had climbed into to see this passing rabbi, Zacchaeus found his whole life touched – and, with it, his money. Proof of change indeed! He said, 'Here and now I give half of my possessions to the poor, and if I have cheated anybody out of anything, I will pay back four times the amount' (Luke 19:8). Can you imagine the cheer that went up in Jericho that day!

While we certainly cannot buy God's favour, showing that we have truly changed will sometimes cost us. For Zacchaeus, it meant giving back what he had cheated people out of; for converts in Ephesus, it meant burning their expensive parchment scrolls about sorcery – fifty thousand drachmas' worth (and since a drachma was a day's wage, that was a huge sum!). But whenever we take this sort of step, there is always a great sense of 'salvation coming to our house', just like Zacchaeus experienced. Sometimes the cost of change seems just too much for some people, like the rich young man who, rather than owning his money, as he thought, found that it owned him and that he could not let it go, and so 'went away sad' (Matthew 19:22).

If God has been challenging you to change in some way, don't go away sad like the rich young man; take the risk, like Zacchaeus, and bring joy to yourself and to others.

'If you want to be perfect, go, sell your possessions and give to the poor, and you will have treasure in heaven. Then come, follow me.'
(MATTHEW 19:21)

The unchanging one

Jesus Christ is the same yesterday and today and for ever.
(HEBREWS 13:8)

We live in a world where things are rapidly changing – so rapidly that at times it is hard to keep up. Consider how computers are now part of everyday life, whereas two decades ago they were still quite rare. Or think about mobile phones: not only now does every young person in the West seem to have one, but they are almost as commonplace on a crowded bus in Kenya or a heaving train in India. Yes, things are certainly changing.

Of course, change is not always for the better, is it? There was a time when we could always trust our pension company, but not any longer; there was a time when we could always trust our employer to provide a job for life, but not any longer; there was a time when we could always trust people who worked with children, but not any longer. The prevailing philosophical view of 'the ascent of man' – the steady, upward progress of the human race – now somehow seems rather shaky. Yes, things have certainly changed.

In the midst of a changing world – both for good and for bad – there is one who never changes, however – and that is Jesus. He is just as faithful, just as dependable, just as kind, just as powerful as he ever was. And because he is the same, he can still meet our needs as much as he ever did. For this Jesus is the *eternal* Son of God, the one who was at the Father's side from before the beginning of time, and so is *eternally* relevant.

You may be facing all sorts of change at this time. But the promise of God is that his unchanging son is with you, bringing to you his unchanging power and purposes for your life. Today, focus not on what is changing all around you, but on him, the unchanging one.

Because God wanted to make the unchanging nature of his purpose very clear to the heirs of what was promised, he confirmed it with an oath. God did this so that, by two unchangeable things in which it is impossible for God to lie, we who have fled to take hold of the hope offered to us may be greatly encouraged.
(HEBREWS 6:17–18)

JANUARY 11

What an inspiration!

All Scripture is God-breathed and is useful for teaching,
rebuking, correcting and training in righteousness, so that the
man of God may be thoroughly equipped for every good work.
(2 TIMOTHY 3:16–17)

One of the reasons we wrote this book (and *The Eagle Handbook of Bible Promises* and *The Eagle Handbook of Bible Prayers* on which it is partly based) is that we love the Bible! We love its stories; we love its truth; we love its revelation about the Father's heart. But not only do we love it, we trust it – and that for one simple reason: it was God himself who was the inspiration behind it; God himself who caused it to be written.

How did he do this? First, he inspired *the writers*. They 'spoke from God as they were carried along by the Holy Spirit' (2 Peter 1:21). The word used for 'carried along' was used of a ship carried along on the sea by the wind. That is how the Scriptures were written; the writers, as it were, 'hoisted their sails' to the Holy Spirit, and were 'carried along' by him, so that what they wrote was exactly what he wanted written. Second, he inspired *the writings*. The words of Scripture are, our verse for today tells us, the very 'breath' of God, timeless truth caught in time by the inspiring work of the Holy Spirit. But then, having done all this, there is a third stage: he inspires *the readers* – us! For without the Spirit's help, the Bible remains a 'closed book'; a fascinating, but not very relevant, piece of ancient literature. But with the Spirit's help, this book comes alive, as it reveals God's heart, purposes, and ways, just as God promised it would.

So as you use this book of ours, reading each day's Scripture verses, don't read it just like any other book. What you are reading is drawn from the inspired word of God! God is sharing his heart with you! And as you read it, God promises it will do its work in you – its work of 'teaching, rebuking, correcting and training in righteousness' – so that *you* can be 'thoroughly equipped' for all the good work that God has for you. Go out today, inspired and strengthened by the word of God.

> *. . . the sword of the Spirit, which is the word of God.*
> (EPHESIANS 6:17)

JANUARY 12

Revival!

*Will you not revive us again, that your people may
rejoice in you?*
(PSALM 85:6)

'Revival' should be a word that excites us all. As we read of revivals,
historical or current, our hearts are hopefully stirred with a longing that
cries out to God to bring revival here. There has been much debate over
whether we should be praying for *renewal*, *revival*, or *restoration*; or
whether we have been through one phase and are entering another. The
more pragmatic approach simply says that, whatever our nation needs, we
want it! We want to see the church come even more alive so that prodigals
come home, sinners are saved, and the nation is changed.

One of the best known revival promises comes from when God spoke
to Solomon at the temple's dedication: 'If my people, who are called by
my name, will humble themselves and pray and seek my face and turn
from their wicked ways, then will I hear from heaven and will forgive their
sin and will heal their land' (2 Chronicles 7:14). While we cannot take
this promise and claim it directly as our own (for our nation is not in a
covenant relationship with God as Israel was when God gave the
promise), there is nevertheless an underlying principle here: revival
begins, not with sinners, but with God's own people. It is as *we* see our
desperate need for God that his Spirit begins to move, first in us, and then
in those around us. Repentance, and returning to God's word and God's
ways, has therefore always been a major feature of any revival.

How very quickly we can need reviving is reflected in the fact that,
even by the last decade of the first century, John was having to call
churches back to their first love for Jesus – the very heart of revival. He
had to challenge them with such words as, 'You have forsaken your first
love' (Revelation 2:4) and 'you have a reputation of being alive, but you
are dead' (Revelation 3:1). To each of the seven churches the challenge
was the same: 'He who has an ear, let him hear what the Spirit says to the
churches' (e.g. Revelation 2:7). That's how revival begins: through
listening to the Spirit, and then doing whatever he says.

O LORD, revive thy work in the midst of the years.
(HABAKKUK 3:2, KJV)

January 13

When weariness sets in

'Come to me, all you who are weary and burdened, and I will give you rest. Take my yoke upon you and learn from me, for I am gentle and humble in heart, and you will find rest for your souls. For my yoke is easy and my burden is light.'
(Matthew 11:28–29)

Jesus spent most of his life as a 'working man'. Brought up the son of a carpenter, he spent many years labouring in the workshop and 'on site' before starting the ministry for which he had come. Over those years, his hands would have no doubt been cut and calloused and his back would have no doubt ached. Like anyone involved with physical labour, he would most certainly have known what it was like to be weary at the end of the day.

But Jesus recognized that there is another weariness that can afflict us all, whatever our task in life. It is the weariness of soul and spirit; a weariness we can all feel when life's pressures and problems relentlessly crowd in and there seems to be no relief. To such people Jesus made his amazingly kind, yet amazingly simple, promise: come to me and I'll lift from your back this load that you have been carrying all by yourself.

But then he says something strange: for not only does he promise to lift our burden from our backs, he then invites us to pick up his burden instead! 'Take my yoke upon you.' What! We've just put one down! Why pick up another again!? But look what he goes on to say: 'Take my yoke upon you and learn from me.' Jesus was thinking here of how animals were trained in those days. One new to the job would be harnessed alongside one that had been doing it for years and that 'knew the ropes'. In this way, the new arrival would learn how to do things so much more quickly and easily.

Jesus says: that's what I want you to do with me. Come alongside me, walk with me, and let me show you how to do things; for as you do, the burden will seem so much lighter. Today, this promise of Jesus still remains for all who will come to him.

He gives strength to the weary and increases the power of the weak.
(Isaiah 40:29)

JANUARY 14

The church, his body

God placed all things under his feet and appointed him to be head over everything for the church, which is his body, the fulness of him who fills everything in every way.
(EPHESIANS 1:22–23)

Ask the average person what they think of when they hear the word 'church', and it will almost certainly be 'a building' – one with funny-shaped windows, and perhaps a tower or spire. Some might think of weddings, brides and confetti; or, less happily, of funerals, coffins and mourners; others might think of the 'denomination' that they grew up in many years ago and its apparent intolerance of 'the others' down the road. All in all, it will be a rather drab and unexciting picture – and a million miles from the truth! For the Bible tells us that 'church' is none of these things. Church is nothing less than a family – *God's* family.

This 'church' exists at two levels. First, the 'Universal Church', made up of everyone who believes in Jesus – a family that spreads through time and space, that cuts across boundaries of colour, race, and class, that bursts through the barrier of death itself. Second, the 'Local Church', expressions of this bigger family made up of believers in a particular area. 'Is it possible to be part of one without the other?' people sometimes ask. New Testament Christians would be astonished at such a question! They had no concept of 'Lone Rangers' who see themselves as part of the 'Universal Church', but who cannot, for some reason or other, settle down into a local expression of it. You simply can't have one without the other!

Indeed, to settle for less is to rob ourselves of many of the riches that God has promised to us. For 'church' is not just a meeting or a group; in fact, it is not even just a family; it is the very 'body of Christ' – a living expression of him, with all his life and power flowing down from him as 'head' to the body's various members – and therefore the sphere of an exciting adventure with God and all his people!

Today, don't neglect – and don't despise – this precious gift of God to you; rather, enjoy it!

Now you are the body of Christ, and each one of you is a part of it.
(1 CORINTHIANS 12:27)

Rejoice in the Lord always

Rejoice in the Lord always. I will say it again: Rejoice!
(PHILIPPIANS 4:4)

It was one of the first occasions when Mike, as a young pastor, had witnessed anyone die. The lady in question had struggled with cancer for some time and, as her death drew closer, her husband phoned to ask Mike to come to their home. It was not long before the end came. As she breathed her last, her husband softly said, 'She's gone!' and dropped quietly to his knees by the bedside. He began to praise God, even through his tears, for the assurance that his wife was now with God, free from pain, and that one day they would be together again. His praise was not dependent on his circumstances; his praise was dependent on his God.

The apostle Paul certainly knew how to set his heart on praising God in difficult times. Yet one of his most famous passages (Philippians 4:4–7) encouraging people to do the same has sometimes been misunderstood. Some people have interpreted Paul as saying, 'Praise God for the bad things that happen in life!' But that is not what he says – indeed, to insist that's what he's saying is to turn God into some sort of monster, sending bad things our way and then expecting us to praise him for them. Paul's exhortation here is not to praise God 'for' everything, but 'in' everything (v. 6) – a small, but very significant, difference. God does not expect us to praise him *for* everything; but he does want us to praise him *in* everything. For when our focus is on him, and not on our problems, things begin to happen.

Let's face it: praising God in hard times isn't easy. In the hard times our praise may not, of course, be as exuberant as it is in the good times. The truth is, it involves a sacrifice; a sacrifice of our own feelings and emotions, of our own questions and answers. Today launch out into praising God, even if you are facing difficult times, and see how things – and you! – begin to change.

Through Jesus, therefore, let us continually offer to God a sacrifice of praise.
(HEBREWS 13:15)

JANUARY 16

Finding God

'You will seek me and find me when you seek me with all your heart. I will be found by you,' declares the LORD.
(JEREMIAH 29:13–14)

'Hide and seek' has always been a popular children's game and one that all of us will have played at some point in our lives. You remember how it goes: one child covers their face (with maybe just the teeniest of peeks between fingers!) while the others hide in as difficult places as they can find, in the hope they will not be discovered. After a certain amount of time (normally counted down as quickly as possible!) the search begins; sometimes those hiding are found, and sometimes they aren't.

Thankfully, God never plays 'Hide and seek' with us. Were he to do so, we would never find him for, as one of Job's friends, put it, 'the Almighty is beyond our reach and exalted in power' (Job 37:23). God knows the best hiding places in the whole universe – places where we would never find him! However, God's great delight is not in *hiding* himself, but in *revealing* himself. He loves to be found, as he has made clear again and again. Moses promised God's people, 'But if . . . you seek the LORD your God, you will find him if you look for him with all your heart and with all your soul' (Deuteronomy 4:29). Paul told the unbelieving, yet searching, people of Athens, that God's heart is 'that men would seek him and perhaps reach out for him and find him' (Acts 17:27).

Today, be assured that God is not hiding from you, though the accusations of your own heart or the difficulties of your circumstances may tempt you to feel that perhaps he is. God is not like some sulking child or disappointed friend who thinks, 'You let me down – so now it's my turn!' Any such thoughts that he is like that come from the devil, who is 'the father of lies' (John 8:44). Believe God's promise and reach out to him today – you *will* find him, for he is truly there to be found.

Those who seek me find me.
(PROVERBS 8:17)

JANUARY 17

Awesome!

*How awesome is the LORD Most High, the great King
over all the earth!*
(PSALM 47:2)

Awesome! Amazing! Fantastic! Wow! (Or, if you belong to a younger
generation: Cool! Magic! – even 'Wicked'!) What words do *you* use when
something is so good it almost takes your breath away? Whatever your
words, that's exactly how the writers of the Bible felt about God. For
them, talking to God didn't demand special or religious language, far
removed from ordinary life; God was so amazing that he was worth telling
so with words that came spontaneously and naturally! The football fan
might shout; the theatregoer might applaud; the nature lover might sigh;
but the worshipper who knows God has real cause for getting excited. For
worship is what we were made for, and worship is what we are called to
spontaneously express.

In some church traditions, services often begin with a 'call to worship' –
generally a Scripture or anthem that focuses on God and that helps us 'tune
in'. The Bible is full of such 'calls to worship', encouraging us to come into
God's presence with a sense of 'wow!' in our hearts as we see stand amazed
once again at how truly awesome he is. Moses reminded God's people in the
book of Deuteronomy that their God was 'a great and awesome God' (7:21),
who does 'great and awesome deeds' (4:34) and 'great and awesome wonders'
(10:21), which is cause indeed for us to 'revere this glorious and awesome
name' (28:58). The Psalms too are full of a sense of God's awesomeness.
Psalm 66, for example, urges us to 'shout with joy to God' (v. 1) and to say,
'How awesome are your deeds!' (v. 3) and invites us to 'come and see what
God has done, how awesome his works on man's behalf!' (v. 5).

God is truly awesome! And we are encouraged to consider the works
of his hands, to remember his faithfulness in the past, to marvel at the
intricacies of his creation, to ponder upon his grace to sinners, to rejoice
in his acts of kindness – and to join with those who say, 'Wow! What an
awesome God you are!'

Go on! Get excited about your God today!

*Who among the gods is like you, O LORD? Who is like you – majestic in
holiness, awesome in glory, working wonders?*
(EXODUS 15:11)

Want to be rich?

My God will meet all your needs according to his glorious riches in Christ Jesus.
(PHILIPPIANS 4:19)

Want to be rich? If your instinctive response was 'Yes please!', then take care! For the Bible tells us that 'people who want to get rich fall into temptation and a trap and into many foolish and harmful desires that plunge men into ruin and destruction. For the love of money is a root of all kinds of evil' (1 Timothy 6:9–10). So, perhaps we need to think again!

Now, the Bible isn't against money. Indeed, God often promises to provide for our needs (though 'need' isn't always the same as 'want'!). David's own testimony, even while experiencing hardship in his life, was that 'the lions may grow weak and hungry, but those who seek the LORD lack no good thing' (Psalm 34:10). The trouble is, so many of us spend so much time thinking about money. In many ways, that's understandable, for we live in the real world and need money to survive. But while we can't live without money, we do need to be careful; for when we start focusing too much on money, it's a sure sign that money, and not God, is becoming our god – and Jesus said very clearly, 'You cannot serve both God and Money' (Matthew 6:24).

Actually, the Bible is very realistic about money, and gives practical guidelines on handling money which help ensure it keeps its proper perspective. We can sum these up like this: (1) *Get your money honestly* (not through dishonest, shady or sharp practices); (2) *Use your money wisely* (by providing for yourself, your family and your future, and not getting into debt); (3) *Handle your money faithfully* (understanding that we are simply stewards of what God has entrusted to us); (4) *Share your money generously* (remembering that 'God loves a cheerful giver', 2 Corinthians 9:7); and finally (5) *Stretch your money amazingly* (through the principle of tithing, which ensures that the nine-tenths you are left with goes further than the ten-tenths you would have had!)

Through our application of these principles, God brings his promised contentment into our lives. Try it and see!

'Seek first his kingdom and his righteousness, and all these things will be given to you as well.'
(MATTHEW 6:33)

JANUARY 19

Is that it?

Then Moses said, 'Now show me your glory.'
(EXODUS 33:18)

Some years ago, Martin compiled a book of verses from the Bible, arranged under particular themes. One of those themes was 'being a Christian'. In this theme, he wanted to give verses that would help someone become a Christian, that would explore the Christian's character, and would see what it meant now that you were a Christian. It all seemed relatively straightforward, until he thought, 'Is that it? Is that all there is? To say I'm saved, I'm a believer, I'm a child of God? That's all great; but surely there must be more?' And then it occurred to him – longing for God. Yes, this is the Christian's deepest experience: longing to know God more. Satisfied with him, yet thirsting for more. Passionate for Christ, but still acutely aware that the flames of our devotional life can all too easily go out.

Right through the Bible this was the longing and experience of true believers. This was Moses' prayer, our verse for today. Moses desperately wanted to know the presence of God, to know God himself, as he led God's people. What does this say to our half-heartedness, we wonder? Likewise, David prayed, 'My soul thirsts for you like a parched land' (Psalm 143:6). What does this say to our spiritual dryness? The apostle Paul knew the way to a full life of the soul with God: 'Be filled with the Spirit' he said (Ephesians 5:18). As Christians we have come to fullness of life in Christ, but still remain half-empty and constantly need to be refilled.

Jesus Christ knew the answer: 'If anyone is thirsty, let him come to me and drink' (John 7:37). How can we live for Christ, serving him and others in a world that is spiritually barren? Only by reaching out to him, receiving more of his Spirit, his refreshment, his life, his very self afresh into our lives today.

So, turn to God right now; tell him that you are dissatisfied with your present spiritual state, with where you are now as a Christian. Ask him to fill you again, to fill you to overflowing, to fill you to love him more deeply and to serve those around you more fully.

I want to know Christ.
(PHILIPPIANS 3:10)

JANUARY 20

Your God is too small!

In him we were also chosen, having been predestined according to the plan of him who works out everything in conformity with the purpose of his will, in order that we, who were the first to hope in Christ, might be for the praise of his glory.
(EPHESIANS 1:11–12)

Have you ever thought that God has a book in heaven with all his plans for your life? If so, your God is too small! For while the Bible speaks of a book that records all that we *have done* (Revelation 20:11–15), there is certainly no mention of a book that records what we *will do*. God is far too big for that!

Whenever we think in those terms, we are reducing the God of the Bible – the LORD, the great 'I AM' – to little more than the Muslim god, Allah. For Muslims, whatever Allah wills, happens, inexorably and relentlessly. It's all written in the book, and all we can do is to submit to it. But such a view of God is most definitely not the God of the Bible.

The Bible is certainly clear that God certainly has an ultimate plan, for his world and for our lives, and that he is constantly working towards its inevitable conclusion. But he brings this about, not through fixed and unchangeable events, pre-arranged and already recorded in a book in heaven, but through dynamic interaction with his people as they share their lives with him. So prayer is not about our resigning ourselves to his will, but about engaging with his heart, discovering what is there, and becoming 'God's fellow-workers' (2 Corinthians 6:1) out of our sharing with him and his sharing with us. God is not static but dynamic and is dynamically working together all things – good and bad, planned and unplanned – towards his end purpose. Like a good chef with his ingredients, he can work everything together to bring a fantastic result at the end. It is not the recipe that makes a good meal, but the chef!

God has not set everything about your life in stone; it is not already written up in his book. Rather, he wants to work interactively with you today!

God causes all things to work together for good to those who love God.
(ROMANS 8:28, NASB)

JANUARY 21

Repentance means happiness!

*Godly sorrow brings repentance that leads to salvation and
leaves no regret, but worldly sorrow brings death.*
(2 CORINTHIANS 7:10)

'Repentance' sounds such a 'heavy' word, doesn't it? Of course, the devil
does a good job here at sowing his lies. He convinces us that 'coming clean'
will be painful and embarrassing; that it will bring misery, not joy; that it
would be better if we just moved on and forgot all about it; that God
'understands' and so doesn't need your repentance. Lies from start to
finish!

The truth is that, yes, repentance may feel painful at first. It may be
embarrassing to acknowledge you were wrong or to start living differently.
It may mean you have some explaining to do, or some righting of a wrong
that you did. But, rather like an operation, the wounding is brief but the
healing is lasting.

Of course, it takes a step of faith to discover that, for the devil is quick
to bring his lies; but that is when we need to stand on the truth of God's
word; to believe that God really means it when he tells us that repentance
is *always* the best way, indeed the only way. His unshakable promise is
that 'if you repent, I *will* restore you that you may serve me' (Jeremiah
15:19).

Sometimes unburdening ourselves with someone that we trust can help
us to 'get it off our chest', and to see that, if they do not condemn us, how
much more will God not condemn us. Hearing someone declare the
Bible's promises of forgiveness over us – such as, 'if we confess our sins, he
is faithful and just and will forgive us our sins and purify us from all
unrighteousness' (1 John 1:9) – can be a powerful and liberating
experience. Little wonder James encourages us to 'confess your sins to each
other and pray for each other so that you may be healed' (James 5:16).

Worldly sorrow – just moping over our sin – gets us nowhere. But real
repentance will always bring us into the joy and peace of God. If there is
something that you have been avoiding repenting about, don't delay any
longer; deal with it today!

*I will turn their mourning into gladness; I will give them comfort and joy
instead of sorrow.*
(JEREMIAH 31:13)

In the blacksmith's workshop

*'Is not my word like fire', declares the LORD, 'and like a
hammer that breaks a rock in pieces?'*
(JEREMIAH 23:29)

A blacksmith needs just three pieces of equipment to do his work: a fire
to heat the metal, a hammer to beat the metal, and an anvil upon which
to shape the metal. As Isaiah put it, 'The blacksmith takes a tool and
works with it in the coals; he shapes an idol with hammers, he forges it
with the might of his arm' (Isaiah 44:12). With these simple tools, he can
make anything. And this, the Bible says, is what God's word is like.

First, the Bible is like *fire* because it reveals what God is like in all his
holiness. But having revealed that holiness, it then points us to the one
who can burn up all that is unholy in our life, refining us like precious
metal and making us ready to be shaped into 'an instrument for noble
purposes, made holy, useful to the Master' (2 Timothy 2:21). Second, the
Bible is like a *hammer*. There are times when God woos our hearts gently;
but there are also times when our hearts become so hard that only a
hammer can crack them open. God's word, Jeremiah says, is such a
hammer. It breaks open rock-like hearts so that his life can burst in.
Third, the Bible is like the *anvil*, where the metal is smoothed and shaped.
This is what Isaiah saw when he said, 'The craftsman encourages the
goldsmith, and he who smooths with the hammer spurs on him who
strikes the anvil' (Isaiah 41:7).

This is what God has promised his word can do in our lives. It can
soften our heart in its fire, purge our impurities, break up our hardness
and shape us into something useful for God. Little wonder the devil tries
so hard to keep us from it!

If God has been bringing down his hammer on your life, if you have
felt as if you have been in the fire or on the anvil, don't resist the work of
God's word, but yield to it. Submit your life today to the work of the
word of God. It will do you good, just as he promised.

'The word of God, which is at work in you who believe.'
(1 THESSALONIANS 2:13)

JANUARY 23

Secure in his hands

*'My sheep listen to my voice; I know them, and they follow me.
I give them eternal life, and they shall never perish; no-one can
snatch them out of my hand.'*
(JOHN 10:27–28)

Have you ever lost something precious? If you have, you'll know what a sense of panic can arise as we desperately hunt for it, hoping we might find it, yet fearful that we may never see it again, that it may simply be gone for good.

Some people get just as fearful of losing their relationship with God. Such fears normally arise, either when things have got on top of us, or when we have committed some sin 'just once too often' (as we might put it), or when we have fallen back into some sinful habit that used to be part of our life before we became a Christian. At such times the devil is all too ready to whisper in our ears, 'That's it! You've lost your salvation now! God will never forgive you now!' And all too often we believe him.

At such times it is so important to listen to God's promises rather than to the devil's lies. Again and again, God has promised to keep safe those who have committed their lives to him. The reason he can make such a rock-solid promise is quite simple: it has nothing to do with us and everything to do with him! Our salvation – whether our initial salvation or our ongoing salvation – is all about Christ and what he did for us on the cross through his once-for-all sacrifice. Nothing can be added to that, and nothing can be taken away from that. *That* is why we can be secure; *that* is why we can be certain that nothing can snatch us out of his hands; for it isn't about us, but about him!

Today, if you have been fearful that you have lost your salvation, or if you are worrying that some circumstance could wrench you from God's hand, take heart! The promise of God is: you are safe and secure! And *no one* can take you from him!

*'And this is the will of him who sent me, that I shall lose none of all that he
has given me, but raise them up at the last day.'*
(JOHN 6:39)

JANUARY 24

The God who guides

Trust in the LORD with all your heart and lean not on your own understanding; in all your ways acknowledge him, and he will make your paths straight.
(PROVERBS 3:5–6)

It's amazing how many people look for guidance each day. Sadly, most of them look in the wrong place. Millions turn to the horoscopes in the nation's newspapers. It really is amazing how people so governed by a 'scientific outlook' in the rest of life can believe that the positions of the planets can affect what might happen to them that day. For Christians, such things are not only forbidden, they are completely unnecessary; for God himself – our Father! – has promised to guide us.

What an amazing thought that is! That the sovereign, eternal God of the whole cosmos has, not just plans – but plans for *us*! And that he wants to guide us into them! Yet this is what the Bible assures us of, as when he said, '"For I know the plans I have for you," declares the LORD, "plans to prosper you and not to harm you, plans to give you hope and a future"' (Jeremiah 29:11).

But God's plans for our life are not something cold and deterministic; and here lies a major difference between 'the God and Father of our Lord Jesus Christ' (Ephesians 1:3) and the Muslim 'Allah'. In Islam, whatever Allah wills, happens; our lot is simply to be in 'submission' to it (which is what the word 'Islam' means). But with Father God, while his will is always carried out, we can, amazingly, be 'God's fellow-workers' in it (2 Corinthians 6:1). We can resist his will or respond to his will; but if God doesn't get to us through the front door, he has a way of coming in through the back door! This is a far more exciting and dynamic view of God and his plans for our lives. Such is how Father deals with his children.

God's promise for each of us today is that, if we will set our heart on him and ask him, he *will* guide us.

The LORD says, 'I will make you wise and show you where to go.
I will guide you and watch over you.'
(PSALM 32:8, NCV)

JANUARY 25

Knowing God by name

'[If] they ask me, "What is his name?"'Then what shall I tell
them?' God said to Moses, '"I AM WHO I AM."'
(EXODUS 3:13–14)

Most parents take great care in choosing names for their children. Some have made the decision long before the child's birth (though, unless a scan has revealed the secret, with both male and female options!); some go weeks after the birth before interpreting those cute smiles and questioning eyes into an appropriate choice of name; some embarrass their children for evermore by naming them after all the players in dad's favourite football team! But however we go about choosing them, names are important, for they reflect so much about us.

One of the ways that God has revealed himself is through his names. In Bible times a name was far more than something to distinguish you from someone else; it summed up who you were and what you were like. God has almost one hundred and fifty different Hebrew and Greek words used to name him in the Bible. That in itself tells us how wonderful he is and how difficult it is to describe him! But when Moses first met him at the burning bush in the sun-scorched desert of Midian, God revealed his 'personal' name, 'the name by which I am to be remembered from generation to generation' (Exodus 3:15). And what an unusual name it was: 'I AM WHO I AM' or 'I AM' for short (Exodus 3:14); the one whom we, God went on to say (verse 15), can call, by a play on words, 'HE IS' ('Yahweh', or 'the LORD' as it is translated in most English versions).

God is saying far more here than simply 'I exist'; he is saying, 'I am always, actively present.' He is promising that he is the one who is *always there* – he always has been, and always will be. He is the God of the past, the present, and the future. He is the God of your today, truly with you. So remember: whatever comes along today, whatever happens, the great 'I AM' – the LORD – has promised to be with you, and always will be.

There Abram called on the name of the LORD.
(GENESIS 13:4)

JANUARY 26

God's called ones

*But you are a chosen people, a royal priesthood, a holy nation,
a people belonging to God, that you may declare the praises of
him who called you out of darkness into his wonderful light.*
(1 PETER 2:9)

The trouble with our word 'church' is that it doesn't convey the richness of the original. The word for 'church' in Greek is *ekklesia*, which comes from a verb meaning 'to call out'. It was used of any group of people who were called to meet together for some purpose. But in the Greek translation of the Old Testament *ekklesia* was used to translate the Hebrew word *qahal*, 'the congregation of God's people'. And it was this word that the early church used of themselves, for they understood they were a people with a special *calling* on their lives together.

First, they understood that they had been *called out* – out of the kingdom of darkness with its rule of sin and death. Second, they knew they were *called for* – called for a relationship with God, called to know him and serve him, not to be a holy club with a list of do's and don'ts. Third, they knew they were *called together*, integral members of God's new community, coming closer to one another as they came closer to him. Fourth, they knew they were *called to* – called to a wonderful future inheritance of a glorious heaven and, ultimately, of God's new creation.

Each of these aspects of being 'called' is part of the package of what it means to be a Christian: called *out*, called *for*, called *together*, called *to*. We cannot pick and choose the bits we like or that seem most comfortable or convenient; we either embrace them all, or we do not embrace them at all. Yet when each aspect is so full of God's promises, how silly it is to leave any of them on the shelf.

Today, ask God to help you see more of the implications of this promise of being 'called'.

*I pray also that the eyes of your heart may be enlightened in order
that you may know the hope to which he has called you, the riches of his
glorious inheritance in the saints, and his incomparably great power
for us who believe.*
(EPHESIANS 1:18–19)

January 27

Come clean, get clean

*He who conceals his sins does not prosper, but whoever confesses
and renounces them finds mercy.*
(PROVERBS 28:13)

Most people in our society don't like the concept of sin; after all, it reminds them that they aren't what they thought they were. So whenever the church makes its stand against some moral or social issue, or dares to say that some particular action or lifestyle is 'wrong', it isn't long before the liberal-minded 'thought police' are telling us that we are being narrow-minded, old-fashioned, and judgmental, and that what we need to do is to be more tolerant of others.

Well, the Bible says God is quite intolerant of sin too! When we do something wrong (or neglect to do something right), when we think or speak in a wrong way, when we break God's commands or push back God-ordained boundaries, it is *sin*. Yes, of course that isn't a popular word; and sometimes even we Christians don't like it. But recognizing sin for what it is, is the key to getting it dealt with. We need to 'come clean' in order to 'get clean'.

Throughout the Bible God is quick to forgive when people are quick to confess. To confess simply means to be real with him about what happened, to admit it, to face up to it – not explain it away or blame others. Confession is often the thing we want to run away from; yet it is the very thing that opens the door for God to come in. That is why Peter could stand so confidently and proclaim the possibility of forgiveness on the Day of Pentecost. As the crowd began to understand what they had done in urging the crucifixion of Jesus, they were 'cut to the heart' (Acts 2:37) and desperate to know what to do. Peter knew the answer: it was the same answer it had always been: 'Repent!' Not even the sin of urging the crucifixion of God's Son lay beyond God's ordained way of people getting clean.

The same still holds true today: it is as we confess our sin that God keeps his promise to forgive. 'Come clean', and you'll get clean!

*'Repent, then, and turn to God, so that your sins may be wiped out, that
times of refreshing may come from the Lord.'*
(ACTS 3:19)

JANUARY 28

The God of all grace

'The LORD, the LORD, the compassionate and gracious God,
slow to anger, abounding in love and faithfulness, maintaining
love to thousands, and forgiving wickedness, rebellion and sin.'
(EXODUS 34:6–7)

'It's not fair!' How many times have you heard (or said!) those words? Perhaps someone got promotion when you felt they didn't deserve it; perhaps you felt someone received a better gift or a better deal than you; perhaps life seemed to serve you a hard blow. Whenever we get less than we feel we should have done, we instinctively cry, 'Unfair!' and think that if only the world were just, then surely everything would be 'fair'.

But here is some shocking news – the Bible tells us that God is not 'fair'! What! How can anyone say that? Well, it's true! For if God were fair, none of us would last a moment; his 'fairness' would judge our sin and wipe us from the face of the earth without a moment's hesitation. But here is the wonderful news: God is not fair; he is *more than fair*. And that is what the Bible means by *the grace of God*.

It was this God of grace that Moses met when he went up Mount Sinai. While hidden (for his own protection) in the cleft of a rock, the glory of God passed in front of him and God spoke such wonderful words! For the *first* words from his lips, describing himself, were 'compassionate' and 'gracious' – though these are never the words the devil would have us remember, especially when we have failed God in some way. But again and again in the Bible, God's people remembered this revelation of God's heart to us and were renewed and encouraged though it.

Remember this yourself today, especially if the devil has been accusing you; for this is God's truth about himself. God truly is 'the God of all grace' and his grace is waiting for *you* today!

'The God of all grace.'
(1 PETER 5:10)

January 29

Praying for ourselves

Don't worry about anything; instead, pray about everything.
Tell God what you need, and thank him for all he has done.
(Philippians 4:6, NLT)

'Isn't praying for yourself rather selfish?' people sometimes ask. Not at all! We should never be embarrassed to bring our personal needs to God. He is our heavenly Father who delights to hear the heart cries of his children and who has committed himself to answering them out of his rich resources. Indeed, we are on very safe ground in praying for ourselves and our own needs, for Jesus modelled this for us in the Lord's Prayer, encouraging us to pray about our present need ('daily bread'), past sin ('forgive us our debts'), and future welfare ('and lead us ...') (Matthew 6:11–13). If all this is good enough for Jesus, then it's good enough for us!

As we look through the Bible, there is an overwhelming breadth of personal needs that people brought to God in prayer: daily provision, finances, health, healing, a marriage partner, children, protection, guidance, direction, understanding, wisdom, forgiveness, strength, boldness, help, victory, rescue ... the list goes on and on! When we are sure of our relationship with God, we can be sure that there is absolutely nothing in life that we cannot bring to him.

So, when we come with our requests, let's pray boldly! Jesus has assured us that it isn't selfish to pray for ourselves (it becomes selfish when we pray *only* for ourselves and never for others) and he has made it possible for us to 'approach the throne of God with confidence' (Hebrews 4:16). So bring bold and big requests to God! Don't be timid! And don't settle for praying unfocused prayers that ask for some vague spiritual blessing for the world at large (it's impossible to know whether such prayers are ever answered!); rather, pray specifically. Remember that both the parable of the neighbour who needed bread (Luke 11:5–10) and the parable of the widow and the judge (Luke 18:1–7) both contained requests for very personal needs. And because the key characters weren't afraid to keep asking, they received exactly what they needed. So why shouldn't you?

Come on! Be creative in what you ask your Father for today!

You do not get what you want, because you do not ask God.
(James 4:2, NCV)

JANUARY 30

The God who is compassionate

The Lord is full of compassion and mercy.
(JAMES 5:11)

Compassion is not the most common quality today. It's what most people know they ought to have more of, but which they relegate to 'special people', like the Mother Theresa's of this world. What a contrast this is to God, who throughout the Scriptures is constantly seen as compassionate.

By the end of this book, you will have read about God's revelation of himself to Moses on Mount Sinai several times. That's because, if there's any passage of Scripture we never get tired of recalling, it's this one; when God said he was 'the LORD, the LORD, the compassionate and gracious God, slow to anger, abounding in love and faithfulness, maintaining love to thousands, and forgiving wickedness, rebellion and sin' (Exodus 34:6–7). And this fantastic truth is picked up again and again.

David recalled it as the basis of his confidence that God forgives sin: 'Have mercy on me, O God, according to your unfailing love; according to your great compassion blot out my transgressions. Wash away all my iniquity and cleanse me from my sin' (Psalm 51:1–2). Isaiah recalled it as the basis of his certainty that God wanted to bless his people: 'Yet the LORD longs to be gracious to you; he rises to show you compassion' (Isaiah 30:18). Jeremiah recalled it as the basis of his prophecy that God would restore his people to their land: 'But after I uproot them, I will again have compassion and will bring each of them back to his own inheritance and his own country' (Jeremiah 12:15). Nehemiah recalled it as he gratefully reviewed the history of God's people, remembering that 'in your compassion you delivered them time after time' (Nehemiah 9:28). Paul recalled it as the basis of his confidence that God is with us in every circumstance of life: 'Praise be to the God and Father of our Lord Jesus Christ, the Father of compassion and the God of all comfort, who comforts us in all our troubles' (2 Corinthians 1:3–4).

God's compassion – not just felt, but demonstrated – is still 'alive and well' and available to each one of us today. Recall it – and claim it!

Return to the LORD your God, for he is gracious and compassionate, slow to anger and abounding in love, and he relents from sending calamity.
(JOEL 2:13)

Counting the cost

'If anyone would come after me, he must deny himself and take up his cross daily and follow me. For whoever wants to save his life will lose it, but whoever loses his life for me will save it.'
(LUKE 9:23–24)

Anything worthwhile in life has a cost. Indeed, if there isn't some cost – not necessarily financial, but perhaps in terms of commitment or time or effort – then it is probably worth very little indeed. Following Jesus, too, has a cost to it – and if it doesn't, we may question whether we have truly found 'the real thing'.

This cost is not the cost of *knowing* him, however – Jesus himself paid that cost through his once-for-all sacrifice on the cross, and there is nothing we can add to that. No, this cost is the cost of *following* him, of learning how to live life his way. It is the cost of being a *disciple*. This cost involves, first and foremost, a change in established loyalties. So, for example, while we are to honour our parents, Jesus said that they can no longer take first place in our lives. And loyalty to such things as our possessions and our money would be challenged too, he said; as well as the need to make sacrifices for his sake – whether sacrifices of time, possessions, comfort, or even life itself.

This is why Jesus said that we need to sit down first and consider whether we're ready for all this! He said we need to be like a man planning a building project, or a king going out to battle, who thinks, 'Can I start what I have finished?' He wasn't looking for a blind and easy commitment that doesn't understand what it is letting itself in for, but a thoughtful consideration of whether we are ready to follow him.

This all could sound rather heavy, couldn't it? But there is another side to the matter! For Jesus said that, though the costs were real, the rewards were amazing! And for those who were ready to follow in this way, Jesus promised them that it would never be to their loss!

'And everyone who has left houses or brothers or sisters or father or mother or children or fields for my sake will receive a hundred times as much and will inherit eternal life.'
(MATTHEW 19:29)

FEBRUARY 1

Never mind the place!

This is what the LORD says: 'Heaven is my throne, and the earth is my footstool. Where is the house you will build for me? Where will my resting place be?'
(ISAIAH 66:1)

Some people get so anxious about doing things 'properly' in life. Of course, what they often mean is 'doing it the way I like it done'! Nowhere is this more unhelpful than in the matter of prayer, for countless people exclude themselves, or are excluded by others, from talking to the Father simply because they think they aren't doing it 'properly' – either in the right place, or at the right time, or in the right way. Over the next three days, we'll look at each of those.

Concerning where we should pray, the Bible never restricts prayer to 'special places'. Prayer could be offered anywhere. Why? Because God himself is everywhere and nowhere is big enough to contain him or grand enough to be worthy of him. There is no 'proper' place to pray and there is no 'better' place to pray. God is everywhere; so everywhere will do.

In fact, the Bible shows us people praying in a tremendously wide variety of places and situations: Daniel prayed at home (Daniel 6:10); Moses prayed up a mountain (Exodus 34:8–9); Elijah prayed while on a journey (1 Kings 19:3–4); Anna prayed in the temple (Luke 2:37); Jesus prayed in the countryside (Mark 1:35); Paul prayed in jail (Acts 16:25) – Jonah even prayed inside a great fish (Jonah 2:1–10)! Whether individually or in groups, whether in public or in private, the Bible makes clear that the location of prayer is completely irrelevant to God. Thoughts that we can only pray 'properly' in a church building are completely alien to the Scriptures. What God is after is not the location but the heart.

From bath tub to bus stop, from car to cathedral, there is nowhere that God cannot be found and therefore nowhere that you cannot talk to him. Don't put off prayer today because you feel you can't find the right place or the right moment. The right place is right where you are; the right moment is right now!

I want everyone everywhere to lift innocent hands toward heaven and pray.
(1 TIMOTHY 2:8, CEV)

FEBRUARY 2

Never mind the time!

Evening, morning and noon I cry out in distress,
and he hears my voice.
(PSALM 55:17)

Yesterday we saw that it doesn't matter to God *where* we pray. Today, we see that it doesn't matter to God *when* we pray. Unlike Islam, which prescribes prayer at five points in each day, the Bible makes no requirements about when or how often we should pray. In fact to answer the question 'When should we pray?' is rather like answering the question, 'How often should I talk to my husband or wife each day?' Prayer is not about *rules*; it is about a *relationship* with the living God; and relationship can never be put into a timetable.

We therefore find a whole variety of prayer patterns in the Bible. Some liked praying in the morning, like Jacob (Genesis 28:18–22), David (Psalm 5:3), Elijah (2 Kings 6:15–17) – and Jesus (Mark 1:35). Others prayed in the evening, like Isaac (Genesis 24:63), Solomon (2 Chronicles 7:11–12), Ezra (Ezra 9:5–15) – and Jesus (Matthew 14:23). Some liked to pray through the night at times, like Anna (Luke 2:36–37), Paul and Silas (Acts 16:25) – and Jesus (Luke 6:12). Sometimes people prayed non-stop over long periods of days, like Nehemiah (Nehemiah 1:4–6), David (2 Samuel 1:11), the church leaders at Antioch (Acts 13:1–3) – and Jesus (Matthew 4:1–2). Sometimes people prayed in crisis moments, like Jacob (Genesis 32:7–12), Hezekiah (2 Kings 19:14–19), Stephen (Acts 7:59–60) – and Jesus (Matthew 26:39). The fact that all these times and periods of prayer are blessed by the practice of Jesus should, in itself, underline to us that all times of prayer are blessed, whenever they are.

Above all, the Bible encourages us to develop an attitude of constant prayer: that is, maintaining an atmosphere of ongoing conversation and intimacy with God throughout our day, and not just confining prayer to set times or places.

Morning or evening; midday or midnight; Sunday or weekday; in crisis or continually; there is no time when we cannot talk to God, for it is never inconvenient to him. And there is certainly no time like the present!

Be cheerful no matter what; pray all the time; thank God no matter what
happens. This is the way God wants you who belong to Christ Jesus to live.
(1 THESSALONIANS 5:16–18, THE MESSAGE)

FEBRUARY 3

Never mind the words!

Do not be quick with your mouth, do not be hasty in your heart to utter anything before God. God is in heaven and you are on earth, so let your words be few.
(ECCLESIASTES 5:2)

When it comes to prayer, as we have seen, the place and time are unimportant. But what about the words? Surely some special vocabulary must be needed? Amazingly, the Bible says that God desires no special language from us at all!

All the major terms used for 'prayer' in the Bible are words drawn from everyday life, just like those used between family and friends. They are ordinary words, as people 'say', 'speak', 'ask', 'request', 'enquire of' or 'call to' God. Unlike other religions, both ancient and modern, there is no 'technical vocabulary' to be mastered, no 'insider jargon' to be initiated into, no language that is different from that of everyday life. Christian prayer is simply conversation with God our Father. Because he is our Father, he wants us simply to express what is in our hearts – and we can't do that if we feel we have to constantly search for the right words, as though we might offend the dignity of his majesty if we get them wrong.

The two key things that the Bible stresses when it comes to prayer are that, first, *the heart is more important than the words.* Through Isaiah God challenged his people: 'These people come near to me with their mouth and honour me with their lips, but their hearts are far from me. Their worship of me is made up only of rules taught by men' (Isaiah 29:13). Second, *reality is more important than ritual.* In both Old and New Testaments, empty ritual is exposed as valueless. As Jesus told his disciples, 'When you pray, do not keep on babbling like pagans, for they think they will be heard because of their many words. Do not be like them, for your Father knows what you need before you ask him' (Matthew 6:7–8).

The right heart is more important than the right words; integrity is more important than impressiveness; reality is more important than ritual. God is your Father, so go on, just talk to him!

Trust in him at all times, O people; pour out your hearts to him . . .
(PSALM 62:8)

FEBRUARY 4

'Here is your God!'

*'Here is your God!' See, the Sovereign LORD comes with power,
and his arm rules for him.*
(ISAIAH 40:9–10)

'Just how big *is* God?' This child's question has no doubt stumped many a parent! But actually, it is a question that many of us ask, consciously or unconsciously, when problems or hard times come our way. 'Is God big enough to deal with this? Does he have the resources to meet my needs?' Of course, we may not always speak the words; but when we do not trust, we are certainly thinking the thoughts.

This is exactly how God's people were thinking in Isaiah's day; but Isaiah knew that if they could only see how big God is, then they would not have to ask the question! Isaiah 40 is a prophecy of God, in all his greatness, coming in power to deal with his people's situation and sin. But can he do it? Of course he can, Isaiah replies! Just look at his majestic acts in creation, he says; but those oceans and mountains are as nothing to him (verse 12)! Now look at the great nations of the world, which seem so powerful; but they are merely a drop in a bucket to God! (verses 15–17). Or think of the world's great leaders: leaders of nations and superpowers they might be, but they are nothing in comparison to him! (verses 22–24). And think about the stars – billions of them, millions of light years away, yet all are made by him and are known to him by name (verse 26). 'And then you ask me if God is big enough to deal with *you* and *your* situation?' asks Isaiah? Of course he can! For he is truly God, and a God who comes in power to his people.

And this is the God who has promised to be with *you* today and to come to your aid in every situation. Whatever you may be facing, whatever opportunities lie ahead, the Sovereign God is with you, ruling in power.

The LORD your God, who is among you, is a great and awesome God.
(DEUTERONOMY 7:21)

FEBRUARY 5

Being real

Because of my chains, most of the brothers in the Lord have been encouraged to speak the word of God more courageously and fearlessly.
(PHILIPPIANS 1:14)

It sometimes seems to us that there are two kinds of Christian: those who when asked, 'How are you?' will always answer, 'Fine!' and those who are more honest and who will sometimes say, 'Well, actually, I'm struggling.' Which are you?

All of us face difficulties of one kind or another – relationships, health, finances, for example; but the question is, what do we do with our difficulties and how do we relate them to our Christian faith? Either we can pretend that everything is going swimmingly and hide our problems; or we can be more realistic and acknowledge them. If we continue along the first road, our faith may eventually collapse when reality at last hits home; but if we go down the second road, we're like the people Paul refers to in today's reading. *Most* of the brothers (and sisters!), he says, were courageous; but that presumably meant, *not all* of them were! There were some who weren't so confident – perhaps like the disciples after the resurrection who 'when they saw him, they worshipped him; but some doubted' (Matthew 28:17). Some doubted! In other words, they were real about their struggles.

So here's an encouragement to us today to be real with Christ in our lives. Whenever Martin finds it difficult to pray, or when he feels he's just not in the right spirits, he begins his prayer by telling the Lord just that. We can take our doubts and feelings to Jesus and discuss them with him. (If we can be sexist for a moment, we would have to say that women are much better than men at opening up about what is really going on in their lives!) But here is an encouragement to us all (men and women!) to be honest and open before the Lord. And remember too that it can be a great help to share our struggles with another trusted friend, who can often be God's gift to encourage us and help show us the way.

Today, be real – with God and with others; for being real is a key part of experiencing the promises of God.

Pour out your feelings to the Lord, as you would pour water out of a jug.
(LAMENTATIONS 2:19, CEV)

FEBRUARY 6

God won't turn us away

*'The LORD your God is gracious and compassionate. He will
not turn his face from you if you return to him.'*
(2 CHRONICLES 30:9)

It's amazing how we hesitate to ask someone for something when we
think their answer will be 'no'. We put it off, make excuses, convince
ourselves we'll manage – anything but go and ask, just in case we don't
get the answer we want. Of course, the answer might turn out to be 'yes'!
But we never find out because we never ask. Thankfully, it doesn't have
to be like that with God. We are never left wondering what his answer
might be if we return to him. Like the father of the prodigal son, he is
always ready to welcome us back, and will never say 'no' to those who
come.

The trouble is, we become convinced his answer is bound to be 'no',
because that's the answer we would probably give! We convince ourselves
we have sinned too badly or have committed that particular sin just once
too often or have drifted away for just far too long. But at such times, our
fearful hearts need to listen to the truth of God's word, not the lies of the
devil. For in his word lies assurance that he *will* welcome us back; an
assurance that is based on three things.

First, God's character. God has revealed himself as gracious and
compassionate – always! In Nehemiah's days, God's people were in
desperate need of coming back to God; and what their leaders recalled at
that time was, 'You are a forgiving God, gracious and compassionate, slow
to anger and abounding in love' (Nehemiah 9:17). Second, God's heart
– a heart that wants everyone to know him. Paul reminded Timothy that
'God our Saviour. . . desires all men to be saved and to come to the
knowledge of the truth' (1 Timothy 2:3–4, NASB). Third, God's
patience. Unlike us, he is patient in his dealings with people. As Peter put
it, 'God is patient, because he wants everyone to turn from sin and no one
to be lost' (2 Peter 3:9, CEV).

This, then, is our confidence that God will receive us and never turn
us away! – no matter what we have done or how far we may have drifted.

'Today, if you hear his voice, do not harden your hearts . . .'
(HEBREWS 3:15)

I will build my church

'And I tell you that you are Peter, and on this rock I will build my church, and the gates of Hades will not overcome it.'
(MATTHEW 16:18)

One of the first verses that Mike learned as a new Christian was this one. And after more than twenty-five years as a church pastor, he is certainly glad that God burned it into his heart at such an early stage; for, let's face it, life in a local church isn't always easy, and there are often lots of challenges and discouragements. But today's promise assures us that, no matter what, Jesus *will* build his church – and *nothing* will be able to stop him!

But on what is our confidence for the success and growth of the church based? Not on what may or may not have happened in our own church this past year (whether good or bad); but rather, on this sure promise of Jesus. Your own church may indeed have struggled to grow, or perhaps your church has even shrunk, this year; but while this has happened, the church in China, for example, has grown by millions. The church of Jesus *is* growing! So let us not get discouraged. He has promised to build his church, and this is a promise he will keep. *Our* part is not to worry about the growth; our part is simply to 'seek first the kingdom' (Matthew 6:33). '*You* seek the kingdom' Jesus says, 'let *me* build the church!'

But our assurance is not just based on *Jesus' promise*; it is also based on *Jesus' action*. For it was his death on the cross that made it possible for sinful people like us to be cleansed and be drawn into God's new and ever-growing family. The cross settled the issue! And if it cost Jesus such a price to bring his church into being, do we really think that he will give up with the job only half done?

If you have felt discouraged recently about the life of your own local church, take hold of this promise of Jesus again – and ask him how you can play your part in seeing it come to pass.

> *. . . the church of God, which he bought with his own blood.*
> (ACTS 20:28)

FEBRUARY 8

Don't take it for granted!

*There by the Ahava Canal, I gave orders for all of us to fast
and humble ourselves before our God. We prayed that he would
give us a safe journey and protect us, our children, and our
goods as we travelled . . . So we fasted and earnestly prayed that
our God would take care of us, and he heard our prayer.*
(EZRA 8:21,23, NLT)

Most of us take our safety for granted. So, when travelling by
bike/bus/car/train/plane (choose your usual modes of transport!), we
probably don't give it a second thought. Indeed, it's only after a crisis or
accident that we consider how fortunate we are to travel all those miles
each year in safety. But visit a developing nation and you will quickly
discover that no Christian starts a journey without committing themselves
to the Lord for protection. Of course, we could dismiss this as being more
necessary there; or we could perhaps consider that the safety to which we
have become accustomed has made us become casual, ungrateful and
presumptuous in what we do and don't pray about.

While we certainly don't need to live fearfully, our safety and daily
protection isn't something that we should take for granted. Indeed,
committing ourselves to God's care is a wise and godly thing to do. Ezra
certainly knew that he needed to do that, not just because the journey
back to the promised land was fraught with dangers and difficulties, but
because he wanted *God* to be seen at the centre of everything he did.

But it's not just protection when we travel that we need. Life itself is
full of all kinds of potential dangers, whether from things or from people.
So wise believers will – without fear or panic, but in an attitude of
dependent trust – commit themselves to the Lord for his protection. After
all, Jesus himself encouraged us to ask God to 'deliver us from evil'
(Matthew 6:13, KJV). Even – perhaps especially – in these days such a
prayer is still wise.

Don't take your safety for granted. Pray about it, thereby showing
your complete dependence on God for all you do.

*And pray that we may be delivered from wicked and evil men, for not
everyone has faith. But the Lord is faithful, and he will strengthen and
protect you from the evil one.*
(2 THESSALONIANS 3:2–3)

FEBRUARY 9

Prayer and fasting

'When you fast . . .'
(MATTHEW 6:16)

'Have whatever you want, whenever you want it' sums up Western consumer society. If you can't afford it now, pay for it later. Don't miss out; you deserve it *now*! Sadly, this attitude spills over into our lives and the thought of denying oneself is anathema to many Christians. Yet the Bible says that denying ourselves can be the very way of receiving what we are looking for! And that's where fasting comes in.

Fasting is *not* simply about skipping a meal (that's either dieting or working too hard!), but about abstaining from food for a period of time in order to focus on *God*. In fact, the Hebrew word means 'humbly submitting oneself to God'. It's a way of saying, 'Lord, there is nothing more important in my life than you – not even eating.'

While fasting was originally voluntary, the Pharisees turned it into a twice-weekly requirement and an outward show of piety. Some Christians have therefore shunned fasting, though it is thoroughly biblical and was practised and encouraged by Jesus. The Bible contains several types of fast: the normal fast (abstaining from food, but not from water); the partial fast (abstaining from particular foods for a period of time); the complete fast (abstaining from both food and water); the special fast (lasting forty days at crisis times). Reasons for fasting included seeking God, humbling oneself, seeking God's help, bringing spiritual release or breakthrough, releasing spiritual power, seeking guidance and demonstrating repentance.

Fasting can help our prayers, for it shows our resolve – though it is not a 'hunger strike' to force God to answer! Because of its potential for outward show, the Bible lays great stress on the inner attitudes that must accompany it. Without the right heart, it is quite meaningless. As John Wesley prayed, 'Let our fasting be done unto the Lord, with our eye singly fixed on Him. Let our intention herein be this, and this alone, to glorify our Father which is in heaven.'

Jesus anticipated that his followers would fast, as our opening verse shows. It is not a duty, however, but a powerful weapon in our prayer armoury, and one that God has promised to bless and use. Is it time for you to use it?

We fasted and petitioned our God about this, and he answered our prayer.
(EZRA 8:23)

God cannot forget!

*Can a mother forget the baby at her breast and have no
compassion on the child she has borne? Though she may forget,
I will not forget you! See, I have engraved you
on the palms of my hands.*
(ISAIAH 49:15–16)

The world is full of cynics – many of them professional, paid to write
sneering columns in a newspaper or to produce a slanted view of life for
TV. But most cynics are just ordinary people – people like you and me,
who have become discouraged or lost their perspective or been
disappointed once too often. Sadly, even God's people can become
cynical when things start to go wrong or when they think that God has
somehow forgotten them. Even the writer of Lamentations hit a low point
when he wrote, 'Why do you always forget us? Why do you forsake us so
long?' (Lamentations 5:20). And what about you? Have you perhaps ever
thought, like God's people were thinking in Isaiah's day, 'My way is
hidden from the LORD; my cause is disregarded by my God' (Isaiah
40:27)? Are you perhaps even thinking like that today?

But stop and think for a moment: can it really be that God is so great
that he could forget us? That he has far too much to do in running the
universe and far too many problems to solve to find time for *us* and our
need, which is so small in the great scheme of things! No! God is simply
too big for that! He cannot *fail* us, because he cannot *forget* us. Unlike us,
God never forgets or never has a momentary lapse of memory; he never
switches off in the middle of your prayer or drifts into thinking about
other things. Indeed, how could he possibly forget or neglect you when,
the Bible tells us, your very name is engraved on the palm of his hand?

Today, remember God's promise that he can never forget you. *Your*
name is engraved on the palm of his hands, and so there is nothing that
can make him forget you.

I have made you, you are my servant; O Israel, I will not forget you.
(ISAIAH 44:21)

FEBRUARY 11

It's not size that counts

'And when you pray, do not keep on babbling like pagans, for they think they will be heard because of their many words. Do not be like them.'
(MATTHEW 6:7–8)

Many of us want to grow in prayer, but often feel overwhelmed by the sheer thought it. We imagine that everyone else's prayers are so much better, so much longer, so much more powerful than our own; and so, defeated already, we never begin. How refreshing it is, therefore, to see that so many powerful prayers in the Bible were unbelievably short! You see, it's not the size that counts; what matters to God is sincerity. And here, to prove it, are some of the Bible's shortest – yet most powerful! – prayers:

'Now show me your glory' (Exodus 33:18); 'O God, please heal her!' (Numbers 12:13); 'Speak, for your servant is listening' (1 Samuel 3:10); 'O Lord, open his eyes so that he may see' (2 Kings 6:17); 'Remember me with favour, O my God' (Nehemiah 13:31); 'For how long, O Lord?' (Isaiah 6:11); 'Lord, you can heal me if you will' (Matthew 8:2, NCV); 'Lord, save us! We're going to drown!' (Matthew 8:25); 'I believe; help my unbelief' (Mark 9:24, NRSV); 'Jesus, Master, have mercy on us!' (Luke 17:13, NKJV); 'Who are you Lord?' (Acts 9:5); 'Come, O Lord!' (1 Corinthians 16:22).

Pretty short prayers, eh? So short that we might think they were useless, that they couldn't possibly achieve anything. But how wrong we'd be! For these prayers proved to be some of the most significant prayers ever made, with results completely disproportionate to their length.

So, in a world where the size of everything seems to matter, remember that, when it comes to prayer, 'size' is completely irrelevant. Don't think your prayers are ineffective just because they seem short. It's not your prayers that matter, but your God! And wherever he sees a genuine heart, he has committed himself to hearing and answering. So, pray those prayers today, short though they may be! They may be more powerful than you think!

The world is full of so-called prayer warriors who are prayer-ignorant. They're full of formulas and programs and advice, peddling techniques for getting what you want from God. Don't fall for that nonsense.'
(MATTHEW 6:7–8, THE MESSAGE)

Selah!

The LORD Almighty is with us; the God of Jacob is our fortress.
Selah
(PSALM 46:11)

Isn't it funny how the little things in life can often be missed or taken for granted? Often they are there, faithfully doing their appointed task; but because they've always been there, we pay little if any attention to them – at least until someone points them out to us again. Well, there's a little word in the Bible just like that.

This little word faithfully gets on with its work, but most of us miss it and the significant thing that it's calling us to do. It's that little word 'selah'. Many of us will have read it again and again, especially when reading the psalms, but will probably have paid little attention to. So, what does it mean?

The short answer is: we don't know! Even the scholars aren't completely sure. But it's generally agreed that it was probably some sort of musical term – perhaps indicating a musical interlude or a change of key – in order to bring emphasis to the words or allow some pause for thought. That's why the New Living Translation translates this word as 'Interlude' – though sadly, some modern translations just omit it completely.

In the light of this, perhaps a good translation of it might be, *'Just think about that for a moment!*' In other words, the psalmist didn't want us just to sing words and pass on quickly; he wanted us to pause and really think about what we'd sung (perhaps the equivalent today of singing a song several times over as some churches do in order to let the words 'penetrate' more deeply).

So, when you're next reading the psalms, try substituting 'selah' with the words, 'Just think about that for a moment!' – and then make sure you do just that! And in the meantime, why not punctuate your day with lots of 'selah' moments? Look at a flower, the clouds, a new-born baby, the glorious sunset, the star-filled sky, and say to yourself, 'Selah! Just think about that for a moment!'

Lift up your heads, O you gates; lift them up, you ancient doors, that the
King of glory may come in. Who is he, this King of glory?
The LORD Almighty – he is the King of glory. Selah
(PSALM 24:9–10)

FEBRUARY 13

The faithful God

Great is your faithfulness.
(LAMENTATIONS 3:23)

'I won't be your friend any more if you don't!' How often we must have heard children saying that to one another. Come to think of it, how often we must have heard adults saying it too – though in a far more sophisticated way, of course!

Thankfully, God's friendship is not like that. His friendship with us is completely unconditional. It is never manipulative or demanding (as the phrase above is); it does not play games with us, or go off sulking if we let him down or don't 'come up with the goods'. God's friendship is simply 'there'.

And the reason for this is that God's friendship is the friendship of *covenant*. Through Jesus, God has made a covenant – that is, a binding commitment with us – promising to stay our friend, come what may, and to work his purposes out in our life, come what may. It is this '*come what may*' that characterizes God's faithfulness towards us. What a wonderful phrase that is: *come what may*! To think that God, who upholds the whole universe, should have promised to be with me and to be for me, *come what may*!

But how can we be sure? The answer is simple: God has already demonstrated his faithfulness and commitment to us in the act of sending his Son to die on the cross to pay the price of our sins – and that is a historical and unchangeable fact! And, as Paul put it, 'Since God did not spare even his own Son but gave him up for us all, won't God, who gave us Christ, also give us everything else?' (Romans 8:32, NLT). Of course he will!

This same God is with you today. His faithfulness is sure – not because of you, but because of Jesus. And that is why you can be confident that you can experience that faithfulness afresh today.

He is the Rock, his works are perfect, and all his ways are just. A faithful God who does no wrong, upright and just is he.
(DEUTERONOMY 32:4)

FEBRUARY 14

Mercy and grace

*Grace, mercy and peace will be with us from God the Father
and from Jesus Christ, the Father's Son, in truth and love.*
(2 JOHN 3, NRSV)

In Victor Hugo's novel *Les Misérables* (currently a successful London
West End show) a kindly bishop takes into his home the French ex-
convict, Jean Valjean, who had been imprisoned for 19 years for simply
stealing bread. The bishop's kindness is rewarded only by Valjean stealing
his silverware and making off with it during the night. Caught by the
police, he is returned to the bishop who not only doesn't press charges,
but tells Valjean that he forgot to take the silver candlesticks with him
when he left. The police, of course, then have to walk away with no
accusation against him.

But what would *you* have said? 'Thank you officers for catching him
and recovering my property'? That's probably the answer most of us
would have given; and that would have been justice, what the man
deserved. But the bishop's answer went way beyond the demands of
justice. For he showed the man mercy; and not only mercy, but grace.
Why did he do that? Because that's exactly how God deals with each of
us – in mercy and in grace.

Grace and mercy are two opposite sides of the coin: mercy is about
our not being given *what we deserve*; grace is about our being given *more
than we deserve*. What Valjean deserved because of his theft was
punishment; but what he got was reward! He received not only mercy,
but grace. And what we deserve because of sin, is God's judgment; but
God doesn't give us that. Rather, as we put our trust in Jesus, he gives us
more than we deserve or could ever hope for; he gives us his grace and
forgiveness. What a God!

Oh, what happened to Jean Valjean? Given a new start, he reformed
and became a successful businessman and mayor of a provincial town.
Now if that isn't a picture of what God does for us, what is?

*'The LORD bless you and keep you; the LORD make his face shine upon
you and be gracious to you; the LORD turn his face towards you
and give you peace.'*
(NUMBERS 6:24–26)

Unforgivable sin?

'I tell you the truth, all the sins and blasphemies of men will be forgiven them. But whoever blasphemes against the Holy Spirit will never be forgiven; he is guilty of an eternal sin.'
(MARK 3:28–29)

Over many years as a pastor, Mike has lost count of the times that someone has come to him, fearful of having committed 'the unforgivable sin'. The things confessed have ranged from the profoundly serious to the rather comical. But the answer given has always been the same: if you're worried you have committed the unforgivable sin, then your very worry assures you that you haven't!

It's important to remember the context in which Jesus said today's opening verses. In both Matthew 12:22–32 and Mark 3:20–30 the setting is Jesus' opponents ascribing his work done by the power of the Spirit to the work of the devil. Mark specifically adds the explanation, 'He said this because they were saying, "He has an evil spirit"' (Mark 3:30).

So, the sin in question is ascribing to the devil what Jesus is doing. Such a sin, Jesus says, can't be forgiven. Why? Because Jesus is the only means of salvation; and if we reject him, then we're rejecting the only basis on which we can be forgiven. If we're worried we might have committed this sin, then we can't have committed it; for the very fact that we are worried shows that we are still sensitive to Jesus and his requirements on our life – the very opposite of those who reject him.

It is therefore important that we do not apply Jesus' judgment upon this particular sin to other sins, whether our own or others'. For no sin is ever too bad that God will not forgive us for it – though the devil tries to convince us otherwise. People like Abraham, Moses, David, Peter and Paul, all committed sin of various and dreadful kinds; yet all found forgiveness. Why? Because they took God at his word.

Don't let past sin, or a fear that God might not be prepared to forgive it, keep you from him. The only sin God will not forgive is the sin that will not be confessed.

Jesus said to them, 'It is not the healthy who need a doctor, but the sick. I have not come to call the righteous, but sinners.'
(MARK 2:17)

Think 'people'!

*Once you were not a people, but now you are
the people of God.*
(1 PETER 2:10)

Trying to change our mindset about things can be difficult. Think of how people must have felt when they discovered that the earth was not flat, or that people could fly, or that pictures could be transmitted through the air. Such things are hard to get your mind around at first! And that's how it is for many people with 'the church'. For many, the church is a *building*. But God wants us to change our mindset; for the church is not about *buildings* but about *people*.

There are many different pictures of the church in the New Testament, each of them emphasizing a particular aspect of what it means to be God's people. Some speak of the corporate nature of the church (such as family, building, people, flock, and nation); some speak of the church's role (such as army, temple and priesthood); some speak of the church's fruitfulness (such as field and branches); some speak of the church's need to stay closely linked to Jesus (such as vine and body). But all these pictures have one thing in common: they are all *corporate* or demand *corporate response*. It is impossible for just one person to be them!

God's plan and promise is for us to know him *together* as his church. The New Testament has no concept of 'go-it-alone' Christians, reflected in the fact that the word 'saint' (a synonym for 'Christian') is *always* in the plural (and even the one apparent singular usage in the KJV is corporate: 'Salute every saint in Christ Jesus', Philippians 4:21, KJV). In the words of Michael Griffiths, 'The concept of a solitary saint is foreign to the New Testament writers.' Being a Christian is, quite simply, about being a part.

So, don't feel you are on your own today (though the devil often tries to get us to think we are). If you are a Christian, then you are a part – part of God's wonderful people, with all the promises that this people receive. Don't stay isolated; be 'a part'!

'I will be their God and they will be my people.'
(JEREMIAH 31:33)

FEBRUARY 17

We interrupt this programme

*'May the LORD, the God of your fathers, increase you a
thousand times and bless you as he has promised!'*
(DEUTERONOMY 1:11)

Martin still remembers sitting in a church service one evening when the
minister suddenly stopped in the middle of his sermon. The reason? An
ambulance went by and the minister interrupted his message to pray for
those involved in the emergency. His sermon was important; but not too
important to be interrupted by a matter of potential life and death. 'We
interrupt this programme' is a phrase that we still sometimes hear on radio
or TV at times of national importance. The normal programme is
suspended and the screen suddenly switches to the newscaster who brings
us the newsflash.

In a similar way, Moses interrupts himself in full flow in
Deuteronomy chapter 1. He reminds the Israelites of 'the story so far'.
'You have stayed long enough at this mountain. Break camp and advance
. . . I have given you this land . . . Go in and take possession . . .' he has
been reminding them God had said (Deuteronomy 1:6–8). But then,
suddenly, he pauses, as it were, and prays for God's promise to be fulfilled
even further. 'May the LORD, the God of your fathers, increase you a
thousand times and bless you as he has promised!' (verse 11). This could
seem a bit like an interruption, a bit like someone 'breaking into the
programme' just at the crucial moment; but his prayer doesn't interrupt
his flow; it supports it.

God's promises are so wide and great, but so often we restrict the
release of his power and his goodness by failing to pray those promises
into being. Has God made promises to you? Pray them into being today!
Pray he will complete what he has promised, what he has started. Pray he
will bless whatever he gives you to do today. Be ready to 'interrupt the
programme' of your day to pray things into being and to ask for more of
God's promises and power in your life! He *is* at work in you – but ask him
for more!

*Work out your salvation with fear and trembling, for it is God who works
in you to will and to act according to his good purpose.*
(PHILIPPIANS 2:12–13)

FEBRUARY 18

Praying for others

'And I will pour out a spirit of compassion and supplication on the house of David . . .'
(ZECHARIAH 12:10, NRSV)

So much of life today encourages us to be self-centred and to think only of 'me'. What a contrast this is to prayer in the Bible, where it focuses not on 'me' but on 'them'.

In the Bible we find a huge range of things that people prayed about for their family and friends. These included things such as: *blessing*, as when 'the priests and the Levites stood to bless the people, and God heard them, for their prayer reached heaven, his holy dwelling-place' (2 Chronicles 30:27); *spiritual growth*, like Epaphras who 'is always wrestling in prayer for you, that you may stand firm in all the will of God, mature and fully assured' (Colossians 4:12); *health and healing*, as when John wrote, 'Dear friend, I pray that you may enjoy good health and that all may go well with you, even as your soul is getting along well' (3 John 2); *protection*, as when 'Peter was kept in prison, but the church was earnestly praying to God for him' (Acts 12:5); *the opening of doors*, as when Paul wrote, 'Pray for us, too, that God may open a door for our message' (Colossians 4:3). And these just scratch the surface of things that people prayed for!

Intercession – praying for others – is something of a mystery; but it is one of the key methods that God uses for the pouring out of his blessing upon people. Intercession gets hold of the heart of God through the nudges and promptings of the Holy Spirit and so sees put into action on earth what the will of God is in heaven. Perhaps sometimes, like Paul, we feel that we don't know what to pray for; but if we will just be still, we will often find that the Holy Spirit drops a thought into our minds about a particular person or situation.

Zechariah saw that the age in which we live would be hallmarked by Spirit-prompted intercession. Let's not miss the chance to catch hold of that today! Listen for his nudges – and then pray!

The Spirit helps us in our weakness; for we do not know how to pray as we ought, but that very Spirit intercedes with sighs too deep for words.
(ROMANS 8:26, NRSV)

FEBRUARY 19

Strength for the days

'As thy days, so shall thy strength be.'
(DEUTERONOMY 33:25, KJV)

We have all no doubt seen people suddenly faced with an issue that they had feared they might never be able to handle – perhaps unemployment, or severe illness, or bereavement, or tragedy. Amazingly they seem to suddenly find a miraculous grace and strength from God for each day, so that they are not just 'dragging themselves through' but are experiencing a special sense of his promised presence and help. Whenever we see this, we are experiencing the truth of today's text: that, as the NIV puts it, 'your strength will equal your days'.

What a wonderful promise of God this is! That he will provide strength for each day and for whatever is needed in that day. This means we don't have to sit and worry whether we will have enough strength for tomorrow or for next year or for ten years' time. God promises us sufficient resources – himself! – for each day as it comes. Now the thing about how God works is this: he doesn't give us that strength *before* we need it, but *as* we need it. Most of us would probably prefer to have a spiritual stockpile of resources 'in case of need'; but it doesn't work like that! If it did, it would rob us of having to walk by faith and having to trust God day by day. Rather, it's *as we need it* that the strength and grace are given.

Being a Christian does not guarantee us immunity from life's pressures, trials and sufferings. Such things are simply part of living in a sin-ridden world. As a pastor for many years, Mike has had to walk through many a crisis with people; but he has also seen them find God's amazing grace and strength in their situation. It is at such times, when something earth-shattering happens, when the bottom falls out of our world, that we need God's strength. And when we need it, God promises, it *will* be there – enough strength for each day and to equal our days.

Whatever you are facing, God's grace and strength is also there for *you* today.

'It is God who arms me with strength and makes my way perfect.'
(2 SAMUEL 22:33)

When the world around you is falling apart

*In the year that King Uzziah died, I saw the Lord seated
on a throne, high and exalted, and the train of his robe
filled the temple.*
(ISAIAH 6:1)

The world must have seemed like it had fallen apart. After a glorious –
and, for those days, enormously long – reign of 52 years, during which
Judah's national pride had flourished and its borders grown, the godly
king Uzziah had at last died. All sorts of questions were now running
through people's minds: what would happen now? Who would take over?
How would things go? What about God's promises in the past? What
about that great superpower Assyria to the east with its territorial
ambitions? With King Uzziah no longer on the throne, now what would
happen to them all?

God's answer for Isaiah's anxious foreboding was quite simple: it was
a revelation of himself. The earthly king might have died; but *the* king,
the king of glory, was still on his throne! – a king high and lifted up, holy
and majestic, worshipped by the hosts of heaven – and a king who was
certainly not about to die! And it was seeing *this* king once again that
would make sense of everything and cause Isaiah to take hold of God's
promises for his people once again.

Isaiah's response to such a vision was at first to run! He felt so
unworthy, so unclean. But God had a plan! He himself would deal with
Isaiah's overwhelming sense of sin; just one touch from a coal from the
heavenly altar and it was dealt with! Now that Isaiah knew who *he* was
and who *God* was and how very much he was loved and forgiven, now he
was ready to look at the world and all its problems with fresh eyes.

It is in encountering that God ourselves today – as a King seated on
his throne, high above everything, yet not so far removed that he cannot
deal with our sin and our circumstances – that we too can stand firm
when things around us fall apart and take hold of his promises anew.

. . . and there before me was a throne in heaven with someone sitting on it.
(REVELATION 4:2)

FEBRUARY 21

Does God listen?

What other nation is so great as to have their gods near them the way the LORD our God is near us whenever we pray to him?
(DEUTERONOMY 4:7)

Have you ever wondered whether God *really* listens to your prayers? Or perhaps thought that he listens to others' prayers, but not yours? After all, you're not worthy, are you? And you've been bad in the past, haven't you? Sounds familiar? But when we talk like this, we haven't understood the first thing about prayer – or about God! For there are two main reasons why God hears our prayers – and neither of them has anything to do with us!

First, God hears our prayers because *he is near*. While God is beyond everything in creation, he is nevertheless near us – both those who are his people and those who aren't yet his people, those who've done well and those who haven't done so well. Paul told the people of Athens, who were very religious, yet who didn't know who they believed in or were praying to, about the living God who is 'the Lord of heaven and earth and does not live in temples built by hands' (Acts 17:24), and yet who 'is not far from each one of us. "For in him we live and move and have our being"'(Acts 17:27–28). God really is near, Paul was saying; and so he really does listen!

Second, God hears our prayers because *he loves us* – no matter what we've done – as the Bible makes clear again and again. Of course, this doesn't mean he's happy with everything in our lives as they are, or that he's content to let us stay the same; but, like any good parent with their child, it means that his first response is always one of love, not judgment, of listening and not being deaf to our cries. We really don't have to be perfect before we can bring our needs to him (if we did, we'd be waiting a long time!), just open and honest.

Does he listen to you when you pray? Of course he does – not because of you, but because of him. He's near, he loves you, he's listening; so tell him what's on your heart today.

We give thanks to you, O God, we give thanks, for your Name is near.
(PSALM 75:1)

The God of all comfort

'Praise be to the God and Father of our Lord Jesus Christ, the Father of compassion and the God of all comfort, who comforts us in all our troubles . . .'
(2 CORINTHIANS 1:3–4)

What do you think of when someone says 'comfort'? Settling down into your favourite armchair? Sitting in the bath away from the kids for half an hour? Munching your way through a box of chocolates to cheer yourself up? Upgrading your car to something a little better? All of these are commonplace expressions of comfort. But all of them quickly pass; and none comes anywhere near what the Bible means by 'comfort'. For true comfort is nothing less than an invasion of God's grace, encouragement, and strength for us in the hard and challenging times of life; not just to 'give us a bit of relief' or to 'keep us going', but to transform us and energize us so that we can come through victoriously on the other side.

The reason such comfort works and lasts is that it is nothing less than the comfort of *God himself.* Through Isaiah God promised his weary people, 'I, even I, am he who comforts you' (Isaiah 51:12). Jeremiah, who certainly went through his fair share of troubles, discovered that it was God himself who was his comfort, even calling him 'my Comforter in sorrow' (Jeremiah 8:18). And of course Jesus promised us that his Father would send his followers 'another Comforter, that he may abide with you for ever; even the Spirit of truth' (John 14:16–17, KJV).

Of course, God also knows that we sometimes need encouragement 'with skin on' – that is, in the shape of a friend. So he often sends someone or gets them to contact us at just the right moment. That was Paul's experience when Titus turned up at just the right time, causing him to say, 'But God, who comforts the downcast, comforted us by the coming of Titus' (2 Corinthians 7:6). It was also David's experience when Jonathan 'helped him to find strength in God' (1 Samuel 23:16).

Whether directly or indirectly, God promises to be *your* comfort today in every situation you face. Believe it, and be ready to receive it – even from unexpected quarters!

'As a mother comforts her child, so will I comfort you.'
(ISAIAH 66:13)

FEBRUARY 23

Come home!

'Return, faithless people; I will cure you of backsliding.' 'Yes, we will come to you, for you are the LORD our God.'
(JEREMIAH 3:22)

There are some people who, though once practising Christians somehow wandered from their faith and become 'backsliders'. Such people are rarely 'anti-God'; it's simply that they started to drift, often imperceptibly at first, until they finally found themselves out of the harbour and adrift at sea, not knowing how to get back. Can such people ever come back? Oh yes!

The Bible has many examples of backsliders, all of whom were given the chance to return. Indeed the prophets promised that God himself would do for them what they couldn't do for themselves, as our verses today show. But doesn't Hebrews suggest that backsliders can never be restored? 'What about people who turn away after they have already seen the light and have received the gift from heaven and have shared in the Holy Spirit? What about those who turn away after they have received the good message of God and the powers of the future world? There is no way to bring them back' (Hebrews 6:4–6, CEV). That seems quite stark, doesn't it? But remember the context. This letter was written to Christians from a Jewish background, some of whom, under pressure, were considering returning to Judaism. So the writer says, 'How can you think of doing that and still hope to be saved? You left Judaism because you saw it couldn't save you; and now you want to go back and think you'll still be saved? That's impossible! Keep pressing on with your Christian faith.' So we must take care not to make this contradict what the Bible says elsewhere about how God gladly receives those who repent and return. As Scripture promises, 'if we are faithless, he will remain faithful, for he cannot disown himself' (2 Timothy 2:13).

If you have drifted away from God, don't doubt he'll take you back! Just like the father welcomed his prodigal son, so your heavenly Father is ready to welcome you – no matter how far you have drifted and no matter what you have done. It is never too late to come home!

'I will save them from all their sinful backsliding, and I will cleanse them. They will be my people, and I will be their God.'
(EZEKIEL 37:23)

FEBRUARY 24

I'm praying for you

'Simon, Simon, Satan has asked to have all of you, to sift you like wheat. But I have pleaded in prayer for you, Simon, that your faith should not fail.'
(LUKE 22:31–32, NLT)

'I'll pray for you.' How quickly those well-intentioned words seem to slip out of our mouths, only to then find that we neglect to pray the promised prayers. Thankfully, the Lord Jesus isn't like that! He has promised to pray for us, and that's a promise that he is keeping right now. Both of us writers find this staggering; it bowls us over. To think that Christ is praying for *us*! It seems incredible – but it's absolutely true!

So, how does Jesus pray for us? First, he's praying for us – just as he prayed for Simon and the other disciples – that our faith may not fail; that we won't lose our faith or give up, but that our trust in him will remain strong, despite all challenges and opposition. Secondly, he prays to the Father that 'you protect them from the evil one' (John 17:15) who 'prowls around like a roaring lion looking for someone to devour' (1 Peter 5:8). Thirdly, he is constantly interceding for us, for he intimately knows our weaknesses and can therefore bring us and them before our Father. He is always praying for us, 'always on the job to speak up for [us]' (Hebrews 7:25, The Message). Fourthly, he prays for us that that we may be united with other believers, 'that all of them may be one, Father, just as you are in me and I am in you . . . so that the world may believe that *you* have sent me' (John 17:21). Wow! All of that, and for you and me!

What does this mean for our lives? That Jesus understands right now what you are facing and going through. As authors of this book we couldn't possibly know the circumstances of every reader; but Jesus does! Let this promise bring deep assurance today: Jesus is praying for you right now, just as he promised!

But because Jesus lives for ever, he has a permanent priesthood. Therefore he is able to save completely those who come to God through him, because he always lives to intercede for them.
(HEBREWS 7:24–25)

FEBRUARY 25

The power of blessing

And he took the children in his arms, put his hands on them and blessed them.
(MARK 10:16)

'Bless you!' While we're all familiar with this expression, our guess is that we are far more likely to hear it as a response to someone sneezing than as a prayer on their behalf. The supposed origins of the phrase are many – everything from a belief that the soul left the body momentarily when someone sneezed and so you blessed them as protection lest the devil sneak in, to a benediction on someone who was about to depart this life having caught the 'Black Death' (a symptom of which was sneezing). But in the Bible, blessing someone was far more serious and powerful than any of this. It was not even the mere offering of 'spiritual best wishes' (which it has often become for Christians today); rather, it was a powerful prayer of declaration based on the promises of God.

Perhaps one of the best known blessings is the one that Moses commanded the priests to use (and one that is still used in many Christian traditions): 'The LORD bless you and keep you; the LORD make his face shine upon you and be gracious to you; the LORD turn his face towards you and give you peace' (Numbers 6:24–26). This was a purposeful declaration over people's lives of what God himself had said he wanted to do for his people, and the priests were thereby saying, 'Let it happen Lord!' And that's what we're saying when we bless someone: let what you have promised happen for them Lord!

But it isn't just our friends we should bless, but our enemies too. Jesus said, 'Bless those who curse you, and pray for those who spitefully use you' (Luke 6:28, NKJV). What a difference it would make in our workplace if, instead of holding grudges or trying to 'get our own back', we spoke words of blessing over those who oppose us, and then do all we can to bring that blessing about!

Who knows what a difference it could make today if we were to exercise the power of blessing others! Try it and see!

After spending some time there, they were sent off by the brothers with the blessing of peace to return to those who had sent them.
(ACTS 15:33)

I can call him Father!

When you pray, say 'Father . . .'
(LUKE 11:2)

All across the world, millions of children are growing up without fathers. For some, it is because of AIDS or war; for others because of a broken marriage or an 'absent father'; for others, because their fathers were themselves not fathered properly and so have no concept of fathering. In such a world of 'fatherlessness', then, Jesus' teaching that we can know God as Father comes as a breath of fresh air.

Seeing God as 'Father' is not simply a human projection or personification; rather, it is the other way round: the human race has fatherhood only because God himself is a Father. One of Paul's prayers puts it like this: 'For this reason I kneel before the Father, from whom his whole family in heaven and on earth derives its name' (Ephesians 3:14–15). There is a play on words in the Greek here; the word for Father is 'pater' and the word for family is 'patria'. Paul's argument is that 'patria' flows out of a 'pater', not the other way round. If there is no 'pater', there can be no 'patria'; if there were no 'Fatherhood' in God, there could never have been fatherhood (and family) in human society. This understanding of God as 'Father' is, then, not simply a reflection of patriarchal society nor a human projection; it is a fundamental assurance of what God is like and therefore of how we may approach him; it is an assurance of his fatherly care and loving authority.

Calling God 'Father' doesn't mean he is 'male' of course (indeed, when he created us, it needed both male and female to even begin to reflect his image); nor does it mean he is a bigger version of our own earthly father. (You may have had a good father; but he wasn't good enough in comparison to God! You may have had a bad father and may still have unhappy memories of that, but God certainly isn't like that.)

To know what God's fatherhood is truly like, think of how Jesus related to him and trusted him, loved him and was loved in return. That's how God wants to relate to each of us today!

'I thought you would call me "Father" and not turn away from following me.'
(JEREMIAH 3:19)

FEBRUARY 27

But will he listen?

Then you will call, and the LORD will answer; you will cry for help, and he will say: 'Here am I'.
(ISAIAH 58:9)

'Prayer wouldn't work for me'. Such comments are usually made, not because people wonder whether God is there, or even whether he answers prayer, but because they doubt whether *their* prayers would be answered. Such fears are groundless; for prayer is God's gift to *everyone*. But here are some reasons why people don't pray:

• '*I'm not a Christian.*' But the Bible says God loves to hear everyone's prayers, Christian or not! 'O you who hear prayer, to you all men will come' (Psalm 65:2).

• '*It's a long time since I prayed.*' It was probably a long time since the robber who was crucified with Jesus had prayed; but he was still heard, for Jesus assured him, 'I tell you the truth, today you will be with me in paradise' (Luke 23:43).

• '*I don't feel good enough.*' That's the whole point! None of us is! The psalmist said, 'If you, O LORD, kept a record of sins, O Lord, who could stand? But with you there is forgiveness; therefore you are feared' (Psalm 130:3–4).

• '*I'm not sure if God is there.*' Well, the Bible says, 'try him out' and see! 'Taste and see that the LORD is good' (Psalm 34:8).

• '*I feel so flat*'. But prayer doesn't depend on *our* feelings, but on *God's* faithfulness. Jeremiah, who often felt depressed, said, 'I remember my affliction and my wandering, the bitterness and the gall. I well remember them, and my soul is downcast within me. Yet this I call to mind and therefore I have hope: Because of the LORD's great love we are not consumed, for his compassions never fail. They are new every morning; great is your faithfulness' (Lamentations 3:19–23).

• '*I've drifted away from God.*' But Jesus says, 'Listen! I am standing and knocking at your door. If you hear my voice and open the door, I will come in and we will eat together' (Revelation 3:20, CEV).

Whatever reason you might have had for not praying, forget it right now! Will your father listen to *you*? Of course he will!

I call on you, O God, for you will answer me; give ear to me and hear my prayer. (PSALM 17:6)

FEBRUARY 28

No hiding place!

'Can anyone hide in secret places so that I cannot see him?'
declares the LORD. 'Do not I fill heaven and earth?'
declares the LORD.
(JEREMIAH 23:24)

Try as we might, there is simply nowhere that we can hide from God.
Many years ago, when Mike was living in France, a young Australian
woman arrived at the same school where he was teaching at that time. She
had come half way round the world to run away from God – but God had
arranged to put her with a Christian, the only other person who spoke
English for miles around! God had certainly determined that, for her,
there would be no hiding place!

We may not run to the other side of the globe; but many of us try to
hide from God, especially when things have gone wrong or when we have
'messed up' in life. And while that is the very moment we need him,
everything within us wants to run and get away from him. Even the great
King David walked this path. After his adultery with Bathsheba, he tried
to cover it up; but he could not run from God, who sent the prophet
Nathan to confront him with a word that pierced his heart. And at that
moment, David discovered the solution: he simply said, 'I have sinned
against the LORD' (2 Samuel 12:13). He stopped running, owned up
before God, and the matter was forgiven! He discovered that God keeps
his promise to forgive those who confess their sin. As he wrote in his
psalm about this incident, 'Then I acknowledged my sin to you and did
not cover up my iniquity. I said, "I will confess my transgressions to the
LORD" – and you forgave the guilt of my sin' (Psalm 32:5).

To know that there is no hiding place from God could sound a
frightening thing (and the devil will certainly try to get you to think it is!);
but it is not. It is not frightening, but freeing! Don't run from God today;
talk to him – yes, with all your failures. He knows them all and has already
promised to forgive them. You simply need to ask!

Nothing in all creation is hidden from God's sight. Everything is uncovered
and laid bare before the eyes of him to whom we must give account.
(HEBREWS 4:13)

MARCH 1

Worship God alone

'I am the LORD your God, who brought you out of Egypt, out of the land of slavery. You shall have no other gods before me.'
(EXODUS 20:2–3)

Revelation is an amazing book. But imagine how amazing, how overwhelming it must have been for John when he first received that revelation. Overcome by the vision he had experienced, he fell down at the angel's feet to worship, but was quickly stopped with the words: 'Do not do it! . . . Worship God!' (Revelation 22:9). And this is the constant theme of the Bible: God and God alone is to be worshipped; and therefore false gods and idols are to be avoided at all costs.

This is made clear in the first commandment (our verse for today), a commandment God gave his people after they had left Egypt, a land full of gods and idols. But it would be a commandment repeated again and again at various stages in Israel's history, especially by the prophets when Israel became enticed by the gods and idols of the Canaanites with their highly sensuous fertility worship.

For most of us in the West worshipping a stone or wooden carving is not an issue; but less obvious forms of idolatry certainly are. Whatever we give most of our energy, passion and time to is our idol. As Jesus put it, 'For where your treasure is, there your heart will be also' (Luke 12:34). Our Western idols are often things like our job, our family, our car, our holiday, our football team, our hobby, our computer games; these are what so often have 'number one' place in our life – the place that God says belongs to him alone. Whenever we live like that, we have just bowed down to an idol.

What excites you the most? If the answer isn't 'God', then your answer is an idol! For what I really get excited about is what I really worship. If today you recognize that something has gradually – perhaps almost imperceptibly – pushed God from the central place in your life, then sort it out quickly, for idolatry is something that God truly hates, for it robs us of him – the greatest delight of life.

O LORD, our God, other lords besides you have ruled over us,
but your name alone do we honour.
(ISAIAH 26:13)

MARCH 2

The God of holiness

'Holy, holy, holy is the LORD Almighty; the whole earth is full of his glory.'
(ISAIAH 6:3)

If you have ever had to pick up something completely filthy when you are clean and in smart clothes, you'll know how absolutely disgusting it can feel. Everything within you cries 'Yuk!' and wants to drop it as fast as you can, as you run for the wash basin to get clean again.

The Bible says that this is exactly how God feels about sin. He is so clean, so 'holy' (to use the Bible's word), that he cannot bear the sight of it. As Habakkuk put it, 'Your eyes are too pure to look on evil; you cannot tolerate wrong' (Habakkuk 1:13). This in itself is bad news: that God cannot bear the sight of us; but there's worse to come! For not only can God not bear to look at sin, his perfect justice demands that he also judge it.

But now for the good news! For God's judgment is not his last word, but rather his mercy. God does not simply tell us to be holy, and then leave us to it; he himself provides the means of our becoming holy. This is what Isaiah discovered when his vision of the holy God made him to want to run, but then God stopped him. An angel touched his sinful lips with a coal from the altar and said, 'See, this has touched your lips; your guilt is taken away and your sin atoned for' (Isaiah 6:7). God himself dealt with the problem!

Still today we do not need to run from our holy God, though our sin may often make us feel like doing so. No matter what we have done, or failed to do, God himself has promised to deal with our sin through the death of Christ. The promise of his word is that his forgiveness is still available to us today. As Peter put it on the Day of Pentecost, 'The promise is for you and your children and all who are far off' (Acts 2:39). Those 'far off' include you! And that means that, right now, you can call on God and know again the reality of God himself making you clean. Don't wait – just do it!

I am the LORD, who makes you holy.
(LEVITICUS 20:8)

69

MARCH 3

The friendship of Jesus

'I have called you friends'
(JOHN 15:15)

All of us know what it is like to have friendships, perhaps even a 'special friend' – one with whom we can really be ourselves; one with whom we can laugh and cry; one we trust implicitly through thick and thin; one who loves us enough even to tell us the truth!

The Bible says that this is the sort of relationship that God wants with people – ordinary people like you and me. In fact, this was one of the things that marked Jesus out. He was a real 'people person'. He loved making friendships – not with the 'religious specialists' of his day (in fact, they found him quite difficult to be with), but with ordinary people. He was a *friend* to them, and they felt at ease in his presence because of it, no matter what their life had been like in the past. Little wonder that 'the common people heard him gladly' (Mark 12:37, KJV). For Jesus, being people's friends, and helping them to discover the friendship of God, was one of the most important things in life.

This friendship was no ordinary friendship, however. It was the friendship of *covenant*. In Bible times a 'covenant' was a committed promise, a binding and unbreakable contract - a hard concept for us to grasp these days, when we are so used to slick lawyers being able to break anything! But God says: the sort of agreement I want to make with people is one that can't – and won't – be broken, no matter what happens; and an agreement that is no mere legal contract – technical, hard, and cold – but a contract of intimacy, loyalty, and true friendship.

Today God wants you to experience and enjoy this promise of a covenant of friendship with him for yourself, being at ease in his presence and sharing the day with him, whatever it may bring. Today, he promises to be our friend!

'Greater love has no-one than this, that he lay down his life for his friends.
You are my friends if you do what I command.'
(JOHN 15:13–14)

MARCH 4

Handling enemies

'Love your enemies, do good to those who hate you, bless those who curse you, pray for those who ill-treat you . . . Then your reward will be great, and you will be sons of the Most High, because he is kind to the ungrateful and wicked.'
(LUKE 6:27–28, 35)

Praying for our friends isn't that great a burden really, is it? Sure, we might forget to pray for them as much as we would like; but at the end of the day, it is no great hardship to pray for God's blessing on those that we love. 'Ah!' says Jesus. 'Then now it's time to move on and to bless those you don't love, those who are your enemies!'

Our enemies? Yes! That's exactly what the Bible tells us to do. Even in the Old Testament, which so many people think of as being 'harsh' in comparison to the New, God's people are commanded, 'Do not seek revenge or bear a grudge against one of your people, but love your neighbour as yourself. I am the LORD' (Leviticus 19:18). The book of Proverbs, full of God's wise ways for living, says, 'Do not say, "I'll pay you back for this wrong!" Wait for the LORD, and he will deliver you' (Proverbs 20:22), and 'If your enemy is hungry, give him food to eat; if he is thirsty, give him water to drink. In doing this, you will heap burning coals on his head, and the LORD will reward you' (Proverbs 25:21–22). If this is the high standard set under the Old Covenant, then it shouldn't surprise us to find Jesus setting the standard even higher for those who are his followers and who are filled with his Spirit!

But why should we live like this? Why should we even pray for those who oppose us, let alone do good to them? Because when we do, we are reflecting the character of our compassionate God and so are giving him opportunity to deal with people in his own way. Moreover, doing things this way carries God's commanded blessing for us!

So, has someone been opposing you, or speaking against you or trying to undermine you? If so, let go of your resentment and hostility and start to pray for God to bless them. Then be ready for things to change!

Bless those who persecute you; bless and do not curse.
(ROMANS 12:14)

MARCH 5

Get wisdom!

Do not forsake wisdom, and she will protect you; love her, and she will watch over you. Wisdom is supreme; therefore get wisdom. Though it cost all you have, get understanding. Esteem her, and she will exalt you; embrace her, and she will honour you.
(PROVERBS 4:6–8)

When did you last pray for wisdom? Probably some time ago, as it doesn't figure high on most prayer agendas, other than in crisis situations. Yet requests for wisdom – the ability to do the *right thing* in the *right way* at the *right time* – are often found in Bible prayers, and Proverbs in particular has many encouragements to pursue wisdom.

One of the best-known requests for wisdom is King Solomon's. When God told him in a dream to ask for whatever he wanted, Solomon asked, not for great riches or power for himself, but for 'a discerning heart to govern your people and to distinguish between right and wrong' (1 Kings 3:9). This pleased God, who said, 'Since you have asked for this and not for long life or wealth for yourself, nor have asked for the death of your enemies but for discernment in administering justice, I will do what you have asked. I will give you a wise and discerning heart, so that there will never have been anyone like you, nor will there ever be. Moreover, I will give you what you have not asked for – both riches and honour' (1 Kings 3:11–13). By asking for wisdom, Solomon got it, but far more besides; for wisdom is the key to everything.

In the New Testament, Jesus himself 'grew in wisdom and stature, and in favour with God and men' (Luke 2:52); those chosen to distribute food were men 'who are known to be full of the Spirit and wisdom' (Acts 6:3); of Stephen it was noted that 'they could not stand up against his wisdom or the Spirit by whom he spoke' (Acts 6:10); in 1 Corinthians 12 the word of wisdom is one of the gifts of the Holy Spirit. Wisdom was clearly seen as important!

Wisdom is part of the character of God, and he wants it to be part of our character too. Are *you* asking for more of it?

If any of you lacks wisdom, he should ask God, who gives generously to all without finding fault, and it will be given to him.
(JAMES 1:5)

MARCH 6

'Us' or 'them'?

We are the temple of the living God. As God has said: 'I will live with them and walk among them, and I will be their God, and they will be my people.'
(2 CORINTHIANS 6:16)

Are you an 'us' person . . . or a 'them' person? . . . Let's explain what we mean!

Martin was once at a church meeting where the speaker asked everyone to write just one sentence about 'the church'. Most people began their reply with the word 'It' or 'They'. They got it wrong! If they were being truly biblical in their thinking, their answer should have begun with the word 'We' ('*We* are God's people . . . *We* are the bride of Christ . . .). The church is not 'them', but 'us'!

While ever we think of the church as something 'out there', separate from us, we will miss so much – and be far quicker to criticize what is wrong than to play our part in putting it right. (For who in their right mind would criticize themselves without doing something about it?) God wants us to understand that '*we* are the temple of the living God'; that it is among *us* that he has promised to live and work. Changing our mindset on this would bring about some amazing changes in our personal and corporate life!

The prophet Zephaniah has a beautiful picture of this corporate togetherness that God promises for his people. He saw God's people as standing together 'shoulder to shoulder' (Zephaniah 3:9). This is the sort of intimacy, the sort of togetherness that God has promised to his people; so to settle for anything less is to miss out on his promises and our birthright.

So today, remember that you are not destined to live as an isolated believer (even though the devil may have been trying hard to make you feel isolated). The church is not 'them' but 'us' – and *you* are part of that 'us' – an 'us' that is the very temple of God where he promises to come and walk among us.

'Then will I purify the lips of the peoples, that all of them may call on the name of the LORD and serve him shoulder to shoulder.'
(ZEPHANIAH 3:9)

God's power for weary people

He gives strength to the weary and increases the power of the weak. Even youths grow tired and weary, and young men stumble and fall; but those who hope in the LORD will renew their strength. They will soar on wings like eagles; they will run and not grow weary, they will walk and not be faint.
(ISAIAH 40:29–31)

Ever felt tired or weary? We'd be surprised if you hadn't! Whether it is the weariness of the mother of young children at the end of the day, or the weariness of the elderly as they start the day; the weariness of the manual worker with aching limbs, or the weariness of the executive with an aching head; all of us hit times of weariness, when we have simply had enough and feel we cannot do any more or carry on any longer.

At times like that it's good to remember that God never gets weary. That's hard for our minds to grasp – but it's absolutely true! Even when God rested after creation, it wasn't because he was tired; it was simply that his work was done! God never gets weary! Isaiah put it like this: 'Do you not know? Have you not heard? The LORD is the everlasting God, the Creator of the ends of the earth. He will not grow tired or weary, and his understanding no-one can fathom' (Isaiah 40:28). Indeed, he is so full of energy that he 'he who watches over Israel will neither slumber nor sleep' (Psalm 121:4).

Well, that's all well and good for God; but how does that affect us? Well, here's the good news: God has promised to share his divine energy with us! We may get weary – even the youngest and most energetic of us; but as we put our trust in God each day we can know *our* weakness being exchanged for *his* strength and can soar above pressures and problems like an eagle soaring far above! All we need to do is to stop (one of the hardest things in life to do!) and to call on God's promise of that divine energy for ourselves today! So why not do that right now?

The God of Israel gives power and strength to his people.
(PSALM 68:35)

MARCH 8

The delight of discipline!

'Blessed is the man whom God corrects; so do not despise the discipline of the Almighty. For he wounds, but he also binds up; he injures, but his hands also heal.'
(JOB 5:17–18)

Few of us like discipline – at least, when it is headed in our direction! Yet discipline plays an important part in shaping our character and lives. Any athlete knows how important discipline is if they want to succeed; any parent knows how important discipline is if they want their children to mature, and not turn out as spoilt brats. Discipline is good for us. And God thinks that too. The Bible tells us that he is not afraid to discipline his children. Why? Because he is angry with us? No – because he loves us! God's discipline in our lives is always for our good, never for our harm.

This is why the writer of the letter to the Hebrews – Christians who were experiencing discipline through opposition and persecution – went to such lengths to reassure them of the blessing and the promise that discipline conveys. First, he reassured them that 'the Lord disciplines those he loves' (Hebrews 12:6); second, that discipline meant 'God is treating you as sons' (verse 7), and not as illegitimate children (for a father disciplines his own children, not someone else's); third, that 'God disciplines us for our good' (verse 10). He acknowledged the obvious: that 'no discipline seems pleasant at the time, but painful' (verse 11); but then he got them to lift their eyes to God's purpose through it: 'Later on, however, it produces a harvest of righteousness and peace for those who have been trained by it' (verse 11).

If you have been going through hard times, don't see it as God's punishment (though the devil will try to convince you that it is!). It isn't his punishment, but his promise – his promise to treat you as a son, his promise to do you good through it, his promise to bring a harvest of righteousness and peace. So don't despise his discipline; but instead seek his grace to walk through it.

'My son, do not make light of the Lord's discipline, and do not lose heart when he rebukes you, because the Lord disciplines those he loves, and he punishes everyone he accepts as a son.'
(HEBREWS 12:5–6)

MARCH 9

Stand firm!

'Therefore put on the full armour of God, so that when the day of evil comes, you may be able to stand your ground, and after you have done everything, to stand.'
(EPHESIANS 6:13)

'There are two equal and opposite errors into which our race can fall about the devils. One is to disbelieve in their existence. The other is to believe, and to feel an excessive and unhealthy interest in them,' wrote C.S. Lewis in *The Screwtape Letters*. Some Christians, who cannot accept anything that science cannot explain, dismiss any thoughts of devils or spiritual warfare as merely a primitive worldview; while others find 'demons under every bed' and minister to others until Mary Magdalene, 'from whom seven demons had come out' (Luke 8:2), looked like a mere beginner in the realm of demonization. But somewhere between these two extremes, a real warfare is taking place – a warfare we need to be aware of, but not afraid of.

When Jesus came to earth, he entered a battle zone, for the devil had no intention of giving up conquered territory. From his birth to his death, the devil opposed Jesus at every twist and turn. And that battle was very real; for it was a battle not just against people or political and religious institutions, but against 'the rulers, against the authorities, against the powers of this dark world and against the spiritual forces of evil in the heavenly realms' (Ephesians 6:12).

But that battle was not just his – it's ours too! Jesus warned his followers that they too would be persecuted, opposed, and face many hardships as the devil tried to resist God's advancing kingdom. The battle is real – and that's why the church is described as an army, with you and I as its soldiers. But here is the good news: we already know who wins! For at the cross, Christ 'disarmed the powers and authorities' (Colossians 2:15) – and *that* is why we can stand firm today: because of Jesus.

Today, don't focus on the devil, focus on Jesus. As you do, giving the devil neither too much credence nor too much disregard, you will be able to stand firm!

'Your enemy the devil prowls around like a roaring lion looking for someone to devour. Resist him, standing firm in the faith.'
(1 PETER 5:8–9)

MARCH 10

Help in temptation

'For we do not have a high priest who is unable to sympathise with our weaknesses, we have one who has been tempted in every way, just as we are – yet was without sin. Let us then approach the throne of grace with confidence, so that we may receive mercy and find grace to help us in our time of need.'
(HEBREWS 4:15–16)

If someone tells you that they are never tempted, feel free to be sceptical! For the Bible tells us that temptation is something we all experience, no matter how mature a Christian we might be. Even Jesus himself was tempted (despite being God's Son and having all the resources of heaven at his disposal); so it is even more likely that we ourselves will be.

Right at the start of his ministry, having just been baptized in water and filled with the Holy Spirit, Jesus experienced a profound period of temptation in the wilderness for over forty days. The New Testament tells us that it was the Holy Spirit himself who led Jesus there (which in itself shows that, while the devil means temptation for our harm, God can use it for our good). Despite day after day of temptation, Jesus stood firm, however. Not once did he respond to the temptation; not once did he entertain it or linger over it or say 'yes' to it. Through it all, he remained sinless by finding strength in God to resist it.

We need to remember that *experiencing* temptation is not the same thing as *yielding* to it. As the saying goes: 'You can't stop crows from flying over your head, but you can stop them from making nests in your hair.' In other words, it's not experiencing temptation that is wrong (for we can't stop it happening), but rather responding to it. This is important, for the devil often tries to make us believe that even experiencing temptation is sinful (how can it be? – Jesus experienced it!) in the hope that we will become despondent and so turn the thought into practice anyway.

It is because Jesus himself was tempted that he really can help us when we are tempted. We simply need to ask him to keep his promise!

'And now that Jesus has suffered and was tempted, he can help anyone else who is tempted.'
(HEBREWS 2:18, CEV)

MARCH 11

Forgiven people, fallen world

Then David said to Nathan, 'I have sinned against the LORD.'
Nathan replied, 'The LORD has taken away your sin.'
(2 SAMUEL 12:13)

Have you ever experienced this scenario? You are truly a born-again Christian, living your life for Christ each day as best you can when – suddenly – you fall flat on our face, or you stumble into some sin, or you do or say something that pulls you up with a start. You are shocked! How could you do or think such a thing?! Have you been play-acting, not really living out the Christian life, all along? Have you been deceiving yourself or perhaps been a hypocrite? No, not at all. You are simply discovering the reality of living as *forgiven people* while still remaining in a *fallen world* – and you are not on our own!

The truth is, all God's people fall at times. In fact, some of the greatest saints in the Bible failed God terribly at certain points in their life – so much so that, if they hadn't done so, we would have had a very thin Bible indeed! Think of some of the great figures in the Old Testament: people like Abraham, Isaac, Jacob, Moses, Samuel, and David; or from the New Testament think of Peter, James, John, Thomas, Paul; all these were great figures who were significantly used by God; but they also struggled and stumbled at times, sometimes really badly – deceiving, lying, scheming, doubting, even murdering – but God still used them.

The apostle Paul certainly knew an inner struggle against sin at times, as he describes in Romans 7. He says that he didn't always do what he wanted to do, and sometimes he did what he didn't want to do, just like you and me; but he also knew the answer to this struggle: it was to keep his eyes focused on Jesus! For it is in focusing on Jesus that we remember that forgiveness can always be found – a forgiveness that has already been won for us through his death on the cross. Don't doubt this promise of God's word, but take it and use it today.

What a wretched man I am! Who will rescue me from this body of death?
Thanks be to God – through Jesus Christ our Lord!
(ROMANS 7:24–25)

MARCH 12

Friends!

Two are better than one, because they have a good return for their work: If one falls down, his friend can help him up. But pity the man who falls and has no-one to help him up!
(ECCLESIASTES 4:9–10)

The Bible contains such lofty themes. But then it surprises us by coming down to earth so hard that we can hardly believe it. Paul, for example, explored divine mysteries; yet he it was who wrote in 2 Corinthians, 'I still had no peace of mind, because I did not find my brother Titus there' (2:13) and 'God, who comforts the downcast, comforted us by the coming of Titus' (7:6). How 'ordinary'! To worry about a friend and need him to come and cheer you up! Paul clearly understood the blessing of friends!

Friends stand by us, especially in hard times. As Solomon put it, 'A friend loves at all times, and a brother is born for adversity' (Proverbs 17:17). But real friends are also not afraid to challenge us and tell us the truth; and if we are wise, we will listen. As Solomon put it again, 'Wounds from a friend can be trusted' (Proverbs 27:6).

The Bible contains many examples of good friendships that we could study to good profit: people like Ruth and Naomi (Ruth 1:15–18), David and Jonathan (1 Samuel 18:1–4), Elijah and Elisha (2 Kings 2:1–14), Jesus and the Twelve (John 15:9–17), Paul and Luke (Colossians 4:14), Paul and Timothy (2 Timothy 1:2–5).

Sadly, the church is often seen by many as an institution or organization, rather than what God intends it to be: a *family* (e.g., Matthew 12:46–50; Galatians 6:10; Ephesians 2:19) and *a friendship group* (e.g., John 15:13–15; 1 John 3:1–3; Jude 1–3). This is why the New Testament letters were written, not to a 'flock' or a 'group', but to 'friends'. (Do a word search around 'friends' and you will quickly see!)

Today, be grateful for your friends and pray for them. Don't take them for granted, but tell them you appreciate them. Thank those who have loved you enough to tell you the truth about yourself. And don't sit waiting for people to come and be a friend to you; go out and be a friend to them!

'Dear friends, since God so loved us, we also ought to love one another.'
(1 JOHN 4:11)

MARCH 13

The secret of strength

'Surely God is my salvation; I will trust and not be afraid. The
LORD, the LORD, is my strength and my song.'
(ISAIAH 12:2)

'Lord give me strength!' the cry often goes up. In many cases, it is simply a cry of exasperation in trying circumstances, rather than a genuine prayer. Yet it is a prayer that God is happy for us to make. For the Bible is full of promises of strength for those who come to God acknowledging that they have no strength of their own.

And what is the secret of that strength? That's what Delilah, sent by the Philistines to ensnare Samson, wanted to know when she asked him, 'Tell me the secret of your great strength' (Judges 16:6). At a superficial level, the apparent source of his strength was the Nazirite vow to which he had been dedicated from his conception; but the true source of his strength was not the vow, nor his unshorn hair that reflected it, but the God to whom he had been dedicated. Still today the God of Samson promises to come to people, bringing his supernatural strength into our lives for every need and circumstance.

Paul too discovered this secret of strength. His apostolic ministry led him to face many challenging situations in his life – mentally, physically and spiritually – but he came through them all by focusing on God and looking to him for strength. Writing to the Philippian church while under house arrest in Rome, his confident declaration, even in the light of an uncertain future, was still 'I can do everything through him who gives me strength' (Philippians 4:13).

Perhaps today you feel weary and at the end of your own resources; perhaps you are facing some seemingly insoluble problem in your family or some opposition at work; perhaps some new challenge lies ahead of you that you have not faced before; perhaps you are unsure if you can press on, or even feel like 'giving up'. Whatever your situation, the word of God promises that God himself will be your strength. Turn to him and ask him to fill you with that promised strength once again.

'The Sovereign LORD is my strength! He will make me as sure-footed as a
deer and bring me safely over the mountains.'
(HABAKKUK 3:19, NLT)

MARCH 14

Follow me!

'I am the light of the world. Whoever follows me will never walk in darkness, but will have the light of life.'
(JOHN 8:12)

Mike was sitting by the window as his plane came in to land at Dubai. A few hundred feet from the ground, he saw that a mist was creeping in from the desert; fifty feet from the ground, it was clear that it was now moving rapidly and becoming thicker; as the plane touched down, they were suddenly surrounded by a pea-soup fog. The pilot pulled off the runway and stopped the plane. Then came the announcement: 'Well, we just made it! The airport is now closed and there are an awful lot of planes up there circling around! However, I don't actually know where I am! So we'll just have to wait until they send a fire truck out to guide us in.'

A few minutes later Mike could see on his seat-back screen (set to give a pilot's eye view) the flashing lights of the fire truck and the sign on top of it saying 'Follow me'. The plane slowly began to creep forward; but then the lights of the truck seemed to get dimmer, until they eventually disappeared completely. The captain came back on: 'Well, sorry, ladies and gentlemen, but I've lost him! So rather than roll around blind, I think we'll just wait till he comes back and finds us!' Sure enough, a few minutes later, the welcome 'Follow me' sign came into view again and, tucked in close this time, the plane found its way at last to the stand.

Such an amazingly equipped plane, but brought to a halt by little drops of water vapour in the sky! Rendered completely useless, until a little fire truck came along saying 'Follow me'!

That's really rather like us, isn't it? Such amazing creatures, yet so easily paralysed, so easily lost, through even the smallest things in life. To people who recognize they get lost in the fog of life at times, Jesus comes along and simply says, 'Follow me – I'll get you there!' Today, hear his promise and stay close to him in all you do – and you'll get there too!

The people walking in darkness have seen a great light; on those living in the land of the shadow of death a light has dawned.
(ISAIAH 9:2)

MARCH 15

Why worship?

Jesus answered, 'It is written: "Worship the Lord your God and serve him only."'
(LUKE 4:8)

The worship of God has always been challenged. Right at the beginning Satan, formerly God's highest angel, somehow got it into his heart that he deserved to be worshipped, just like God. Christians have long seen in Isaiah's depiction of the King of Babylon a prophetic insight into Satan's heart at that time as he said, 'I will ascend to heaven; I will raise my throne above the stars of God; I will sit enthroned on the mount of assembly, on the utmost heights of the sacred mountain. I will ascend above the tops of the clouds; I will make myself like the Most High' (Isaiah 14:13–14). Thousands of years later he was still challenging Jesus in the wilderness over who deserved worship. Two thousand years on, and he's still doing the same, whether through atheistic politics or diverse human philosophies. But more subtly, his challenge can even come through the thoughts in our own heart: 'Why worship God?'

Let's be clear first of all that God doesn't *need* our worship. He's not some sort of 'divine battery' that needs recharging nor some inadequate being who needs 'pumping up' through worship. God needs nothing - that's why he's God! No, it's not *God* who needs our worship; it's *us*!

We need to worship, first, because it's what we were made for. Peter says that the very reason for our life is 'that you may declare the praises of him who called you out of darkness into his wonderful light' (1 Peter 2:9). St Augustine summed it up like this: 'You have made us for yourself and our hearts are restless till they find their rest in you.' Second, we need to worship because worship is the proper response to God's love. How can we think of our Father's love in sending Christ to the cross for us and not worship? It would be churlish! But third, we need to worship because worship keeps us in our proper place. It reminds us that the universe does not revolve around us and our plans; that there is someone greater; that we are not God!

Why worship? It's what you were made for and how you live best!

'Let my people go, so that they may worship me.'
(EXODUS 8:1)

MARCH 16

Forgiven and forgiving

'And when you stand praying, if you hold anything against anyone, forgive him, so that your Father in heaven may forgive you your sins.'
(MARK 11:25)

Just how much do we appreciate God's forgiveness? Asked that question 'in a vacuum', all of us would no doubt come up with the right answer, even if we found it hard to find words that were adequate to explain it. Of course, not only is it hard to sometimes put our appreciation into words, it is often hard to put into practice too. That is why Jesus said that one very tangible measure of how much we really appreciate God's forgiveness is how forgiving we ourselves are towards others.

Jesus taught that there is simply no place in our lives for anger or judgmental attitudes towards others who are simply as flawed as us; no place for feelings of hurt, injury, or resentment towards others who have wronged us; no place for clinging on to old wounds and grievances. For, if we have truly understood and received forgiveness ourselves, anger will be replaced by affection. Left to our own resources, of course, this is quite impossible; but we are not left alone – God has promised us his grace.

The truth is, it can sometimes be hard to find the grace to live like this, however – especially when people have hurt us. But this is the very point at which this teaching needs to be implemented! Anyone can believe it in the comfort of a sermon or in the theoretical setting of a group discussion. But God wants us to implement it in life – at the very moment when it *is* hard to do! For that is the very moment at which his promises work!

God's grace to forgive can be found, for God has promised it in his word – and it can be found by you today as you take God at his word and ask him to help you let go of your hurt and offence (which, after all, is only an expression of pride). Forgive today, and Jesus promises that you will truly know what it is to be forgiven!

For if you forgive men when they sin against you,
your heavenly Father will also forgive you.
(MATTHEW 6:14)

An unshakable kingdom

Therefore, since we are receiving a kingdom that cannot be shaken, let us be thankful . . .
(HEBREWS 12:28)

Ask any football supporters whether they prefer their team to win or lose, and the answer is obvious. We all love to be winners, and there's tremendous satisfaction in knowing that 'our team won'. And that's exactly how it is for us as Christians; we can get excited because our 'team' is unstoppable; our team is assured of winning!

The team in question is not us, and it's not even the church; it's the kingdom of God. Jesus said that this kingdom would be *all-growing*, nothing would be able to stop it as it moved towards ultimate, total triumph, as the parables in Matthew 13 (the sower, the weeds, the mustard seed and the yeast) all make plain. Second, he said that this kingdom would be *all-embracing*, that there would be nothing and no one it couldn't reach. Every aspect of life would be touched and transformed by it and people 'from every tribe and language and people and nation' (Revelation 5:9) would be part of it. Third, he said that this kingdom would be *all-pervading*. Like sand at the seaside, the kingdom gets absolutely everywhere! There is nothing powerful enough to resist it or keep it out. Like yeast, it pervades everything it touches. Like a multi-national corporation it is not confined by governments or borders. Limited to no one place or nation, yet having an all-pervading influence in and beyond them all, there is nothing and nowhere it cannot reach. Fourth, he said that this kingdom would be *all-victorious*. Human kingdoms may rise and fall, but God's kingdom cannot fail to be victorious. It is, like Daniel saw in his vision, a rock that 'became a huge mountain and filled the whole earth' (Daniel 2:35). Truly this is a kingdom that cannot be shaken!

In the light of all this, what confidence we should have today! No matter what circumstances or pressures you or your church might be facing, you are on the winning side! As long as we 'seek first his kingdom and his righteousness' (Matthew 6:33), we cannot fail, for his kingdom cannot fail!

'The kingdom of the world has become the kingdom of our Lord and of his Christ, and he will reign for ever and ever.'
(REVELATION 11:15)

MARCH 18

In the nitty-gritty of life!

'My ears had heard of you but now my eyes have seen you.'
(JOB 42:5)

Listening to stories about God's power and faithfulness is wonderful. How a testimony of some great healing or miraculous intervention by God builds up our faith! How exciting it is to hear someone's story of God's provision for them in some fantastic way, and at just at the right moment! But while such stories may do us good, they don't in themselves bring about change in us. For that to happen, we have to encounter God for ourselves in the 'nitty-gritty' of life.

No one ever learned about God's faithfulness in the classroom or from reading Christian books or from watching Christian TV. Rather, it is in the 'nitty-gritty' of life, with all its troubles, all its rough and tumble, all its hard knocks, that we prove God's faithfulness for ourselves. As with anything else in life, it is only when something is 'put to the test' that we can see if it really works and make it our own.

That's what Abraham discovered when God put him to the test by asking him to sacrifice his long-awaited, promised son, and then miraculously intervening at the last moment. What Abraham had to learn that day was that it was not his son that God wanted, but his heart! This is what Job learned too when, after much questioning from his own heart and many answers from his friends, every issue was settled in just one real encounter with the living God.

Neither of these men learned about God's faithfulness from a book; they had to walk through life and make the promises their own. And so it is for us. It may be that you are facing some challenges or difficulties at this time. Don't see this as God's abandoning of you, but simply his opportunity for you to discover him again for yourself in the 'nitty-gritty' of life and to discover that his promises work, not just for others, but for you!

> *'We no longer believe just because of what you said;*
> *now we have heard for ourselves . . .'*
> (JOHN 4:42)

MARCH 19

A broken spirit

*The sacrifices of God are a broken spirit; a broken and
contrite heart, O God, you will not despise.*
(PSALM 51:17)

Over the years the various cars that Martin has owned have broken down
a few times; not many, but enough to be recalled fairly easily: a clutch
failing at a roundabout; a flat tyre on a motorway; an undiscovered cause
in the middle of the country. This last one was particularly interesting as,
when Martin went to the nearest house, on the wall by the phone (this
was before the era of mobile phones!) was a list of phone numbers of the
local garages and breakdown trucks. Clearly, others had broken down on
the same road before him!

Today's verse reminds us that it is all right to be 'broken down' before
God. In fact, the best offering we can bring to God isn't money or
possessions; it is 'a broken and contrite heart'.

This strikes at two things: our outer actions and our inner lives. We
all too often think that we can please God by our outward actions when
the inner attitude of our heart is not right. Are we truly sorry for our sin?
Are we real in wanting to stop sinning? Then what really pleases God is a
humble attitude of deep sorrow at that sin, not a quick and easy prayer
that ignores our intention of carrying on doing that particular thing. Of
course, repentance strikes right at the heart of our human pride: when we
think we know best, that in ourselves we are good enough without God,
that our natural achievements can secure us a firm place in heaven; all that
has to go if we are to be truly broken before God.

Martin well remembers the challenge given by one of the former
pastors of the church that he is a member of. 'When was the last time you
repented? Last year, last month, last week?' A good question! Let's
remember today that in Jesus' parable of the Pharisee and the tax
collector, it was the latter who 'went home justified before God', for it was
he who called out, 'God, have mercy on me, a sinner' (Luke 18:13–14).
Such calls are *never* left unanswered!

> *'Everyone who exalts himself will be humbled,
> and he who humbles himself will be exalted.'*
> (LUKE 18:14)

Praying for the nation

*'Seek the peace and prosperity of the city to which I have
carried you into exile. Pray to the LORD for it, because if it
prospers, you too will prosper.'*
(JEREMIAH 29:7)

Would you love to see our nation both blessed by God and living in more
godly ways? A nation living by the Ten Commandments, where love for
God and one's neighbour is the norm rather than the exception? If your
answer is 'Yes', then ask yourself: how often do you pray for that? How
often do you pray for our nation and government (whatever political party
you might support)? Apart from those who pray briefly as part of their
church's liturgy, we suspect that the answer is, 'Not very much.' So, maybe
it's not very surprising that our nation is not as godly as it might be.

David encouraged people to 'pray for the peace of Jerusalem' (Psalm
122:6). In Bible times a capital was often used to symbolize the nation
(just as today we speak of 'Washington' when we mean the USA). Because
we are no longer part of the Old Covenant, we aren't obliged to pray for
'Jerusalem' as such. But the underlying challenge remains: if you want
your nation to be blessed, pray for it!

In praying for blessing on our own nation, we are wanting people to
experience more of God and so have opportunity to turn to him. That's
what Jeremiah, in today's opening verse, encouraged his compatriots in
exile to do. He didn't tell them to retreat into their own little enclaves,
leaving Babylon to its own godless ways, since it was destined for
destruction one day; rather, he told them to pray for it and do all they
could to bless it. That's exactly what Daniel did, praying for openings and
serving King Nebuchadnezzar in a way that led to an increased awareness
of the living God in Nebuchadnezzar's life (Daniel 2:46–47; 4:34–37)
and to new openings for Daniel and his friends.

Don't grumble about your nation or government; bless it and pray for
it! Like Daniel, we *can* make a difference.

*I urge, then, first of all, that requests, prayers, intercession and thanksgiving
be made for everyone – for kings and all those in authority, that we may live
peaceful and quiet lives in all godliness and holiness.*
(1 TIMOTHY 2:1–2)

MARCH 21

A Sacrifice of Praise

Through Jesus let us always offer to God our sacrifice of praise,
coming from lips that speak his name.
(HEBREWS 13:15, NCV)

Let's face it: praising God in hard times or when things aren't going well isn't always easy. The truth is, it involves a sacrifice; a sacrifice of our feelings and emotions, of our questions and answers. But whenever people in the Bible chose to make this sacrifice, they always found that God did not disappoint them and that joy was always the final outcome. As God promised through Jeremiah, 'Again there shall be heard in this place . . . the voice of joy, and the voice of gladness, the voice of the bridegroom, and the voice of the bride, the voice of them that shall say, Praise the LORD of hosts: for the LORD is good; for his mercy endureth for ever: and of them that shall bring the sacrifice of praise into the house of the LORD' (Jeremiah 33:10–11, KJV).

Of course, our praise may not be as exuberant in the hard times as in the good times. But that's not the point. What matters is not the volume, but the sincerity; not the outward manifestation, but the inward heart. We aren't praising because we *feel* like it (we probably don't!), but because of what we know about God.

So, why can we praise in hard times? Well, it's not because we're 'burying our head in the sand' or 'whistling in the dark'. It's because we have come to see that we can trust God, who is the sovereign LORD. Even when things seem to be going wrong, he is still on his throne, still in control, still causing 'everything to work together for the good of those who love God' (Romans 8:28, NLT). When we moan rather than praise, what we're saying is, 'God, I really don't think you know what you're doing!' But when we praise rather than moan, we're saying, 'God I may not understand you; but I do commit myself to trusting you as I wait for your outcome!'

Remember: we may not always be able to rejoice in *the circumstance*, but we can always rejoice in *the Lord*. Set your heart to bring him your sacrifice of praise today.

I will bless the LORD at all times: his praise shall continually be in
my mouth.
(PSALM 34:1, NRSV)

MARCH 22

The God who gives hope

But now, Lord, what do I look for? My hope is in you.
(PSALM 39:7)

'I'm keeping my fingers crossed for you!' No doubt we have all heard people say that many times. But when you think about it, what a silly thing that is for rational people to say! As though putting one finger over another could make the least scrap of difference to anything that happens in life! Of course, for many people, what they really want to say is, 'I'm praying for you!' – though in modern western society that is far too embarrassing and risky a thing to commit oneself to!

Let us be clear: there is absolutely no hope in crossing one's fingers! But where there *is* hope is in the living God! David (who wrote the verse above) faced many difficult situations in life, both before and after becoming king – situations that at times, from a human point of view, seemed quite hopeless. For example, though he was at first liked by King Saul, he soon found himself on the run from him once Saul started to see him as a threat and a rival. David then had to spend some ten years hiding in the deserts, hills and caves; at one point he even had to take refuge in the heart of the Philistine camp, pretending to be mad himself in order to save his life. And even after he became king, life did not always go smoothly for him, and on one occasion he even faced a civil war that seemed to drain all hope out of him.

But despite the difficulties and challenges that he faced, David didn't give up hope, for he had discovered the God of hope. 'My hope is in you' he would say again and again; and on each occasion, he would find that God was true to his promise, as he came to rescue David from whatever faced him.

Today, this same God of hope is with you in whatever challenges and opportunities are facing you. Look to him – and find your hope!

Why are you so downcast, O my soul? Why so disturbed within me? Put your hope in God, for I will yet praise him, my Saviour and my God.
(PSALM 42:5)

MARCH 23

Jesus, the focus of God's promises

The promise of life that is in Christ Jesus.
(2 TIMOTHY 1:1)

'A man apt to promise is apt to forget,' said Thomas Fuller. 'Promises and pie-crust are made to be broken,' said Jonathan Swift. However we word it, we're probably all too familiar with people's broken promises, and we have no doubt all been disappointed many times. But with God, things are really quite different. His promises are not mere 'wishful thinking', vague hopes or empty words; they are firm declarations of intent that he has committed himself to fulfil in Christ.

When Mike was a school teacher, if ever there was trouble in a particular class, he always knew where to look. There were always one or two individuals who (no matter what the issue) would be involved. All the experience and all the evidence always pointed to them! And that's exactly how it is with Jesus and the promises of God; everything points to him. He is their origin, their fulfilment, their goal. It is he himself who *is* 'the promise of life' (2 Timothy 1:1).

Paul put it like this: 'No matter how many promises God has made, they are "Yes" in Christ' (2 Corinthians 1:20). What he meant was that, first, Christ is God's 'Yes' to all the promises of Scripture. That is, they all point to him and are fulfilled in him. So if our understanding or claiming of God's promises leads us to anything or anyone other than Christ, then our interpretation is, quite simply, wrong. Second, Paul was saying that Christ himself is God's 'Amen' to all the promises of Scripture. As we claim these promises for ourselves, we are simply adding our 'Amen' to the 'Amen' that is Jesus himself. We are not trying to wrestle anything out of his hands; we are simply agreeing with what he has said he wants to do!

Today, you don't have to wrestle the promises from God's hands; they are freely given to you in Christ, God's ultimate promise. So let Jesus help you to claim, boldly and confidently, whatever promises you need today, and let them lead you closer to him.

Through the gospel the Gentiles are heirs together with Israel, members together of one body, and sharers together in the promise in Christ Jesus.
(EPHESIANS 3:6)

MARCH 24

In remembrance of me

The Lord Jesus, on the night he was betrayed, took bread, and when he had given thanks, he broke it and said, 'This is my body, which is for you; do this in remembrance of me.' In the same way, after supper he took the cup, saying, 'This cup is the new covenant in my blood; do this, whenever you drink it, in remembrance of me.'
(1 CORINTHIANS 11:23–25)

Sometimes the simplest things can carry the most powerful memories. A letter, a photograph, a news cutting, a trinket; as we look at them again, memories come flooding back. And that's what exactly the Lord's Supper is meant to do.

Instituted by Jesus on the night before his death, 'the breaking of bread' (Acts 2:42) – also called the Lord's Supper, Communion, or Eucharist – became a central part of early church life. It was a wonderful opportunity to remember what Jesus had done for them at the cross and to do four things:

First, it was a chance to *look back*, remembering how Jesus gave his life for us, and to thank him. Second, it was a chance to *look in* and to confess any sin; for how can we thank Jesus for saving us if we're harbouring sin in our heart? Anyone who does so simply 'eats and drinks judgment on himself' (1 Corinthians 11:29). Third, it was a chance to *look round*, recognizing that those eating were brothers and sisters in Christ and that 'we, who are many, are one body' (1 Corinthians 10:17). Fourth, it was an opportunity to *look forward*, anticipating Christ's future return, for we share this meal together only 'until he comes' (1 Corinthians 11:26).

All this seems to have happened in the context of a meal in homes. Perhaps somewhat unfortunately, it has become almost exclusively part of Sunday services, and a part where most churches become more solemn than at any other point in the meeting. It is certainly serious, but that doesn't mean it has to be miserable! In fact, Paul's constant theme about the Lord's Supper in 1 Corinthians is 'thankfulness'.

Who knows what life and joy might be released among us if we were to take this 'memorial' back into homes in the context of a meal. Perhaps you could try it and see!

Remember Jesus Christ, raised from the dead.
(2 TIMOTHY 2:8)

MARCH 25

What a price!

For you know that it was not with perishable things such as
silver or gold that you were redeemed from the empty way of
life handed down to you from your forefathers, but with the
precious blood of Christ, a lamb without blemish or defect.
(1 PETER 1:18–19)

Hardly a month goes by without a report of some fantastic price paid for a work of art. Often it will go into millions of pounds or dollars – and for what? At one level, simply a bit of paint on canvas or a bit of marble sculpted to some form. So, why do people pay such fantastic prices? Because, quite simply, it was worth it to them.

And that really sums up why God paid such a fantastic price for us – because he felt we were worth it! He loved us that much – even 'while we were still sinners' (Romans 5:8) – that he was prepared to pay the ultimate price for us – the price of the life of his own dear Son. God's forgiveness of us was not brought about by his simply 'waving some magic wand' in heaven or by his saying, 'Let's just forget about it'. Our forgiveness cost him the life of his Son – the only ground, according to the New Testament, upon which it could happen. God himself paid the price of satisfying his own righteous anger against our sin by sending his Son, not to somehow vaguely die *for us*, but to die in *instead of us*, to die *in our place*, to be an 'atoning sacrifice' (NIV, NRSV) or 'propitiation' (KJV, NASB) for our sin – that is, a sacrifice that really worked, dealing with the sin once and for all.

Just think: God loved *you* that much that he paid for you with the costliest thing he had – his priceless son! What a price! What a God! Be encouraged today that this is how much he loves you and is committed to you. And be assured that 'he who did not spare his own Son, but gave him up for us all – how will he not also, along with him, graciously give us all things?' (Romans 8:32). This is God's promise to us today!

But God demonstrates his own love for us in this: While we were still
sinners, Christ died for us.
(ROMANS 5:8)

MARCH 26

The peace of God

He himself is our peace.
(EPHESIANS 2:14)

Martin was once involved in some trade-union negotiations. The atmosphere was tense and stifled; there certainly wasn't peace. There was a stiffness in the atmosphere until everything got resolved (which happened on a day when he wasn't there!). Peace reigned – at least for a while! We are reminded of the cynic's definition that peace 'in international affairs is a period of cheating between two periods of fighting' (Ambrose Bierce, *The Devil's Dictionary*).

People generally negotiate a peace; but God's peace is quite different. Jesus didn't *negotiate* peace between God and us; he was the peace! 'He himself is our peace,' wrote Paul. Peace is not a 'thing' or an atmosphere, but a *person* – the person of the Lord Jesus Christ. It was Jesus himself who 'destroyed the barrier, the dividing wall of hostility' (Ephesians 2:14). The barrier Paul was thinking of was the wall that separated the Court of the Gentiles from the Court of Israel in the temple at Jerusalem. Signs stood at the gate between the two: 'Gentiles keep out on pain of death'. But through his death, ripped that wall down, as it were. He made it possible for both Jews and Gentiles alike to come close to God so that they could know his peace – with him and with one another.

Peace is the birthright of every believer. God wants us to know his peace, not just as theological truth, but as a reality; a peace in our relationship with him and with each other; a peace that abides in face of difficulty, hardship, and even death. But how do we maintain such a peace? Through trusting in the Lord, and not ourselves; through staying close to him and depending on his Spirit; through keeping our minds fixed on him and putting God's word into practice.

Christ's life was characterized by a calm, unruffled, unflappable spirit. Just think, for example, of how he simply walked through a mob anxious to kill him or waited in Gethsemane for his betrayer to arrive. It is this sort of peace, a peace that knows God is with us even in the pressurized times, that Jesus promises to each of us today.

The peace of God, which transcends all understanding, will guard your hearts and your minds in Christ Jesus.
(PHILIPPIANS 4:7)

MARCH 27

The gift of hindsight

And beginning with Moses and all the Prophets, he explained to them what was said in all the Scriptures concerning himself.
(LUKE 24:27)

It's easy at times to read the New Testament and think, 'How stupid those first disciples were!' After all, Jesus spoke to them again and again about his impending death and resurrection, but they never seemed to understand what he was talking about. And even after the resurrection, it still took some time for 'the penny to drop'. Of course, it's so much easier for us to see it all now with the wonderful gift of hindsight. But gradually, after the resurrection, the disciples began to see it too, as Jesus appeared to them and showed them how it had all been prophesied and promised long ago.

In many ways, the New Testament itself is God's gift of hindsight to us. When we read it, it is like putting on our 'Jesus spectacles' that brings everything in the Old Testament into focus. It helps us look back and see how so much planning and preparation had gone into the coming of Jesus; how events, laws, sacrifices and festivals all pointed to him and prepared for his promised coming. It was some of these Scriptures that Jesus took and explained to the disciples on the Emmaus road on Easter Day. The strange thing is, they didn't recognise that it was him at first, because of his transformed resurrection body. But as he broke bread with them later that evening, their eyes were suddenly opened and they understood at last. 'Were not our hearts burning within us while he talked with us on the road and opened the Scriptures to us?' (Luke 24:32) they said to one another.

Still today our own hearts can 'burn within us' as we read the Old Testament, by simply asking Jesus to interpret it to us through his Holy Spirit and to show us how it all relates to him and how all the promises are fulfilled in him. He is the one who now gives us the gift of hindsight that makes sense of it all.

'We have found the one Moses wrote about in the Law, and about whom the prophets also wrote – Jesus of Nazareth, the son of Joseph.'
(JOHN 1:45)

Salvation!

The LORD your God is with you, he is mighty to save.
(ZEPHANIAH 3:17)

Nowadays 'salvation' is what a financier brings to a troubled business or a football manager brings to a struggling team; but salvation in a religious sense, well, that's just old hat, isn't it? But if we think like that, we've been robbed! For 'salvation' needs reclaiming and putting where it belongs: in the realm of people's relationship with God.

Perhaps the reason we don't use the word 'salvation' very much is that we don't really understand how rich a concept it is. In the Bible, salvation is never an 'airy-fairy' thing; it was always very specific: people are saved *from* something and *for* something. God's salvation includes, among many others, things like –

• *salvation from sin.* 'Trust the LORD! He is always merciful, and he has the power to save you. Israel, the LORD will save you from all of your sins' (Psalm 130:7–8, CEV).

• *salvation from circumstances.* 'Then they cried to the LORD in their trouble, and he saved them from their distress. He sent forth his word and healed them; he rescued them from the grave' (Psalm 107:19–20).

• *salvation from despair.* 'The LORD is close to the broken-hearted and saves those who are crushed in spirit' (Psalm 34:18).

• *salvation from sickness.* 'He was pierced for our transgressions, he was crushed for our iniquities; the punishment that brought us peace was upon him, and by his wounds we are healed' (Isaiah 53:5).

• *salvation from enemies.* 'In you our fathers put their trust; they trusted and you delivered them. They cried to you and were saved' (Psalm 22:4–5).

Do I really believe that God can save me from *everything*? Do I look to him to save me in situations at work, with my family, with my health? Or is my faith for salvation restricted solely to 'spiritual' things? Do I look to myself and my own resources and abilities before looking to God, leaving him as little more than a 'last resort'? Or is God the first one that I turn to in every circumstance to be my saviour?

Don't try to be your own saviour today – let him be!

Turn to me and be saved, all you ends of the earth; for I am God, and there is no other.
(ISAIAH 45:22)

MARCH 29

Lost and found

I will search for the lost and bring back the strays.
(EZEKIEL 34:16)

Have you ever been lost and not known where you were or how to get back home? Mike once found himself in such a situation in one of the developing nations. Along with a colleague, they had been visiting a pastor on the edge of town, but it was now getting late and time to head for home. With the darkness drawing in, they decided to try to save time by taking a short cut. They presumed that if they just took any of the roads that headed down the hill, it would meet up with the main road at the bottom and save them time by not having to go the long way round. That's where their misfortune began!

The trouble was, the road they chose didn't go straight down the hill; it meandered all over the place! And then there were the junctions and crossroads – not to mention the dead ends! After thirty minutes, they were well and truly lost – and since the civil war had only ended recently, and there was still lawlessness around at times, they were feeling far from confident! Having no idea where they were, and unsure even if it was safe to get out and ask the way, they decided they needed to pray. And what heartfelt prayer it was: 'Oh God – we've been stupid and we're lost – help!' Fortified by prayer, they gingerly set out again. And, guess what? Within minutes they were on the right road and safely bound for home again.

Actually, we don't have to travel far at all to end up 'lost'. It is all too easy to feel lost in the midst of a loving family or a lively crowd or a bustling office. Everything and everyone can 'be' there; but inside, we can feel so 'lost', so empty, so lacking in direction, so unsure of which way to go. At such times it is good to remember God's promise that he loves to come looking for the lost! All we need to do is to call out to him: 'Oh God – I've been stupid and I'm lost – help!' – and God himself will come running to our rescue!

For the Son of Man came to seek and to save what was lost.
(LUKE 19:10)

MARCH 30

Learning through failure

'Simon, Simon, Satan has asked to sift you as wheat. But I have prayed for you, Simon, that your faith may not fail. And when you have turned back, strengthen your brothers.'
(LUKE 22:31–32)

There are few worthwhile things in life that we do, or at least do well, at the first attempt. Even such basics as eating, speaking, and writing took lots of attempts (and lots of failures!) before we mastered them. And think of more challenging things, like learning to drive. Those of us who have done this will know what a challenge that was to co–ordinate hands and feet and eyes to do quite different things at the same time.

Being a Christian is no different. The Bible describes becoming a Christian as being 'born again' (John 3:3). As such, we are new babies who need to learn lots of new skills for our new life – and it doesn't come easily. Jesus' programme for our learning all this is 'discipleship'; and, just as in everything else in life, this learning never stops. In fact, the day we stop, we die! Discipleship is for life.

Discipleship, by its very nature, will involve failure – and that's where we find it hard! For few of us like to fail; and even fewer like to admit our failure. Our whole society is geared to 'success' not 'failure', and those who do fail are often dealt with mercilessly. So to find we have failed as Christians can sometimes be hard for us. But when we look at the New Testament, we find that Jesus' twelve disciples failed often! They failed to trust him, to obey him, to believe in him, to love him – the list could go on. But this is the very heart of discipleship: learning through failure. The issue is not have we failed, but have we learned?

Remember: no matter how many times his disciples failed him, Jesus never gave up on them, never sent them back home, never said, 'Let's find a better bunch of people to work with'. Rather, he lovingly and patiently kept working with them until they had learned, until they got it right. And that is his commitment to each of us today.

I applied my heart to what I observed and learned a lesson from what I saw.
(PROVERBS 24:32)

MARCH 31

Anyone and anything

*I am the least of the apostles and do not even deserve to be
called an apostle, because I persecuted the church of God. But
by the grace of God I am what I am.*
(1 CORINTHIANS 15:9–10)

If it's amazing to discover that God loves to forgive, it's even more amazing
to discover that he loves to forgive *everyone*. Our minds can just about
grasp that he forgives the very religious, or those who pray a lot or who
haven't sinned too badly. But God does more than that! The Bible
promises that he will forgive *absolutely anyone* for *absolutely anything*. All
we need to do is to confess: that is, not just say 'I'm sorry' but 'I did it!'

As we see in the Bible the broad range of people and their sin that God
forgave, it really is quite mind-blowing. It should certainly convince us
that, if God forgave them, he can surely forgive us. The list includes
people like King Manasseh who engaged in idolatry, star worship, sorcery,
divination, spiritism, witchcraft, and who even sacrificed his son to pagan
gods – clearly a man most of us would have written off! But this was also
a man that God forgave, as he 'humbled himself greatly before the God
of his fathers. And when he prayed to him, the LORD was moved by his
entreaty and listened to his plea; so he brought him back to Jerusalem and
to his kingdom. Then Manasseh knew that the LORD is God' (2
Chronicles 33:12–13). If God can forgive Manasseh, he can certainly
forgive you!

Or consider Paul who, before his conversion, had led the persecution
against the Christians, playing a part in Stephen's stoning and being
responsible for the arrest and death of many other Christians. Yet God
forgave him for it all as he repented, and his grace transformed him into
one of the most effective apostles.

Both these men, like so many others, discovered the kindness and
mercy of God when they came to him and said, 'I did it!' God is still the
same, still the God who 'forgives *all* your sins' (Psalm 103:3). That 'all'
includes all *your* sins – no matter what they might be or how guilty you
might feel because of them. Believe it!

'No matter how deep the stain of your sins, I can remove it.'
(ISAIAH 1:18, NLT)

The priority of life

*'Seek first his kingdom and his righteousness, and all these
things will be given to you as well.'*
(MATTHEW 6:33)

We all give priority to what is important to us in life. In fact, it is amazing
what even the busiest of us can squeeze in if we really want to! For all of
us, the issue is not one of 'time', but 'will'; not what we *can* do, but what
we *choose* to do.

For us as Christians, we have a new, and very simple, priority
however. Jesus said that it was to seek first *God's* kingdom. He said this in
the context of telling his disciples not to worry about such basic things in
life as food and clothing – the very things that *are* our priorities so often,
especially in our modern, pressurized society. But if we get this new
priority in place, Jesus said, then all these other things will fall into place
as well. Of course, this doesn't come naturally to us, for we have all been
taught that if we don't provide for ourselves, then nobody else will, and
that to 'look after number one' is eminently sensible.

How Jesus' simple command cuts across this! Don't seek what *you*
want first; seek what *God* wants first, he says. It sounds tremendously
challenging, doesn't it? – if not downright scary! But the challenge has a
promise attached to it: a promise that if we do seek first God's kingdom,
then all the practical necessities of life will fall into place. We might not
have everything we *want*, but we will certainly have everything we *need*.

So, what should our new priorities be? Jesus said things like: seeking
to become more like him, letting him be Lord in all we say and do,
keeping his commandments, loving one another, being a faithful witness,
being fruitful for him, not looking back to our old life, giving up our own
ways. The key is deciding where our treasure is; because wherever our
treasure is, Jesus said, our heart will follow after it.

So, a challenging command, but an exciting promise! And the only
way to see if it works is to *try it*!

For where your treasure is, there your heart will be also.
(LUKE 12:34)

Breaking the chains

You have freed me from my chains.
(PSALM 116:16)

'Do I suffer for the sins of my family before me?' is a question people sometimes ask, particularly when things are going badly in life. After all, doesn't the Bible say that God 'punishes the children for the sin of the fathers to the third and fourth generation' (Numbers 14:18)? Surely this means there's no hope for me, that I must pay for my forefathers' sins. When we put our trust in Jesus, the answer is: not at all!

This truth of the fathers' sins being visited on the children signifies not divine arithmetic, but divine observation. What God is saying is that those who break his law inevitably pass on those ways to their families; and so they end up living the same way, often for generations to come. But Jeremiah saw that life wouldn't always be like that, but that a time would come when 'people will no longer say, "The fathers have eaten sour grapes, and the children's teeth are set on edge." Instead, everyone will die for his own sin; whoever eats sour grapes – his own teeth will be set on edge' (Jeremiah 31:29–30).

When Jesus came, this inexorable causal chain would at last be broken. Indeed, this was one of the first things he said he had come to do: 'to proclaim freedom for the prisoners . . . to release the oppressed' (Luke 4:18). No longer would sin – our own or our forefathers – be able to continue to imprison us in its terrifying grip. At the cross, he broke its power and set us free. That's why Paul could confidently declare: 'If anyone is in Christ, he is a new creation; the old has gone, the new has come!' (2 Corinthians 5:17).

We really don't have to live under the shadow and influence of our forbears and their ways. If you've been doing so, bring it to Jesus right now. Declare that you believe he died to break the chains of the past, and claim the power of the cross that sets you absolutely free.

Shake off your dust; rise up, sit enthroned, O Jerusalem. Free yourself from the chains on your neck, O captive Daughter of Zion. For this is what the LORD says: 'You were sold for nothing, and without money you will be redeemed.'
(ISAIAH 52:2–3)

APRIL 3

Tearing up the list

Love doesn't keep score of the sins of others.
(1 CORINTHIANS 13:5, THE MESSAGE)

Have you noticed how easy it is to 'keep a list' of the wrongs that people have done to us? And even when we try to forget, that wonderful computer of ours (the brain) has a way of remembering what we want to forget (and an equal ability to forget what we want to remember!). But the Bible urges us to tear up those 'lists'!

Of course, everything within us at times feels we have a right to 'keep a list'. And Peter felt he was being very spiritual when he was prepared to let the list get to seven offences (seven being the 'perfect' number in Judaism) before feeling he had a right to not tear the list up! But Jesus' answer surprised him. 'I tell you, not seven times, but seventy-seven times' (Matthew 18:22) – that is, an endless number of times; or, to put it another way, just don't keep a list, Peter! For forgiveness is not something we can 'count'; forgiveness is the very atmosphere of God's kingdom. True forgiveness means tearing up the list and leaving things to God.

In fact, Jesus went further in this area than anyone ever before or since; for not only did he call us to unconditionally love and forgive our friends and to tear up the list of their sins and failings, he called us to do the same with our enemies! 'You have heard that it was said, "Love your neighbour and hate your enemy." But I tell you: Love your enemies and pray for those who persecute you, that you may be sons of your Father in heaven' (Matthew 5:43–45).

What about you? Do you have a mental list of where others have hurt, disappointed or wronged you? If you do, tear it up! Leave God to deal with the issue, and with them. He'll do a far better job!

Do not repay anyone evil for evil. Be careful to do what is right in the eyes
of everybody. If it is possible, as far as it depends on you, live at peace with
everyone. Do not take revenge, my friends, but leave room for God's wrath,
for it is written: 'It is mine to avenge; I will repay,' says the Lord.
(ROMANS 12:17–19)

The depth of his friendship

*'I am the good shepherd. The good shepherd
lays down his life for the sheep.'*
(JOHN 10:11)

How do you show how much you love someone? TV advertisements tell us that it is by giving your beloved their favourite – or last – chocolate, or by buying your family that new car, or by taking them to this 'must-have' holiday destination. So many things are seen as the ultimate expression of love or friendship. But for the Son of God, showing how very much he loved us was nothing so trivial!

Jesus said that the ultimate expression of love was to 'lay down his life for his friends' (John 15:13). And of course, that is exactly what he would do for them, only hours later. We can perhaps understand how a true friend might be prepared to sacrifice his life for someone he really loved; or how a parent would gladly risk their own life to save that of their child who had wandered in front of a car. But the Bible says Jesus did far more that. For the great wonder is that our heavenly friend died on the cross, not for his friends, but for his *enemies!*

The New Testament constantly stresses that it was 'while we were still sinners' (Romans 5:8), while we were 'alienated from God' (Colossians 1:21), that Christ died for us. He didn't wait for us to become his friends before he acted; he acted so that we could become his friends! The apostle Paul discovered this truth and was transformed by it. As a Pharisee, he had dedicated himself to the eradication of the church, helping in the stoning of Stephen and going from house to house to find Christians and to drag them off to jail. And yet, this self–sworn enemy of Christ was transformed that day he met him and found his life turned around - not when he had become his friend, but while he was still a sinner.

Today, we do not have to try to win Christ's friendship; we already have it! He showed it to us while we were still sinners; how much more will he show us that friendship, just as he promised, now that he has made us his friends.

*While we were God's enemies, he made friends with us
through the death of his Son.*
(ROMANS 5:10, NCV)

Hallelujah!

*After this I heard what sounded like the roar of a great
multitude in heaven shouting: 'Hallelujah! Salvation and glory
and power belong to our God.'*
(REVELATION 19:1)

'Much dreaming and many words are meaningless. Therefore stand in awe
of God' wrote King Solomon (Ecclesiastes 5:7). And Jesus hit a similar note
when he said, 'When you pray, don't talk on and on as people do who don't
know God. They think God likes to hear long prayers' (Matthew 6:7,
CEV). Of course, it's not that God doesn't like long prayers; there are lots
of them in the Bible. But 'many words' have a way of crowding out the
heart of things; and certainly the Pharisees of Jesus' time had turned prayer
into something of 'a theatrical production' (Matthew 6:7, The Message).
But both Old and New Testaments bring home the message that it's not
the length of a prayer that is important, but the heart behind it.

Which leads us nicely to the Bible's shortest prayer: the simple word,
'Hallelujah!' This is a Hebrew expression – 'Hallelu Yah' – meaning
'Praise the LORD' ('Yah' being a shortened form of 'Yahweh', God's
covenant name that he revealed to Moses). Its presence isn't always easy
to recognize in English Bibles because most versions translate the phrase,
rather than reproduce it. (For example, the NIV has retained the word
only four times, while the King James Version doesn't use it at all.) But it
is an expression that we find in the context of worship, in the Psalms and
in Revelation. In Revelation its use precedes the climactic return of the
Lord Jesus – something worth getting excited about! In the Psalms, on all
but one occasion (Psalm 135:3), it is always found at either the beginning
(e.g. Psalms 111–113) or at the end (e.g. Psalms 115–117) of the psalm.
In other words, it was a great way to set you off in praise or to bring your
praise to a resounding end.

This expression brings home to us that sincere praise does not always
need many words! Of course, 'hallelujah!' can become a mere catchphrase,
glibly used without much thought. But it doesn't have to be that! It is a
thoroughly biblical way of expressing gratitude to God in a simple way.
Try using it more yourself and see!

Hallelujah! For our Lord God Almighty reigns.
(REVELATION 19:6)

APRIL 6

When God seems distant

My God, my God, why have you forsaken me? Why are you so far from saving me, so far from the words of my groaning?
(PSALM 22:1)

When life gets hard, a common cry is, 'Where is God in all this?' Even the psalmists, who clearly enjoyed wonderful intimacy with God, had times when they felt God was a million miles away and didn't hesitate to tell him so, as in our opening verses today.

But while it can feel lonely, even fearful, not sensing that God is around, such times can prove precious, for they do a number of things. First, they strengthen our faith, for we have to trust what we cannot 'feel'. Second, they remind us not to take God for granted, as though he were merely some friend who calls when needed rather than the Lord of glory. But third, they make us appreciate so much more the times of God's presence. And it is often when we feel that he is absent, that things that have lain hidden in our souls for years (like anger, fear, resentment, or pain) come to the surface. And when that happens, God can, at last, deal with them.

But remember this: God is *always* there, even if we do not *feel* his presence or *see* his activity at that moment. There is nowhere his presence cannot be found; so we need not fear we have been abandoned. The solution is simply to keep waiting for him. How long? Well, quite simply, 'until he comes' (Hosea 10:12).

Our verses were not just spoken by David, however. They were repeated by Jesus on the cross, when he so experienced the weight of the sin of the world that he felt completely forsaken by his Father. But another cry followed: 'It is finished!' (John 19:30), meaning, 'It's all paid for!' His death is our assurance that, as we trust in him, we will never be cut off from God; for the only thing that can keep us from him is our sin; and Christ has paid for that sin once and for all.

No matter how you might feel today, God *is* with you. The cross is your assurance of it!

I will wait for the LORD, who is hiding his face from the house of Jacob.
I will put my trust in him.
(ISAIAH 8:17)

APRIL 7

Left to its own devices

He himself bore our sins in his body on the tree, so that we might die to sins and live for righteousness; by his wounds you have been healed.
(1 PETER 2:24)

We have to be honest: not all of God's promises are exciting! For example, God makes some promises about what sin does to us – and they do not make for pleasant reading! But we are foolish not to listen to what God says about it and its consequences.

The Bible sums up the consequences of sin in a number of ways: it says, for example, that it puts us out of relationship with God; that it makes us slaves to our actions and habits, so we cannot stop doing things we know are wrong, even if we want to; that it renders us helpless, incapable of doing anything about our situation, even though we might want to. But one of the worst things is that, through sin, 'this people's heart has become *calloused*' (Matthew 13:15); that is, hard and insensitive. We no longer have a conscience about the thoughts we have or the things we do, and what used to trouble us does so no more. So, sin has done its dirtiest trick: it has got us to do wrong and then hardened our hearts so we don't even feel bad about it!

But even worse is to follow! For ultimately, left to its own devices, this disease leads inexorably to death – for every single one of us. The Bible sees death as, not merely an inevitable end to life, but the direct consequence of sin. And, as a result of that sin, death itself is followed – not by 'nothing' – but by judgment.

Thankfully, this is not the end of God's promises! For God has also promised that there is a way out from all of this. God himself has provided the answer; for by means of Christ's death on the cross our whole condition is changed. Sin need no longer be left to its own devices – and nor need we. Today, let's take hold of God's promises that, through Christ, our sin has been completely dealt with and that it need no longer reign over us.

For Christ died for sins once for all, the righteous for the unrighteous, to bring you to God.
(1 PETER 3:18)

APRIL 8

God's courtroom

'[God] commands all people everywhere to repent. For he has set a day when he will judge the world with justice by the man he has appointed. He has given proof of this to all men by raising him from the dead.'
(ACTS 17:30–31)

High above the buildings of the Old Bailey law courts in London stands the golden statue of 'Justice' with a sword in her right hand and scales in her left hand, symbolizing the justice promised in the courts below. Sadly human courts are not always just, for a whole variety of reasons. But there is one courtroom in which all of us will one day stand where justice will be absolutely impartial: the courtroom of God at the end of the age.

The fact of judgment, uncomfortable as it is to us, is clear throughout the Bible. For example, the prophets foresaw that God, the righteous judge, would bring his judgement upon sinners on 'the day of the Lord'. As Obadiah put it, 'The day of the LORD is near for all nations. As you have done, it will be done to you; your deeds will return upon your own head' (Obadiah 15). In the New Testament, the writer of Hebrews put it like this: 'Nothing in all creation is hidden from God's sight. Everything is uncovered and laid bare before the eyes of him to whom we must give account' (Hebrews 4:13). All of this could sound a very frightening prospect, for none of us likes the idea of being judged, least of all by God.

Thankfully, God has made such wonderful promises that we need not fear this coming judgment at all! For the Bible promises us that, at the very moment we put our trust in Christ, we are 'justified' – that is, we receive his 'Not Guilty!' verdict right there and then. We don't have to wait till Judgment Day to wait and see what that verdict will be; we can know what it is right here and now – and know that this is God's last word on the matter!

This doctrine of 'justification of faith', lost under centuries of church tradition but rediscovered at the Reformation, is a wonderful promise that gives us great hope, encouragement and security. Live in the light of that promise today!

Therefore, there is now no condemnation for those who are in Christ Jesus.
(ROMANS 8:1)

No big surprise!

For what I received I passed on to you as of first importance:
that Christ died for our sins according to the Scriptures.
(1 CORINTHIANS 15:3)

Jesus made many promises to his disciples during the three years that they spent together; some of those promises they received with great joy; others they struggled with; while still others they never understood at all. Among these were the promises he made concerning his death and resurrection.

After Peter's confession of Jesus as the Christ as Caesarea Philippi, Jesus spoke with increasing clarity about what was going to happen to him in Jerusalem so that it would be no big surprise to them; but Luke tells us that 'the disciples did not understand any of this' (Luke 18:34).

In fact, the Old Testament was full of prophecies about detailed events surrounding the death of Jesus. For there we read about: his betrayal by a friend, the falling away of his disciples, his being sold for thirty pieces of silver, the purchase of a potter's field, his suffering, his suffering in the place of others, his silence before his accusers, his disfigured face, his being beaten and spat upon, his being nailed to the cross, the mocking of him by those around, the abandoning of him by God, the offering of wine vinegar to him, the dividing up of his clothes, his prayer for those who crucified him, his death, his bones not being broken, the piercing of his side, his burial and his ultimate resurrection. Wow! What a list and what amazing detail!

Either all of it is the most amazing coincidence (on a level with the proverbial chimpanzee banging on the keys of a computer and happening to type out the *Encyclopaedia Britannica*!); or Jesus was indeed the promised Saviour. In many ways, his death should have been no great surprise to his disciples. The trouble was: they just weren't expecting God to do it that way!

Be open today for God to do what he has promised he will do. And when he does, don't let it be a big surprise.

The Son of Man will go just as it is written about him.
(MATTHEW 26:24)

APRIL 10

New bodies for old!

We ourselves, who have the firstfruits of the Spirit, groan inwardly as we wait eagerly for our adoption as sons, the redemption of our bodies.
(ROMANS 8:23)

Remember the story of Aladdin and his magic lamp that was inadvertently given to his evil uncle, disguised as a trader offering 'new lamps for old'? The Princess swapped Aladdin's old lamp, much to his dismay, for it wasn't a good deal at all. But there is an exchange coming that will be amazingly good: the exchange of our old bodies for new ones when Jesus returns!

The Jewish concept of the 'afterlife' had been very limited. At death everyone, good and bad alike, simply went to Sheol (in Greek, 'Hades' – not the same as 'hell'). Sheol was a gloomy half–life; a place of darkness and lack of knowledge of God. Only occasionally were there glimpses of real hope, as when Job declared, 'After my skin has been destroyed, yet in my flesh I will see God' (Job 19:26). What a contrast, then, when we come to the New Testament! For Jesus confidently proclaimed, not some vague immortality, but the resurrection of the body – and then proved it in his own life! Don't forget: our ultimate destiny is not to 'go to heaven' – for us heaven is but a glorious 'waiting room' – but to be given a resurrection body, like that of the resurrected Jesus himself – 'physical' (for he could walk and eat), but transformed and so gloriously 'spiritual' that his disciples didn't recognize him at first.

But why the need for such a transformation? Simple: a new environment demands a new kind of body, as Paul argues in 1 Corinthians 15. Our bodies are going to be transformed! For our more youthful readers, that may not sound very exciting; but for those of us who are getting older, with the increasing aches and pains this brings, this is a fantastic promise! Today, if your body is not as sprightly as once it was, if you are sick or incapacitated, then rejoice in this wonderful promise: you're getting a new body one day!

Our earthly bodies, which die and decay, will be different when they are resurrected, for they will never die. Our bodies now disappoint us, but when they are raised they will be full of glory . . . full of power.
(1 CORINTHIANS 15:42–43, NLT)

Peace with God

Therefore, since we have been justified through faith, we have peace with God through our Lord Jesus Christ.
(ROMANS 5:1)

'All I want is a bit of peace!' How often have you said those words? Even in our hi-tech world, with all its 'mod cons' and labour-saving devices, 'a little bit of peace' can often seem hard to find, can't it? For the parent with a toddler, for the executive with a schedule, for the student with a deadline, for the salesperson with a target, finding a few minutes' peace would be wonderful. And as for those in war-torn areas, peace would be worth anything.

Even when we find peace, it seems as if everything that can spoil it will try to. In the week that Mike wrote this, for example, his peace was severely challenged when, not only did his computer keep crashing, but he also got himself trapped on a train heading for a place he didn't want to go to at a time when he had no time to spare!

God wants us to experience peace, and to experience it in every circumstance of daily life. The Bible tells us that such peace doesn't depend on where we are or what's going on around us; true peace can be found anywhere; for true peace is found in the heart, and the heart is something that no one can touch.

Some peaces in life can be negotiated; but not God's peace! There is no bargaining or negotiating in the world that could let us arrange terms with God and find his peace. The only way peace could be made was when Christ died on the cross to pay the price of our sin. God himself was the one making the peace for us, even though the hostilities began on our side!

Today, let's thank God for Jesus, who brings us peace with God; and let's claim God's promise that this peace is for enjoying in every circumstance of life – even those that face you today.

And through Christ, God has brought all things back to himself again – things on earth and things in heaven. God made peace through the blood of Christ's death on the cross.
(COLOSSIANS 1:20, NCV)

APRIL 12

Worship that releases power

Let the high praises of God be in their mouth, and a two-edged sword in their hand.
(PSALM 149:6, KJV)

In so many of our Western churches worship can be a very 'tame' affair. This really comes home to you when you travel to non-Western nations and touch something of the vibrancy and power of their worship. And that's exactly how we find worship to be in the Bible at times, especially when it is used to enforce God's victory into difficult (if not impossible!) situations. Whenever people focused on God in worship, there was a breakthrough in the spiritual dimension of life. Hindrances were removed, difficulties overcome, problems resolved and enemies defeated.

Our introductory verse today is deliberately chosen from an older translation to retain the phrase 'high praises'. There are times in life when 'ordinary praise' just won't do and when we really need to 'give it all we've got' – in volume, in passion, in faith, in the Spirit – and attain a 'higher level' of praise to God that breaks through spiritual barriers. Daniel discovered something of those barriers when fasting for three weeks to seek God's revelation. At the end of that period, God's angelic messenger finally broke through, explaining that 'the prince of the Persian kingdom resisted me twenty-one days' (Daniel 10:13) and saying that it was only when the archangel Michael came to his aid that there had been a breakthrough.

'High praise' is what often helps bring about such breakthroughs. It engages things at a spiritual level in the 'Heavenly realms' (Ephesians 6:12), the realm where we can't see unless our eyes are opened. That's what happened to Elisha's servant. He couldn't see what Elisha was seeing; but then Elisha prayed for him and 'the LORD opened the servant's eyes, and he looked and saw the hills full of horses and chariots of fire all round Elisha' (2 Kings 6:17). In Psalm 149, the psalmist recognizes that such divine breakthroughs can as easily come through the mouth full of praise as by the hand with a sword.

Today, if you are facing what seem to be insuperable obstacles, let 'the high praises of God' fill your mouth. Give it all you've got – and expect a breakthrough!

I call to the LORD, who is worthy of praise, and I am saved from my enemies.
(2 SAMUEL 22:4)

Utterly abandoned

About the ninth hour Jesus cried out in a loud voice, 'Eloi, Eloi, lama sabachthani?' – which means, 'My God, my God, why have you forsaken me?'
(MATTHEW 27:46)

All of us experience loneliness at times; but how very dark things are when we feel, not just lonely, but desolate – utterly abandoned by everyone. That's how Jesus felt on the cross; so abandoned that he cried out in the words of our opening verse.

These words had such an impact on his followers that the very Aramaic phrase he used was remembered. They couldn't believe what they were hearing! Jesus, who had taught them so much about trusting God as Father, was now asking why that Father had abandoned him! His cry was from the opening words of Psalm 22, a prayer written by David a thousand years earlier. 'My God, my God, why have you forsaken me? Why are you so far from saving me, so far from the words of my groaning?' the psalm begins (v. 1). It goes on to express, in amazing detail, so much of what Jesus experienced on that first Good Friday. 'All who see me mock me; they hurl insults, shaking their heads' (v. 7); 'I am poured out like water, and all my bones are out of joint' (v. 14); 'dogs have surrounded me; a band of evil men has encircled me, they have pierced my hands and my feet. I can count all my bones; people stare and gloat over me. They divide my garments among them and cast lots for my clothing' (vv. 16–18). What amazing prophecy this was!

But when Jesus recited these words, it was not merely as poetic language; some graphic way of describing how very alone he felt. It expressed the reality of his abandonment by the Father. For as 'he himself bore our sins in his body on the tree' (1 Peter 2:24), the Father turned away from his beloved Son, unable to look upon the sin that he was carrying.

This was the ultimate abandonment! And Jesus embraced it for us, so that we might never be abandoned again. What a Saviour! And what a Father who, on Easter Sunday, kept his promises and raised his Son from the dead!

'[Jesus] was not abandoned to the grave, nor did his body see decay. God has raised this Jesus to life.'
(ACTS 2:31–32)

APRIL 14

A worldwide epidemic!

There is no difference, for all have sinned and fall short of the glory of God, and are justified freely by his grace through the redemption that came by Christ Jesus.
(ROMANS 3:22–24)

Imagine the headlines if a killer disease were to sweep across the continents, devastating nations and decimating populations. Imagine how TV companies and journalists would all be out there, trying to catch the latest breaking news. Such an event would certainly grab the 'number one spot' in all the headlines.

But actually, such a killer disease *is* at work in the world, and has been so for centuries. But because it does its work silently and surreptitiously, no one hardly notices it is there, though its symptoms and signs are around for all to see. It is what we might call these days a genetic disease, for it goes right back to the first parents of the human race who have passed it on to every one of their descendants ever since. It is the disease is that the Bible calls 'sin'.

Like any diagnosis of a serious illness, the identifying of this most basic human condition is not popular; for being called 'sinners' hits right at our pride. Yet it is only when we recognize that our most fundamental problem is sin that we can begin to see a way out. For, the good news is – there is a cure! (Imagine the headlines now: 'Miracle cure discovered – world saved!'). God himself has provided a cure for this condition, just as he promised on the very day that Adam and Eve first sinned. The cure is his own Son, the Lord Jesus Christ; the dosage is to believe what he did for us when he died on the cross in our place and dealt with our condition once and for all.

No matter how you may feel you have failed God, no matter how bad you have been, the epidemic of sin in your life has been dealt with by Jesus. All you need to do is to reach out to him once again and enjoy the relief of being cured!

Therefore, there is now no condemnation for those who are in Christ Jesus, because through Christ Jesus the law of the Spirit of life set me free from the law of sin and death.
(ROMANS 8:1–2)

What a Saviour!

This grace was given us in Christ Jesus before the beginning of time, but it has now been revealed through the appearing of our Saviour, Christ Jesus, who has destroyed death and has brought life and immortality to light through the gospel.
(2 TIMOTHY 1:9–10)

'Hallelujah! What a Saviour!' ends each verse of the old hymn 'Man of sorrows'. What a Saviour indeed! For Jesus our Saviour came, not to live, but to die. True enough, his life and teaching powerfully demonstrated his ability to save people – from their sin, their sickness, their circumstances, the devil's grip. But the heart of God's plan of salvation could only happen through his death, not his life.

The first Christians were quite convinced that his death was the focal point of his ministry. Everything before it simply pointed to and prepared for that moment. Because of his sacrificial death, he was now 'Saviour' (a title used in the Old Testament of the Father, but one they had no hesitation in applying to the Son); and not just one saviour among many; but the *only* Saviour. 'Salvation is found in no-one else, for there is no other name under heaven given to men by which we must be saved,' declared Peter (Acts 4:12).

But it was not just his death, but his resurrection too that was key to this salvation; it was what assures us that his sacrifice had been accepted by the Father. The first Christians were convinced that, though unmistakably dead on Friday, Jesus walked out of his tomb on Sunday, gloriously conquering death. Indeed they were so convinced of this that Paul said that 'if Christ has not been raised, our preaching is useless and so is your faith' (1 Corinthians 15:14).

Of course, this death and resurrection are amazing – almost unbelievable. But who wants a saviour who can do little more than we can do? Better a saviour in God's image than in ours! Hallelujah – what a Saviour!

We preach Christ crucified: a stumbling-block to Jews and foolishness to Gentiles, but to those whom God has called, both Jews and Greeks, Christ the power of God and the wisdom of God.
(1 CORINTHIANS 1:23–24)

A case of heartburn

They asked each other, 'Were not our hearts burning within us
while he talked with us on the road
and opened the Scriptures to us?'
(LUKE 24:32)

One of Martin's favourite Bible stories is from that first Easter Sunday evening when the two disciples accompanied the risen Jesus to Emmaus, not knowing who it was until he broke bread with them. They had spent the day listening to him as he opened up Old Testament passages about the Messiah; but it was only when their eyes were opened to see who this stranger really was that they suddenly realized why they had felt so different when he had been speaking. 'Didn't we feel on fire as he conversed with us on the road, as he opened up the Scripture for us?' (Luke 24:32, The Message).

God doesn't want this to stay a 'nice story', however; he wants it to be the experience of each of us. So here's a little question: when did your heart last burn as the Scriptures were opened up, either in a sermon or in something you saw in your own Bible reading? Like the psalmist, can we say, 'As I meditated, the fire burned'? (Psalm 39:3). The 17th-century Puritan minister, Thomas Watson, wrote: 'Meditate for as long as it takes for you to find your heart warm. Don't leave off reading the Bible till you find your hearts warmed. Let the Bible not only inform you, but let it also inflame you . . Christian, if your heart is cold, stand at the fire of meditation until you find your affections warmed, and you are made fit for spiritual service . . . I will never come away from your presence without you.'

So, how are the fires of our own devotional life? Roaring and aglow with the Spirit? Steady but unexciting? Barely lit? Wherever we are at, our heavenly Father invites us to delight ourselves in him again as we reflect on him and on what he has promised and done. For as we do so, our hearts will burn and our confidence will grow.

One thing I ask of the LORD, this is what I seek: that I may dwell in the
house of the LORD all the days of my life, to gaze upon the beauty of the
LORD and to seek him in his temple.
(PSALM 27:4)

APRIL 17

It's all uphill!

'Come, let us go up to the mountain of the LORD, to the house of the God of Jacob.'
(ISAIAH 2:3)

We often use the phrase 'it's all uphill from here' to mean that it's going to be a really hard slog from now on. But there is a going up the hill, the Bible promises, that is a delight, not a drudge. It's the going up the hill to meet with God.

The temple in Jerusalem was on a hill, so to get to it you had to 'go up' the hill or 'ascend' – a phrase that often appears in worship contexts in the Old Testament. But just as going up a natural hill can be hard work sometimes, so can 'going up the hill' to meet with God, if we're honest. It doesn't always come easily or naturally to us, and we sometimes need help to 'get going' or 'keep going'. So Psalm 100 has a simple pattern to help us: come . . . know . . . thank . . . praise.

'*Come* before him' (v. 2) is an invitation, and an invitation is the assurance we are welcome. But we now have to make the decision and go. We have to *choose* to throw off the things that have filled our minds, captivated our hearts and demanded our time, and say 'I'm going!' As we do so, we need to '*know* that the LORD is God' (v. 3); that is, to start focusing on him and not ourselves, remembering what he has done for us and that there is no one like him. This in turn will cause us to 'enter his gates with *thanksgiving*' (v. 4), as we remember all that God has done. And this in turn helps us to 'enter . . . his courts with *praise*' (v. 4), rejoicing in who God is and what he is like – the climax of our journey up the hill, which brings its own reward.

Don't stop halfway up the hill. Don't give in, but press on. Try using this pattern from Psalm 100 of 'come . . . know . . . thank . . . praise' to help you today as you 'go up the hill'. You're invited, and he's waiting to meet with you!

Let us know, let us press on to know the LORD.
(HOSEA 6:3, NRSV)

APRIL 18

The power of doxologies

To him who is able to keep you from falling and to present you before his glorious presence without fault and with great joy – to the only God our Saviour be glory, majesty, power and authority, through Jesus Christ our Lord, before all ages, now and for evermore! Amen.
(JUDE 24–25)

Scattered throughout the Scriptures are lots of 'doxologies'. The word comes from two Greek words: *doxa* (meaning 'glory') and *logos* (meaning 'word or speech'). A doxology, therefore, is an exclamation of praise that glorifies God. Such prayers have often been used liturgically; but perhaps more importantly they serve as models to us of how to call out to God in praise, briefly but powerfully, in all sorts of circumstances.

In the Bible we see doxologies not just in 'religious' or worship settings, but in the ordinary routine of everyday life. For example, the birth of a new baby is always a cause for joy; but in the Bible, it is a cause for joy before God. So, when the sad story of Naomi and Ruth comes to its happy conclusion as Ruth marries Boaz and gives birth to a son (the grandfather of the future King David), the women-folk of the town spontaneously exclaim, 'Praise be to the LORD, who this day has not left you without a kinsman-redeemer' (Ruth 4:14). When Elizabeth gives birth to her long-awaited child, then her husband Zechariah, seeing the fulfilment of God's word to him, exclaims, 'Praise be to the Lord, the God of Israel, because he has come and has redeemed his people' (Luke 1:68).

But it was not just in speech, but also in writing that doxologies could also be found. For example, Paul concludes his testimony to Timothy with the words, 'Now to the King eternal, immortal, invisible, the only God, be honour and glory for ever and ever. Amen' (1 Timothy 1:17). Peter ends his second letter with the words 'Grow in the grace and knowledge of our Lord and Saviour Jesus Christ. To him be glory both now and for ever! Amen' (2 Peter 3:18).

Whether through spoken or written words, God's people in the Bible were not afraid to let their spontaneous praise to God be known. What about us?

To our God and Father be glory for ever and ever. Amen.
(PHILIPPIANS 4:20)

APRIL 19

A call and a promise

'Come, follow me,' Jesus said, 'and I will make you fishers of men.'
(MARK 1:17)

Jesus is not looking for Christians – he is looking for *disciples*. This was what lay at the heart of his ministry. It is how it began, as he called those fishermen and said, 'Come, follow me' (Mark 1:17); it is how it ended, as he sent out those same disciples, now themselves equipped to 'make disciples of all nations' (Matthew 28:19). In the intervening three years, he had called all sorts of people to be disciples too, from all walks of life: fishermen, tax collectors, homemakers, religious experts, freedom fighters, soldiers, prostitutes – a whole cross-section of society. There really was room for everyone in Jesus' school of discipleship. And as each one followed him and became a disciple, their life was changed.

Discipleship remains Jesus' primary call today. But it is not just a call – it is a promise! It involves three things. First, it is a call to *decision*. When Jesus said, 'Come!' a decision had to be made; a decision that would change the life of the one who made it. Second, it was a call to *difference*, for we cannot 'follow' while staying where we are! As they followed, change occurred, for they saw something better and wanted it in their own lives. Third, it is a call to *destiny*, for Jesus wants to bring us into God's eternal purposes for our life, making us into something beyond what we could have ever imagined!

Paul received a tremendous promise when called by Jesus, being told he would take the good news to the Gentiles – the very people he had formerly despised. But this was no penance for him – no punishment for having hated them. Rather, it became his joy and delight. For that is what discipleship does: it changes us and brings us into what God has promised.

Today, this promise and this call are still as real, still as powerful, still as effective for all who will pick up the challenge. How will we respond to Jesus' call, 'Come, follow me'?

For I am the least of the apostles and do not even deserve to be called an apostle, because I persecuted the church of God. But by the grace of God I am what I am, and his grace to me was not without effect.
(1 CORINTHIANS 15:9–10)

APRIL 20

Happiness and holiness

Christ loved the church and gave himself up for her to make her holy.
(EPHESIANS 5:25–26)

Probably the greatest priority of people in the West is 'being happy'. What a shock it is, therefore, to discover that God's priority for us is not happiness, but holiness – though, strangely, when we pursue the latter we find the former! At first sight, holiness and happiness might seem the very opposite of one another. Yet if we see holiness as simply 'becoming like Jesus', we will understand that it is when we are at our holiest that we are also at our happiest.

All of us have heard children saying, 'When I grow up, I want to be a . . .' Mike wanted to be a train driver (but never became one), while Martin wanted to write dictionaries (and certainly did). Whether we become what we imagined or not, such desires are part of growing up. Likewise, every Christian should have a desire to grow up – not into our own plans and ambitions, but into becoming like Jesus. Look at his life and it's clear that no holier a man ever lived; there wasn't a trace of sin in him. Yet Jesus lived life to the full and thoroughly enjoyed it. Surely this must tell us something about holiness.

The problem starts when we see holiness as 'yet another demand' on our already-busy lives, something else we have to 'do'. But if we think like that, then we have lost before we have even begun. Left to ourselves and our efforts, holiness is an impossible task, for how can unholy people make themselves like the holy God? And whenever we try to, we simply fall into a religion of works and effort, and end up disappointed, defeated and frustrated. That is why it is important to remember that '*Christ* loved the church and gave himself up for her to make her holy'. In other words, this is all about him! It is Jesus who not only died for us, but who works his holiness into us, as we allow his Holy Spirit to rule our lives. Our part is simply to believe his promise and co-operate with him! Try it today and see!

It is God who saved us and chose us to live a holy life.
(2 TIMOTHY 1:9, NLT)

The God who comes to help

'God has come to help his people.'
(LUKE 7:16)

Christianity stands out from every other religion in the world; for where they have people reaching up to find God, Christianity has God coming down to find and help people! This is a theme that we see again and again throughout the Bible. For example, when the Israelites were in slavery in Egypt, God heard their cry, saw their suffering and took action. He called Moses, saying to him, 'I have indeed seen the misery of my people in Egypt. I have heard them crying out because of their slave drivers, and I am concerned about their suffering. So I have come down to rescue them . . .' (Exodus 3:7–8). '*I have come down to rescue them.*' That simple sentence sums up how God would act again and again for his people throughout the Old Testament, for his very nature is to be a redeeming God.

It should not surprise us, therefore, to find that when Jesus, the Son of God, came to this world, the same theme was found on his lips. In fact, at the start of his ministry in the synagogue at Nazareth, he read from the prophet Isaiah, proclaiming how God's anointed one would come in the power of the Spirit to bring help to God's people through bringing to them freedom from imprisonment, sight for blind eyes, and release for the oppressed. Truly, this was 'the year of the Lord's favour' (Luke 4:19) – a time when God had come down to help his people.

The same message is brought home to us in the story of the raising of the widow of Nain's son. What drama there must have been in town that day as the wailing of bereavement gave way to shouts of joy as the young man sat up in his coffin! The people lifted their voices in praise to God and declared, 'God has come to help his people' (Luke 7:16).

This promise still holds true for us today. God does not stand afar off, but he is the one who comes to help his people – even you!

'Praise be to the Lord, the God of Israel, because he has come and has redeemed his people.'
(LUKE 1:68)

APRIL 22

The generosity of God

> *. . . the riches of God's grace that he lavished on us with all wisdom and understanding.*
> (EPHESIANS 1:7–8)

In the week that Mike wrote this, he and his wife were on the receiving end of a substantial gift from someone who wanted to share an inheritance with them. How grateful they were for the donor's generosity! But then God reminded Mike of how he had felt when a colleague had received a gift earlier in the year but when he hadn't. He remembered that he hadn't been as excited about generosity on that occasion!

We all love generosity – as long as it is we who are on the receiving end. Jesus told a parable that touched on this attitude in Matthew 20. A caring landowner gave work to those who needed it and agreed to pay them a fair wage: a day's pay for a day's work. As the day went on, however, he became more and more generous. Each worker, regardless of how long he worked, was paid a day's wages. Each received what he needed in order to keep his family, not what he deserved on a strict hourly rate. Those who didn't start work until the eleventh hour (5pm by our reckoning) were excited by such generous treatment – though those who had worked from the beginning of the day complained it wasn't 'fair'. But the landowner simply replied that he wasn't being unfair, but more-than–fair. His generosity had exposed the hearts of mean-minded people.

God is still as generous today. The riches of his grace are freely promised and available to all, regardless of what we have been or done. The miracle of grace is that he doesn't deal with us according to what we deserve or have 'earned', but simply according to his kindness and generosity – a generosity that is still available to all today.

> *'If you, then, though you are evil, know how to give good gifts to your children, how much more will your Father in heaven give good gifts to those who ask him!'*
> (MATTHEW 7:11)

Finding our destiny

For he chose us in him before the creation of the world to be holy and blameless in his sight. In love he predestined us to be adopted as his sons through Jesus Christ, in accordance with his pleasure and will.
(EPHESIANS 1:4–5)

Think of destiny, and we instinctively think of great men and women like Churchill, Martin Luther King or Mother Teresa; people who changed the face of history or impacted whole nations and times. While such 'big names' have undoubtedly played key roles in human history, it is easy to forget that the Bible promises that each one of us – ordinary Christians! – has a destiny too – a destiny that is far greater than that of some of the great names of life!

God's ultimate destiny for each of us is to become his 'sons' (Ephesians 1:5) – part of 'the family of believers' (Galatians 6:10) and 'co-heirs with Christ' (Romans 8:17), enjoying fulness of life with him that begins now, continues through heaven, and finds ultimate expression in his new creation at the end. But while that is our *general* destiny, each of us has a *particular* destiny, with its own particular 'shape' for each one of us here and now. Finding our destiny is about *finding what we were made for.*

In the film *Chariots of Fire* Eric Liddell spoke of how he felt God's pleasure when he was running. In doing what he was made for, he knew that his true self was being realized. For Eric, it was running; for Peter, it was building the church; for Paul, it was preaching the gospel; for one of the authors of this book, Martin, it is in compiling and editing reference books!

But each of *us* has a destiny in God too. Ask him to show you what it is – it will often be to do with what you enjoy doing most and what you are most fruitful in. Then give yourself to the process of letting God shape you and make you even more fruitful in that area, so that you might come into the destiny that God has for your life, just as he has promised to do.

Not that I have already obtained all this, or have already been made perfect, but I press on to take hold of that for which Christ Jesus took hold of me.
(PHILIPPIANS 3:12)

APRIL 24

God's big family

For this reason I kneel before the Father, from whom his whole family in heaven and on earth derives its name.
(EPHESIANS 3:14–15)

When God revealed himself to Abraham and called him to go to Canaan, he made a covenant with him. He promised that he would give him many descendants and that, through those descendants, he would build a big family for himself. The Old Testament is the story of how God patiently grew that family, preparing for the coming of his Son into it, through whom he would expand it to 'every nation, tribe, people and language' (Revelation 7:9).

It should not surprise us, therefore, to find that, in the New Testament, the church is often described as a 'family'; for, in the church, God is continuing the story that he began with Abraham. So, we find Paul speaking of the church as 'the family of believers' (Galatians 6:10) and as 'God's household' (1 Timothy 3:15), and Peter calling us 'the family of God' (1 Peter 4:17). 'Family' speaks of being together and being at ease. The church should be, in the words of Michael Griffiths, 'a place where we feel safe, can be ourselves, and have no need to be boarded up behind a façade, a place where we are cared for and care for one another'. It should be a place where we can be ourselves, rather than where we feel we have to 'perform'; for the church is God's 'family', and 'family' is all about being 'at home'.

This is why it is so good that many churches have re-discovered the importance of using homes, for it helps build a sense of real family. Homes were a key feature of early church life; in fact, when Paul was persecuting the church, it wasn't to some central building that he went to round up believers, but rather 'from house to house' (Acts 8:3). Homes played a key part, not simply because they didn't have buildings yet, but because they really helped to express 'family'.

God has promised to build a family - and he wants *you* (and your church) to be a part of it! Don't take this promise for granted; rather, enjoy your church family today!

Consequently, you are no longer foreigners and aliens, but fellow-citizens with God's people and members of God's household.
(EPHESIANS 2:19)

Beautiful feet!

'Everyone who calls on the name of the Lord will be saved.'
(ROMANS 10:13)

We only have to watch the TV or read the newspaper to see the mess the world is in. At every level – politically, economically, morally, and spiritually – the human race seems to lurch from bad to worse. Even creation itself, the Bible tells us, is eager to be 'liberated from its bondage to decay' (Romans 8:21). Of course, the world's basic problem is not economics or politics or ecology, but *sin*. It is because of sin that people 'love darkness instead of light', and 'do evil' (John 3:19–20). Yet despite this dark picture, God promises that 'everyone who calls on the name of the Lord will be saved.' Which is where the beautiful feet come in!

For people to be saved they first need to *hear* the good news that can save them; and that in turn means people going and telling it to them. This is why Paul writes: 'How, then, can they call on the one they have not believed in? And how can they believe in the one of whom they have not heard? And how can they hear without someone preaching to them? And how can they preach unless they are sent? As it is written, "How beautiful are the feet of those who bring good news!"' (Romans 10:14–15).

God is looking for those who will believe his promise about beautiful feet! Those who will go and tell will find that his anointing is with them as they do. This doesn't mean having to go to some far-flung nation; mission begins right on our own doorstep – among our unsaved family and friends, with neighbours, at school or college, at our workplace. As we are faithful in going and telling, God promises to add his blessing.

So, why not claim his promise today of having 'beautiful feet'? That is, of people thinking it fantastic that you went to them and brought the good news of Jesus that alone can rescue them from a messed-up world. God's heart is to see everyone saved; will you play your part in giving someone a chance for that to happen?

We have put our hope in the living God, who is the Saviour of all men, and especially those who believe.
(1 TIMOTHY 4:10)

APRIL 26

The day everyone prayed

*Many peoples and the inhabitants of many cities will yet come,
and the inhabitants of one city will go to another and say, 'Let
us go at once to entreat the LORD and seek the LORD Almighty.
I myself am going.'*
(ZECHARIAH 8:20–21)

The prophets were people of enormous vision. Despite many challenges and obstacles, they still saw God's purposes, prayed in faith and prophesied amazing things. One of the most significant things they prophesied was the exile and return from it. But they also saw something greater: the coming of Messiah and the ultimate deliverance that he would bring. And when this happened, they saw, there would be a great turning of hearts to God – not just among Jews, but among all the nations – and a passionate desire to rush into God's presence and pray.

Jesus prefigured this desire in his own ministry. All sorts of people (not just the religious and not just Jews) felt able to sit in his presence and talk to him. Think, for example, of the Greek woman who came to Jesus begging him to free her daughter from demonic control. 'First let the children eat all they want," he told her, "for it is not right to take the children's bread and toss it to their dogs." "Yes, Lord," she replied, "but even the dogs under the table eat the children's crumbs.' Then he told her, 'For such a reply, you may go; the demon has left your daughter." She went home and found her child lying on the bed, and the demon gone' (Mark 7:27–30). Through his apparently reluctant answer, he had pushed her into faith to ask, and her faith was rewarded.

You may sometimes feel alone when you are praying or alone in what you are praying for. But remember this: all around the world, there are God's people who are praying; in heaven, the angels and Jesus himself are praying; and one day, the nations of the earth will flock into his presence to praise and pray. Let this thought strengthen you as you turn to him in prayer today!

*Many nations will come and say, 'Come, let us go up to the mountain of the
LORD, to the house of the God of Jacob. He will teach us his ways,
so that we may walk in his paths.'*
(MICAH 4:2)

APRIL 27

Seeking signs

Gideon replied, 'If now I have found favour in your eyes, give me a sign that it is really you talking to me.'
(JUDGES 6:17)

When younger, Martin was once on a train journey, praying and agonizing over whether to marry a particular girl. Eventually he asked God to intervene miraculously and to show him his will through 'a sign'. There was suddenly a dramatic intervention when cows invaded the railway line and brought the journey to a complete standstill. The trouble was: Martin wasn't quite sure whether this was God answering his prayer or not – and if it was, what the sign meant anyway! And so he (wisely!) decided that perhaps this wasn't quite what God meant by seeking his guidance!

While there are times in the Bible when God gave 'signs' to assure people of his presence, guidance or activity – such as the sign given to Hezekiah that Assyria would not prevail (2 Kings 19:29) or to the shepherds that they had indeed found the new-born Messiah (Luke 2:11–12) – asking for signs is generally seen as a *lack* of faith rather than a mark of faith (e.g. Exodus 4:1–17; 2 Kings 20:8–11); and *demands* for signs were certainly always resisted (e.g. Matthew 12:38–40).

Gideon's laying out of a sheep's fleece has often been taken by Christians as a 'model' of how to receive guidance (see Judges 6:36–40); but it is clear from the context that, for a man who had just encountered the angel of the LORD, had been commissioned by him, had experienced a miracle and had received an empowering of the Holy Spirit, his exercise with the fleece – just to make sure! – was a measure of his *lack* of faith, not the abundance of it.

So, is God angry with us if we ask for signs? We doubt it! But as Christians we do not need to look for such external 'signs' (even if God graciously has given us one in the past!). Through God's word, God's Spirit and God's people, God has provided ample means for us to receive his promised guidance. Why look for 'things' to guide us when we have God himself!?

I will lead the blind by ways they have not known, along unfamiliar paths I will guide them; I will turn the darkness into light before them and make the rough places smooth.
(ISAIAH 42:16)

APRIL 28

Little faith, big God!

'If you have faith as small as a mustard seed, you can say to this mulberry tree, "Be uprooted and planted in the sea," and it will obey you.'
(LUKE 17:6)

God's promises can seem quite staggering at times, almost too good to be true – especially if we have just failed God in some way. But this is when we need to remember this simple truth: God's promises aren't dependent on *us*, but on *him*! We may feel that our faith is so small; but it's not the smallness of our faith that counts; it's the bigness of our God!

So often, we feel we can't match big promises from God's side with big faith from our side; so we give up before we start, or we get weary half way through, or we embrace the devil's accusations and drop the whole idea. But Jesus said that it isn't the *amount* of faith that is the issue. Twice, when his disciples were challenged by their own lack of faith, he said that all they needed was faith the size of a mustard seed (which is very small indeed!).

The issue is not the *amount* of faith, but the *object* of faith; not *how much* faith you've got, but *where* the faith that you have got is focused. To put it a different way: there is no power in 'faith'; there is only power in Jesus. Faith needs to be faith in him, not faith in 'faith'. Faith isn't what makes the promise happen; faith is simply what keeps us focused on God who alone can make it happen. And this is why we can hold on to the promises, even when we have messed up; for, ultimately, it is not about us, but about him.

What this means practically is that we have to face up to the reality of our situation, but at the same time keep hold of God's promise, constantly bringing it back to him, reminding him of what he said and telling him we aren't going away until he has done what he has promised, no matter how long we have to wait.

So, whatever you are waiting for, let your faith today be focused on your God, not on your faith!

So those who have faith are blessed along with Abraham, the man of faith.
(GALATIANS 3:9)

APRIL 29

Strongest when weak

'You come against me with sword and spear and javelin, but I come against you in the name of the LORD Almighty, the God of the armies of Israel, whom you have defied. This day the LORD will hand you over to me . . . All those gathered here will know that it is not by sword or spear that the LORD saves; for the battle is the LORD's.'
(1 SAMUEL 17:45–47)

Our text today comes from the well-known story of David and Goliath. While everyone else in Israel was too afraid to take up Goliath's challenge to settle the outcome of the war by one-on-one combat, David was incensed by his audacity. 'Who is this uncircumcised Philistine that he should defy the armies of the living God?' he declared (1 Samuel 17:26). And with that, he resolved to do the job himself.

At first, his brothers laughed at him and King Saul was ready to dismiss him. But David pressed his case, confident that 'the LORD who delivered me from the paw of the lion and the paw of the bear will deliver me from the hand of this Philistine' (1 Samuel 17:37). Saul wanted to put his own armour on David (one of the few sets that Israel possessed), but since David was still a teenager at this time, it hung off him like an oversized jacket and David couldn't move around in it easily. Of course, Saul meant well; he was trying to give David the best protection and equipment available. But David knew that this wasn't where to find it. He knew that the place to find it was in God alone – and the rest is history.

To an outside observer David seemed desperately weak, and indeed, he was. But he knew where real strength was to be found – not in himself, but in his God. He felt terribly weak; but he knew that it was in such times of our weakness that the strength of God really comes into its own – and he was proved right!

Feeling weak today? Good! For the weaker we are, the better; because the more aware we are of our weakness, the more God can show his power, just as he promised.

'For the foolishness of God is wiser than man's wisdom, and the weakness of God is stronger than man's strength.'
(1 CORINTHIANS 1:25)

Question . . . or trust!

'But I trust in you, O LORD; I say, "You are my God."
My times are in your hands.'
(PSALM 31:14–15)

None of us gets through life without meeting trouble or sorrow at some time. As one of Job's friends put it, 'Man is born to trouble as surely as sparks fly upward' (Job 5:7). At such times we may wonder where God is and may even ask, 'Why?' Certainly people in the Bible did. The psalmist asked God, 'Why do you hide yourself in times of trouble?' (Psalm 10:1); Jeremiah asked, 'Why is my pain unending?' (Jeremiah 15:18); and Habakkuk asked, 'Why are you silent while the wicked swallow up those more righteous than themselves?' (Habakkuk 1:13). So when we ask similar questions we aren't on our own! And the fact that these questions are recorded in Scripture shows us that God doesn't mind us asking them.

But ultimately, the answer to the question 'why?' remains a mystery. The problem, at its most basic level, is that we live in a fallen world, one originally made good but spoilt by sin, and one in which, as a result, things go dreadfully wrong at times. So, while suffering may sometimes be the consequence of our own sin or bad choices, more often than not, it is simply 'one of those things' in life in a fallen world.

That is why endlessly asking 'why' doesn't get us very far. In fact, those who asked this question in the Bible rarely got an *answer*. What they got instead was an *encounter* – an encounter with the living God who brings his strength and encouragement in the midst of our troubles so that we can walk through them and come out on the other side. Rather than pour our emotional and spiritual energy into a question that ultimately has no answer, therefore, how much more worthwhile it is to turn to God and say, 'I don't understand what I'm going through, and I don't like what I'm going through; but I choose to put my trust in you, despite everything.' When we do this, we begin to see indeed that 'in all things God works for the good of those who love him' (Romans 8:28). Trust that God again today!

'The eternal God is your refuge, and underneath are the everlasting arms.'
(DEUTERONOMY 33:27)

Lead kindly Light

Whether you turn to the right or to the left, your ears will hear
a voice behind you, saying, 'This is the way; walk in it.'
(ISAIAH 30:21)

'Lead, kindly Light, amid the encircling gloom, Lead Thou me on.' So begins one of Cardinal John Henry Newman's famous hymns, written over a century ago. He was expressing his faith that, though the way ahead may not always seem clear, he was confident that God would lead him – a confidence based on the sure promises of the Scriptures.

All of us face times when we have to make decisions about the way ahead. Some of those decisions are ordinary and run-of-the-mill; but some are much more significant, even life-changing. It can be easy to feel somewhat paralysed at such times, overwhelmed by the possibilities or the uncertainties. That's when it's good to remember two things: First, that God *wants* to guide us. The constant testimony of Scripture is that God loves his people and guides his people. Even with an unknown wilderness ahead of them that they needed to cross, Moses and Miriam could sing, 'In your unfailing love you will lead the people you have redeemed' (Exodus 15:13). And God really wants to guide us too!

Second, that God knows all the 'what ifs . . .' of life. Sometimes we can be paralysed by thinking, 'But what if this ….' or 'What if that …?'. That's when it's good to remember that God, who is outside of time, knows all the 'what ifs' of life. He already knows all the possibilities and conceivable options – and he has a plan 'up his sleeve' for every one of them! *We* may not be able to see around the corner, but *God* can! That's why we can be sure that he will guide us and that, as long as we are seeking to follow him, even if we get it wrong, he is the God who 'causes everything to work together for the good of those who love God' (Romans 8:28, NLT).

Whatever decisions you need to make, whatever uncertainties may lie ahead, God will be your kindly light. Simply claim his promises of guidance – then trust him!

For this God is our God for ever and ever; he will be our guide even to the end.
(PSALM 48:14)

MAY 2

Lost and found

'For this is what the Sovereign LORD says: I myself will search for my sheep and look after them.'
(EZEKIEL 34:11)

Some years ago Mike and his wife 'lost' one of their children. The minute they realized it, they informed the manager of the store where they were shopping. A guard was put at the entrance and the staff set about searching the premises. Thankfully, their daughter was quickly discovered (sitting happily on a shelf!), but the dread panic of those few minutes was not something they would want to repeat.

As it happened they had another of their daughters with them at the time. So can you imagine everyone's horror if they had failed to find the missing daughter but said, 'Well, never mind everyone – we tried! Thanks for looking – but we've still got another daughter here, so we'll cut our losses and call it a day!' Nothing on earth would have made them act like that; they would have simply kept on looking until the lost one was found, no matter how long it took.

If that is what we would do, why should it surprise us to find that God promises to do the same? In Luke 15, we find three parables about 'lost things' – a lost sheep, a lost coin, and a lost son. In each case, the one who had lost them wouldn't give up until they were found. The shepherd left his other sheep and went to find the stray; the woman turned the house upside down until she found the lost coin; the father waited for the son to come to home, and was ready with a party when he did.

All of these stories are, of course, pictures of us: it is we who are lost and need to be found. But equally, they are pictures of God and what he is like – a God who refuses to give up on people, no matter how 'lost' they might be. The promise of Jesus to go and find the lost still holds true today. It is a promise that he holds out to each one of us; but also one that he invites us to share in as we join him in looking for others too.

'In the same way your Father in heaven is not willing that any of these little ones should be lost.'
(MATTHEW 18:14)

Seeing the invisible

'Don't be afraid,' the prophet answered. 'Those who are with us are more than those who are with them.' And Elisha prayed, 'O LORD, open his eyes so that he may see.'
(2 KINGS 6:16–17)

Imagine the scenario: you are the prophet Elisha's servant and you wake up early, as usual, to start the tasks of the day. But as you do so, you discover the town is surrounded by your enemies, the Arameans. For years there have been border skirmishes of varying intensity between them and Israel, which Israel had been doing rather well in, thanks mainly to Elisha whose prophetic insights had kept giving the king 'inside information'. But finally, the King of Aram had had enough and had sent an army of soldiers, horses and chariots to capture Elisha. In panic, you run to awaken Elisha and tell him the bad news. And he's as calm as anything!

'Don't be afraid,' he tells you (for you clearly are afraid, as any sane person would be in such a situation!). 'Those who are with us are more than those who are with them.' 'What on earth is he talking about?' you think. 'The dear man has flipped at last! The pressure has got to him.' And then he prays for your eyes to be opened – and you suddenly see! You see 'the hills full of horses and chariots of fire all round Elisha' (2 Kings 6:17). The enemy is completely outnumbered! Now, at last, you can see why Elisha isn't panicking!

We too, the New Testament tells us, are in the midst of a battle – a spiritual battle that we cannot see with human eyes, but which God has promised to help us discern through his Holy Spirit. This battle has always been there; it's just we never understood it before we became a Christian; and even now, we sometimes miss it or forget it. If things have been going wrong in your life, if problems have crowded in, then ask God to open your eyes so you can 'see' what he can see. Ask him to show you what is going on spiritually. He will hear and answer your prayer!

'Call to me and I will answer you, and will tell you great and hidden things that you have not known.'
(JEREMIAH 33:3, NRSV)

MAY 4

Removing the clutter

What is more, I consider everything a loss compared to the surpassing greatness of knowing Christ Jesus my Lord, for whose sake I have lost all things. I consider them rubbish, that I may gain Christ.
(PHILIPPIANS 3:8)

One of the current 'reality television' shows is 'Life Laundry' (forgive us if you are reading this in twenty years' time when this seems very outdated!). The programme's aim is to remove the clutter that we all so easily accumulate in our homes. You know the sort of things: keepsakes from past holidays, old school books, long-playing vinyl records, things we can't bring ourselves to throw away. In the programme, all of this junk (for that is what it really is!) is put on the lawn (a lawn which, remarkably, whenever Martin has watched it, has always been dry!). Then presenters sit down with the owners who have to justify why they want to keep the various items. You can imagine some of the inventive reasons that people come up with when challenged!

Well, here's a challenge to us. Do we need a spiritual 'Life Laundry', a spiritual spring-clean? Is there spiritual clutter that we need to get rid of? Are there things that hinder us from loving Christ more, or things that crowd him out or that have taken his place? Are there things which, though once useful, have now passed their 'sell-by' date and serve no purpose to either God or man? It could be money, ambition, pride: it could be an obsession or persistent habit; it could be a problem with a personal relationship, excessive pressure from work, family or church; it could be laziness, or a host of smaller things that stifle our love for Jesus. Paul considered as rubbish absolutely anything that got in the way of him and Jesus!

God wants our devotion to him to be pure and wholehearted. Like weeds in the garden, the cares of life tend to grow naturally and persistently. So we need to take time to remove the weeds so that the Spirit can produce his fruit in our lives instead. Ask God to show you your clutter and to help you walk in his ways today.

Teach me your way, O LORD, and I will walk in your truth; give me an undivided heart, that I may fear your name.
(PSALM 86:11)

MAY 5

Praying in Jesus' name

'And I will do whatever you ask in my name, so that the Son may bring glory to the Father. You may ask me for anything in my name, and I will do it.'
(JOHN 14:13–14)

Prayer isn't 'magic' – though it's amazing how we fall into the trap of seeing it as such, especially when we want something. In magic, saying the right formula brings the required result, and Acts tells us about some Jewish exorcists who saw Christian prayer in that way. 'They would say, "In the name of Jesus, whom Paul preaches, I command you to come out"' (Acts 19:13). But seven sons of Sceva tried it and found they had 'bitten off more than they could chew' when an evil spirit answered them, 'Jesus I know, and I know about Paul, but who are you?' (v. 15), and promptly gave them a good beating. They certainly learned that praying 'in Jesus' name' wasn't some magic formula that achieved its required end just because you used it.

So what does it mean to pray 'in Jesus' name'? First, it's about praying on the basis of *who Jesus is.* In Bible times, someone's name summed up who they were and what they did. So praying 'in Jesus' name' recognizes that, while we have no claims in our own right when we approach God, we are coming on the basis of who Jesus is.

Second, it's about praying on the basis of *what Jesus has done.* We are remembering his death on the cross, where he defeated sin and Satan, and remembering that our sins have been dealt with and that the devil now has no grounds for accusing us as we pray.

Third it is about praying on the basis of *what Jesus is like.* The 'anything' that Jesus promised has first to get past the 'everything' that Jesus is. He is holy; so can we ask him to answer some unholy request? He is compassionate; so can we ask him to answer some unkind and uncaring prayer?

No, praying in Jesus' name certainly isn't magic – but it is powerful! And recalling who he is, what he has done and what he is like will always affect our prayers.

'I tell you the truth, my Father will give you whatever you ask in my name.'
(JOHN 16:23)

MAY 6

Two-way conversation

'Come now, let us reason together,' says the LORD.
(ISAIAH 1:18)

Ever had a conversation with someone who doesn't listen? All they do is talk; and even if you do get a word in, the conversation quickly gets round to them again. But have you ever thought whether your talking to God is rather like this? All talking and no listening? In the Bible, it's two-way conversations that often prove to be the best prayers, as people 'talk things through' with God.

One of the longest prayer-conversations is in Exodus 3:1–4:17, where God calls Moses to lead his people and where Moses finds lots of excuses for not being suitable for the job. Just look at some of the ones he comes up with:

' "Who am I, that I should go to Pharaoh and bring the Israelites out of Egypt?" And God said, "I will be with you." (3:11–12) . . . "Suppose I go to the Israelites and say to them, 'The God of your fathers has sent me to you,' and they ask me, 'What is his name?' Then what shall I tell them?" "God said to Moses, "I AM WHO I AM." (3:13–14) . . . "What if they do not believe me or listen to me and say, 'The LORD did not appear to you'?' Then the LORD said to him, "What is that in your hand?" (4:1–2) . . . Moses said to the LORD, "O Lord, I have never been eloquent . . ." The LORD said to him, "Who gave man his mouth? . . . Is it not I, the LORD? Now go; I will help you speak and will teach you what to say." (4:10–12) . . . But Moses said, "O Lord, please send someone else to do it." Then the LORD's anger burned against Moses and he said, "What about your brother, Aaron the Levite? I know he can speak well . . ."' (4:13–14).

What a conversation! And how our own praying might be transformed if we prayed a bit more like that, seeing prayer as a two-way conversation, listening and responding, until the issue is clear. Try it today – as you walk, as you travel to work, as you drive the car, as you stand at the sink. God invites you to do it!

For God does speak – now one way, now another – though man
may not perceive it.
(JOB 33:14)

Open our eyes Lord!

See, a king will reign in righteousness and rulers will rule with justice. Each man will be like a shelter from the wind and a refuge from the storm, like streams of water in the desert and the shadow of a great rock in a thirsty land. Then the eyes of those who see will no longer be closed, and the ears of those who hear will listen.
(ISAIAH 32:1–3)

'They can't see the wood for the trees' is often said about someone who is missing something obvious. Of course, it's always more obvious to those who are looking on than to those who are trying to see! But some people, of course, just don't want to see; they don't want their eyes opening to truth, preferring to live in their own little world with its familiar, cosy parameters.

Sadly, even God's people can sometimes be like this: blind – blind to what God is doing. In the Bible we frequently find God challenging his people's blindness and deafness, telling them to 'Hear, you deaf; look, you blind, and see!' (Isaiah 42:18). Leaders, sadly, can sometimes be the most blind of all, and Jesus called the religious leaders of his day 'blind guides' (Matthew 15:14), for they were the most resistant to God, 'change', or anything that they could not yet 'see'.

However, God promised through the prophets that when Messiah came, he would open blind eyes so that people could 'see' once again; and Jesus confirmed this when he spoke of how he had come to bring 'recovery of sight for the blind' (Luke 4:18).

Perhaps there is something that you have not been 'seeing' recently. Perhaps it has caused you to be frustrated or confused or even angry. If so, stop fighting (you might be fighting against God!). Instead, claim his promise that those who know him will 'see'. Ask him to open your eyes, just as Elisha prayed for his servant – and then be open to what he shows you. Knowing God, it will almost certainly be different to what you expect! So be ready to see - and change!

And Elisha prayed, 'O LORD, open his eyes so that he may see.' Then the LORD opened the servant's eyes, and he looked and saw the hills full of horses and chariots of fire all round Elisha.
(2 KINGS 6:17)

MAY 8

Prayer walking

'What do you see, Amos?' he asked. 'A basket of ripe fruit,' I
answered. Then the LORD said to me,
'The time is ripe for my people Israel.'
(AMOS 8:2)

'In the past God spoke to our forefathers through the prophets at many times and in various ways' (Hebrews 1:1). So begins the writer as he reflects on the different ways in which God spoke to people in the past. For some, it was through visions, or dreams, or an audible voice; but for others, it was often through what they 'saw'. They would be walking along when God suddenly interrupted their thoughts and asked, 'What do you see?', just as he did with Amos in our opening verse today. As the prophets looked and reflected, God would speak to them, interpreting the physical reality before them in terms of the spiritual reality to which it pointed.

God still loves to do the same today. The trouble is, we are often so busy that we just don't hear what he's saying; and so we miss so many opportunities to receive God's revelation or to hear what is on his heart. But one way to begin to train ourselves to hear him better is to 'prayer walk'. Prayer walking is simple and is something that both of us as writers enjoy doing. It can be done as a specific exercise in its own right (perhaps walking round the streets in your neighbourhood or near your church) or while on the way to work. As you walk, what do you *see*? It may be something obvious: you walk past the police station, so pray about law and order; you walk past a school, so pray for the teachers and children there.

But sometimes something more 'supernatural' happens. You are walking down a certain street and suddenly feel burdened to pray about – marriage! You hadn't been thinking about that before; in fact, the thought came from nowhere. But our experience is that this often proves to be a real need in that area at that time. So trust the Holy Spirit, and pray!

Why not try some prayer walking today, either alone of with a friend? What do you 'see'? . . . Then pray about it!

'I tell you, open your eyes and look at the fields! They are ripe for harvest.'
(JOHN 4:35)

MAY 9

Ever felt jealous?

'Are you envious because I am generous?'
(MATTHEW 20:15)

There is a shop in Martin's town where they know him by name, say hello cheerily as he enters, and treat him really nicely. They make him feel important! But one day he noticed that the assistants were acting like this with other people too. His reaction? He felt cheated! Why? Because he wanted to be the only one who received special treatment! At that moment, he had forgotten the meaning of grace.

Actually, all of us can feel like this at times when God treats others just like us. Well, treating them just like us, we can just about bear; it's when he starts to treat them in ways that seem better than the way he treats us that it gets really hard! (Go on! – be honest! – you must have felt like this at times!)

But how unreasonable it is of us to complain at how God treats others. He can treat us however he wants: he is, after all, God! So who are we to question him? As Paul put it, 'But who are you, O man, to talk back to God? . . . Does not the potter have the right to make out of the same lump of clay some pottery for noble purposes and some for common use?' (Romans 9:20–21)

God is not unfair to any of us; for if he treated any of us on the basis of what is fair, the only outcome would be that all of us would be condemned to hell! But in his *mercy*, God does not give us what we deserve (which is judgment); rather, in his *grace* he gives us more than we could ever deserve (forgiveness!).

Grace is the free gift of God, given freely, as God chooses, to those who deserve the opposite. So, don't focus on the grace that he has been giving to others – that only leads to jealousy; but rather focus on the grace that he has promised is yours today.

Resentment kills a fool, and envy slays the simple.
(JOB 5:2)

MAY 10

The door to safety

Seek the LORD while he may be found; call on him while he is near. Let the wicked forsake his way and the evil man his thoughts. Let him turn to the LORD, and he will have mercy on him, and to our God, for he will freely pardon.
(ISAIAH 55:6–7)

If you have ever seen someone with a placard proclaiming the word 'Repent', or listened to a street preacher calling out to passers-by to do the same, you will no doubt have noticed the reaction of most people. There is an obvious embarrassment, an eagerness to look the other way, an urgent need to cross to the other side of the road. Being reminded there might be things in life that we need to repent of leaves most people feeling distinctly uncomfortable.

How sad this is, for the call to repent is one of God's kindest invitations to us! The word *repent* originally meant 'to change one's mind' – what we might describe today as 'doing a U-turn'. It is about recognizing that we have been going about things the wrong way; and the most logical consequence of that is to stop, turn round and start doing things God's way instead. Repentance is the decision we make that moves us from the wrong way to the right way, from our way to God's way. In the delightful phrase of J. A. Motyer, 'Repentance is the door into safety.'

What a wonderful picture that is! If you were in a room full of danger and there, in the corner, stood a door marked 'way out', what would you do? Without a moment's hesitation you would go through the door to escape. In the same way, God's escape door to safety is his gift of repentance. The trouble is, it is a door that is hard for us, for it requires that we admit we got things wrong – a difficult thing for us humans to do! Yet God promises that those who walk through this door *will* find him and, with him, life and forgiveness.

Today, as you turn to him, you can find his kindness and goodness once again.

Don't you know that the reason God is good to you is because he wants you to turn to him?
(ROMANS 2:4, CEV)

MAY 11

The Spirit of sonship

For you did not receive a spirit that makes you a slave again to fear, but you received the Spirit of sonship. And by him we cry, 'Abba, Father.'
(ROMANS 8:15)

We have probably all heard children say to one another – perhaps in an attempt to settle some dispute – 'My dad is bigger than your dad!' What they're really saying, of course, is, 'I'm not scared of you – because I've got someone to back me up!' And that's exactly what the Holy Spirit does for us whenever we are afraid or in difficulties. He comes and whispers, 'Remember who your Dad is!'

Paul had left his young associate Timothy in charge of the large, flourishing church at Ephesus. Reading Paul's letters to him, it is clear that it hadn't been too long after his departure before some members of the church were letting Timothy know that he wasn't doing quite as good a job as the previous pastor and were starting to 'flex their muscles' in all kinds of ways. Not surprisingly, Timothy got rather anxious about all this. But Paul reminded him that he needn't be anxious or afraid, for he had the Holy Spirit with him, constantly reminding him of his Father in heaven. And this Spirit, Paul told him, is not 'a spirit of timidity, but a spirit of power, of love and of self-discipline' (2 Timothy 1:7). He is there within us, encouraging us to be 'strong in the Lord and in his mighty power' (Ephesians 6:10) as he reminds us of who we are in Christ and of the resources of heaven that we can call upon.

As God's people, we do not need to be 'like cowering, fearful slaves' (Romans 8:15, NLT). We aren't slaves any longer, but 'sons' – part of God's family. God himself is our Father – a Father bigger than anything that might stand against us; and the Holy Spirit is his promised gift to us to enable us to remember this truth and to live in the good of it today.

Since you are God's children, God sent the Spirit of his Son into your hearts, and the Spirit cries out, 'Father'. So now you are not a slave; you are God's child, and God will give you the blessing he promised, because you are his child.
(GALATIANS 4:6–7, NCV)

Two aspects of prayer

I urge you, brothers, by our Lord Jesus Christ and by the love of the Spirit, to join me in my struggle by praying to God for me.
(ROMANS 15:30)

'It's the thought that counts!' people often say, meaning it's not the size or cost of the gift that matters, but the heart that lies behind it. And the Bible agrees wholeheartedly with that when it comes to worship and prayer. It's the thought, the heart, what's going on inside, that counts. But if that's the case, is there a place for corporate prayer and worship? Or should it simply be kept just 'between God and me'?

Never to worship or pray alone certainly robs us of the opportunity to be intimate with God, to tell our heavenly Father the things that are hidden away in the depths of our heart, that no one else knows. But equally, never to worship or pray with others robs us of the blessing and power that the Bible shows us is released when God's people come together. (Indeed, if public worship and prayer were removed from the Bible, it would be very much thinner!) Much Old Testament worship was certainly a corporate affair, bringing home that *together* they were the redeemed people of God. Jesus himself said, in the context of teaching about prayer, that 'where two or three come together in my name, there am I with them' (Matthew 18:20). And the early church had some powerful moments when they prayed together, such as in Acts 4 where 'after they prayed, the place where they were meeting was shaken' (Acts 4:31).

Paul certainly anticipated that true believers would participate in both private and corporate prayer. In today's verse, he urges the Christians at Rome to 'join me in my struggle by praying to God for me'. Obviously he himself had been praying; but he recognized that to see the breakthrough he was longing for, he needed them to join in with him in prayer too.

If we are going to be a true follower of Jesus, both private and corporate prayer will be an indispensable part of our life. Which of these aspects do you need to give more attention to at this time?

Friends, please pray for us.
(1 THESSALONIANS 5:25, CEV)

MAY 13

Failed again?

Learn to do right!
(ISAIAH 1:17)

If you are anything like us, you will often feel that you fail in your life of discipleship. It may be through some act of disobedience or fear; or perhaps through not being as radical as we should be; or perhaps through trying to 'serve two masters' (Matthew 6:24) and having seen – once again! – that it just doesn't work. We all fail to hit the target at times. So when we do, it is encouraging to remember that we are in good company.

Consider those first disciples of Jesus. The Gospels show us that they didn't always understand what Jesus said; they didn't always use the power that was theirs – and even when they did, it wasn't always in the right way or with the right attitude; they failed Jesus at the crucial moment, fleeing in Gethsemane; and to crown it all, Peter was even once told by Jesus that he was doing Satan's work for him! Hardly a great portrait of success, is it?

But we need to remember that discipleship is a process. The word 'disciple' means a *learner* or *apprentice*. An apprentice is someone who comes alongside someone with a particular skill to watch how they do it, then to 'have a go' themselves, to get tuition along the way, until eventually they can do it themselves. That's how Jesus wanted his disciples to see their life with him. Of course he knew they wouldn't get it right at first; of course he knew they would make mistakes – sometimes, big ones. But that's what an apprentice does; that's how an apprentice learns.

For all of us, learning as his disciples will mean failing at times, as well as succeeding. But every failure can be the seed-ground of the success of the next attempt. The fact that God tells us to 'learn to do right' means he knows that doing right does not always come instinctively to us, and that we will sometimes get it wrong as we seek to do so. He promises to 'give us space' today – space to fail, in order to train us to succeed.

Simon, Simon, Satan has asked to sift you as wheat. But I have prayed for you, Simon, that your faith may not fail.
(LUKE 22:31–32)

MAY 14

Look out!

'All authority in heaven and on earth has been given to me.
Therefore go and make disciples of all nations . . . And surely
I am with you always, to the very end of the age.'
(MATTHEW 28:18, 20)

Everything that is healthy in this world relates to something beyond itself; what is concerned only for itself ultimately dies. A doctor sees this in the human body, where a cell that cares only for itself becomes cancerous, and its very attempts to survive kill the whole body. A pastor sees this in human lives, where people who think only of themselves become the most unhappy of people. What cares only for itself, dies; what looks beyond itself, lives.

The same is true for the church. Before Jesus ascended to heaven, he gave his disciples both a command and a promise: the command was to go into the world and make disciples; the promise was that, *as they did so*, he would be with them. The church in Jerusalem found that difficult, struggling to look beyond itself and its narrow horizons. As a result, it was ultimately sidelined in God's bigger plan, while the church at Antioch looked beyond itself and became one of the most significant churches in the early centuries of church history.

Sometimes we forget that Jesus' promise to be with us was not a promise for 'staying' but a promise for 'going'. It is *as we go* and put our faith to the test that we experience his promises in ways that we could never do by simply sitting at home. It was as those first disciples responded to his promise to send them out as witnesses 'in Jerusalem, and in all Judea and Samaria, and to the ends of the earth' (Acts 1:8), that they experienced his presence and power in amazing ways and with amazing results.

God wants us to 'look out' not 'look in'. This is a time, not for endless spiritual navel-gazing, but for 'going', knowing that as we do, he will surely be with us. Today, as you 'go', claim his promise that he will be with you.

'I will also make you a light for the Gentiles, that you may bring my
salvation to the ends of the earth.'
(ISAIAH 49:6)

MAY 15

A promise of old

'And afterwards, I will pour out my Spirit on all people.'
(JOEL 2:28)

'Always vote for the man who promises the least; that way, you'll be disappointed the least.' So goes a rather cynical (but perhaps fairly accurate!) comment about politics today. We are all accustomed to politicians (of whatever persuasion) making promises of what they will do if only we will vote for them; but we all know that, by and large, we will almost certainly end up disappointed. However, you can never say this about God. What he promises, he does – every time.

One of the promises that God made in the Old Testament concerned a new experience of the Holy Spirit for his people; and, unlike our politicians, he did not disappoint us. In Old Testament times, experience of the Spirit was the preserve of leaders or 'special' people – people like elders, judges, kings, priests, and prophets. Even then, he generally 'came and went' as his presence, power or wisdom was needed; he never 'stayed around' for too long! In fact, King David was probably one of the few to experience a more permanent presence of the Spirit (and hence his cry to God not to take his Spirit from him in Psalm 51).

However God promised that a day was coming when he would give his Spirit, not just to 'special people', but to *all* his people; and at Pentecost he kept that promise. The disciples were once again praying, after the return of Jesus to the Father, when they were suddenly overwhelmed – 'baptized' – with the Holy Spirit, just as Jesus had promised ten days before. One of the first things that Peter wanted the gathering crowd to know was that what they were seeing was what God had promised through the prophet Joel over eight hundred years earlier. And you can experience this too, he went on to tell them.

Still today, this promise of God holds true – all we need to do is ask! And whoever asks will have an experience of the Spirit, not that 'comes and goes', but which is lasting, transforming and empowering. This is the promise of the Father!

Exalted to the right hand of God, he has received from the Father the promised Holy Spirit and has poured out what you now see and hear.
(ACTS 2:33)

MAY 16

Stepping out with God

*[Abraham] did not waver through unbelief regarding the
promise of God, but was strengthened in his faith and gave
glory to God, being fully persuaded that God had power to do
what he had promised.*
(ROMANS 4:20–21)

'Trust' is a rare commodity these days. Can we trust politicians, newspapers, our employer, our pension company, our friend? It can sometimes be hard to know. But often, their 'track record' is a good indicator, for if they haven't been trustworthy in the past, it is unlikely that they will be in the future.

God is certainly not afraid of our looking at the 'track record' of how he has acted and how he has kept his promises. Indeed, as we begin to grasp what the Bible says about him, we see that it is the most natural thing in the world to step out and trust him for our own lives and future.

But when Abraham first stepped out with God, he had absolutely nothing to go on. For Abraham, God had no track record! But he steadily learned from experience that you really can trust God and his promises. Like so many of us, Abraham started out by *not* believing in God. Coming from the city of Ur, a centre of Moon worship, he was almost certainly a 'pagan'. But God broke in to his life and told him to 'go to the land I will show you' (Genesis 12:1) – though he didn't tell him which one! Only when he got to Shechem did God eventually say, 'This is it!' Abraham had to leave his home, his family, his friends, his old way of life, and step out into an unknown world. But if he hadn't stepped out in faith and trusted God's promise, he would never have known whether it was true or not. Faith doesn't drop out of the sky; it grows as we risk stepping out with God.

Today, we can look at God's track record in the Bible in a way that Abraham never could. As you consider that track record, let it strengthen your resolve to step out with God today into whatever he brings before you as you take hold of his promises.

Build yourselves up in your most holy faith.
(JUDE 20)

MAY 17

Floodlight ministry

'He will bring glory to me by taking from what is mine and making it known to you.'
(JOHN 16:14)

Floodlights have transformed the world of sport. At one time, an international match or tournament would have been suspended as the light faded, or a local sports team would not have been able to practise during winter evenings; but now, floodlights mean that play can happen any time. Floodlights make a difference.

But while floodlights are important, they aren't the focus of our attention. When did you last say, 'Oh look at those lovely floodlights'? Floodlights are there, not to draw attention to themselves, but to the pitch they are directed to. And so it is with the Holy Spirit: he is, as it were, the floodlight shining onto Jesus, directing our attention, not to himself, but to him.

In fact, as you read the New Testament, it becomes clear that *everything* the Spirit does seems to point away from himself and towards another. We read that he convicts us of sin. Why? To point us to Jesus who alone can forgive it. He brings new spiritual birth as we trust in Christ. Why? So he can bring us to the Father. He lives within us. Why? So that we can lead a life that pleases the Father. He inspired and interprets the Scriptures. Why? So we can know what the Father is like and what he wants for us in our daily lives. He gives his gifts to the church. Why? So he can see us built up and made strong for the work we are called to do. From start to finish, everything the Spirit does – like our floodlights – is not for himself but for others.

Today God still wants each one of us to be filled with his promised Holy Spirit. But as he comes and fills us, it is not to draw attention to himself or to have us caught up in him; it is so that we can see Jesus and become more like him. Ask the Holy Spirit to work this promised floodlight ministry for you today.

. . . the mystery of Christ, which was not made known to men in other generations as it has now been revealed by the Spirit to God's holy apostles and prophets.
(EPHESIANS 3:4–5)

MAY 18

Be chosen!

You did not choose me, but I chose you
(JOHN 15:16)

There is a wonderful scene in the movie *Toy Story* where lots of little round creatures get excited about being chosen. They are squashed together inside one of those arcade machines often found at funfairs where a miniature crane drops a claw to grab a prize (and which, more often than not, misses!). In the movie, the creatures see the crane begin to move. The moment is here! 'Be chosen! Be chosen!' they all begin to cry out, believing it is a profound privilege to be picked up and taken to the place 'up there'. They may not have understood what was going on; but they certainly believed in the privilege of being chosen.

We too have the privilege of being chosen – not by some unfeeling mechanical arm from the sky, but by the heart of a loving heavenly Father. Some have seen this choice as an arbitrary decision by God: 'I'll have you . . . but not you.' But that is not at all the spirit of things. The Bible tells us that God's choosing of us was planned in eternity; it was before we knew anything about it, which underlines how very much our salvation has nothing to do with us! Then it stresses that his choosing of us is not because we were special or good; it is a choice made entirely by *his* mercy, grace and love, not based on anything *we* have done. And yet, this choosing of us does not undermine our own responsibility; we are not lost or saved against our will! No one is 'forced into heaven'; and no one is chosen 'not to have an opportunity'. All are invited to respond.

This promise of being chosen underlines how very much salvation is *God's* doing. And this is the basis of our certainty. If our salvation was dependent on us, who of us could ever be sure of making it to heaven? Our being chosen should not be a ground for pride, but it most definitely should be a ground for confidence!

Today, let God's loving choice of *you* be a source of confidence for all you face and do.

From the beginning God chose you to be saved through the sanctifying work of the Spirit and through belief in the truth.
(2 THESSALONIANS 2:13)

MAY 19

The wind of God

The wind blows wherever it pleases.
(JOHN 3:8)

By and large, we are very 'cerebral', mind-oriented, in the West; everything has to be understood before we can accept it or believe it is real. This can make us very sceptical, if not downright cynical, about anything 'unusual' or 'different' or that cannot be 'explained' – hardly a good basis for a supernatural faith!

What a contrast this is to what we see in the Bible! For here we often see God moving in strange ways – his wind blowing where and how he wills – to achieve his purposes. The Holy Spirit certainly did some very 'strange things' in the early church. In the book of Acts we see that he came in wind and fire, shook rooms, did miracles, suddenly transported individuals from where they were, gave strange visions, rescued people miraculously from prison, gave gifts of tongues and prophecy. The list of 'the unusual' is so long that, if we exclude such things from happening today, or if we are fearful when they do, we may well be in danger of missing a key aspect of what the Spirit may want to do among us. And not only that, but if our God can only do what we can understand or do ourselves, then what a small God he is!

The secret to being ready for God's wind to blow is to 'be filled with the Spirit' (Ephesians 5:18). This statement is actually as much a promise as it is a command, for it is in the passive tense: 'be being filled'. Being filled is something 'done to us' rather than our 'doing something'. We are commanded to seek it; but we cannot 'make it happen'. Our part is to *allow* the Spirit to fill us, by being clean, obedient, available – *and* ready for whatever he may want to do.

Today, be open to God and the blowing of the wind of his Spirit in your life; be ready for the unusual. Tell him that you want to be 'being filled' with the Spirit throughout the day, so that you can be open to his wind blowing wherever and however he wills.

I will put breath in you, and you will come to life.
(EZEKIEL 37:6)

The promise of fruitfulness

But the fruit of the Spirit is love, joy, peace, patience, kindness, goodness, faithfulness, gentleness and self-control.
(GALATIANS 5:22–23)

One of the great delights of children is to find the 'Pick and Mix' counter when out shopping with their parents. These counters (strategically placed by the entrance or the cash desk to produce maximum enticement!) are full of a dazzling and colourful array of various kinds of sweets. Armed with tongs or scoop, you pick out what you want, and leave the rest. The end result is a bag of sweets (always weighing far more than you thought!) made up of just your favourite things.

While picking sweets like this might be great fun, it is a disastrous way to live our Christian life – picking out those bits that we like and leaving the rest. That is why Paul wrote about the fruit (singular), not the fruits (plural), of the Spirit. For Paul, the nine things he lists are not nine separate fruits, but just one. Unlike our Pick and Mix counter, you can't take some and leave others; they *all* belong together for they are *all* what God is looking to grow in us through his Holy Spirit. The 'fruit of the Spirit' are those things that grow naturally if only we will let *him* be in control.

'Fruit' finds expression in a number of ways in the New Testament: through the life we live, the words we speak, the service we offer, the prayers we pray, the witness we bear, the gifts we give. In fact, bearing this sort of fruit is so natural to God's people that, throughout the Bible, fruit-less-ness is seen as something shameful. But with the Spirit helping us, there is simply no need for it. In fact Jesus said that, 'A good tree cannot bear bad fruit (Matthew 7:18)' – it's impossible! On the contrary, if we abide in him, we *will* bear much fruit.

God's promise to us is that, as we abide in Jesus, we *will* be fruitful. Why not pray through Paul's list of nine Christ-like characteristics and ask that God will help you show each one of them today.

'I am the vine; you are the branches. If a man remains in me and I in him, he will bear much fruit; apart from me you can do nothing.'
(JOHN 15:5)

MAY 21

The person and the power

'But you will receive power when the Holy Spirit comes on you;
and you will be my witnesses in Jerusalem, and in all Judea
and Samaria, and to the ends of the earth.'
(ACTS 1:8)

A person's final words always have special significance – whether it is those of a politician leaving office, or of a loved one slipping from this world to the next. Final words are always special words, something to be kept and remembered. Likewise the final words of Jesus before his ascension must have powerfully engraved themselves on the minds of his disciples for the rest of their lives. For those final words were not simply 'words'; but words that became reality. For the following ten days the disciples must have wondered what Jesus meant; but then, at Pentecost, it happened; the Holy Spirit came. The promise was kept; the *person* and the *power* had arrived!

It is so important that we remember the link between the *person* and the *power*. God's power is not some 'thing' that can be manipulated like primitive magic, as Simon Magus discovered to his cost. He saw Peter praying for the believers in Samaria to be filled with the Spirit – and he wanted 'it'. But this wasn't about an 'it'; it was about a 'him'. God's power comes in the package of a *person* – the person of the Holy Spirit - whom we therefore need to respect and call upon in the right way.

We so easily forget that the Holy Spirit is a *person*. Perhaps it is because of the images that are sometimes used to describe him when he comes, especially in the Old Testament. For example, he comes in the form of wind, fire, water, oil, and at Jesus' baptism, as a dove – hardly images that make us think of a person. But all these images describe more what the Spirit has come to *do*, rather than who he is.

Don't go looking for the power of God; look for the person of God! For when you do, he will come – just as Jesus promised!

'He is the Holy Spirit, who leads into all truth. The world at large cannot
receive him, because it isn't looking for him and doesn't recognise him. But
you do, because he lives with you now and later will be in you.'
(JOHN 14:17, NLT)

MAY 22

Power!

I want to know Christ and the power of his resurrection.
(PHILIPPIANS 3:10)

From start to finish the Christian faith is about 'power'. Indeed if we don't believe in the power of God – witnessed to in Scripture and still available today – then it is somewhat doubtful whether we have experienced authentic Christianity, which is about the power of God from start to finish. Well-known author Jim Packer puts it like this: 'Supernatural living through supernatural empowering is at the very heart of New Testament Christianity, so that those who, while professing faith, do not experience and show forth this empowering are suspect by New Testament standards' (*Keep in Step with the Spirit*). What a challenge that is! But also, what a promise!

It really is quite impossible to read about the New Testament church – whether through the book of Acts or through the letters – and not see this power as a normal part of their everyday life. Paul recognized that any effective ministry through him had been entirely 'by the power of signs and miracles, through the power of the Spirit' (Romans 15:19); that the gospel had been preached by him 'not with wise and persuasive words, but with a demonstration of the Spirit's power, so that your faith might not rest on men's wisdom, but on God's power' (1 Corinthians 2:4–5); that even his 'thorn in the flesh' helped him to experience more of God's power as he learned that, 'My grace is sufficient for you, for my power is made perfect in weakness' (2 Corinthians 12:9). Here was a man who believed in the power of the Spirit! And he taught his churches to do the same, warning them to have nothing to do with those 'having a form of godliness but denying its power' (2 Timothy 3:5).

We cannot dismiss these demonstrations of supernatural power, or confine them to a narrow band of time or people, or say that 'this was just for those days'. The *power* of the Spirit is always available, for the simple reason that the *person* of the Spirit is always available.

Today, don't be afraid of God's power, but be expectant of encountering his power, just as he promised – it really is quite 'normal'!

'Not by might nor by power, but by my Spirit,' says the LORD Almighty.
(ZECHARIAH 4:6)

The flow from within

On the last and greatest day of the Feast, Jesus stood and said in a loud voice, 'If anyone is thirsty, let him come to me and drink. Whoever believes in me, as the Scripture has said, streams of living water will flow from within him.'
By this he meant the Spirit, whom those who believed in him were later to receive.
(JOHN 7:37–39)

The Feast in today's reading was Tabernacles, one of three occasions when all Jewish men had to worship at the temple in Jerusalem. The festival commemorated God's provision, not only through the recent harvest, but also during Israel's wilderness wanderings. It was one of the most popular festivals of Jesus' day, full of joy and ceremony, including the highlight of priests taking a jug of water from the Pool of Siloam and going in procession to the altar in the temple where the water was poured out. This ritual happened every day for a week; but on the last day of the festival ('the last and greatest day'), water was neither collected nor poured. It was, instead, a day of 'sacred assembly' (Leviticus 23:36). And it was on that day, when religion had run out, as it were, that Jesus invited men and women to come to him for an experience of the Spirit that would never run out and never run dry.

This is why any worship and prayer that discounts the Spirit, or that solely pays lip service to him, or that gives mere theological credence to him, is going back to the old ways that Jesus brought us out of. For he said that we should expect the Spirit's life to 'flow from within' (John 7:38). This is something we are meant to *experience*, not just to think about. He wants us to know the Spirit's presence, joy, promptings, gifts and guidance – yes, even as we pray today!

If you have never experienced that promised 'flow' of the Spirit, why not ask Jesus to release it within you today? If you have, ask him to let it flow again today!

'Did you receive the Holy Spirit when you believed?' They answered, 'No, we have not even heard that there is a Holy Spirit'... When Paul placed his hands on them, the Holy Spirit came on them, and they spoke in tongues and prophesied.
(ACTS 19:2,6)

MAY 24

Being there

'I will not leave you as orphans; I will come to you.'
(JOHN 14:18)

Knowing that someone is *there* can make such a difference. Think of the mother giving birth, or the aged person dying, or the child learning to ride a bicycle; just having someone nearby is so reassuring at such times. *Being there* makes such a difference at such times.

How good it is to remember, then, that our God is 'the God who is there' – 'there' upholding the universe; but also 'there' right alongside us mere mortals, moment by moment and day by day. What an amazing God! 'There' in the great things; and 'there' in the small.

But not only is he 'there'; he is there as *a friend*. When Jesus came into his world, he came as a friend. Not only was the word 'friend' often found on his lips, he acted as a true friend to everyone he encountered, especially to those who felt they did not deserve it – even to the one who betrayed him! Such is the depth of his friendship.

So, when the disciples became anxious at his talking about leaving them, he knew that what they needed more than anything was the reassurance of his ongoing presence, and it was in this context that he made his promise: 'I will not leave you as orphans; I will come to you.' He was looking beyond his death that would bring them to despair; beyond his resurrection that would bring them to joy; beyond his return to the Father that would bring them to anticipation. He was looking to the Day of Pentecost when he would baptize them with his Holy Spirit and when, through this life-giving and empowering experience, they would know for sure that Jesus was truly 'there' – with them for ever; not limited now by space or time; but with each of them, wherever they went, in the power of the Spirit.

Let us remember that Jesus is still 'there' for each one of us. His promise is that he will not leave us as orphans; and through his Holy Spirit, he wants to make that real to each of us today.

'I will live among the people of Israel and never forsake my people.'
(1 KINGS 6:13, NLT)

All change!

'I tell you the truth, unless you change and become like little children, you will never enter the kingdom of heaven.'
(MATTHEW 18:3)

In a world that has become increasingly smaller, most of us will have travelled to another country at some time. An indispensable part of the journey is converting our money from our own currency to that of the nation we are visiting. Only when we have done so can the fun of the holiday begin. Well, just as our money can 'be converted', so people can 'be converted' too, the Bible tells us. For conversion is about change.

Conversion is far more than simply making a decision to follow Jesus (though that is the indispensable beginning!). It is about *being changed*. This change is not brought about by self-effort or by 'pulling ourselves up by our bootstraps', however. It is a change that happens in the heart, a change brought about by the Spirit of God working within us, just as Jeremiah and Ezekiel prophesied. It is not something we ourselves can bring about; it is a change done to *us*, not *by* us. It has nothing to do with self-effort or self-improvement techniques, as both Nicodemus and Paul discovered. As Pharisees, they had been committed to the punctilious and legalistic fulfilment of the Jewish Law, in all its minute details and all its various interpretations; but they both discovered that it simply didn't work; it didn't change a thing – least of all, them.

No, this new beginning, this 'change', is *God's* work from start to finish; it is *God alone* who can transform us. All we need to do is to call out to him, believing that Christ has already done all that is needed to bring about that change in us.

Today don't try to change by self-effort. Rather, call out to Jesus to work in you by his Spirit; for only in this way can true change begin – and continue!

'I will give you a new heart and put a new spirit in you; I will remove from you your heart of stone and give you a heart of flesh. And I will put my Spirit in you and move you to follow my decrees and be careful to keep my laws.'
(EZEKIEL 36:26–27)

Quenching your thirst

*'Come, all you who are thirsty, come to the waters; and you
who have no money, come, buy and eat! Come, buy wine and
milk without money and without cost.'*
(ISAIAH 55:1)

Mike was recently on a ministry trip in Europe when he suddenly found himself lost in a town that he thought he was starting to get to know quite well. He knew he wasn't a million miles away from where he needed to be; it was just that he didn't know exactly where he was! And unfortunately, in the night gloom, all the streets looked so similar. So, he had no alternative but to backtrack to his friend's house so that he could start the journey all over again.

The first step to finding our way to somewhere is always to find out where we are now; or, to put it a different way, the first step to solving a problem is to see the need. The same is true with our lives. The Bible pictures our need, or 'where we are now', in many different ways: it sees us as being hungry, weary, blind, lost, poor, to name but a few. But in our verse today, God sees his people as being thirsty – thirsty for reality and thirsty for him. The solution, he tells them, is not to keep pressing on regardless, hoping that 'something might turn up', but to turn back to where they had started, with God himself.

Perhaps you are feeling spiritually thirsty or dry today. Don't keep busily pressing on with life regardless, filling your life with all kinds of busy-ness in the hope it will 'do the trick'. It's time to stop and to hear the invitation of God to come and drink from his well; for his promise is that all who do will truly find their thirst quenched.

*Jesus answered, 'Everyone who drinks this water will be thirsty again, but
whoever drinks the water I give him will never thirst. Indeed, the water I
give him will become in him a spring of water welling up to eternal life.'*
(JOHN 4:13–14)

A promise kept

'Wait here to receive the promise from the Father which I told you about. John baptised people with water, but in a few days you will be baptized with the Holy Spirit.'
(ACTS 1:4–5, NCV)

No matter how well-intentioned we might be, we all fail to keep our promises at times. Perhaps circumstances were against us; perhaps resources ran dry; perhaps hopes were greater than abilities; but for whatever reason, we failed to do what we promised we'd do. But this was never true of Jesus! Every promise he made, he kept – though sometimes his followers had to wait a little while!

Pentecost was a wonderful example of this. After Jesus' return to the Father on Ascension Day, the way was open for the promised baptism with the Holy Spirit to happen, for Jesus had told them that, 'Unless I go away, the Counsellor will not come to you; but if I go, I will send him to you' (John 16:7). And so they waited . . . and waited . . . and waited. Ten days passed by; ten days of praying and waiting; ten days of wondering what exactly it was that Jesus was going to give them. And then, suddenly – it happened! On the Day of Pentecost itself, a day associated with God's provision for his people, the promised Holy Spirit came – and with external signs so amazing that there could be no doubting his arrival – 'a sound from heaven like the roaring of a mighty windstorm in the skies above them' (Acts 2:2, NLT), 'what seemed to be tongues of fire that separated and came to rest on each of them' (verse 3), and 'all of them were filled with the Holy Spirit and began to speak in other tongues as the Spirit enabled them' (verse 4). There was absolutely no doubt that the promise had been kept!

But Pentecost was just the start! For this experience was not meant to be a 'one-off' for the church, something to 'get it going'. Rather, it is a promise to every believer who will ask Jesus to keep his promise to them too. Ask him – he will not ignore you!

'The promise is for you and your children and for all who are far off – for all whom the Lord our God will call.'
(ACTS 2:39)

MAY 28

The anointing of the Spirit

'The Spirit of the Lord is on me, because he has anointed me to preach good news to the poor. He has sent me to proclaim freedom for the prisoners and recovery of sight for the blind, to release the oppressed, to proclaim the year of the Lord's favour.'
(LUKE 4:18–19)

'Anointing' is not something that forms part of ordinary life these days – which is perhaps why so many Christians misunderstand it. To many Christians, 'the anointing' is some sort of 'mystical feeling', 'spiritual intensity' or 'special presence' that marks someone out as special or that indicates that God is about to do something special. But this really isn't its meaning at all in the Bible.

In the Bible, anointing is, quite simply, God's promised empowering to get the task done. That's why they anointed prophets, priest, kings, leaders – they wanted to see God's task done for God's people in the power of God's Spirit. It was something that was very much action-based, not feeling-based. So, when Jesus came into the synagogue at Nazareth and read from the prophet Isaiah, claiming that 'today this scripture is fulfilled in your hearing' (Luke 4:21), he was saying, not that he now 'felt good' (for there would be many times when he didn't!), but rather that God's empowering presence was now upon him to do the work for which he had come – things like preaching, proclaiming freedom, healing, releasing the oppressed – that would let people know that 'the year of the Lord's favour' was at last here.

But this 'anointing' is not simply something that God has kept for Jesus. He has promised to give it to us too – to us who believe in Jesus. All we need to do is to ask him for it! Remember: 'anointing' is not a feeling and not an experience (though we recognize that for many there is a powerful moment of first encountering the Holy Spirit); it is the ongoing, indwelling, promised presence of the Spirit of God within you, given to get on with the task. That anointing is with *you* as you step out to do all that he brings before you today.

As for you, the anointing you received from him remains in you . . .
(1 JOHN 2:27)

MAY 29

The promised baptism

*For John baptised with water, but in a few days you will be
baptised with the Holy Spirit.'*
(ACTS 1:5)

If any promise of Jesus has caused misunderstanding between fellow
Christians, it is this one. For while it is clear that Jesus expected his
followers to be baptized with (or 'in' or 'by') the Holy Spirit, Christians
have had different understandings about what this means. For some,
Spirit baptism is an aspect of what it means to become a Christian; for
others, it is a distinct experience *after* becoming a Christian to empower
us. Opposing positions have been taken up – sometimes acrimoniously –
while the devil has been laughing as the church has been kept from one
of the most powerful promises that Jesus ever made.

Of the seven references to being 'baptized with the Holy Spirit', six are
in the Gospels, contrasting John the Baptist's ministry (baptizing with
water) with Jesus' ministry (baptizing with the Spirit). The seventh (in 1
Corinthians 12) describes the unity of the experience of the Spirit of all
believers. This suggests that 'baptism with the Spirit' is, at heart, an
integral aspect of what it means to become a Christian, and that it is
something each of us is meant to experience.

However, while this 'Spirit baptism' was expected as the norm,
whenever there was a lack in understanding or experience, the apostles
took immediate steps to rectify the situation, so that a 'baptism' – an
immersing, a drenching, a soaking (for this is what the Greek word
means) – was *exactly* what people experienced. Jesus doesn't want us to
just *believe* in baptism with the Spirit; he wants us to *experience* it! As Peter
made clear, this promise wasn't just for the early church, but 'for you and
your children and for all who are far off – for all whom the Lord our God
will call' (Acts 2:39). And since we are most certainly 'far off' – in time
and distance – this certainly includes us.

If, for whatever reason, you feel you are lacking a true 'baptism' of the
Holy Spirit, then the most obvious thing is to ask Jesus to fulfil his
promise and to rectify that for you right away!

'He will baptise you with the Holy Spirit and with fire.'
(LUKE 3:16)

MAY 30

Praying in the Spirit

Pray in the Spirit at all times with all kinds of prayers, asking for everything you need.
(EPHESIANS 6:18, NCV)

Probably all of us have times when we find praying hard work. That's when it's good to remember Jesus' promise to send the Holy Spirit to be our 'helper' (John 14:26, NCV). In fact, without the Spirit, we could never pray.

Having already urged the Ephesians to 'be filled with the Spirit' (Ephesians 5:18), Paul now encouraged them to 'pray in the Spirit'. He probably meant a number of things by that: that we should expect the Spirit to remind us of our relationship with our Father, from which a strong basis of prayer comes; to convict us when there is sin in our life, so that nothing hinders our prayers; to show us God's heart and truth, so that we know what to pray about; to be the one who 'helps us in our weakness' (Romans 8:26). This expression literally means 'he takes hold of us at our side'. The Spirit really will support us in our praying, if only we will ask!

One further thing that Paul may be referring to is praying in tongues. Our experience as authors is different in this area: Martin doesn't exercise the gift, whereas Mike does; but both see it is a genuine gift of the Spirit (see 1 Corinthians 12:4–11,27–31; 14:1–33). While in corporate gatherings, praying in tongues requires interpretation to be of benefit (1 Corinthians 14:13–17), in private use it needs no interpretation, for it is a means of personal edification and of being able to pray beyond our knowledge or understanding (especially useful when we don't know the details of a particular situation). Paul believed in the value of praying both 'with my mind' (i.e. in our own language) and 'with my spirit' (i.e. in tongues) (1 Corinthians 14:15). So if God has given you this gift, use it. (And if he hasn't, why not at least ask him for it?) Your intercession on behalf of others in this way may well be expressing things that your natural mind could never think of nor could ever know.

We are not on our own in our praying! The Spirit of Jesus is truly with us; so ask him for his help and direction.

Pray in the Holy Spirit.
(JUDE. 20)

MAY 31

The promised Helper

*'And I will ask the Father, and he will give you another
Counsellor to be with you for ever.'*
(JOHN 14:16)

When we hear the word 'counsellor' these days, we are unlikely to picture what Jesus had in mind when he promised to send his disciples someone who would be this to them. For us, a counsellor is either someone from whom we get help with our problems, or (if we live in North America) our lawyer. But both of these meanings are a long way from what Jesus was thinking of when he promised to send the Holy Spirit as our 'counsellor'.

An illustration from the Bayeux Tapestry, portraying the Norman invasion of Britain in 1066, might help. In one scene an English bishop is prodding his spear into the backside of a soldier, and underneath it says: 'He comforts his troops.' That may seem a strange way of 'comforting'! But what he was doing was saying, 'Go on; you can do it! Don't give in now!' And that is exactly what the Holy Spirit does for us. He is there within us saying, 'Go on – you can do it! I'm here! I'll help you! Don't give in now!' He is '*the one who comes alongside us to help us*' – which is the literal translation of the word used for 'counsellor' in the Greek New Testament. Because it is quite difficult to express that idea in just one word in English, it has been translated in several ways – 'Comforter' (KJV), 'Helper' (NASB, NKJV, NCV), 'Advocate' (NRSV, The Jerusalem Bible), 'Friend' (The Message), 'Someone to stand by you' (JB Phillips). But whatever word we use, the message is the same: we are not left alone! The promised Holy Spirit is always there, right alongside us in all we do.

This promise of the Holy Spirit is not automatic however, Jesus said. He said that the Father would give him, first to all who *believed*, and second, to all who *asked*. Fulfil these two conditions, Jesus promised, and you will never be alone; for the promised Helper *will* surely come!

*But I tell you the truth: It is for your good that I am going away.
Unless I go away, the Counsellor will not come to you;
but if I go, I will send him to you.*
(JOHN 16:7)

JUNE 1

An undivided heart

'I will give them an undivided heart and put a new spirit in them; I will remove from them their heart of stone and give them a heart of flesh.'
(EZEKIEL 11:19)

In Martin's early years as a Christian it was verses from Ezekiel that greatly helped him understand the work of the Holy Spirit. In particular he gained from this book the understanding that the Holy Spirit wants to give us a new heart, a new inner life that is responsive to God.

The truth is, all too often things come into our lives that we let harden us against him and his will. Things such as a spirit of criticism, the cares of this world, unresolved problems from our past, can all too easily come in and choke our new life in Christ and challenge our allegiance to him.

The way out of this isn't by a 'heart by-pass' operation. No. What it needs, rather, is 'open-heart surgery.' King David grasped this when he cried out to God, 'Teach me your way, O LORD, that I may walk in your truth; give me an *undivided heart* to revere your name' (Psalm 86:11, NRSV). He desperately wanted to have a sincere, godly, pure inner life that was centred firmly on the Lord alone.

The opposite of being 'undivided' is being 'double-minded' (James 1:8), adrift and tossed about in the uncertain seas of life, swayed by this pressure and that pressure, by this opinion and that opinion. If we sense that this is how we have become, we need to turn afresh to God in repentance and faith, seeking him and his fullness, asking for a new heart. When we turn to him, he promises that he really will give us that new heart, a heart that wants to obey him so that our deepest desire is to delight to do his will. And he gives us what is best: a fresh vision of himself.

Let's turn to him again right now; let's seek him and ask him to give each one of us an undivided heart today so that he and he alone is our passion and our joy.

'I will give them singleness of heart and action, so that they will always fear me for their own good and the good of their children after them.'
(JEREMIAH 32:39)

JUNE 2

Not a power but a person!

*'He is the Holy Spirit . . . he lives with you now
and later will be in you.'*
(JOHN 14:17, NLT)

Listen to many Christians and it won't be too long before they start
speaking of the Holy Spirit as little more than the power or presence of
God – some 'thing' to be called upon in time of need. But whenever we
talk like that, we are still living as Old Testament believers, with their
limited appreciation of who the Spirit was. And who wants to live with an
old revelation when a far better one has come along?

Throughout the Old Testament, the Spirit was rarely seen as a *person*,
but more as the *power* or *presence* of God. By the New Testament,
however, he is seen, not as some impersonal force, but as the third person
of the Trinity. He is constantly referred to as *he*, not *it* - even though the
Greek word for 'Spirit' is a 'neuter' gender, grammatically requiring the
use of 'it'. (In other words, they were so convinced the Spirit was a person
that they broke the rules of grammar to make their point!) As a *person* the
Spirit is seen doing what a person does: he thinks, loves, decides, hears,
speaks, helps, gives gifts, gets hurt … Get the message? The Spirit is no
impersonal force – a mere 'it'. He is a *he*, a person of the Trinity, *God* at
work among us.

If he is a person, then we should be careful not to treat him as some
'commodity' to be used at our command. That was the lesson that Simon
the sorcerer had to learn. When he saw how the Spirit was given as the
apostles prayed for people, he wanted 'it' too. 'Give me also this ability so
that everyone on whom I lay my hands may receive the Holy Spirit' (Acts
8:19). But Peter's harsh rebuke could not have left him in any doubt
about such an attitude.

If you have been seeing the Holy Spirit more as a power than a person,
then you are living under the old covenant rather than the new! Don't do
that today; rather ask *him* to come, just as Jesus promised, and help you
see who he really is.

And do not make the Holy Spirit sad.
(EPHESIANS 4:30, NCV)

JUNE 3

The Spirit who helps us

The Spirit helps us in our weakness.
(ROMANS 8:26)

'Can I help you?' How many times has someone asked you that and you've answered, 'Oh no, that's fine! I can manage!' Or perhaps they heard (after the event) that you had needed some help and said, 'Why didn't you ask me?' and you replied, 'I didn't want to trouble you.' For many of us, talking like this is a way of life.

The trouble is, we give these answers to God too! The Holy Spirit comes and helps us and we say (by action if not by word), 'I can manage all right by myself, thanks!' But it's impossible to answer God like that, and be a Christian! For Christians are those who *know* they need the Father's help through the Spirit to live their life in Christ. Paul learned this lesson the hard way. He had always been an independent man, able to stand on his own feet. But through a process of hardship, God gradually knocked the independence out of him. In 2 Corinthians he lists some of the hardships he went through in his ministry; but he begins the letter by recognizing that these things happened 'that we might not rely on ourselves but on God, who raises the dead' (2 Corinthians 1:9). God wanted him to learn that he couldn't do it on his own – and eventually, the lesson hit home.

Perhaps this is why we find so much stress in Paul's letters on the way that the Spirit helps us. He says that the Spirit helps us in our knowing, making us confident about our relationship with the Father. He helps us in our understanding, giving us insights into the Father's heart and giving spiritual gifts to us. He helps us in our praying, showing us *what* to pray for and *how* to pray for it. He helps us in our witnessing, enabling words and lifestyle that speak for him.

The promise of the Spirit's help still remains for us today. There is one simple condition, however: we have to acknowledge *our* weakness! Only then, will the Spirit come in with *his* strength, just as Jesus promised.

'My grace is sufficient for you, for my power is made perfect in weakness.'
Therefore I will boast all the more gladly about my weaknesses, so that
Christ's power may rest on me.
(2 CORINTHIANS 12:9)

The Spirit of God

In the beginning God created the heavens and the earth. The earth was barren, with no form of life; it was under a roaring ocean covered with darkness. But the Spirit of God was moving over the water.
(GENESIS 1:1-2, CEV)

To listen to some Christians, you could almost think that the Holy Spirit had never been heard of until the Day of Pentecost; (and to listen to others, that he has never been heard of since!). But the Bible is clear that the Holy Spirit has always been there and always will be. He is an integral part of our three-in-one God – God, in the person of the Spirit.

We first meet him on the opening page of the Bible. There he is, before creation, eagerly waiting to bring about Father's creation. We then find him constantly at work throughout both Old and New Testaments in many ways. And as we get to the last page of the Bible, who is still there? Yes – the Spirit – inviting all to 'Come!' From start to finish, the eternal Spirit is present and is at work.

It shouldn't surprise us therefore to discover that the Bible has no uncertainty in declaring who this Spirit is. He is seen, not merely as the *presence* or the *power* of God; he *is* God! He is constantly equated with God, and passages referring to the Father in the Old Testament are unashamedly applied to him in the New. He is seen as having all the characteristics of God – omnipresent (being everywhere), omniscient (knowing everything), omnipotent (able to do everything) and eternal (without beginning or end). He is seen as doing the works of God – creating, working miracles, giving new birth, bringing life to the dead, inspiring Scripture – things that only God can do. In fact, he is even called 'God'.

What this means is this: in dealing with the Holy Spirit, we are dealing with *God*. The one whom Jesus promised to send to you is not some mere power or presence; some 'spiritual uplift' to get you through the day. It is *God himself* who has come to live within you, just as he promised! What a joy – and what a provocation – that should be to us today!

. . . the Spirit of God lives in you.
(ROMANS 8:9)

JUNE 5

The Spirit of truth

'But when he, the Spirit of truth, comes,
he will guide you into all truth.'
(JOHN 16:13)

'What is truth?' (John 18:38) Pilate asked Jesus at his trial. Did he mean, 'What does truth matter?' or 'How can any of us know what truth is?' or 'What truth are you talking about?' We will never know. But whatever he exactly meant, it was the sort of attitude that we often meet in our post-modern, Western world, where the greatest 'wrong' is to dare to suggest that there is 'a' truth – absolute truth – truth that has a legitimate call upon everyone.

In stark contrast to this, Jesus came into this world, not simply *bringing* the truth, but *being* the truth. 'I am the way and the truth and the life,' he boldly declared – and as God, he had every right to! And so it should not surprise us to find him describing the Holy Spirit, whom he promised to send to be everything to his disciples that he himself had been, as 'the Spirit of truth'.

This truth is not just about *right doctrine*, however - important as that is; it is also truth in terms of *right living*. Truth is not a concept but a person; and so our living in truth is about our living out our life with this person of the Holy Spirit. There is little that rings 'true', therefore, if we 'stand up for truth' – perhaps defending some doctrine or action or position – but are arrogant and ungracious in the way we do so; there is little that rings 'true' if we condemn the sins of others, but then live in secret sin ourselves.

Do I want to *stand up* for truth in the world? Then I will look to the Spirit of truth to lead me. Do I want to *live out* the truth? Then I will obey the Scriptures that the Spirit of truth inspired. Do I want to *grow in the truth*? Then I will respond to the way the Spirit of truth leads me. For truth is for living, not just for learning.

Today, ask the Holy Spirit to lead you into truth, just as Jesus promised he would – and then do whatever he tells you.

. . . the Spirit is the truth.
(1 JOHN 5:6)

JUNE 6

One Spirit, one body

'We were all baptised by one Spirit into one body – whether Jews or Greeks, slave or free – and we were all given the one Spirit to drink.'
(1 CORINTHIANS 12:13)

For all of us, there are occasions in our life that are engraved on our memories, events we will never forget. One such event for the disciples would undoubtedly have been Pentecost. Of course, they had seen many Pentecosts, for it was one of the great festivals for which they were required to go up to Jerusalem. But *that* Pentecost had been so different! For just as Jesus had promised, the Holy Spirit had fallen on them.

One of the first things that happened as they were baptised in the Spirit was that a tremendous unity was released among them. And this Spirit-given unity had a powerful effect that cut across their natural human selfishness. We read that 'all the believers were one in heart and mind. No-one claimed that any of his possessions was his own, but they shared everything they had' (Acts 4:32). And as a result of this, 'with great power the apostles continued to testify to the resurrection of the Lord Jesus, and much grace was on them all' (Acts 4:33).

Paul was convinced that this Spirit baptism was what took such diverse people – men and women, Jew and Gentile, slave and free – and put them into Christ's body. At last, all the great barriers of the ancient world were broken down as the Spirit baptized them into unity in the body of Christ. How sad it is, then, when we allow the Spirit's work among us today to do the very opposite at times.

Becoming one body with God's people is not some vague wish, but the promise of Scripture. Let us do all within our power today to live as members of that body, not despising our Spirit-given unity, but doing all we can to strengthen it. Let us speak well today of all God's people!

'Make every effort to keep the unity of the Spirit through the bond of peace. There is one body and one Spirit–just as you were called to one hope when you were called– one Lord, one faith, one baptism; one God and Father of all, who is over all and through all and in all.'
(EPHESIANS 4:3–6)

JUNE 7

The outer fringe

'By his breath the skies became fair; his hand pierced the
gliding serpent. And these are but the outer fringe of his works;
how faint the whisper we hear of him! Who then can
understand the thunder of his power?'
(JOB 26:13–14)

Have you ever stood and marvelled at beautiful sunsets? Aren't they fantastic? That kaleidoscope of colours splashed across the evening sky. At times it can almost look like the sky is on fire, or as if some abstract painter has thrown their colours on the cosmic canvas. Anyone who can look at sunsets and not be moved needs a heart transplant!

Job was a man who, even in the midst of all his troubles and questions, couldn't get away from the wonders of creation. In chapter 26 he scans God's handiwork: the mystery of a sky held up by nothing; of clouds full of water yet not bursting under their weight; the beauty of the moon; the horizon that separates sky and oceans; the boundaries of light and dark; the mysteries of the ocean; the beauty of the skies. And then, having marvelled, he comes out with that striking phrase: 'And these are but *the outer fringe* of his works'. Imagine that! So fantastic – but just the outer fringe! Job's God was big!

Today, we know far more than Job ever did about the wonders of the cosmos: the mysteries of the farthest extent of space to the deepest depths of the oceans. Amazing technology allows us to see things that human eyes have never seen before: the beauty of God's intricate creation, brought about for his glory. But here is the amazing thing: even when we've finished marvelling at all those discoveries, they are still only 'the outer fringe of his works'! In other words, we haven't even started to scratch the surface of God's mysteries!

Next time you stand amazed at some aspect of creation, join Job in marvelling before God that this is nothing but 'the outer fringe of his work' – and stand in awe!

'You alone are the LORD. You made the heavens, even the highest heavens,
and all their starry host, the earth and all that is on it, the seas and all that is
in them. You give life to everything, and the multitudes of heaven
worship you.'
(NEHEMIAH 9:6)

Your will be done

'Father, if you are willing, take this cup from me; yet not my will, but yours be done.'
(LUKE 22:42)

Jesus' anguish must have been enormous. Indeed, it was so great that 'his sweat was like drops of blood falling to the ground' (Luke 22:44). What caused this wasn't merely the thought of a martyr's death, but knowing that he was about to carry the weight of the world's sin and drink what the prophets had called the cup of God's wrath (e.g. Jeremiah 25:15–16). This cup symbolized God's righteous judgment that was being stored up, ready to be poured out on sinners at the End; but here is Jesus preparing himself to take that cup and drink it dry for us. Little wonder, as he reflected on this, that he prayed the words of our opening verse, knowing what the personal cost would be, and yet committing himself to doing his Father's will.

Sadly, Jesus' submission of his prayer to the condition 'if it be your will' has sometimes become little more than a 'lazy cop-out' for many Christians. That is, we can pray for whatever we like; but add the postscript 'if it be your will Lord', and then we won't have to discover what God's will is before we pray, and nor will we have to worry if our prayers aren't answered, as we can always put it down to, 'Ah well, it wasn't God's will anyway'.

The far more exciting and faith-building approach to prayer is to take time to seek to discover what God's will is first – through the Bible, through abiding in Jesus, through prophecy, through waiting upon God, and so on – and then to pray it into being. If we find out what God wants in this way, then we can be confident our prayers will be answered, for our thoughts will be in line with his thoughts, and we won't have to keep adding 'if it be your will, Lord'.

So, what about you? Do you use phrases like 'if it be your will'? And if so, how do you use it? As a 'cop-out' from seeking God, or as an 'opt-in' to truly wanting his will for your life?

This is the confidence we have in approaching God: that if we ask anything according to his will, he hears us.
(1 JOHN 5:14)

JUNE 9

Christ's wonderful body

*The body is a unit, though it is made up of many parts; and
though all its parts are many, they form one body.
So it is with Christ.*
(1 CORINTHIANS 12:12)

One of Martin's friends once broke her little toe. Not only was it very painful, it made her far less mobile. Even when something so small is out of joint, the whole body cannot function properly. And so it is with the Body of Christ, the church. Paul wrote that no member of it is unimportant or unnecessary; and no member is more important than another; all are needed differently, but equally.

Yet if you asked many Christians what the most 'important' jobs in the church are, they would probably reply 'preaching' or 'pastoring'. But the Bible says: the most important tasks are – all of them! Just think of a church service: we might thank the preacher; but what about those who helped him preach by putting out the chairs, operating the PA equipment, playing the instruments, serving the tea, and sweeping up our mess at the end? *All* of them are important; *all* need each other; *all* have a vital and promised place in the Body; and *all* are valued by Christ, the Head of the Body, for their service to him.

So, what is the role of leaders? Well, the Bible says they are *not* there to 'do the work'! Rather, their role is to 'equip the saints for the work of ministry, for building up the body of Christ' (Ephesians 4:12, NRSV). Don't expect your leaders to do everything – that's not what they are there for! God gives them to us to ensure *the Body* functions, not so that the Body has a rest!

God has promised that he will build his church as the very Body of Christ. As a believer, *you* are part of that Body and *you* have a function in it. Don't believe the devil's lies that you are useless and that there is no place for you. Your congregation is the poorer without you! So, go and make a difference!

*Just as each of us has one body with many members, and these members do
not all have the same function, so in Christ we who are many form one
body, and each member belongs to all the others.*
(ROMANS 12:4–5)

June 10

Comparisons

If anyone thinks he is something when he is nothing, he deceives himself. Each one should test his own actions. Then he can take pride in himself, without comparing himself to somebody else, for each one should carry his own load.
(GALATIANS 6:3–5)

'Comparisons are odorous,' wrote William Shakespeare in 'Much ado about nothing', making a pun on the more usual saying 'comparisons are odious'. Clearly he thought that comparisons just stank! But falling into comparing ourselves with others is so easy these days, isn't it? After all, advertisements constantly provoke us to do it. 'Are you really happy that you're looking your best? Just see how this famous person looks when wearing this!'

The trouble is, this then spills over into spiritual areas of our life too, and we start to fall into making comparisons here too. Why did God answer their prayer and not mine? Why can they afford a nicer house and car than we can? Why is it that they can go abroad every year for a holiday and we can't? In short, why does God seem to be blessing them more than us? And before long, we feel completely 'hard done by'.

While we would never acknowledge it, of course, such questions are fundamental challenges to God; because when we start thinking like that, we're telling him that he doesn't know how to run our lives (though we will, of course, piously sing on Sunday that he knows how to run the world!). But a truly thankful and committed heart to God is one that trusts his purposes, that gratefully receives whatever he gives us at this time (without comparing it with others), and that trusts him even when things aren't working out in quite the way we would have liked them to.

If you have fallen into the trap of comparing yourself with others or longing for what they have, just stop it! God loves you exactly as you are, and is providing for you in exactly the way that is right for you at this time. The only person you should be comparing yourself with is – yourself! – seeking to be a better Christian than you were this time last week, last month, last year. Only this comparison bears fruit for God!

A heart at peace gives life to the body, but envy rots the bones.
(PROVERBS 14:30)

JUNE 11

Just stand!

*'Submit yourselves, then, to God. Resist the devil, and he will
flee from you.'*
(JAMES 4:7)

When we typed the word 'bullying' into an Internet search engine, it
came back with 593,000 pages worldwide and 160,000 pages in the UK
alone. Clearly this is a subject of some interest these days! But of course,
there is nothing new about bullying. It is as old as the hills. And the
solution to bullying is just as old too. As the old saying puts it: stand up
to a bully and he will back down.

The Bible says that this is true of the biggest bully of all – Satan. Satan
is undoubtedly powerful – though we should never imagine that he is
anywhere near as powerful as God! So, while we should be careful of him,
we by no means need to be afraid of him, for Christ has stripped him of
his power at the cross. But Satan doesn't give up easily! He still 'prowls
around like a roaring lion looking for someone to devour' (1 Peter 5:8).
But he really is just a bully, trying to throw his weight around, trying to
get us to believe that he has more power than he really does, trying to
convince us that we have to do what he says or wants – but with
absolutely no authority to do so!

The New Testament's solution to this spiritual bully is simple: stand
up to him! Not in our own strength, of course, but in God's strength.
That's why James tells us that the first step is to 'submit to God' – that is,
to make God and God's will our focus and our intent. Paul says that we
then need to 'put on all of God's armour' – the Greek word he used
meant the full armour a Roman soldier wore for going into battle. That
armour, he said, are things like truth, faith and prayer. With those in
place, all we then need to do is to simply *stand!* Stand up against the bully;
and as we do so, the Bible promises, the devil really will flee! Try it today
and see.

*Put on all of God's armour so that you will be able to stand firm against all
strategies and tricks of the devil.*
(EPHESIANS 6:11, NLT)

JUNE 12

God loves enthusiasts!

They sought God eagerly, and he was found by them.
(2 CHRONICLES 15:15)

Have you noticed how easy it is to feel embarrassed by enthusiasts? Whether in the church or the workplace, enthusiasts can … well, just go over the top, can't they? Of course, the real reason we find enthusiasts hard to cope with at times is because they reveal our own lack of enthusiasm. The problem is not theirs, but ours.

So perhaps it might come as a surprise to discover that God loves enthusiasts! He loves people who seek him eagerly, worship him eagerly, serve him eagerly. In fact, the Bible speaks positively of such people and promises a blessing for 'the eager', for 'fanatics'. So we find the Bereans studying the Scriptures daily 'with great eagerness' (Acts 17:11); the Corinthians being commended for how they 'eagerly wait for our Lord Jesus Christ to be revealed' (1 Corinthians 1:7); Paul reminding Titus that Jesus wants 'a people that are his very own, eager to do what is good' (Titus 2:14); Peter reminding his readers to be 'eager to serve' (1 Peter 5:2). In short, eagerness seems to get a pretty good press!

Eagerness and enthusiasm should characterize every aspect of our life – including the way we search out and claim the promises of God. There is a wonderful passage in Job 28 which describes a miner at work deep underground, and which says that this is how we should search for God's wisdom, God's word, God's promises. Just like mining, it may be hard work at times; but it is always worth it, for it 'brings hidden things to light' (v. 11). It goes on to say that wisdom, 'hidden from the eyes of every living thing' (v. 21), can be discovered only by those who come 'digging' into God, for 'God understands the way to it and he alone knows where it dwells' (v. 23). This is the sort of eager, searching, and expectant heart that God wants to find in us as we come looking for his word and his promises.

Ask God to help you to eagerly pursue him and his ways today; for in doing so, there is the promise of great blessing.

Follow the way of love and eagerly desire spiritual gifts.
(1 CORINTHIANS 14:1)

JUNE 13

God's comfort principle

'He comes alongside us when we go through hard times, and before you know it, he brings us alongside someone else who is going through hard times so that we can be there for that person just as God was there for us.'
(2 CORINTHIANS 1:4, THE MESSAGE)

The last thing that any of us wants to be in times of trouble is 'glib comforters'; you know, people who come with their trite truths, dispensed without real thought or feeling, trying to 'cheer us up' or telling us that it will 'be all right'. Job had friends like that – and he described them as 'miserable comforters' whose 'long-winded speeches never end'! (Job 16:2–3).

But this doesn't mean that there isn't a very real way in which we can share with others in their hard times out of what we ourselves have been through. Once we have 'come out the other side', we often find that we can help those who are going through the same things. We can share our first-hand experience of God's comfort and help with real understanding; and as long as we do so with sensitivity and a caring heart, it will be appreciated and do its work.

Paul experienced many times what it was both to comfort and be comforted, grasping the clear link between the two and seeing it as a principle of how God works among us. There was one particular time when he felt greatly in need of comfort. Besides the usual pressures of his work, he had become anxious about a number of things, especially about what was happening in the church at Corinth. He desperately wanted some news; and it was right at that point that God's 'comfort principle' sprang into action, as 'God, who comforts the downcast, comforted us by the coming of Titus, and not only by his coming but also by the comfort you had given him' (2 Corinthians 7:6–7). Comfort all round!

No matter what our situation, God has comfort appropriate to it. He wants us to get hold of that – and then to pass it on. Today, resolve to both be comforted and to be a comfort, thereby releasing more of God's promised comfort among his people.

'And Saul's son Jonathan went to David at Horesh and helped him to find strength in God.'
(1 SAMUEL 23:16)

June 14

God's house

You also, like living stones, are being built into a spiritual house to be a holy priesthood, offering spiritual sacrifices acceptable to God through Jesus Christ.
(1 PETER 2:5).

'This is God's house; please keep quiet.' You will perhaps have seen such signs at the entrance to some great cathedral or religious building. It is a sign that strikes us as odd, for it suggests that perhaps God is somehow offended by conversation as people walk around. But not only is it odd, it is inaccurate! For actually, the 'house of God' is not a building, but 'people'. We are his house!

In the Old Testament King David wanted to build a 'house' for God – a temple that he felt would be worthy of such a great God. But God said to him, 'I don't want you to build a house for me – I'm going to build a house for you instead!' Initially a 'royal house' or dynasty, it would eventually become a vast family through King David's descendant, the Lord Jesus. You see, God has always had it in his heart to have a house, not of *stones*, but of *people*.

But this house of God is not yet complete. Paul told the Ephesians that 'you too are being built together to become a dwelling in which God lives by his Spirit' (Ephesians 2:22). Note how he says we *are being built*. The work is still in progress and the building is still under construction! This means, first, that we will have to exercise patience and tolerance with one another at times (ask anyone who has worked on a building site!); and second, that we need to take care how we build together, co-operating with one another rather than working against one another.

God's promise is that he is building a house for himself – and *we* are a part of that. He has not saved you in order to leave you as some lonely brick on the building site, put to one side while more important parts are set in place; there is a place for you too! Believe his promise, take your place – and be gracious with the other bricks!

For we are . . . God's building.
(1 CORINTHIANS 3:9)

JUNE 15

An encounter with holiness

*'Woe to me! . . . I am ruined! For I am a man of unclean lips,
and I live among a people of unclean lips, and my eyes have
seen the King, the LORD Almighty.'*
(ISAIAH 6:5)

There are some things in life we just try to avoid. Sometimes it's
something simple, like those little jobs we hate doing; but sometimes it
can be deeper issues we avoid, knowing that if we 'dig too deep' there
might be things we have to deal with. Something we often try to avoid in
our spiritual life is the reality of God's holiness, fearing what it might be
too uncomfortable. But Isaiah discovered that, while at first he thought
encountering God's holiness would kill him, it was in fact the very thing
that changed him and turned his life around.

This encounter with God's holiness 'in the year that King Uzziah
died' (Isaiah 6:1) did three things for him. First, it reminded him of God's
uniqueness. Faced with the death of his earthly king, he saw that there was
a king like no other, one who would never pass away, who alone was 'the
King, the LORD Almighty' (Isaiah 6:5). Second, it revealed his sinfulness.
God's holiness inevitably shows up what is wrong in our lives; and our
first response, like Isaiah, is to withdraw: 'Woe to me!' he cried. 'I am
ruined! For I am a man of unclean lips, and I live among a people of
unclean lips, and my eyes have seen the King, the LORD Almighty' (Isaiah
6:5). But that's not where God left him; for the third thing that happened
was that it released God's cleansing. He discovered that God's holiness
doesn't 'stand at a distance', accusing us of our sin; rather, it takes action
to come and change us. 'See, this has touched your lips; your guilt is taken
away and your sin atoned for' (Isaiah 6:7). And having been cleansed, he
was commissioned to go and take this good news to others. What a
wonderful revelation this was: that God shows us our sin, only to himself
come and deal with it!

Don't run from God's holiness today; it's here to do you good!

*Consecrate yourselves therefore, and be holy; for I am the LORD your God . . .
I am the LORD; I sanctify you.*
(LEVITICUS 20:7–8, NRSV)

JUNE 16

Praying in faith

'I tell you the truth, if you have faith as small as a mustard seed, you can say to this mountain, "Move from here to there" and it will move. Nothing will be impossible for you.'
(MATTHEW 17:20)

As we get older, most of us discover that muscles that were once firm begin to weaken; and before we know it, the person in the mirror just isn't us. Something happened to the muscles along the way! And that's what can happen to our 'faith muscles' too. The trouble is, the longer we are a Christian, the easier it is to stop exercising those muscles and to become lazy or even presumptuous. But we won't see our prayers answered unless our faith remains functioning, as the disciples discovered.

When Jesus came down the mountain after the transfiguration, he discovered that the disciples had experienced an embarrassing failure: a man had brought his demonized son to them, 'but they could not heal him' (Matthew 17:16). Jesus rebuked them for their failure and then healed the boy instantly. When they asked why it hadn't worked for them, Jesus replied, 'Because you have so little faith', and then added the words of our opening verse.

What can we learn from this? First, that *past authority* is no substitute for present faith. Jesus had already given them 'authority to drive out evil spirits and to heal every disease and sickness' (Matthew 10:1), but they hadn't taken hold of that right now when it was needed. Second, that *past experience* is no substitute for present faith. Having been given Jesus' authority, they had gone out and used it, 'preaching the gospel and healing people everywhere' (Luke 9:6). They returned excitedly saying, 'Lord, even the demons submit to us in your name' (Luke 10:17). So, what had gone wrong? It seems they had become presumptuous because of their very success, and so had ended up not exercising faith.

Remember: we never get beyond the stage where we have to exercise our 'faith muscles' daily. Don't rely on past authority or past experience; exercise those faith muscles today! For with faith, anything can happen; but without it, only dismal failure awaits us.

And without faith it is impossible to please God, because anyone who comes to him must believe that he exists and that he rewards those who earnestly seek him.
(HEBREWS 11:6)

A job for everyone!

The Lord's hand was with them, and a great number of people believed and turned to the Lord.
(ACTS 11:21)

When Mike travels to other nations, one of the things he loves doing is to 'people watch'. There is one nation in particular that he visits quite often where his 'people watching' has revealed what is almost a national characteristic: men sitting around watching other people doing work! They will happily sit on their haunches for hours, offering the odd bit of (contradictory!) advice, reflecting on life, and generally watching the world go by. Sadly, some of God's people can be like that. They are not actively involved in the life and work of their church; but they will happily sit around for hours commenting on deficiencies or pointing out what 'they' ought to be doing – while never getting off their spiritual haunches and doing it themselves.

One church in the New Testament that was most definitely *not* like that was Antioch. At Antioch, *everyone* was involved, not just the leaders – especially when it came to sharing their faith. When persecution arose in Jerusalem, the main leaders had stayed there, while the 'ordinary' Christians were scattered, some ending up in Antioch where they preached the gospel and where many responded. There were no 'big names'; no well-known convention speakers or international evangelists; even Barnabas didn't come till later when the apostles heard what was going on. The growth happened quite simply through 'ordinary' believers 'getting on with the job', sharing the gospel naturally and telling people the good news about Jesus.

And what about us? Do we leave it to 'the experts' or the paid staff of the church? Do we think it's enough just to live a good Christian life and never *talk* to anyone about Jesus? Our lifestyle is indeed often a key in preparing the ground for the seed of the word; but ultimately, the seed must be sown, as we *speak out* the gospel. Sharing the good news about Jesus is a job for *everyone*; and Jesus promises that his Spirit *will* be with us when we 'get to work' in this way.

'Say whatever is given you to say at that time, because it will not really be you speaking; it will be the Holy Spirit.'
(MARK 13:11, NCV)

JUNE 18

Trust in action

*Hezekiah received the letter from the messengers and read it.
Then he went up to the temple of the LORD and spread it out
before the LORD.*
(ISAIAH 37:14)

How easy it is to say to someone, 'I trust you!' – until the situation demands that we put that trust into action. That's when we can start to have second thoughts, isn't it? We wonder if our words were somewhat rash. But real trust demands action! And sometimes, God puts us into situations to see whether we will turn our declared trust into action; whether our trust is real or it is just empty words; whether we will 'nail our colours to the mast' and 'burn our bridges'.

That's exactly what King Hezekiah had to do when he received a threatening letter from the King of Assyria, demanding that Jerusalem surrender to him. But what Hezekiah did was not to panic (though if ever anyone had grounds to do so, it was him at that moment!), but rather to turn his trust of God into action. He got hold of that letter and marched straight off to the temple. There he 'spread it out before the LORD'. It was his way of saying, 'Do you see this letter God? Do you see what these idol-worshipping unbelievers are wanting to do to the people and the city you love?' And as he spread out the letter, he began to pray, focusing on the greatness of God, seeing him as the God of heaven and all the kingdoms of the earth, and stressing how the letter was an insult to the living God. And then came his final act of trust as he spoke these words: 'Now, O LORD our God, deliver us from his hand, so that all kingdoms on earth may know that you alone, O LORD, are God' (Isaiah 37:20).

At a time like that, those were no mere empty words, but trust in action.

We don't know what situation you find yourself in at this time; but whatever it is, look today for how you can put your trust into action. As you do, it will change things, just as it did for Hezekiah.

*'When this is done, I will go to the king, even though it is against the law.
And if I perish, I perish.'*
(ESTHER 4:16)

JUNE 19

Externals and internals

Search me, O God, and know my heart; test me and know my anxious thoughts. See if there is any offensive way in me, and lead me in the way everlasting.
(PSALM 139:23–24)

How much do externals matter to you? If your answer is, 'Not at all', you're certainly an exception! Externals drive so much of life today and keep our economies going. Wearing 'designer labels', having the latest fashions, updating the car to the latest model, being seen with 'the right people' or in 'the right places'; all of these are externals that most of us embrace at times. What a contrast to how God sees things! For God is not interested in externals; what matters to him is *the heart.*

Throughout Scripture, God prioritizes the heart over everything. So, a bad heart always leads to judgment; like when he saw 'how great man's wickedness on the earth had become, and that every inclination of the thoughts of his heart was only evil all the time' (Genesis 6:5) and so had to send the flood; or that 'these people come near to me with their mouth and honour me with their lips, but their hearts are far from me' (Isaiah 29:13) and so had to send his people into exile.

But a good heart always opens the door for God to act; like when Samuel, when looking for King Saul's replacement, was reminded, 'Do not consider his appearance or his height, for I have rejected him. The LORD does not look at the things man looks at. Man looks at the outward appearance, but the LORD looks at the heart' (1 Samuel 16:7); or when Josiah was told that it was 'because your heart was responsive and you humbled yourself before God' (2 Chronicles 34:27) that his prayers were heard.

Having a good heart isn't about being perfect. After all, David was seen by God as 'a man after his own heart' (1 Samuel 13:14), and yet he failed dismally many times in life. Having a good heart is about knowing that it's the inside that matters more than the outside, and letting God in to deal with it, just as David did in today's introductory prayer. It's a prayer that the wise among us will still pray today.

Above all else, guard your heart, for it is the wellspring of life.
(PROVERBS 4:23)

JUNE 20

Belt up!

'Stand firm then, with the belt of truth buckled round your waist . . .'
(EPHESIANS 6:14)

We live in a world where there is often little regard for truth. 'Bending the rules', 'little white lies', 'fixing the books' – such things are commonplace today. But truth, the Bible tells us, is foundational to how God's people are to live – and it is a foundation that promises a blessing.

Paul encouraged believers to put on 'the full armour of God' (Ephesians 6:11) to be able to stand for Jesus. He imagined a Roman soldier putting on his armour piece by piece. The first thing he put on was his belt, into which he tucked his long garment, then buckling it tight so that there would be no risk of him getting tripped up as he went into battle.

That's how it needs to be for us, Paul says. There are things we need to get in place *now* 'so that *when* the day of evil comes' (Ephesians 6:13), we will be ready. (Note that 'putting on the armour' is not a prayer to be said before 'spiritual warfare', but part of a whole lifestyle we adopt so that we are always ready!) The first thing we need to ensure is in place, Paul says, is truth. Unless we are people of truth, integrity, honesty, sincerity, eager to live according to God's word, we will most certainly get tripped up, opening the door to the devil's accusations and robbing our testimony of effectiveness.

Sometimes it is not easy to stand in truth; but God always honours us when we do. In the week we wrote this, one of Mike's church members came to him saying that he needed to tell his boss that he had lost a large amount of money in the accounts. They agreed together that it was important to 'own up', whatever the outcome (possibly the loss of his job). But as the man set his heart to do this, guess what happened? On the very day he had the appointment with the boss, the money turned up! God had honoured his integrity, and he was not 'tripped up'.

Belt up today with 'truth' – God promises to honour you as you do.

'The man of integrity walks securely, but he who takes crooked paths will be found out.'
(PROVERBS 10:9)

JUNE 21

Anything goes!

You say, 'I am innocent; he is not angry with me.' But I will
pass judgment on you because you say, 'I have not sinned.'
(JEREMIAH 2:35)

In today's world the concept of 'sin' is a rather quaint idea. These days 'anything goes', as long as it 'doesn't harm anyone else'. So, we talk about mistakes, or momentary lapses, or errors of judgment, or little character weaknesses – but never 'sin', for sin is far too judgmental a word. The trouble is, all these expressions 'let us off the hook'. So, the husband doesn't need to say 'sorry', the politician doesn't need to resign, the wrongdoer doesn't need to own up. At best, it was always someone else's fault (an excuse that goes right back to Adam and Eve!); at worst, it was just one of our little weaknesses.

All of this, however, underplays what the Bible means by *sin*. Sin isn't a momentary lapse in my morals, behaviour or deeds; sin is *an offence against God*. 'Against you, you only, have I sinned,' said David when his adultery was uncovered (Psalm 51:4). This comes out in the words the Bible uses for 'sin', all of which concern *God*. In the Hebrew and Greek, the words used for sin imply things like: missing the target, stepping over the boundary, twisting the standard, rebellion. In all of these pictures it is *God* who is at the centre: it is *God's* target that is not hit, *God's* law that is broken, *God's* purpose that is twisted, *God's* will that is defied. Sin is not just some lapse of good judgment; it is going against *God*. It is living for ourselves and not for him – and then wondering why life doesn't turn out right! And it is in this state of sin that we all naturally find ourselves.

Thank God, he has promised us a way out! And the way out is not to pretend sin isn't there, but to 'own up', to 'come clean', to acknowledge what we have – for in doing so, we find, not God's judgment, but God's mercy. See for yourself today!

If we confess our sins, he is faithful and just to forgive us our sins,
and to cleanse us from all unrighteousness.
(1 JOHN 1:9, KJV)

JUNE 22

The power of unity

The LORD said, 'If as one people speaking the same language they have begun to do this, then nothing they plan to do will be impossible for them.'
(GENESIS 11:6)

The well-known story of the tower of Babel is a classic example of human arrogance. Wanting to celebrate their growing skills and power so they would be 'noticed', its citizens resolved to build a huge ziggurat 'so that we may make a name for ourselves and not be scattered over the face of the whole earth' (Genesis 11:4). But while that is the part of the story we remember, there is a part we often forget – yet a part that contains a powerful principle.

God's response to their plans is fascinating: 'If *as one people* . . . they have begun to do this, then nothing they plan to do will be impossible for them' (Genesis 11:6). What God was underlining here was *the power of unity* – here, of course, for evil; but the opposite is just as true. Again and again the Bible promises that God releases his power through the unity of his people. It says that unity frees him to command his blessing among us; it enables him to answer our prayers; it allows the Holy Spirit to move; it frees us to use our gifts without vying with one another so that the church can be built up; it pushes us outwards into the world. Little wonder, then, that the devil doesn't like unity and does all he can to keep us from it! And little wonder that Paul tells us to 'make every effort to keep the unity of the Spirit' (Ephesians 4:3).

What might this mean practically for us? Well, we could start by resolving not to pass on gossip (even if it is true!); not to be negative about others; not to speak badly of other churches or leaders; not to look down on others who do things differently. It was because the early church was so united that it experienced the presence and power of God and made such a powerful impact on the world around it. So why not resolve today to discover for yourself more of God's ordained power of unity?

'When Jesus had called the Twelve together, he gave them power and authority . . .'
(LUKE 9:1)

JUNE 23

Vaguely hoping?

*Now faith is being sure of what we hope for and certain of
what we do not see.*
(HEBREWS 11:1)

Sometimes people speak about 'faith' as though it were some sort of mysterious heavenly substance that you have to get hold of by some great act of self-effort, or something that drops out of heaven and takes hold of you in some way, lifting you to a higher spiritual plane, or something that fills up the empty jug of our hearts and that then never runs dry. But faith isn't like that! Faith is not a *commodity*, it is a *relationship* – a relationship of daily trust as we walk with the Living God and believe his promises to us.

Whenever God calls people to have 'faith', it is never to something vague; it is always faith *in* him *for* something – and that 'something' is always quite specific. Think of perhaps the most famous example of faith in the Bible: when Abraham believed God for the first time in Genesis 12. But what was it that God asked him to believe? It wasn't belief in something vague, but rather in something very specific and tangible. God told him to look at the stars in the clear night sky – and all of us know what that is like: the more you look, the more you see. And as he saw more and more of the myriads of stars in the heavens, God promised him, 'That's how many descendants you're going to have!' And Abraham simply said, 'I believe it Lord!' – despite circumstances that seemed completely hopeless from a human point of view. He wasn't vaguely hoping; his faith was in the specific promise God had made; and, armed with that, he started the journey of faith that led to the promised outcome.

Today, don't vaguely hope for things; take hold of God's specific promises and believe. Let your faith be *in him* and *for* that which he has promised to you.

*By faith Abraham, even though he was past age – and Sarah herself was
barren – was enabled to become a father because he considered him faithful
who had made the promise.*
(HEBREWS 11:11)

JUNE 24

Ask Jesus first!

Are any among you sick? They should call for the elders of the church and have them pray over them, anointing them with oil in the name of the Lord. And their prayer offered in faith will heal the sick, and the Lord will make them well.
(JAMES 5:14–15, NLT)

Even a quick glance through the Gospels shows that a major part of Jesus' ministry involved healing the sick. How sad it is, therefore, that praying for healing is often the very last thing we think of doing these days. Far ahead of prayer, for most of us, is the bottle of tablets or the doctor's appointment.

While we should be grateful for both tablets and doctor, isn't it at least worth giving Jesus a chance to heal us *first*? If we take the Bible's record and promises seriously, shouldn't we go to Jesus before anyone or anything else? And if we're not healed the first time of asking, isn't it worth asking him again? (After all, we go to the doctor again if we don't get better straight away!)

In the week we wrote this, a bus driver from one of the churches that Mike leads did an emergency stop to save someone's life. It cost him personally, for the steering wheel crashed into his ribs and he was taken to hospital with severe bruising. He had only just become a Christian a few days earlier (and so had none of the hang-ups that many of us have about asking God for things!). So, while out walking a few days later, he decided to 'give God a chance' and asked him for healing. He suddenly felt a warmth in his chest; so he poked his ribs – softly at first, but then harder and harder. He could feel no pain! When he lifted his shirt, the bruising had completely gone – instantly and miraculously. He had been healed!

Yes, we know it doesn't always happen like that when we pray for healing. But we also know that not enough Christians pray enough for healing! Why some get healed instantly and some don't, remains a mystery (though the help of Jesus can be found whatever the outcome of our prayers). But maybe we would *see* more healing if we *prayed* for more healing! Why not try it?

'I am the LORD, who heals you.'
(EXODUS 15:26)

Thank you!

Let the peace of Christ rule in your hearts . . . and be thankful.
(COLOSSIANS 3:15)

Martin had the privilege of being a school governor for nine years. What with school inspections to bring the school out of its 'serious weaknesses' category and several changes in head teacher, it was certainly a challenging role. But one of Martin's abiding memories is that, at the end of lengthy governors' meetings, the head teacher never failed to say, 'Thank you'. Two simple, quick words: an acknowledgement of work done and time given, and an encouragement to carry on!

How often does each of us say 'thank you', we wonder? Perhaps to the preacher (whose hours of study are unseen beneath the final message); or to the worship group (whose choice of songs we may criticize more readily than appreciate); or to those who keep the 'wheels' of church life turning smoothly? Or to the bus driver or the shopkeeper? *Thank you*: two little words that provide an encouragement to carry on.

Perhaps we may think that we are only an 'ordinary Christian' or are new to the church, so who are we to say thank you to someone else? Might it not sound presumptuous or patronizing? But such thoughts shouldn't stop us from expressing gratitude to others; for gratitude is an immensely Christ-like quality.

We may need to creatively think of ways of saying thank you. When Martin recently finished work on a Study Bible, he gave copies to others who were part of the team: not just to colleagues who had helped work on it, but also to the couple who run the Post Office from where the material was sent out (not everything can be done by e-mail!), to the courier who regularly delivers his books, and to the proprietor of the local Chinese takeaway which his family regularly patronizes! These were all part of the team, so why not say thank you to them?

Above all, we should be grateful to God, the giver of all things, who generously provides what we don't deserve. Today, will you be one of the 10% who acknowledge with thanksgiving the Lord's answer to prayer (see Luke 17:11–19)? For with Christ-like gratitude comes Christ-like peace in our hearts.

Be joyful always; pray continually; give thanks in all circumstances,
for this is God's will for you in Christ Jesus.
(1 THESSALONIANS 5:16–18)

JUNE 26

Never turned away!

All that the Father gives me will come to me, and whoever
comes to me I will never drive away.
(JOHN 6:37)

Have you ever been turned away? If you have, you'll know how disappointing it can be. In the week that we wrote this, Mike and his wife were turned away from a cinema where they had hoped to see a movie that was extremely popular. Mike had been abroad for three weeks, and he had promised his wife this night out on his return. But when they arrived at the cinema, the queue at the ticket office was enormous. They inched their way forward in the queue, and were just six people away from the desk, when the manager announced, 'This film is now sold out for tonight!' To get turned away when they were so close, and after all that queuing, was so disappointing – and cost Mike a grovelling apology!

Thank goodness, when it comes to the promises of God, no one is ever turned away! For his promises, though made in time, have an eternal quality, for he is 'the LORD, the Eternal God' (Genesis 21:33) whose heart is unchanging and whose purpose is unchanging from one generation to another. This is why we can trust him and trust his promises, why we can believe that we will never be turned away.

Jesus told a parable about a man who received a late-night visit from a friend on a journey. It was midnight, and he had no food for his guest; so he knocked on his neighbour's door (which he wasn't very pleased at as the family was now in bed!). But while he might not have wanted to get up, he didn't turn his friend away; he got up and gave him what he asked for, simply because of his boldness. Jesus was saying that, if even a neighbour wouldn't turn the man away, do you really think your heavenly Father would do any less?

Today, whatever need you have, whatever promise you need to claim, call upon the Father; he will not turn you away.

'Ask and it will be given to you; seek and you will find; knock and the door
will be opened to you. For everyone who asks receives; he who seeks finds;
and to him who knocks, the door will be opened.'
(LUKE 11:9–10)

Breaking point

*'This job is too much for me . . . If this is the way you're going
to treat me, just kill me now and let my miserable life end.'*
(NUMBERS 11:14–15, CEV)

Have you ever felt that the pressure in some situation was so great that
you hit breaking point and felt you wanted to give up? If so, you'll
identify with how Moses felt as he led the Israelites to the promised land.
Life in the desert proved to be hard, and it wasn't long before people were
grumbling and wishing they were back in Egypt. 'We remember the fish
we ate in Egypt at no cost – also the cucumbers, melons, leeks, onions and
garlic. But now we have lost our appetite; we never see anything but this
manna!' they said (Numbers 11:5–6). (It's amazing what short memories
people have, isn't it? They had forgotten the reality of slavery, beatings
and hardships!) Eventually, it got too much for Moses and he hit breaking
point. But rather than let himself 'go down the tube' (which is what so
many people do at such times) he brought the matter to God, sharing not
only the problem, but also exactly how he felt.

Moses asked God bluntly why he had brought all this trouble his way;
what he had done to displease him to get such a burden; why he should
care about them anyway; where on earth God expected him to find food
for them all; how he was expected to bear their constant complaints. Little
wonder he ended his prayer by praying the words of our opening verses.

But although Moses' complaint was forthright, God didn't rebuke
him for it. He recognized that this was the cry of someone who had come
to breaking point. So he responded by providing a very practical solution.
Moses had made himself almost indispensable; so God simply told him to
share the load around a little, just like he'd already told him to.
(Sometimes the solution to a spiritual problem can be very practical!)

If you're at breaking point, don't keep it to yourself. Do what Moses
did: take it to God. Off-load your burdens onto him – and then do
whatever he tells you.

*I was pushed back and about to fall, but the LORD helped me. The LORD is
my strength and my song; he has become my salvation.*
(PSALM 118:13–14)

JUNE 28

Be still!

*'Be still, and know that I am God; I will be exalted among the
nations, I will be exalted in the earth.'*
(PSALM 46:10)

As we look back to the times when our children were little, we've lost count of the number of times we had to say to them, 'Be still!' Perhaps it was while sitting at the meal table, or when sitting next to someone on a bus, or while watching a TV programme with them. But when you're young, life always seems so exciting and full that 'being still' is the last thing you want to do. But come to think of it, isn't that rather like most of us? Isn't there always the next thing to do, the next meeting to be dashed to, the next crisis to be solved, the next meal to be prepared? 'Being still' is often the very last thing we want to do.

Perhaps one of the best-known Bible verses about 'being still' is our verse for today. It comes from Psalm 46, a psalm that was written at a time of some unknown pressure or crisis for God's people. The temptation at such moments, of course, is to go into over-drive with our plans and activity. But the psalmist's solution was simple. 'Be still! And focus on God!' was his cry.

Other English versions, bringing out different emphases of the Hebrew text, translate this verse as: 'Calm down and learn that I am God! (CEV); 'Be quiet and know that I am God' (NCV); 'Pause a while and know that I am God' (JB Phillips); 'Stop fighting, and know that I am God' (Good News Bible).

Stop fighting! But that's what so many of us do in life, isn't it? Something goes wrong or some pressure comes, and we start to 'fight' – anybody and anything! But God's solution is not for us to get into 'fight mode', but for us to learn how to be still. For only when we are still can we hear the heartbeat and the gentle whispers of our Father God.

*'Do not be afraid. Stand firm and you will see the deliverance the
LORD will bring you today . . . The LORD will fight for you;
you need only to be still.'*
(EXODUS 14:13–14)

JUNE 29

Listen and learn!

*'Listen, listen to me, and eat what is good, and your soul will
delight in the richest of fare. Give ear and come to me;
hear me, that your soul may live.'*
(ISAIAH 55:2–3)

Any husband will tell you that a frequent complaint of his wife is that he
doesn't listen when she's speaking. (It's not really that bad, is it guys?) Not
listening to our partners is bad enough; but not listening to God – well,
that's just plain stupid!

The importance of listening to God is seen in the Bible's many
exhortations to listen – and learn! – and the many warnings that we fail to
listen to our loss. For example in Deuteronomy 28 Moses says 'all these
blessings will come upon you and accompany you if you obey the LORD your
God' (v. 2), followed by a list of blessings and the promise that 'if you pay
attention to the commands of the LORD your God that I give you this day
and carefully follow them, you will always be at the top, never at the bottom'
(v. 13). But then he adds, 'However, if you do not obey the LORD your God
and do not carefully follow all his commands and decrees I am giving you
today, all these curses will come upon you and overtake you' (v. 15), and
there follows a list of curses. In other words, he's saying: listen – and learn!

But how do we listen? One of the main ways, of course, is through the
Bible. But along with Scripture, God also speaks through the Spirit's gifts
(such as prophecy), the counsel of other Christians, the promptings of the
Spirit in our heart, and through our circumstances. But while he's eager
for us to listen, there are some things God expressly forbids, because of
their link to occult powers, including astrology (e.g. Deuteronomy 4:19;
17:2–5), consulting mediums or spiritists (e.g. Leviticus 19:31; 20:6),
divination of any sort (e.g. Deuteronomy 18:10–12; 2 Kings 21:6) and
magic (e.g. Ezekiel 13:18–20; Acts 8:9–13). Many 'New Age' practices
fall within these bounds, so beware of them. They may sound 'spiritual',
but they don't come from God.

In one way or another, take time to listen to God today – and in
listening, learn.

*Blessed is the man who listens to me, watching daily at my doors,
waiting at my doorway.*
(PROVERBS 8:34)

JUNE 30

The watchful guide

The LORD will watch over your coming and going both now and for evermore.
(PSALM 121:8)

How do I know which job to take? Where to live? What to study? Whom to marry? For all these sort of questions – as well as the routine issues of everyday life – we need the guidance of God. And the truth is, it's not always easy to be sure of what that guidance is. But the *guidance of God* becomes clearer the more we get to know *the God of guidance*. The more we learn about him, the more we learn about his ways and the more we know instinctively what is right to do. Knowing what to do only assumes enormous proportions if we are uncertain about God himself or our relationship with him. If we see him merely as some sort of celestial careers adviser, then we're missing the point! He is our loving Father who is constantly 'there' for us, constantly watching over us. We don't have to persuade him to guide; he is always the watchful guide.

The Bible tells us that this watchful Father brings his guidance through many ways; through things like God's word (the Bible), God's people (both leaders and friends, and the counsel they bring), God's gifts (such as prophecy or words of knowledge), God's voice (that quiet inner conviction in our heart that we can't explain), God's hand (as he shapes circumstances, carefully opening and closing doors for us). And when several of these means of guidance all come in to line, that is when it is most safe to step out.

Of course, we also need to remember that there are some means of guidance that the Bible clearly forbids, because of their link to occult powers; things like horoscopes, astrology, magic and consulting mediums and spiritists. (So if you've used any of these things, you need to repent of them and ask God to forgive you.)

If you are seeking God's guidance at this time, be encouraged that the Watchful Guide is always with you. He has a plan for your life, and he *will* lead you into it.

In your unfailing love you will lead the people you have redeemed. In your strength you will guide them to your holy dwelling.
(EXODUS 15:13)

JULY 1

Friendship with God

And the scripture was fulfilled that says, 'Abraham believed
God, and it was credited to him as righteousness,'
and he was called God's friend.
(JAMES 2:23)

To know someone famous as a friend would probably give all of us something of a thrill. Just think – to be the friend of a film star, or TV personality, or millionaire philanthropist! How people might then sit up and take notice of us and want to be our friends too! But actually, we have an even better friendship than any of those: if you are a Christian, then you are among those who have a friendship with God!

Abraham was one of the first to be known as God's friend. That meant that he had got to know God; that there was a closeness between them; that they shared their lives together. And as God's promises became increasingly part of his life over the years, and as God himself became more and more precious to him, so Abraham learned to trust God his friend who had made him such amazing promises.

That's why Abraham didn't give up, even when everything seemed impossible and to be against him; that's why he could pick himself up and start again when he tried to 'help God out' and found he only made a mess of things; that's why he could hang on to the very end. For what he had was not some dry religion or head knowledge of God; he had truly developed a relationship of friendship with him.

Developing friendship with God is a key to experiencing his promises and to keeping going when things don't seem to be working out. Like any friendship, it requires time spent talking and an openness of heart. Why not make today a day when – whatever you might be doing – you look to grow your friendship with God through sharing everything with him as you go through the day and to opening your heart to listen to, and act upon, whatever he might have to say.

He who loves a pure heart and whose speech is gracious
will have the king for his friend.
(PROVERBS 22:11)

JULY 2

Prayer changes situations

He answered their prayers, because they trusted in him.
(1 CHRONICLES 5:20)

'Can you prove that prayer makes a difference?' the sceptics ask. 'And how do you know that what you prayed for wouldn't have happened anyway? Maybe it was just a coincidence.' Well, maybe it was. But our own experience as writers, along with countless Christians throughout the ages, is that a remarkable number of coincidences seem to happen when we pray! Prayer is not a meaningless spiritual exercise; it really is effective! God hears our prayers, God answers our prayers, and those answers change things and people.

The Bible is full of examples of prayer changing situations; people like Moses, who saw God's people rescued as he raised his staff and called out to God (Exodus 14:21–22); Hannah, who saw her barrenness ended through faithful, persistent prayer (1 Samuel 1:27); David, who saw a national situation changed through prayer (2 Samuel 24:25); Elijah, who saw countless miracles as he called out to the living God to show his reality and power in the face of godless people (e.g. 1 Kings 18:41–45); Hezekiah, who saw his lifespan extended as he prayed (2 Kings 20:1–6); Nehemiah, who saw amazing doors opened for him because he prayed (Nehemiah 2:4–6); Daniel, who influenced a whole nation because he prayed (e.g. Daniel 6:10–28); Peter, who experienced a miraculous escape from jail as a result of the prayers of others (Acts 12:5–19); Paul, who saw prayer do everything from changing the whole outlook of a church (Acts 13:1–3) to bringing about miracles (e.g. Acts 28:1–9) to rescuing him again and again from danger (e.g. 2 Corinthians 1:10–11).

This brief overview Scripture should convince us that prayer changes things in a wide variety of contexts and for a wide variety of people. And God wants us to believe that the same thing can still happen – through you! He is still looking for men and women who, like Moses, will pick up the staff of prayer, who will listen to him, and then come with bold prayers, expecting things to change as they do. Will we pick up that staff of prayer today?

Prepare a guest room for me, because I hope to be restored to you
in answer to your prayers.
(PHILEMON V. 22)

JULY 3

God's comfort in our fear

'The LORD is my light and my salvation – whom shall I fear?
The LORD is the stronghold of my life – of whom shall I be
afraid?'
(PSALM 27:1)

Fear is a powerful emotion – for good or for bad. At its best, it prompts great acts of courage; at its worst, it causes panic and paralysis. Thankfully, the Bible is full of prayers from people in situations of fear and – even better! – full of God's promises for those in the midst of it!

David, the author of our text, faced countless situations of fear, especially while on the run from King Saul. But he also the learned the secret of handling fear: it was, quite simply, to press into God. As surely as people ran into a 'stronghold' when an enemy came, so David learned the secret of running into God's presence as his spiritual stronghold. Many of us no doubt do the same; but so often, it's the *last* thing we do, not the *first*. Something happens that causes us to fear. We try everything: we try to 'forget it'; we try to 'fix it'; we try to change it - but still the fear is there. And so, when everything else has failed, we go to God! But what God wants is for us to come to him *first*, finding as we do so his promised comfort in our fear.

When Paul began to preach in Corinth, he experienced real opposition – though it wasn't as bad as in Iconium where they stoned him and left him for dead! Paul (being human!) would no doubt have experienced fear at such times; it would have been a natural reaction. But, like David, he too pressed into God again and again; and that night, the Lord said to him, 'Do not be afraid; keep on speaking, do not be silent. For I am with you, and no-one is going to attack and harm you' (Acts 18:9–10).

God truly brings his comfort in times of fear. If you are in such a time, stop and turn to him right now, and claim his promised presence, comfort and grace. With this, who or what can ultimately harm you?

So we say with confidence, 'The Lord is my helper; I will not be afraid.
What can man do to me?'
(HEBREWS 13:6)

JULY 4

Why say sorry?

I will declare mine iniquity; I will be sorry for my sin.
(PSALM 38:18, KJV)

When our children were young, one thing we worked hard on was getting them to say 'sorry'. Such a small word, yet one that it could be so difficult to extract at times! Of course, adults are no different; it's just that we are far more subtle in how we avoid saying it. But knowing how to say 'sorry' is one of the most important things in life.

First, saying 'sorry' reminds us *who God is*: that he is holy and cannot bear the sight of sin. This is hard for us to grasp, for we have all learned to live too easily with sin. But just as we instinctively feel repulsed when seeing scenes of slaughter on the TV news, so that is how God feels when he sees sin. He feels revolted and sickened by it – even by what we might see as 'trivial' sin – for it offends his holiness, his love of what is good and right. Acknowledging his holiness and our sinfulness, therefore, is the first step to receiving forgiveness.

Second, saying 'sorry' reminds us *who we are.* We can so easily lose a proper perspective of ourselves and become convinced of how important and indispensable we are. How fortunate my employer is to have *us* working for them! How blessed the church is to have *us* as a member. But owning up to our sin has a way of healthily putting things back into perspective again.

Third, saying 'sorry' reminds us *who others are.* Sometimes we hurt others. Careless words, thoughtless actions, ungrateful attitudes, can all cut deep into the hearts of family, friends and colleagues. When we recognize that's what we've done, we need to say 'sorry' quickly (both to God and to them), for this reminds us that we are no different from them and that they too are made in the image of God and are to be treated as such.

Saying 'sorry' isn't always easy; but when we do, it is the most liberating thing on earth! Is there someone you need to say 'sorry' to today?

'So I confessed my sins and told them all to you. I said, "I'll tell the LORD each one of my sins." Then you forgave me and took away my guilt
(PSALM 32:5, CEV).

July 5

Encouragements to pray

When Jacob awoke from his sleep, he thought, 'Surely the LORD is in this place, and I was not aware of it.' He was afraid and said, 'How awesome is this place! This is none other than the house of God; this is the gate of heaven.'
(GENESIS 28:16–17)

Have you ever felt sometimes that prayer seems so difficult? Or that God seems so distant? If so, remember Jacob. He simply went to sleep one night – and found that God was there! The presence of God had come in the night and God had spoken to him. What a picture of how easy it is to relate to our heavenly Father! Jacob's encounter brings home three things to remember as we come to pray.

First, remember that *God is with us.* As David put it, 'The LORD is near to all who call on him, to all who call on him in truth' (Psalm 145:18). And Zephaniah said, 'The LORD your God is with you, he is mighty to save. He will take great delight in you, he will quiet you with his love, he will rejoice over you with singing' (Zephaniah 3:17).

Second, remember that *God wants to be found.* Since God is spirit, we could never discover him by ourselves. But he doesn't play 'Hide and Seek' with us; rather he does everything possible to make himself known. That's why Moses said, 'If . . . you seek the LORD your God, you will find him if you look for him with all your heart and with all your soul' (Deuteronomy 4:29). It's why God himself says, 'You will seek me and find me when you seek me with all your heart. I will be found by you' (Jeremiah 29:13–14).

Third, remember that *God wants to answer.* He not only hears prayers, but answers them. He himself promised, 'I am the LORD their God and I will answer them' (Zechariah 10:6); and David confidently declared, 'I call on you, O God, for you will answer me' (Psalm 17:6).

With these promises in our hearts, prayer will be spontaneous and natural.

'I revealed myself to those who did not ask for me; I was found by those who did not seek me. To a nation that did not call on my name, I said, "Here am I, here am I"'
(ISAIAH 65:1)

JULY 6

The God of truth

Though everyone else in the world is a liar, God is true.
(ROMANS 3:4, NLT)

'WYSIWYG' – 'What You See Is What You Get' – is a familiar expression to computer users. It means that what shows on your computer screen is exactly what you get when it is printed out on paper, so that you know where you stand and what you can expect. And this is exactly how it is with God: what you see is what you get! With him, there is no distortion, no trickery, no nasty surprises, no lies; just absolute truth.

Of course, the concept of 'absolute truth' doesn't sit easily in postmodern, Western society. 'What sort of truth do you mean?' 'It may be truth for you, but is it truth for everybody?' are the sort of questions that are often asked. And so the suggestion that there might be any kind of absolute truth – 'the' truth, truth that has a legitimate call upon everyone – is strange indeed.

But this is exactly what God is – absolute truth. His very nature and character is 'truth'; he is absolutely upright, with nothing unjust, crooked or unreliable about him. And therefore his words and promises are absolutely true; what he says, he means; what he says, he does. He is completely dependable and reliable, unchanging and unchangeable.

What this means is that we don't find that God is one thing today but something else tomorrow, or that he revealed himself as one thing in the Old Testament but as something different in the New. Nor does he appear as one thing in Bible times but as something utterly different today. Unlike moving shadows, he doesn't change, as he himself assures us: 'I the LORD do not change' (Malachi 3:6). His promises of old still hold true now, for he himself is truth, eternal truth.

Of course, the devil tries to get us to doubt God, especially when we are looking to lay hold of his promises. Don't listen to 'the father of lies' (John 8:44); listen to the Father of Truth, your unchanging, faithful God; the 'God who does not lie' (Titus 1:2). Take hold of his unchanging truth again today!

Every good and perfect gift is from above, coming down from the Father of the heavenly lights, who does not change like shifting shadows.
(JAMES 1:17)

JULY 7

What's in it for me?

He is your praise; he is your God.
(DEUTERONOMY 10:21)

'But what's in it for me?' How many times you have heard (or perhaps even asked!) that question. It's a question that reflects the utilitarian society that we live in these days: what will *I* get out of it? Everything must have an immediate purpose or return – preferably in some way that will benefit me.

Worship, however, cuts right across this utilitarian instinct, for it promises nothing for *me*; it is something given solely to *God*. This isn't because God *needs* our worship in some way. He isn't 'lessened' if we don't bring worship to him; and nor is he 'greatened' if we do. The fact that he doesn't need our worship is reflected in the way that, time and time again, he refuses to accept worship at any price. 'The multitude of your sacrifices – what are they to me?' (Isaiah 1:11), he said to a people who thought that the mere externals of worship were sufficient to keep him on 'their side'. If the heart wasn't right, then God wasn't interested. (In fact, it's interesting to note that God says far more in the Bible about unacceptable worship than he does about acceptable worship!)

God doesn't want our worship at any price then. And yet, our worship is certainly something that he desires. For worship does two things: First, it pleases God. He has revealed himself to us as our Father; and as a Father, he just loves to hear his children bring their expressions of delight to him. But second, worship honours God. Our word *worship* comes from an Old English word, *worth-ship*. When we worship, we are telling God how much he is worth to us and giving him the honour that is rightfully his.

And yet, here is the strange thing: when we give ourselves to worshipping him, things happen to me and for me, for I am drawn into his sphere. 'What's in it for me?' Nothing – and yet everything! Such is the mystery of worship. Give yourself to it once again today, and experience the mystery anew.

He who sacrifices thank-offerings honours me, and he prepares the way so that I may show him the salvation of God.
(PSALM 50:23)

JULY 8

United we stand, divided we fall

'You are all sons of God through faith in Christ Jesus, for all of you who were baptised into Christ have clothed yourselves with Christ. There is neither Jew nor Greek, slave nor free, male nor female, for you are all one in Christ Jesus.'
(GALATIANS 3:26–28)

Imagine a new community where all divisions have been removed; where every barrier – whether racial or religious, social or sexual – are broken down. That's what the body of Christ is destined to be like, Paul tells us in today's text. However, that theory needs turning into practice; and the truth is, the early church didn't always achieve that. We often find disunity raising its head among them; and while some of that disunity was over fundamental doctrine, most of it was to do with ethnic tensions, naked ambition, pride, greed, favouritism and personal opinion – hardly appropriate to the body of Christ, is it? Which is all the more reason for us to learn from their mistakes.

There is an old saying: united we stand, divided we fall. That's certainly true in the church. Division robs us of our power and effectiveness. It is a 'spoiler'; it spoils our own life, producing bad attitudes within us. It spoils others' lives, because of the way our attitudes affect them. It spoils the life and witness of the church as we pour energy into criticizing one another rather than getting on with the real job. Little wonder, then, that Paul was constantly appealing to his churches to make a priority of unity.

Divided we fall. But united, we most definitely stand! It was when the disciples 'were all with one accord in one place' (Acts 2:1, KJV) that the Holy Spirit of God fell upon them in power, transforming them and thrusting them out to change the world. Their unity provided a powerful platform from which God could work, fulfil his promises and reveal his plans. It still does the same today. Give yourself to it and see!

'My purpose is that they may be encouraged in heart and united in love, so that they may have the full riches of complete understanding, in order that they may know the mystery of God, namely, Christ, in whom are hidden all the treasures of wisdom and knowledge.'
(COLOSSIANS 2:2–3)

JULY 9

Our friend in times of trouble

O LORD, how many are my foes! How many rise up against me!
Many are saying of me, 'God will not deliver him.'
But you are a shield around me, O LORD; you bestow
glory on me and lift up my head.
(PSALM 3:1–3)

Have you noticed how some of the psalms have a title to them? Psalm 3, from which today's verses come, is one of those: 'A psalm of David. When he fled from his son Absalom.' So few words; but such a story behind them! For David had had to flee from his kingdom when his very own son, Absalom, led a coup against him – a coup that looked like it might succeed. There were indeed 'many foes' against him (v. 1), and they were trying to discourage him by saying he could forget any ideas of God coming to his rescue (v. 2). All in all, a nasty situation.

The details of this story in 2 Samuel 15–18 show us that this was a really difficult – even depressing – time for David. Yet nevertheless he turned in prayer to God and expressed his confidence in him once again. David understood that speaking out what God has shown us of himself in the past is a key to our faith being strengthened at such times; and in Psalm 3 he goes on to speak of who God is, what he has done, and how he has answered and blessed in the past. All of this strengthened him and helped him declare in faith that, 'I will not fear the tens of thousands drawn up against me on every side' (v. 6). Lifting our eyes from our circumstances to our God is always a key to experiencing God's shield around us.

And then, having done all this, he boldly calls out, 'Arise, O LORD! Deliver me, O my God!' (v. 7). God loves such bold praying from us; and the more we take time to get to know our heavenly friend in times of peace, the more bold we can be with him in times of trouble.

If you are facing trouble at this time, do what David did: remember God's blessings in the past – and then be bold in praying about the present and the future!

God is our refuge and strength, an ever-present help in trouble.
(PSALM 46:1)

When faith is tested

*Consider it pure joy, my brothers, whenever you face trials of
many kinds, because you know that the testing of your faith
develops perseverance. Perseverance must finish its work so that
you may be mature and complete, not lacking anything.*
(JAMES 1:2–4)

Have you noticed how much easier it is to see faith tested in others than
in yourself? And how much easier it is to stand with others in their
difficulties than to stand in your own? But the time inevitably comes
when it is our turn to face the challenges and tests of life. Then how do
we react when God tests our faith, and when trusting him seems to be the
last thing that we want to do? It is at such times that we need to remember
two key promises from God's word.

The first promise is that God tests us, not because he doesn't love us,
but because he does. Trials and tests prove that 'God is treating you as
sons' (Hebrews 12:7). God wants us to grow – and to grow up. Just as a
young sapling grows into a sturdy mature tree by putting down roots,
growing in the face of the wind and rain, so God wants his people to
grow, putting their roots down into him.

The second promise is that God won't test us beyond what we can
bear. Being asked to offer up his son wasn't the only test of Abraham's
faith, but it was certainly the most stretching. Yet because Abraham had
trusted God over many years, he was now ready for such a test. God's tests
are always appropriate to the stage where we are at in our journey of faith;
he never stretches us beyond what he knows we can carry.

If you are going through a difficult, challenging and testing time at
this moment, remember these two promises And above all, remember that
God is with you today in all that you face, wanting to work through
everything for your good.

*No temptation has seized you except what is common to man. And God is
faithful; he will not let you be tempted beyond what you can bear. But
when you are tempted, he will also provide a way out
so that you can stand up under it.*
(1 CORINTHIANS 10:13)

July 11

Anyone can pray

*And foreigners who bind themselves to the LORD to serve him,
to love the name of the LORD, and to worship him . . . these I
will bring to my holy mountain and give them joy in my house
of prayer . . . for my house will be called
a house of prayer for all nations.*
(ISAIAH 56:6–7)

Mike will never forget the lady who just wouldn't set foot inside the church building. She had come to collect her child from the special children's meetings that were being held that week, along with all the other parents; but even though it was pouring with rain, she just wouldn't come inside, despite Mike's warmest invitations. She didn't seem angry with the church or with God (she wouldn't have let her children come if she had been); it seemed she just didn't think that church and God were for people like her. Perhaps she simply felt 'not good enough'. That's how some people feel about prayer too: not good enough. But the Bible tells us that *anyone* can pray!

The prayers of the Pharisees in Jesus' day seemed very impressive; but it didn't impress God, Jesus said. In their desire to be 'noticed', with their wordy prayers, they were a real obstacle to ordinary people praying, who were left feeling that prayer wasn't for 'people like them'. But it's exactly those sort of people that God loves to hear praying, said Jesus. In his parable of the Pharisee and the tax collector, Jesus said that it was the tax collector with his simple words, 'God, have mercy on me, a sinner' (Luke 18:13) whose words were heard, rather than the Pharisee with his long and 'showy' prayers.

The simple truth is: anyone can pray. You don't have to be 'religious'; in fact, being 'religious' can sometimes get in the way! You don't even have to be a Christian to start to pray. In fact, reaching out to God in time of need can often be the beginning of a real relationship with him, as many people have discovered.

Don't feel today that *you* can't pray, for whatever reason. Don't think that God won't be interested in *your* prayers. Just call out to him; use your ordinary words. He is just waiting to hear from you!

'Call to me and I will answer you . . .'
(JEREMIAH 33:3)

JULY 12

Mirror, mirror....

'Anyone who listens to the word but does not do what it says is like a man who looks at his face in a mirror and, after looking at himself, goes away and immediately forgets what he looks like. But the man who looks intently into the perfect law that gives freedom, and continues to do this, not forgetting what he has heard, but doing it – he will be blessed in what he does.'
(JAMES 1:23–25)

'Mirror, mirror on the wall, who is the fairest of them all?' asked the Queen in the story of Snow White. The mirror always gave her the answer she wanted to hear: 'Why, you, O Queen!' But then came the day when a more beautiful woman appeared on the scene – Snow White – and the Queen was furious to hear what the mirror said. But then, that's what mirrors do: they tell the truth.

When we stand before a mirror, we see ourselves as we really are. Mirrors don't lie (except those at funfairs that deliberately aim to distort!); and our mirror, the Bible, is no different. It shows us things exactly as they are. We see God exactly as he is, and ourselves exactly as we are. Of course, we have to trust that the mirror is a true reflection. If we start doubting its reliability or accuracy, how will we ever be sure about what we see? How will we ever face up to its truth and its challenges if we explain away things that are hard or that challenge us? Like the Queen in Snow White, we will want to get rid of the problem rather than see the problem in ourselves.

Today's text brings home the truth that, not only is the Bible a mirror, but that we need to *act* on what we see there. We don't look into a mirror and then forget what we see; we act on it, adjusting our hair or our clothes. Likewise, the Bible calls us not to be casual, passive listeners or admirers of the word, but *doers* of it; to act on what we see.

If you have been putting off obeying something in God's word, just *do it* – you *will* be blessed as you do!

'Do not merely listen to the word, and so deceive yourselves.
Do what it says.'
(JAMES 1:22)

JULY 13

Troubling trouble

About midnight Paul and Silas were praying and singing
hymns to God, and the other prisoners were listening to them.
Suddenly there was such a violent earthquake that the
foundations of the prison were shaken. At once all the prison
doors flew open, and everybody's chains came loose.
(ACTS 16:25–26)

Trouble seemed to follow Paul wherever he went. Not that he went looking for it! He was simply so committed to sharing the gospel that it constantly got him into hot water. It was during his second missionary journey that a vision led to him crossing into modern Europe. Arriving in Philippi, Paul and Silas quickly got into trouble through delivering a slave girl possessed of an evil spirit of fortune-telling. While the girl was no doubt pleased, her owners were livid that their source of income had gone and soon stirred up a riot that led to Paul and Silas being flogged, thrown into jail and put into the stocks.

But rather than fall into self-pity, or waste endless hours asking 'Why?', they began to praise God. And when they did, some amazing things happened. Right in the middle of their praying and singing, an earthquake struck the city, and the prison's foundations shook so much that the doors burst open and the prisoners' shackles broke free. Now, any normal prisoners would have taken the opportunity to escape; but not Paul and Silas – and not, it seems, the other prisoners who there in jail with him. Something strange was surely at work here!

In fact, as we read the account in Acts 16, we see several things happening as the result of their praising: the non-Christian prisoners heard their witness; it released God's hand to act, in quite an amazing way; it produced peace in them rather than panic (just think about it: an earthquake and nobody runs!); and ultimately, it brought the jailer's whole family to faith in Jesus.

Rather than allowing himself to be troubled by 'trouble', Paul went on the offensive and set himself to trouble the trouble through praise. If you are in the midst of trouble at this time, why not set your heart to do the same? It really does release God's hand to do amazing things!

You are my hiding-place; you will protect me from trouble and surround me
with songs of deliverance.
(PSALM 32:7)

July 14

Sin against . . . who?

*'Father, I have sinned against heaven and before you, and I am
no longer worthy to be called your son.'*
(Luke 15:18–19, NKJV)

'As long as what I'm doing isn't hurting anyone else, what's it got to do with
you?' That's the sort of question that sums up many western attitudes today.
It sounds quite plausible as an argument, doesn't it? (though it's utterly
false, for anything that ultimately affects society affects me!). The same sort
of attitude is sometimes directed towards God too. What have my actions
got to do with him? But the Bible tells us that everything we do has to do
with God, who is our creator and to whom we are therefore accountable;
and every wrong thing we do is therefore a wrong against him.

But how does upsetting my friend, arguing with my boss, messing up
my life, affect *God*? Well, it affects him because all these sort of things are
an offence to his holiness and because he has made us to live as his
obedient children, reflecting that holiness. All sin is sin against him,
therefore, whether we see a direct connection to him or not.

This principle comes out in the parable of the prodigal son. When the
wild-living, rebellious son finally realizes what a mess he has made of life,
and that he needs to go back home, he prays the words of our opening
verses today. Note that he sees two dimensions to his sin: it is 'against
heaven' (a common synonym for 'God' in those days) and 'against you'
(his earthly father). But note which comes first: God! God is always far
more offended by our sin than anyone else will ever be. That's what
Joseph acknowledged when Potiphar's wife attempted to seduce him.
'How then could I do such a wicked thing and sin against God?' (Genesis
39:9). The sin, he saw, would not just have been against his master, but
against God himself. It is seeing sin in this bigger context – as something
that offends and hurts God – that helps keep us on the 'straight and
narrow'.

Recognizing that what we have done wrong is a sin against God
himself is a key to finding forgiveness and release. So, any sin to confess
to him today?

'I have sinned against the Lord.'
(2 Samuel 12:13)

JULY 15

God is good . . . all the time!

I am still confident of this: I will see the goodness of the LORD in the land of the living. Wait for the LORD; be strong and take heart and wait for the LORD.
(PSALM 27:13)

Finding things that are good isn't always easy. Do all the research you like to find a 'good' car, but you might still end up buying the 'Friday afternoon' model (the one that often has various things wrong with it as workers' minds begin to drift towards the weekend) and it might not turn out to be so good after all. And as to finding people that are good – well, that can be a nightmare! After all, appearances can be deceptive; and even the best of folk can let you down.

Thankfully, and in contrast to all this, one of the Bible's most basic affirmations is that God is good – all the time. There's nothing 'Friday-afternoon-ish' or unreliable about him. From start to finish, he is good through and through.

His goodness was something that the we find Old Testament prophets frequently stressing. He wasn't like the pagan deities of all the surrounding nations, who were often vacillating in character and attitude and whom you had to take care not to upset. ('Quick! We'd better offer a sacrifice in case he wakes up in a bad mood today!'). No, the living God is good through and through, day after day, year after year; good in both nature and action. That's why the psalmist could declare with such confidence, 'You are good, and what you do is good' (Psalm 119:68). It's why David could say, 'You are my Lord; apart from you I have no good thing . . . LORD, you have assigned me my portion and my cup; you have made my lot secure. The boundary lines have fallen for me in pleasant places; surely I have a delightful inheritance' (Psalm 16:2,5–6). David might have had his ups and downs in life; but, at the end of the day, he was confident that his God was a good God who was committed to doing him only good.

God *is* good – all the time! And God *does* good – all the time! Remember – and enjoy! – his goodness today.

Be at rest once more, O my soul, for the LORD has been good to you.
(PSALM 116:7)

JULY 16

The ministry of compassion

If there is a poor man among your brothers . . . give generously to him and do so without a grudging heart; then because of this the LORD your God will bless you in all your work and in everything you put your hand to.
(DEUTERONOMY 15:7, 10)

When Moses encountered God on Mount Sinai, having asked to see what he was really like, the first words he heard were: 'The LORD, the LORD, the compassionate and gracious God . . .' (Exodus 34:6). It is surely not without significance that the *first* thing God wants us to know about him is that he is *compassionate*. It should not surprise us therefore to find, in both Old and New Testaments, God calling upon his people to be compassionate too – and promising a blessing on those who are.

One church that showed particular compassion was the church at Antioch. Alerted to an impending famine through prophecy, 'the disciples, each according to his ability, decided to provide help for the brothers living in Judea' (Acts 11:29). Note that this was something that was not just done by the church leaders; it was the whole church – 'the disciples' – that were moved by the plight of their brothers and sisters in Christ.

Compassionate ministry is a hallmark of all true biblical faith, for compassion is a hallmark of God himself. So, when Paul went to Jerusalem for discussions with Peter, James and John, they agreed that he should go to the Gentiles, but underlined the need to 'remember the poor, the very thing I was eager to do' (Galatians 2:10).

And here is the amazing thing: when we make sacrifices in order to be compassionate to others, God himself is compassionate to us. Time and time again, we as writers have seen that God has more than repaid us for any kindness we may have extended to others – though, of course, that should not be the reason for doing so! God wants us to be compassionate as a reflection of his heart, not as a way of 'putting his arm up his back' to bless us!

Today, look to be compassionate as God himself is compassionate – for he promises to then be compassionate to you too.

He who gives to the poor will lack nothing, but he who closes his eyes to them receives many curses.
(PROVERBS 28:27)

JULY 17

God uses strange things!

In order to fulfil the word of the LORD spoken by Jeremiah, the LORD moved the heart of Cyrus king of Persia to make a proclamation.
(2 CHRONICLES 36:22)

Israel had been used to God's interventions in its history. *The* great intervention they always looked back to was the exodus, when God rescued them from slavery in Egypt 'by a mighty hand and an outstretched arm' (Deuteronomy 4:34). Looking back to this reminded Israel of the great things God had done for them in the past, and encouraged them to trust for the future. But God had a surprise up his sleeve; he was about to intervene in a very different way.

Seeing themselves delivered *from* the hands of their enemies had always been easy for them to see as God's intervention; but what about being delivered *into* the hands of their enemies? Could that be God too? Oh yes, the prophets answered! God was the God of the nations; and he would use those pagan nations to bring his discipline to his people.

First, the northern kingdom of Israel was defeated and exiled by Assyria, 'the rod of my anger' (Isaiah 10:5), as prophesied by Hosea and Amos in the north and by Isaiah in the south. Later, the southern kingdom of Judah, having failed to learn from the disaster that had befallen their northern neighbour, was also defeated and exiled to Babylon, the new super-power in that part of the world, just as Isaiah and Jeremiah had prophesied. But they also prophesied the ultimate overthrow of Babylon itself too.

But then came the biggest surprise of all: it would be another pagan nation – Persia, the next great superpower – that God would use to intervene in history to bring his people back to the promised land! Cyrus of Persia conquered Babylon; and then God conquered Cyrus, though he did not know it! And not only did he send all the Jews back home, he even financed them to do it!

Surely, God can use strange things and strange people. So don't get disheartened if you can't see how God is going to do something or work something out. God has more ways than one to 'skin a cat'! Trust him!

The LORD controls rulers just as he determines the course of rivers.
(PROVERBS 21:1, CEV)

JULY 18

Lost in wonder, love and praise

Pour out your heart like water in the presence of the Lord.
(LAMENTATIONS 2:19)

Ever tried talking to your children when they're watching their favourite TV programme? Or to your husband when his head is in the newspaper? Or to your wife when a friend brings their newborn baby? The chances are: you won't get through! They're so caught up with what they are focused on that they're lost to the world. It's as if nothing else existed!

And that's what God's heart is for us when we come into his presence: to be so caught up with him that nothing else matters, that everything else fades into insignificance, and that he alone becomes the focus of our attention as we pour out our heart to him. When that happens, we have truly had a foretaste of heaven!

The final verse of one of Charles Wesley's most famous hymns, 'Love Divine,' ends like this: *Changed from glory into glory, Till in heaven we take our place, Till we cast our crowns before Thee, Lost in wonder, love and praise.* 'Lost in wonder, love and praise'. That's how it's going to be in heaven! There will be nothing to distract us, or to worry us, or take our minds from God and his wonderful presence. But we don't have to wait until heaven to start experiencing and enjoying God's presence! Even in the Old Testament, there were times when God's presence came down in a special way, like when Solomon brought the ark into the temple. There was such an outburst of praise that suddenly 'the temple of the LORD was filled with a cloud, and the priests could not perform their service because of the cloud, for the glory of the LORD filled the temple of God' (2 Chronicles 5:13–14). If that was their experience under the old covenant, how much more can we expect the presence of God through Jesus in the power of his Spirit!

God wants us to experience a foretaste of heaven, to be lost in wonder, love and praise – but we have to want it too! God forces nothing on us – least of all, the enjoyment of his presence! So, how much do you want his presence today?

They ate and drank with great joy in the presence of the LORD that day.
(1 CHRONICLES 29:22)

July 19

Be honest!

Strike all my enemies on the jaw; break the teeth of the wicked.
(PSALM 3:7)

Hopefully our introductory verse brought you up with a bit of a jolt! Hopefully you're thinking, 'What on earth are they doing including a prayer like that?' (If you are, good! If you're not, then you're probably still asleep!) But let us ask you a question: have you ever felt you wanted to be honest in prayer? We mean, *really* honest? So often prayers can be wrapped up in such nice, religious language that they lack any reality or 'bite'. We say all the 'right' words, but go away not really having told God what we think. Well, if that's you, then today's verse is for you; for it is an example of one of the prayers in the Bible that are staggeringly honest, to the point of being shocking!

Here is King David, on the run from a coup against him, calling out to God with great trust, but also with great honesty: asking God to strike his enemies' jaws and break their teeth. But surely that isn't very godly, is it? Why is such a prayer recorded in God's word? Well, it's because God wants us to know that we can be utterly honest when we bring our feelings and prayers before him; that he is not shocked by them – indeed, he knew them before we spoke them anyway!

But of course, just because this is what *David* felt doesn't mean it's what *God* felt! But nevertheless God says, 'Come on; get it off your chest; then we can talk about it.' Only as our cries are honest will we ever see God breaking in – and that may be breaking into our own life as much as into the lives of others or the situation that we are complaining about!

God wants us to be honest when we pray, then. He's big enough to cope with whatever we have to say. But then, having said it, we then need to be ready to listen to what *he* has to say in return – and that may be just as strikingly honest too! Come on! Be honest in your talking to God today!

I am sick of life! And from my deep despair I complain to you, my God!
(JOB 10:1, CEV)

JULY 20

The hand of the LORD

. . . the hand of the LORD will be made known to his servants . . .
(ISAIAH 66:14)

In the 1986 World Cup, the famous Argentinean footballer, Diego Maradona, scored a controversial goal by what he later described as 'the hand of God'. What he really meant was that he had cheated! For it had been his hand that knocked the ball into the net (and while he knew that, he wasn't about to own up to it with so much at stake!). There is another hand, however, that is far more trustworthy. It is 'the hand of the LORD'.

The 'hand of the LORD' is an expression used in the Bible to mean 'God's intervention' on behalf of his people. God is not remote and distant, but intimately involved in his world and his people's lives. That is why we see his 'hand' at work bringing deliverance, help or guidance, often through *circumstances*. By 'circumstances' we mean the things that happen around us, opportunities that come our way, doors that open or close, commitments that restrain us, events that suddenly take a turn in an unexpected direction; all these are things that God's hand shapes to lead and bless his people.

For example, Joseph was released from jail and brought to Pharaoh only when God stirred the cupbearer to remember him; Ruth went to glean in the fields, but just happened to find herself in a field that belonged to Boaz, her kinsman-redeemer; Paul, 'tried to enter Bithynia, but the Spirit of Jesus would not allow them to' (Acts 16:7). God is bigger than any of our circumstances, and he can use them all, or override them all, for our good and for his purpose.

Sometimes, God's hand can feel frustrating. So, when God took the Israelites 'the long way round' from Egypt to Canaan, many were quick to complain. But actually, he was helping them avoid the Philistines on the coastal plain by blocking what would have been the obvious way for them to go. We need to learn not to fight God's hand seems to resist our plans at times. For his hand is always a good hand, intimately but powerfully working on our behalf. So ask him to move his hand for you today.

. . . your hand will guide me, your right hand will hold me fast.
(PSALM 139:10)

JULY 21

I am with you

'Do not be afraid; keep on speaking, do not be silent. For I am with you, and no-one is going to attack and harm you, because I have many people in this city.'
(ACTS 18:9–10)

We love the promises of God! That's why we wrote a book about them, and that's why we developed that book into this daily devotional that you are now reading. But we also know that there is something even better than the promises of God. Even better than his *promises* is his *presence!* Knowing that the presence of Almighty God is with us! Knowing that, whatever happens, there is one who is our constant companion! Knowing that, whatever the devil may throw at us, there is one who is our shield and our defender. Grasping hold of this truth is life-changing.

Jesus knew how important this would be for us. That is why the very last thing he promised his disciples, before returning to his Father in heaven, was that he would always be with them. This was certainly a promise that they would need to keep hold of; for as they went out with the good news of the gospel, not everyone was ready to receive it as good news. The disciples would be rejected, persecuted, even put to death, because of their message about Jesus; but Jesus was with them through it all – and it was this certainty that kept them going. Paul too experienced many difficulties, hardships and rejections; little wonder, therefore, that at times he became downhearted. It was on one such occasion, in the city of Corinth where he had met with much hardness of heart, that Jesus spoke to him in the night: 'I'm with you Paul!' Such simple words; yet words that gave him renewed strength and vision – so much so that he would stay on in Corinth for a further eighteen months and continue with the work.

The promise of Jesus to *all* his followers is that he would be with them. Whatever opportunities or challenges you may be facing at this time, this promise still holds true for you today.

'Surely I am with you always, to the very end of the age.'
(MATTHEW 28:20)

JULY 22

Eat up!

'Then he said to me, "Son of man, eat this scroll I am giving
you and fill your stomach with it." So I ate, and it tasted as
sweet as honey in my mouth.'
(EZEKIEL 3:3)

'Eat up!' Parents will have said this many times to their children as they were growing up. Despite all protests, we press our demands, because we know that (no matter what they feel at that moment) they need it, and without it will become weak and will even die. This obvious truth has a spiritual parallel. Just as we need food to live physically, so we need food to live spiritually. Without a regular diet of spiritual food – especially God's word – we will never grow up, but rather will remain weak and sickly.

This food of God's word is described as milk. Peter says, 'Like newborn babies, crave pure spiritual milk, so that by it you may grow up in your salvation, now that you have tasted that the Lord is good, (1 Peter 2:2–3). Just as babies need milk to grow and become strong, so the Bible helps us grow up spiritually.

But just as babies are weaned and move on to solids, so we too need to move on. Hebrews challenges its readers to go on to the 'solid food' of God's word (Hebrews 5:13–14). The writer was sad that so many were not growing up spiritually. He wanted them to start 'getting their teeth into' God's truth; to 'chew it over' and take it in and make it part of themselves. That's what would make them grow up and be useful to God in the world. (So don't give up when you get to the 'more chewy bits' of the Bible. It's as we 'chew it over' that God's Spirit begins to speak to us through it.)

But perhaps one of the best pictures of the Bible is of it as honey. Whenever Martin feels under the weather, he loves a slice of bread and honey. It just cheers him up no end! And that's just what God promises his word is like: it is a sheer delight, to cheer us up, as we grasp it, take it in and grow. Enjoy it for yourself today, and be blessed!

'Blessed is the man who fears the LORD,
who finds great delight in his commands.'
(PSALM 112:1)

JULY 23

The God who rolls his sleeves up

He saw that there was no-one, he was appalled that there was no-one to intervene; so his own arm worked salvation for him.
(ISAIAH 59:16)

'Don't get involved!' How many times have you heard those words? They certainly seem to be the watchword of so many today. But thankfully God isn't like that. God loves to get involved! He isn't some 'remote creator' who stands far off; rather, he 'rolls his sleeves up' to intervene in his world, both in the lives of individuals and the affairs of nations, working towards his end purpose that 'the earth will be filled with the knowledge of the glory of the LORD, as the waters cover the sea' (Habakkuk 2:14).

The Bible sometimes likens God to a potter, carefully shaping the clay on his wheel. The clay is us and our lives, which means that we are both secure in his hands, but also that he can do with us as he pleases! Thankfully, he knows what he is doing and we can trust his intervention completely. As Isaiah confidently prayed, 'Yet, O LORD, you are our Father. We are the clay, you are the potter; we are all the work of your hand' (Isaiah 64:8). When we feel the fingers of the potter going into our lives, we need not fear. God is our Father and we can be confident that 'in all things God works for the good of those who love him' (Romans 8:28), as so many of the stories in the Bible bring home to us again and again.

So if you are sensing God's fingers pressing into the clay of your life at this time, don't be fearful! Perhaps you have been asking him to do it – perhaps you haven't! But, either way, you can trust him. He really is only working for your good. Look back and remember the times that he has rolled up his sleeves and intervened in the past on your behalf; as you do, let it help you to look forward in trusting anticipation of his involvement once again. Remember: his sleeves are only ever rolled up for good for his children!

Since ancient times no-one has heard, no ear has perceived, no eye has seen any God besides you, who acts on behalf of those who wait for him.
(ISAIAH 64:4)

JULY 24

Don't blame-shift!

'I will frown on you no longer, for I am merciful,' declares the
LORD, 'I will not be angry for ever.
Only acknowledge your guilt.'
(JEREMIAH 3:12–13)

Blame-shifting is as old as the hills, going way back to Adam and Eve. When God challenged Adam about his disobedience, he immediately blamed it on his wife. 'The woman you put here with me – she gave me some fruit from the tree, and I ate it' (Genesis 3:12). But Eve was ready with her excuses too. 'The serpent deceived me, and I ate' (Genesis 3:13). (And if the story were being retold today, no doubt the serpent's psychiatrist would tell him it wasn't his fault either, but was due to a traumatic experience when he was younger!)

But Adam and Eve weren't the last; lots of stories reveal people who tried to blame-shift. Abraham blamed the reputation of the local area for lying about his wife; Aaron blamed the people for leading him into idolatry; Saul blamed his soldiers' fear for his disobedience to Samuel's command; Martha blamed Jesus for the death of Lazarus by failing to arrive on time. Blame-shifting certainly seems to be a characteristic of the fallen human race, doesn't it?

But, why do we do it? What is it in us that finds it so hard to 'come clean' and accept responsibility? Sometimes it is because of pride. We are too proud to admit that we made a mistake; or we want to maintain a good appearance and have people think well of us. Sometimes it is because of fear, perhaps from our circumstances or from worrying about the consequences of our sin or even whether God will forgive us for it. But through it all there is the deceitfulness of sin: the hope that 'it will be all right', which is quickly replaced by the discovery that it wasn't all right after all (which we probably suspected all along, but somehow thought it might be different this time!).

Blame-shifting is the one thing that puts us outside the grace of God; for that grace can be found only where people are prepared to own up. Don't blame-shift today; just 'come clean'!

O LORD, we acknowledge our wickedness and the guilt of our fathers;
we have indeed sinned against you.
(JEREMIAH 14:20)

JULY 25

Understanding God's grace

'O LORD, is this not what I said when I was still at home?
That is why I was so quick to flee to Tarshish. I knew that you
are a gracious and compassionate God, slow to anger and
abounding in love, a God who relents from sending calamity.
Now, O LORD, take away my life,
for it is better for me to die than to live.'
(JONAH 4:2–3)

Grace is something that we all appreciate – as long as it's directed towards us. But when grace is shown towards others, our instinctive reaction is to cry, 'That's not fair!' rather than, 'Isn't that great!' Which is the story of Jonah.

Jonah was someone who appreciated God's grace – as long as it was for him and his fellow Israelites. But what he couldn't cope with was the thought of God blessing others. At the time when Amos and Hosea were prophesying to Israel that, unless they repented, judgment would come from Assyria, God called Jonah to go to Nineveh, Assyria's capital, to call them to repent too. But rather than going east, Jonah headed west; not because he was afraid, but because he had a sneaky suspicion that God might just be gracious and the Assyrians might actually repent, which was the last thing he wanted. After a detour via the belly of a great fish, where he at last grasped that 'salvation comes from the LORD' (Jonah 2:9), Jonah eventually went to Nineveh and proclaimed his message. To his surprise (and displeasure!) they repented. And that's when he prayed the words of our opening verses today.

The problem was, Jonah didn't want Nineveh saved; he wanted it destroyed. But God hadn't gone along with Jonah's plan, because God isn't like that. Deep down, Jonah knew this – and didn't like it! So much so, he thought he'd be better off dead. His self-pity and self-concern blinded him to what God is really like. But through a simple withering vine God showed him that if Jonah could be upset about that, then God could certainly be concerned about a perishing people.

When we complain about God's grace, it's generally because we are small-minded and mean-hearted. Thankfully God isn't like that; so ask him for more of his gracious heart today.

Grace to you and peace from God our Father and the Lord Jesus Christ.
(PHILEMON 3)

JULY 26

Thirsty for God

*As a deer longs for flowing streams, so my soul longs for you,
O God. My soul thirsts for God, for the living God.*
(PSALM 42:1–2, NRSV)

Ever felt thirsty? Really thirsty? Perhaps after a stint of hard work in the garden or after a lazy relax by the holiday pool? At such moments, there's nothing we wouldn't do for a long, refreshing, cold drink. My, how it does you good! And God says: that's how I want you to be with me. To be thirsty for me; and then to drink of me until you're satisfied and you know it's done you good.

That's the sort of thirst reflected in our verses today. The psalmist was desperately thirsty for God; he wanted him, longed for him more than anything else; and there was something within him that wouldn't be satisfied until he'd drunk his fill. But of course, such thirst for God can only grow if we've settled our priorities. It goes without saying that there are other important things in life – family, work, friends; but the challenge is: what is *the* most important thing to us? Get that right, and everything else follows. As Jesus put it, 'Seek first God's kingdom and his righteousness, and all these things will be given you as well' (Matthew 6:33).

God is looking for us to abandon our lives to him, to come to the point where we say, '*You* are the most important thing in life to me! You are what I am most thirsty for. Everything else is insignificant in comparison to you.' This means being ready to let go of things that have taken up the most precious places in our hearts, and becoming 'detached from other attachments, whether they are addictive, habitual, enslaving or just plain fascinating' (James Houston). Or, to put that in a prayer of a former time: 'Take from us, O God, the care of worldly vanities; make us content with necessaries' (Edmund Grindal, 1519–83, Chaplain to King Edward VI and Archbishop of Canterbury).

Knowing God's intimate presence begins as we start to be thirsty for it and thirsty for him. What are you thirsty – truly thirsty – for today?

*God, you are my God. I search for you. I thirst for you like someone
in a dry, empty land where there is no water.*
(PSALM 63:1, NCV)

JULY 27

The help of hardship

'Endure hardship as discipline; God is treating you as sons.'
(HEBREWS 12:7)

When Mike visits India he often sees Hindu 'holy men'. Generally dirty and dishevelled, they go out of their way to experience hardship or pain, believing that there is great spiritual benefit in doing so. For a Christian, the sight of them is dreadfully sad, for they are trying to gain by their own efforts what Christ alone on the cross won for us – something that none of us can add to or substitute for.

But actually, some Christians back home aren't much different. They too believe that there is something particularly spiritual about hardship, to the point that they actually go out of their way looking for it. Others believe that there is more blessing in always choosing the hard way over the easy way. But actually, only fools go out of their way to look for hardship! And there is certainly nothing in the Bible that encourages us to do so. Indeed, following such a path shows we have failed to understand something about both the grace of God and the work of Christ.

Yet while it is both foolish and worthless to go looking for hardship, the Bible does tell us that hardship often comes our way – especially when we are seeking to follow Christ. So, when it does come, it shouldn't surprise us. Indeed, if we embrace it with Christ's help, it can even be turned, Paul tells us in Romans 8, to our good. For hardship may help us, through serving as God's loving discipline, leading to a deeper revelation of him, strengthening our character, or bringing an opportunity for his grace to be experienced.

You may be experiencing some hardship at this time and may even be wondering what God is doing. What you can be sure of is this: it is all for your good and not for your harm. So tell him today that you trust him today and that you want to let him do his work in you through the help of hardship. The Bible promises that it *will* turn out for your good!

'The suffering you sent was good for me, for it taught me
to pay attention to your principles.'
(PSALM 119:71, NLT)

JULY 28

Unanswered prayer (1)

'Why do you complain to him that he answers none of man's words? For God does speak – now one way, now another – though man may not perceive it.'
(JOB 33:13–14)

'Why didn't God answer my prayer?' is probably a question that we have all asked at some time or other. But actually, God *always* answers. Sometimes his answer is 'yes'; sometimes, 'no'; and sometimes, 'wait'. He always answers; it's just that we don't always understand – or like! – the answer that he gives. But if we are going to grow in our relationship with him, then it's important we understand *why* he doesn't always answer as we had hoped.

First, prayer sometimes isn't answered as we had hoped because God knows more than us; and it's this knowledge that prevents him from answering. If he did, the outcome might be unhelpful or even disastrous. So God gave Job neither physical relief nor answers to his questions because wider issues were involved and Job had bigger lessons to learn. A quick answer would have 'cut the corners' too much!

Second, prayer sometimes isn't answered as we had hoped, not because what we asked for was wrong, but because the timing wasn't right. When Mary and Martha asked Jesus to come and heal their brother Lazarus, Jesus didn't respond immediately but rather delayed his journey, because he knew that God had a greater miracle in store, which would never have happened had he rushed to answer. Only later on did the sisters see God's bigger purpose. It's at such times, when God's answer is, 'Wait', that we need to trust him, for his timing is always perfect.

Third, prayer sometimes isn't answered as we had hoped because we simply don't understand God's bigger plan. It was only at the end of thirteen years, during which things kept constantly 'going wrong' for him, that Joseph finally saw what God had been doing and why he had not rescued him earlier: it was so that God's people could be brought to safety and avoid the famine in Canaan.

Perhaps you feel that God does not seem to be answering your prayer at this time. If so, keep trusting him. There *will* be a good reason – you'll see!

But as for me, I trust in you.
(PSALM 55:23)

July 29

Unanswered prayer (2)

Three times I begged the Lord to make this suffering go away.
But he replied, 'My kindness is all you need.
My power is strongest when you are weak.'
(2 Corinthians 12:8–9, CEV)

Let's continue with yesterday's theme and consider now some reasons from our side why prayer doesn't always seem to be answered.

First, because we sometimes ask for wrong things. Some requests are obviously wrong, if only we stopped and thought. We can't expect God to answer such requests, only those in line with his will. 'We can be confident that he will listen to us whenever we ask him for anything in line with his will' (1 John 5:14, NLT).

Second, because sometimes we ask for the right thing, but with wrong motives. 'When you ask, you do not receive, because you ask with wrong motives, that you may spend what you get on your pleasures' (James 4:3). Because God is far more interested in our hearts than anything else, he sometimes refuses our requests to help us see more important issues.

Third, because of lack of faith. When Jesus' disciples asked why they couldn't cast out a demon, he replied, 'You didn't have enough faith' (Matthew 17:20, NLT).

Fourth, because of a lack of prayer. James wrote, 'You do not have, because you do not ask God' (James 4:2). We all know how much easier it is to talk about praying, or to promise to pray, than to actually do it!

Fifth, because of sin. Of course, if God were to wait until we were sinless before he could answer, he would wait a long time! But the harbouring of serious or ongoing sin inevitably hinders what he can do through us. 'If I had cherished sin in my heart, the Lord would not have listened' (Psalm 66:18).

Finally, because of our need to stay humble. We would probably become unbearable if all our prayers were answered every time. Why, God might even have to move sideways on his throne! Not having prayer answered sometimes, therefore, can help keep us humble and dependent on God, as Paul discovered.

If some of your prayers haven't been answered recently, why not ask the Holy Spirit to show you if any of these issues might be the cause.

God examine me and know my heart.
(Psalm 139:23, NCV)

JULY 30

Unanswered prayer (3)

'Since the first day you began to pray for understanding and to humble yourself before your God, your request has been heard in heaven. I have come in answer to your prayer. But for twenty-one days the spirit prince of the kingdom of Persia blocked my way.'
(DANIEL 10:12–13, NLT)

Let's look today at a third category of reasons why our prayers aren't always answered. These are to do with the devil.

From the day of his expulsion from heaven, Satan has constantly opposed God and his purposes. So when Jesus came to earth, Satan did all he could to oppose him: trying to kill him at birth, tempting him to disobey his Father, stirring up a lynch mob against him, inspiring Judas to betray him, and provoking the authorities to execute him. Because he opposes God and his purposes, he inevitably opposes God's people too in every way he can, both corporately and individually. So how should we respond to his opposition, especially when we sense he is hindering our prayers?

It is at such times that the Bible calls us to engage in 'spiritual warfare'. While some Christians turn this into binding and loosing all sorts of demons, the Bible's approach seems, perhaps surprisingly, to be much more 'down to earth'. It says that spiritual warfare involves such things as: *praying and fasting* as Daniel did for revelation (Daniel 10:1–19); *submitting to God* and seeing the devil flee as we do so (James 4:7); being *self-controlled and alert* for the devil prowls around looking for prey to devour (1 Peter 5:8–9); *recalling Christ's victory at the cross*, where Satan and all his hosts were stripped of their power (Colossians 2:13–15); *changing ways of thinking* which have become strongholds that need demolishing (2 Corinthians 10:3–5); *putting on 'the armour of God'* (Ephesians 6:10–18), not as a spiritual exercise just before battle, but as a lifestyle that prepares us for such times; *getting back to our first love*, as the seven churches in Revelation were called to do (Revelation 2:1–3:22).

Are there any of these expressions of spiritual warfare that you sense the Holy Spirit is reminding you that you have been neglecting? They may be the very thing that are hindering your prayers!

Surrender to God! Resist the devil, and he will run from you.
(JAMES 4:7, CEV)

JULY 31

From mountaintop to valley

*'I have had enough, LORD,' he said. 'Take my life; I am no
better than my ancestors.' Then he lay down under the tree
and fell asleep.*
(1 KINGS 19:4–5)

Admitting you feel depressed almost seems a taboo among some
Christians. It's seen as a sign that you haven't trusted God enough (and if
you had, you wouldn't be feeling like this). That sounds a nice theory; but
life isn't always that straightforward, is it? In fact, depression – that feeling
of deep sadness and an inability to do anything about it – was experienced
by many people in the Bible: David, Hagar, Job, Jonah, Joshua, Moses,
Naomi, Paul – all had their desperately low points. But perhaps one of the
best-known examples is Elijah.

Having challenged the prophets of Baal to a contest on Mount Carmel
to determine who was truly God, and their frantic efforts having had no
effect, Elijah had built his altar to Yahweh, prayed to him, and seen fire
fall from heaven. The people had repented, the false prophets had been
killed and King Ahab had been challenged. Elijah's emotions were now
running high. But he hadn't counted on the wicked Queen Jezebel, whose
threats suddenly threw him into the valley of despair. He fled for his life
into the desert, where he sat down under a tree and, in the words of our
opening verses, prayed to die.

This story illustrates how there is often no rational explanation for
depression. Elijah had just seen God's power demonstrated in an amazing
way; but now, after just one threat, he plummets into the depth of
despondency. But God doesn't rebuke him for this; and nor will he
rebuke us. In fact, God deals with him in a tremendously tender way,
giving him sleep, getting him to eat properly, encouraging him to express
his feelings, meeting with him gently, getting him to do something
practical, giving him a friend and successor in Elisha, reassuring him he is
not alone – then sending him back to get on with life.

God didn't rebuke Elijah for feeling low; he simply drew him out of
it step by step. And God can do the same for us.

*To all who mourn in Israel, he will give beauty for ashes,
joy instead of mourning, praise instead of despair.*
(ISAIAH 61:3, NLT)

AUGUST 1

The God who changes his mind

'If at any time I announce that a nation or kingdom is to be uprooted, torn down and destroyed, and if that nation I warned repents of its evil, then I will relent and not inflict on it the disaster I had planned.'
(JEREMIAH 18:7–8)

Let's face it: some things in life are a mystery. Most men put women into that category – and most women put men there too! But when it comes to God, everything is a mystery; not least, why he seems prepared to 'change his mind' when people pray.

In saying that God sometimes changes his mind, the Bible doesn't mean that he is unreliable or that we can't take him at his word. He is always trustworthy and true. But in order to maintain that 'truth' towards his character and purposes, there are times when he changes his declared plan – though not because we have somehow 'won him over' (like a nagging child overcoming its parents 'No'). This is not about *our overcoming his reluctance*; it is about *his winning our hearts*. God changes his mind when we grasp his bigger purposes and appeal to him to do what he always wanted to do all along – to do good and to save people!

That's what Jeremiah discovered when, although he had been proclaiming the certainty of judgment, he declared God's promise in our opening verses, reflecting the depths of God's heart in wanting sinners to repent and be saved. It's what Amos discovered when his vision of God's coming judgment led him to cry out, 'Sovereign LORD, I beg you, stop! How can Jacob survive? He is so small!' So the LORD relented. "This will not happen either," the Sovereign LORD said' (Amos 7:5–6). It's what Jonah discovered when he announced the impending destruction of Nineveh but discovered that 'when God saw what they did and how they turned from their evil ways, he had compassion and did not bring upon them the destruction he had threatened' (Jonah 3:10).

Is there some situation that you would like to see changed? Then ask God! Who knows whether he may not change his mind if you will 'stand in the gap' and pray that more of his graciousness might be seen.

'I searched for someone to stand in the gap in the wall . . .'
(EZEKIEL 22:30, NLT)

AUGUST 2

Straight talks with God

O LORD, you deceived me, and I was deceived;
you overpowered me and prevailed.
(JEREMIAH 20:7)

Jeremiah exercised a difficult ministry. A prophet for some forty years leading up to Babylon's invasion of Judah in 586 BC, his message – that Jerusalem would be destroyed unless God's people repented – was bitterly opposed. He had nowhere to turn but to God. In what have been called his 'Confessions' (though they might be better described as 'Straight talks with God'), Jeremiah laid bare his feelings. He was a man of strong emotions: he wept much, despaired of finding any comfort, cursed the day he was born, prayed for judgment upon his opponents, and frequently wanted to give up his ministry but couldn't. Perhaps there have been days when you felt like that too!

On one occasion, having been beaten and put into the stocks because of his prophecies, he complained bitterly to God, even accusing him of deceiving him, as in our opening verse. These are strong words indeed! And then he went on to complain that if he tried to keep quiet, 'his word is in my heart like a fire, a fire shut up in my bones. I am weary of holding it in; indeed, I cannot' (Jeremiah 20:9). What he was saying was, 'This isn't fair God! I didn't sign up for all this; but I can't get out of it now! You've deceived me!' But this was then followed by a surge of faith: 'But the LORD is with me like a mighty warrior; so my persecutors will stumble and not prevail' (Jeremiah 20:11). Then no sooner has he declared this than he curses the day he was born!

But isn't this so true to life? Don't our feelings and emotions go up and down in stressful times? But Jeremiah's example highlights two important things. First, he knew he could be utterly honest with God, bringing all his emotions, questions and frustrations before him. Second, his *decisions* weren't governed by his *emotions*. What he *did* and what he *felt like doing* weren't necessarily the same. Despite everything he was experiencing, he 'got things off his chest' and then pressed on with doing God's work.

Actually, that's quite a good policy to follow. Try it yourself today and see.

'If you repent, I will restore you that you may serve me.'
(JEREMIAH 15:19)

AUGUST 3

Who cares?

Cast all your anxiety on him because he cares for you.
(1 PETER 5:7)

'Who cares?' The question sums up so much of the prevailing attitude in society today. 'As long as I am OK, who cares?' Thankfully, the Bible tells us that *God* cares! In fact, there is *nothing* that he doesn't care about, and *no one* that he doesn't care for.

Jesus' disciples were starting to get anxious one day about the basic necessities of life: things like food and clothing. In many ways, this was quite understandable, for they had left their homes, families and jobs to follow him; and that meant no pay cheque at the end of the week! Either God now provided – or they were sunk! Well, on this particular day they were obviously having a bad time of it; worry seems to have got on top of them (something we can no doubt identify with!).

Jesus dealt with their worries in a devastatingly simple way. He told them to look at the birds. 'They do not sow or reap or store away in barns, and yet your heavenly Father feeds them. Are you not much more valuable than they?' (Matthew 6:26). 'Of course you are,' was his point. 'Oh, and look at the flowers and grass too,' he went on to say. If God cares about all these things, don't you think he might just care about you?

Of course, the reality is that anxieties do come our way; whether it's cares about our health, our family, our work, our future. Experiencing such cares coming to our life isn't sinful; it's what we do with them that counts! That's why our text today is so powerful. Peter tells us to 'cast' (the word means 'throw' or 'hurl') all our cares, all our anxiety on to God. Why? Because he cares for us! And he cares like no one else on earth or in heaven.

When problems come, we can't always just deal them; but what we can do is to 'hurl' the cares and anxiety that comes with them on to God, assured of his promise that, as we do so, he *will* sustain us.

> *Cast your cares on the LORD and he will sustain you;*
> *he will never let the righteous fall.*
> (PSALM 55:22)

AUGUST 4

The God who hears

How gracious he will be when you cry for help! As soon as he hears, he will answer you.
(ISAIAH 30:19)

Mike remembers how, when he was younger, it was easy to get impatient with older folk who didn't hear what you said first time. Now that he is getting older and is starting to miss things himself, he is suddenly very sympathetic! Not being able to hear is a real hindrance; things so easily get missed or misunderstood. But thankfully, we have a God who is neither deaf nor hard of hearing. He is the God who hears.

The Bible is full of testimony to the fact that God really does hear when we call out to him. Abraham became so convinced that God hears us that he called his first-born son 'Ishmael' ('God hears'). David's testimony was, 'I waited patiently for the LORD; he turned to me and heard my cry, (Psalm 40:1). Isaiah said, 'How gracious he will be when you cry for help! As soon as he hears, he will answer you' (Isaiah 30:19). The testimony of all these, and countless others, is that God is a God who hears.

In fact, in the Old Testament, 'not hearing' was seen as a characteristic of deaf and dumb idols and the false gods they represented. That's why Elijah taunted the prophets of Baal on Mount Carmel when their gods didn't answer. '"Shout louder!" he said. "Surely he is a god! Perhaps he is deep in thought, or busy, or travelling. Maybe he is sleeping and must be awakened." So they shouted louder and slashed themselves with swords and spears, as was their custom, until their blood flowed. Midday passed, and they continued their frantic prophesying until the time for the evening sacrifice. But there was no response, no-one answered, no-one paid attention' (1 Kings 18:27–29).

In contrast to this, the living God is the God who always hears, just as he did when Israel cried out to him in slavery 'and their cry for help because of their slavery went up to God. God heard their groaning and he remembered his covenant with Abraham, with Isaac and with Jacob' (Exodus 2:23–24).

Don't doubt today that God hears – and that God hears *you*

. . . he hears us.
(1 JOHN 5:14)

AUGUST 5

The God who can be trusted

He who dwells in the shelter of the Most High will rest in the shadow of the Almighty. I will say of the LORD, 'He is my refuge and my fortress, my God, in whom I trust.'
(PSALM 91:1–2)

Few of us go through life without facing difficulties: family worries, financial problems, unemployment, sickness, bereavement. Life in a fallen world throws up plenty of challenges. At such times we can do one of two things: we can either turn *against* God, blaming him for what happened; or we can turn *to* God, trusting him and claiming the promises of his word for our situation. That's certainly what the psalmist did who wrote Psalm 91, a wonderful testimony to how God can keep us safe through all the varied troubles of life.

In fact all the psalms are a rich source of God's promises for life's varied situations. Are we facing trouble? Then let us remember: 'The LORD hears his people when they call to him for help. He rescues them from all their troubles' (Psalm 34:17, NLT). Are we experiencing fear? Then let us remember: 'The LORD is my light and my salvation–whom shall I fear? The LORD is the stronghold of my life–of whom shall I be afraid?' (Psalm 27:1). Are we running out of our own strength or resources? Then let us remember: 'My flesh and my heart may fail, but God is the strength of my heart and my portion for ever' (Psalm 73:26). Are people working against us? Then let us remember: 'Though I walk in the midst of trouble, you preserve me against the wrath of my enemies; you stretch out your hand and your right hand delivers me' (Psalm 138:7, NRSV). Are we in a situation of danger? Then let us remember: '"Because he loves me," says the LORD, "I will rescue him; I will protect him, for he acknowledges my name. He will call upon me, and I will answer him; I will be with him in trouble, I will deliver him and honour him"' (Psalm 91:14–15).

Whatever your situation or need, God is the God who can be trusted in it. Claim his promise today!

'Call upon me in the day of trouble; I will deliver you, and you will honour me.'
(PSALM 50:15)

The path to forgiveness

I confess my sins; I am deeply sorry for what I have done.
(PSALM 38:18, NLT)

One of the most famous psalms in the Bible is Psalm 51, written after David's adultery with Bathsheba. In early Christian tradition it was used as a penitential psalm, since it provided a classic insight into how to find the path to forgiveness. What does it say?

First, begin with God. David began by focusing on God not himself, remembering that he is a God of 'mercy . . . unfailing love . . . great compassion' (v. 1). If we don't start here, our confession will be little more than a rehearsal of self-pity; but with this in place, we can press on with the harder bit of 'coming clean', sure that God will forgive us.

Second, confess the sin. David faced up to what he'd done, describing it as 'transgressions . . . iniquity . . . sin' (vv. 1–2). But as he reflected on his sinful action, he saw that the issue went far deeper. It wasn't just that he had *sinned*; it was that he was a *sinner*, and had been from his earliest days (vv. 5–7); so he couldn't even excuse it as a 'one-off'. Sin had been the story of his life!

Third, ask for forgiveness. Having confessed his sin, David called out for God to cleanse, wash and renew him (vv. 7–9). The Hebrew word 'cleanse' literally means to 'un-sin'. 'Oh God, get this sin out of me!' was his desperate cry.

Fourth, ask for a change of heart. David knew how all too easily he could go away and do the same thing again, unless God changed his heart. He therefore asked for a pure heart (so that he wouldn't want to do this again) and a steadfast spirit (so that he would have the strength to stay on the straight and narrow).

Finally, look to the future. David looked ahead, to having a testimony that he could share with others (v. 13), to being able to praise God once again (vv. 14–15), and to being able to walk more humbly with his God out of the whole experience (vv. 16-17). The devil loves nothing more than trying to get us to look back at our past sin and failings. But when God has forgiven it, it is forgiven!

These steps still work! For God is still the same. What do you need to do today?

'God, have mercy on me, a sinner.'
(LUKE 18:13)

AUGUST 7

Thankfulness for creation

O LORD, our Lord, how majestic is your name in all the earth!
You have set your glory above the heavens.
(PSALM 8:1)

Imagine the scenario: there was the psalmist, standing outside one evening, looking up at the stars. It was a perfectly clear night; and so, the more he looked, the more he saw. And the more he saw, the more gratitude arose in his heart towards God for his wonderful work of creation. And then, he went inside and wrote Psalm 8.

The psalm begins with the words 'For the director of music. According to gittith.' The reference to the director of music suggests that 'gittith' was probably a musical term. The Septuagint (the Greek translation of the Hebrew Old Testament) associates this word with the Hebrew for 'winepress'. So David was writing: 'A song of the winepress'. Was this a type of tune? Or was it to be sung in a certain way? Whichever it was, perhaps it arose from the overwhelming 'pressing down' that David felt within his heart as he stood, so small and insignificant, in God's vast universe. But David's wonder did not stop at the starlit sky; he saw beyond the glory of the stars to the glory of the God who had made them. Such splendour is so obvious, he wrote, that even children can see it and praise God; and their instinctive awe and praise silences those who have lost the ability to wonder at anything (v. 2).

But this wonderful creation did not just 'happen'; it was brought about by God himself, which is why David describes the heavens as 'the work of your fingers' and speaks of 'the moon and the stars which you have set in place' (v. 3). It didn't just 'happen'; *he* made it happen! He alone is 'the Maker of heaven and earth' (Psalm 124:8).

Because of all this, the Bible sometimes calls on creation itself to praise God for his creative work. In fact, Jesus once said that if *we* don't give praise to God, then 'the stones will cry out' (Luke 19:40) – which somehow puts us in our place! Don't let stones beat you today; thank God for his creation!

They raised their voices in prayer to God. 'Sovereign Lord,' they said, 'you made the heaven and the earth and the sea, and everything in them.'
(ACTS 4:24)

AUGUST 8

Companion, or friend?

'Our friend Lazarus . . .'
(JOHN 11:11)

No doubt all of us have at some time been on a journey where we found a travelling companion – someone with whom we shared life stories, or with whom we complained about the delays, or possibly with whom we even shared the gospel. A complete stranger can become, for a little while at least, a worthwhile travelling companion; but while it may have been enjoyable and helped to pass the hours, enduring friendship is unlikely to arise from it.

Thankfully, that is not how it is with Jesus! For Jesus is not merely some *companion* – someone who is simply 'there' with us on the journey. No! He is far more than that; he is our *friend.* This is what he underlined to his followers again and again. He told the Twelve that they were his *friends*; he spoke of Lazarus as his *friend*; he was known (disparagingly by his opponents) as 'a friend of the worst sort of sinners' (Luke 7:34, NLT); and he wants to be our friend too!

When Mike was young, he had a friend whose parents owned an ice-cream factory. During the school holidays, they would often go in to the factory to help out – and, of course, to get the occasional treat! How exciting it was to be drawn into such a business for a day, and all because of a friend! But what Jesus offers is far better than that. Through friendship with him, we are drawn not just into a business (though the Father indeed has a 'business'!) but into a family – a family that stretches into eternity!

Let's ensure we aren't settling for mere companionship with Jesus – someone with whom we merely pass the time of day or have the odd chat; someone with whom we share only the superficial things of life and then hurry on. Rather, let us respond to his promise that he wants to be our friend, sharing the heart and the secrets of the Father with us. Let us live with him today as our *friend.*

'I no longer call you servants, because a servant does not know his master's business. Instead, I have called you friends, for everything that I learned from my Father I have made known to you.'
(JOHN 15:15)

AUGUST 9

The God who catches us up

So Jacob was left alone, and a man wrestled with him till daybreak. When the man saw that he could not overpower him, he touched the socket of Jacob's hip so that his hip was wrenched as he wrestled with the man.
(GENESIS 32:24–25)

Every area of life has its 'rogues'; those who 'duck and dive', who seem to get away with anything. But while they may seem to do so for a while, God has a way of catching up with them. One such character was Jacob, a real rogue, who even cheated his own brother out of his birthright. But God caught up with him.

The first time he did so was when Jacob was deceived by Laban into marrying Leah rather than Rachel (thick wedding veils would help the trick!), even though he had served Laban seven years for Rachel. Another seven years' hard work for Rachel gave him plenty of time to realize that even the most slippery characters get their just deserts in the end! Yet through it all, God was still with him. His family increased, his flocks grew, and he became wealthy. But God hadn't finished with him yet.

He had had a special encounter with God in a dream some years earlier, in which he saw a stairway reaching up to heaven, with angels going up and down it and God standing at the top. He had discovered that day how very close God could be. But now he needed to learn something else: that God doesn't simply want to meet us; he wants to change us. This happened through wrestling with a man one night – and then discovering that 'the man' was God himself! He came out of the incident different, as 'a man with a limp', not just physically, but metaphorically; for he would never be the same again. And God changed his name from Jacob ('heel-grabber' or 'deceiver') to Israel ('he struggles with God'). He had been caught up with at last!

If you sense that God has been 'catching you up' in some area of your life, don't keep running; stop and let him wrestle it out of you. It will only be for your good!

As a man he struggled with God . . . He found him at Bethel and talked with him there – the LORD God Almighty.
(HOSEA 12:3-5)

AUGUST 10

The fear of the Lord

Always be zealous for the fear of the LORD. There is surely a future hope for you, and your hope will not be cut off.
(PROVERBS 23:17–18)

Fear is a powerful emotion. At its best, it can preserve our life; at its worst, it leads to lying and cheating, to death and destruction. But there is a fear in life which, if we understand it properly, always works for good, and never for harm. It is 'the fear of the Lord'.

By 'the fear of the Lord' the Bible doesn't mean 'being afraid' of him; indeed if we have trusted in Jesus, we have no need to fear for we have come to understand that 'there is now no condemnation for those who are in Christ Jesus' (Romans 8:1). Rather, what it means is that we should have a proper respect of and reverence for God and his commandments. Of course God wants us to be his friends! But we shouldn't reduce that to the mere level of 'being pals' that leads us to treat him lightly or with no sense of 'healthy respect'. True fear of God is about remembering who God truly is, and living in the light of that.

As we do so, a whole number of blessings follow, the Bible promises. In fact, in the book of Proverbs alone we are told that 'the fear of the LORD is the beginning of knowledge' (1:7); that 'the fear of the LORD adds length to life' (Proverbs 10:27); that 'the fear of the LORD is a fountain of life, turning a man from the snares of death' (14:27); that 'the fear of the LORD teaches a man wisdom' (15:33); that 'through the fear of the LORD a man avoids evil' (16:6); that 'the fear of the LORD leads to life: then one rests content, untouched by trouble' (19:23); that 'the fear of the LORD bring wealth and honour and life' (22:4). Little wonder then that the writer urges us to 'always be zealous for the fear of the LORD' (23:17).

Don't be afraid of God today; but do have a healthy respect for him and his word. If you do, it will go well with you!

But the eyes of the LORD are on those who fear him, on those whose hope is in his unfailing love.
(PSALM 33:18)

AUGUST 11

Me, me, me . . .

*Not to us, O LORD, not to us but to your name be the glory,
because of your love and faithfulness.*
(PSALM 115:1)

Me, me, me . . . That sums up so much about Western society today: it is utterly 'me' orientated. Just look at the world of advertising: most of it is about how 'I' can feel better, how 'I' can look better, how 'I' can be thought of better by others. Or consider people's attitudes: 'I' have a right to this or that; 'I' have a right to sue someone else; 'I' have a right to certain luxuries in life. Me, me, me . . .

The trouble is, this so easily spills over into our spiritual life. Consider, for example, some of our modern hymns and songs (many of which, we hasten to say, we love!). So many of them focus on 'me'; on how *I* feel in God's presence; on how *I* need God's love; on how *I* respond to Jesus – rather than being God-focused. Worship then so easily becomes about 'me' and not about him at all.

And the same can be true of our praying. It's so easy to rush into God's presence thinking only of ourselves and our requests – and then wonder why we didn't 'break through' to God but came away feeling empty. We went looking for God as the divine 'Father Christmas', and were surprised to find he was not at home that day. What a contrast this is to how Jesus taught us to begin our praying: 'Our Father in heaven . . .' Real prayer begins with the Father, not with me, me, me . . .

So, when praying today, don't start with 'me'; start with 'him'. It will put things wonderfully in perspective. And if your thoughts wander back to yourself all too soon, then take hold of them; 'take captive every thought to make it obedient to Christ' (2 Corinthians 10:5); for focusing on God, on his character and nature, rather than on our own sin or needs, is what transforms our praying.

*'If anyone would come after me, he must deny himself and take up his cross
and follow me. For whoever wants to save his life will lose it, but whoever
loses his life for me will find it. What good will it be for a man
if he gains the whole world, yet forfeits his soul?'*
(MATTHEW 16:24–26)

AUGUST 12

Where are you God?

The LORD himself goes before you and will be with you;
he will never leave you nor forsake you.
(DEUTERONOMY 31:8)

'Where are you God?' Ever found yourself thinking like that? Perhaps through some crisis bursting into your life, or through some ongoing situation that steadily wearied you? And now, it seems like God is a million miles away and your prayers just seem to hit the ceiling and bounce back again. The God you have known, the God whose promises you have always trusted, seems so very distant.

If you have felt like this, be encouraged that there were people in the Bible who felt the same – and who came through it! David, for example, knew what it was to enjoy God's intimate presence; but he also knew times when God seemed so far away; so far away that he once wrote, 'My God, my God, why have you forsaken me? Why are you so far from saving me, so far from the words of my groaning? O my God, I cry out by day, but you do not answer, by night, and am not silent' (Psalm 22:1–2).

It is at such dark times that we need to trust God's promises, rather than our feelings (which can be so unreliable). This is actually what David went on to do in the psalm. For what immediately follows his doubts is the word, 'Yet . . .'. And as he starts to go over all the 'yets' of life – things like God's faithfulness to his people over generations, his answering of their prayers, his care of David since his birth – he suddenly finds that he has things to praise God for, no matter what might be happening at that moment. And as he sets his eyes on the King who is still on his throne, his perspective began to change and his spirits began to lift, even in the midst of his situation.

If God seems far away today, focus on *his* promises rather than *your* feelings. Look back over the 'yets' of life and remember all he has done thus far. Above all, remember his promises that he will *never* leave you – not matter what you feel!

'So do not fear, for I am with you; do not be dismayed, for I am your God.'
(ISAIAH 41:10)

August 13

The challenge of suffering

*Why is my pain unending and my wound
grievous and incurable?*
(Jeremiah 15:18)

Let's face it, there is a lot of suffering in life; and people (generally those who spend most of their lives saying they don't believe in God) are quick to blame God for it. But actually, the main reason for suffering is – us! So often it is the direct result of our own *actions* (like smoking leading to lung cancer), *emotions* (like anger leading to violence), *selfish passions* (like lust leading to adultery), *stupidity* (like drinking and driving), or *lifestyle* (like using fossil fuels which affect global weather patterns). And then we turn round and blame God for the things that *we* have done! But having said all that, some suffering seems quite inexplicable and unfair: earthquakes, disease, freak accidents. And these often cause people to ask God, 'Why?'

The Bible tells us that, while all suffering is rooted, ultimately, in human sin that has invaded both the very fabric of our life and creation itself, God does not stand indifferent to it: he comes and strengthens us in it, identifies with us in it through his own Son's suffering on the cross, and promises to rid the world of it when Jesus returns at the end of human history.

Through all our sufferings, the Bible encourages us to keep focused on him and to be open to receive the grace and strength that he has promised to those who call on him. As the psalmist writes, 'Cast your cares on the Lord and he will sustain you' (Psalm 55:22); 'My comfort in my suffering is this: Your promise preserves my life' (Psalm 119:50). And with hindsight we can often look back and see that suffering actually brought some good. King Hezekiah suffered greatly with his illness; but at the end of it all he could look back and say, 'Surely it was for my benefit that I suffered such anguish' (Isaiah 38:17).

When we have asked all our questions and expressed all our frustration and anger, what better can we do but say, 'God I will continue to trust you; for life is better with you than without you'.

*Why are you downcast, O my soul? Why so disturbed within me? Put your
hope in God, for I will yet praise him, my Saviour and my God.*
(Psalm 42:11)

AUGUST 14

The friend who sticks by us

. . . there is a friend who sticks closer than a brother.
(PROVERBS 18:24)

Friendship means different things to different people: from deep commitment to casual acquaintanceship; from fun to formality; from confidante to companion – all of us have different ideas and expectations of what 'friendship' means.

But Jesus' friendship with us is not one thing to one person and something different to another. Whatever our human experiences and expectations (or lack of them!), the Bible promises us that Jesus' friendship is solid and secure, unchanging from one day to the next – a friendship that 'sticks by us' come what may.

Jesus sticks by us, no matter how we might let him down. He will never leave us, never let us down – even when we have failed him, as Peter discovered. Three times Peter vehemently denied Jesus at the end; but Jesus forgave him and, to wipe out that three-fold denial, gave him a three-fold commission after the resurrection to care for his sheep. This friend sticks by us, even when we do not do stick by him.

Jesus sticks by us, even when others don't. He knows what it is to be deserted by friends, for they all left him in Gethsemane as the soldiers came to arrest him, fleeing for their lives; but he will never do that to us. Paul discovered this for himself one day. He recounts to Timothy of how, when on trial, 'no-one came to my support, but everyone deserted me . . . But the Lord stood at my side and gave me strength' (2 Timothy 4:16–17).

Jesus sticks by us, no matter what we might be facing. Whatever the issue, Jesus has been through it – and has come out on the other side, victorious. He faced temptation, weariness, misunderstanding, false accusation, rejection – that's why he understands it and can stick by us and help us as we walk through it.

Whatever we are facing at this time, Jesus our friend has promised to 'stick by us', come what may. Through his Spirit he will be with us and will help us face whatever today might bring.

I will never leave you nor forsake you.
(JOSHUA 1:5)

Prayer changes people

Satan's angel did his best to get me down; what he did in fact was push me to my knees. No danger then of walking around high and mighty! At first I didn't think of it as a gift, and begged God to remove it. Three times I did that, and then he told me, 'My grace is enough; it's all you need.'
(2 CORINTHIANS 12:7–9, THE MESSAGE)

'Prayer changes things,' it is often said – and it's true! But just as true is the fact that prayer also changes *people*. In fact, the change in people is often far more significant. In the Bible, when people's prayers didn't seem to be answered, it was often because God was working some change in *them* rather than in what they were praying about. Once *they* were changed, anything could happen!

The Bible contains many examples of people who were changed as they prayed: Jacob, whose life was so completely changed as he wrestled with God that he was given a new name and left with a limp (Genesis 32:24–32); Hannah, whose deep sadness of spirit at her barrenness was changed as she persisted in prayer (1 Samuel 1:3–2:1); Job, whose self-righteousness was knocked out of him through suffering until he understood his rightful position before God (Job 42:1–6); Jonah, whose attitude to sinners was changed to become more like God's own attitude (Jonah 4:1–11); Zechariah, whose unbelief at the promise of answered prayer had to be borne through dumbness until his barren wife bore him a son (Luke 1:5–20,57–64); Stephen, whose attitude to his persecutors was miraculously changed as he prayed (Acts 7:59–60); Peter, whose attitude to Gentiles, so long despised by him, was transformed as he encountered God in a vision (Acts 10:9–48); Paul, whose attitude to weakness changed when God didn't remove his problem but instead gave him his grace to go through it (2 Corinthians 12:7–10).

All of these bear witness to the fact that prayer changed, not just their circumstances, but *them*. Hearts were softened, preconceptions challenged, attitudes changed and unbelief dealt with. If you have been praying about something that hasn't happened yet, stop and ask God whether it is because there is some change that he is looking for in you first.

I heard about you from others; now I have seen you with my own eyes.
(JOB 42:5, CEV)

Upside-down or right way up?

'These people who have been turning the world upside down
have come here also.'
(ACTS 17:6, NRSV)

Martin recalls once watching ducks on the River Thames. Most of them were paddling upstream against the flow. They were huffing and puffing away (or whatever it is that ducks do!), making very heavy weather of it all, expending a lot of energy but making little progress. However, some of the ducks were 'going with the flow' of the river. They were paddling, just like the others, but in a natural and easy way. And, not surprisingly, they were the ones making progress and not getting worn out. And Martin thought to himself: which ducks are paddling the way God intended? The ones paddling downstream, of course; the ones 'going with the flow' of the river. How strange, therefore, that we humans at times don't do the same!

As human beings – the crown of God's creation – we have been designed to live for God. His intention has always been that we should 'go with the flow' of his river, that is his Spirit, whom Jesus described as 'streams of living water' (John 7:38); for as we do, we learn from him 'the unforced rhythms of grace' (Matthew 11:29, The Message).

Still today, as in the book of Acts, the world can think that Christians have got everything upside-down and back-to-front; that we are like ducks paddling the wrong way. Not at all! The Christian way is the right way up, the one 'going with the flow' of God's life. It's the people of the world that are upside down and are struggling against the current. So we don't need to envy what they have or what they do; it's all destined to perish one day, for it's all heading in the wrong direction.

Don't be embarrassed about going with God's flow today!

'Are you tired? Worn out? Burned out on religion? Come to me. Get away
with me and you'll recover your life. I'll show you how to take a real rest.
Walk with me and work with me – watch how I do it. Learn the unforced
rhythms of grace. I won't lay anything heavy or ill-fitting on you. Keep
company with me and you'll learn to live freely and lightly.'
(MATTHEW 11:28–30, THE MESSAGE)

The Lord and giver of life

'Naked I came from my mother's womb, and naked I shall depart. The LORD gave and the LORD has taken away; may the name of the LORD be praised.'
(JOB 1:21)

This prayer of Job's was an amazing prayer indeed. He had just been through a whole string of disasters: enemies had stolen his livestock and killed his servants; lightning had struck his flocks; more enemies had stolen his camels and killed more of his servants; and now, the crowning disaster: his children had been killed in a freak accident as a tornado hit the house they were in. But despite all this, Job fell to the ground in worship and prayed the words of our opening verse today.

What enabled him to do this? It was a profound sense that God was indeed 'the Lord and giver of life', to use a phrase found in many prayer books. He knew that it was within God's sovereign power to give life; later he will say, 'The Spirit of God has made me; the breath of the Almighty gives me life' (Job 33:4). But he also knew that it lay within that same God's power to take away life. And it is when we can trust that he does both with nothing but loving intent that we can rest secure in him.

The Bible reassures us that God knows the number of our days and it invites us to rest secure in him because of that. Our end cannot come too early, and nor can it come too late! So we are certainly meant to live *in the light of it*, but not *in the fear of it*! That's why David said, 'Show me, O LORD, my life's end and the number of my days; let me know how fleeting is my life . . . But now, Lord, what do I look for? My hope is in you' (Psalm 39:4,7).

Today, don't live in the fear of life's end; live in the light of it. For your loving Father has promised to be with you.

How do you know what will happen tomorrow? For your life is like a morning fog – it's here a little while, then it's gone. What you ought to say is, 'If the Lord wants us to, we will live and do this or that.'
(JAMES 4:14–15, NLT)

AUGUST 18

Getting it off your chest

Finally, I confessed all my sins to you and stopped trying to hide them. I said to myself, 'I will confess my rebellion to the LORD.' And you forgave me! All my guilt is gone.
(PSALM 32:5, NLT)

Have you ever had to tell someone something that you didn't want to? You can often feel churned up inside until it's over; but once it's said, what a relief! And that's exactly how it is with us and God when it comes to 'getting it off our chest' where sin is concerned. But when we don't take God at his word and believe that he really wants to forgive our sin, but keep hiding it or explaining it away instead, it affects us in a number of ways.

First, unconfessed sin eats us up inside. The Bible, anticipating the insights of psychology, says that when we have unresolved conflicts or guilt, it eats away at us. In Psalm 32 David contrasts his experience of hiding his sin with the joy that followed once he confessed it. 'When I kept silent, my bones wasted away through my groaning all day long . . . my strength was sapped as in the heat of summer' (Psalm 32:3–4). But when he at last acknowledged his sin, our opening verse today says, he experienced freedom and relief at last.

Second, unconfessed sin hinders our prayers. It stops us praying boldly (for we are still hanging our heads in shame) and it stops God answering as he would like to. As Isaiah put it, 'Your iniquities have separated you from your God; your sins have hidden his face from you, so that he will not hear' (Isaiah 59:2); and as Jeremiah said, 'Your sins have deprived you of good' (Jeremiah 5:25). God doesn't look for us to be perfect before he can answer prayer; but he does expect us to be humble and quick to confess our sins when we get things wrong so that we clear the spiritual airwaves.

If you have things that you need to 'get off your chest', don't put it off any longer. Do it right now!

If I had cherished sin in my heart, the Lord would not have listened; but God has surely listened and heard my voice in prayer.
(PSALM 66:18–19)

AUGUST 19

Tested for purpose

*'But he knows the way that I take; when he has tested me,
I shall come forth as gold.'*
(JOB 23:10)

Ask most people what the story of Job is about, and they will answer, 'Suffering'. But while suffering is clearly a major theme, the real issue tackled is not suffering, but righteousness. One of Job's first questions is, 'How can a mortal be righteous before God?' (Job 9:2). He had lived all his life as righteously as he could – 'righteous and blameless' (12:4), 'pure and without sin . . . clean and free from guilt' (33:9) – and still things went badly for him. *Why?*

In the midst of all his struggles and complaints, we get glimpses of how he holds on in faith. Right at the beginning, having lost everything, his response is: 'Naked I came from my mother's womb, and naked I shall depart. The LORD gave and the LORD has taken away; may the name of the LORD be praised' (1:21). When afflicted by painful sores and encouraged by his wife to 'curse God and die' (2:9), he replies, 'Shall we accept good from God, and not trouble?' (2:10). And throughout the rest of the story, we see ongoing glimpses of his trust in God, even in his darkest days, such as when he says, 'Though he slay me, yet will I hope in him' (Job 13:15), and his ultimate declaration of trust: 'I know that my Redeemer lives, and that in the end he will stand upon the earth. And after my skin has been destroyed, yet in my flesh I will see God; I myself will see him with my own eyes – I, and not another' (19:25–27).

But these sufferings were not an end in themselves. They were designed to drive Job to God; to help Job see that you could be the most righteous person on earth, and you still wouldn't deserve anything from God! Only when he sees this, at the end of the story, does God restore him again.

The message of Job is that those who trust God in hard times keep their focus on him and, in so doing, on the one solution to their circumstances: the God who alone makes people righteous. Focus on him today!

The Lord knows how to rescue godly men from trials too small.
(2 PETER 2:9)

AUGUST 20

The Lord, my lover

His mouth is sweetness itself; he is altogether lovely.
This is my lover, this my friend.
(SONG OF SONGS 5:16)

Sadly, western Christianity has often reduced faith to little more than an intellectual acceptance of truth, and any thoughts of 'emotion' have been seen as excess or belonging to the fringe of Christian experience, rather than being right at the centre of it. But Christian faith is not about our heads being filled with knowledge, but our hearts being filled with love. When we come into God's presence, we should expect something to happen, to receive a fresh infilling of his love.

One whole book of the Bible is given over to the intimacy of love: Song of Songs (or, Song of Solomon). At its most fundamental level, it is a collection of love songs between a man and a woman, depicting love in all its power and wonder. But many have seen in it parallels to the love between Christ and his church, bringing home how very much he wants to be not just our Saviour and our Lord, but also our lover and our friend. Church leaders throughout the centuries have stressed the importance of receiving God's love. For example, St Francis of Assisi prayed: 'May the power of your love, Lord Christ, fiery and sweet, so absorb our hearts as to withdraw them from all that is under heaven; grant that we may be ready to die for love of your love, as you died for love of our love. Amen.'

What about you? Have you ever considered the Lord as your lover? A striking image, we grant; but one that brings home the depth of his love for you far more than the simple phrase 'the one who loves you'. Don't be afraid of being intimate with him; it opens the door for his love to flood in so that you too can say, 'My beloved is mine and I am his' (Song of Songs 2:16, KJV).

Like an apple tree among the trees of the forest is my lover among the young men. I delight to sit in his shade, and his fruit is sweet to my taste. He has taken me to the banquet hall, and his banner over me is love.
(SONG OF SONGS 2:3–4)

An attitude of gratitude

Give thanks to the God of heaven.
(PSALM 136:26)

Imagine how you would feel if someone said 'Thanks' but then left and did something that proved the opposite. Perhaps they had said, 'What a wonderful present! Thank you so much!', but then you discovered they had thrown it in the bin. How would you feel? Probably not too pleased! This really would be a case of 'actions speak louder than words'. But that's exactly how God must feel when we go to church, pray in our groups or pray alone, but then don't back up 'thanks' expressed in words by 'thanks' lived out in life.

What God wants from us is 'an attitude of gratitude': a life where we are constantly grateful, to God and to others; a life where our *first* response is gratitude rather than grumbling; a life where thankfulness permeates everything we are and do and pray; where appreciation – of God, his people and his world – is the very atmosphere we breathe.

But for most of us, this doesn't come instinctively. We can work at it, however! For example, we can ensure that our prayer times are filled with gratitude and aren't just 'shopping lists'. We can ensure we are grateful in the daily run of life – in the office, at college, in the shop, on the bus – looking constantly to use those little words 'thank you'. We can ensure that an attitude of gratitude pervades our conversations, so that people leave us feeling better rather than worse (and the workplace is a great place to do that, for if anywhere can be negative, it is often there). In short we can give ourselves to being a people of 'thanks-living' and not just 'thanks-giving'. As Matthew Henry, the eighteenth-century Bible commentator put it, 'Thanks-giving is good, but thanks-living is better.' And as George Herbert, the seventeenth-century poet and hymn writer, prayed, 'Thou that hast given me so much … Give me one thing more – a grateful heart.'

So, what about me? Do I model 'thanks-giving' or 'thanks-living' in my life? Do I seek to maintain 'an attitude of gratitude'? Am I a grumbler or am I grateful? A worrier or a worshipper? Today is as good a day as any to start doing things differently!

Whatever happens, keep thanking God.
(1 THESSALONIANS 5:18, CEV)

AUGUST 22

Does anyone know the way?

I am the way and the truth and the life. No-one comes to the Father except through me.
(JOHN 14:6)

Mike's teaching ministry often takes him to the Developing World. Wherever he goes, he can be sure of being pestered by street traders to buy bargains he does not need or by unofficial guides to visit sights he does not want to see. The thing about such guides, especially in some parts of the world, is that they often have no idea at all of where they are taking you, or even of how to direct you to get to somewhere. But since it is deemed rude not to know or not to tell, they will guide you anyway! The philosophy seems to be: going somewhere is better than going nowhere!

Going somewhere is better than going nowhere. That seems to sum up so much religion today. And since, we are constantly told, that 'all roads lead to God in the end, don't they?', then why worry anyway? 'None is wrong, and none is right; they are just different,' is the theme of the age. 'So, choose which ever feels best for you.'

But the Christian has to disagree with this post-modern view of life, for Jesus disagreed. In fact, Jesus was quite stark in this matter: he said that *he* was the only way to God. But how do we know he was right? Well, Christianity is unique among world religions, for it alone has its God coming to look for people, rather than the other way round. Jesus was no mere teacher, prophet, guru, or guide; he is God himself, God come to us in person. And that is why he, and he alone, is the only guide worth trusting, the only one who knows the true way to God, and whose promise to lead us into fellowship with the Father can be trusted.

Does anyone know the way? Yes! Jesus does! And he promises to lead on it all who will follow him. Today, stay close to him and you will most certainly find the Father.

'Only Jesus has the power to save! His name is the only one in all the world that can save anyone.'
(ACTS 4:12, CEV)

AUGUST 23

Just look!

From the time the world was created, people have seen the earth and sky and all that God made. They can clearly see his invisible qualities – his eternal power and his divine nature. So they have no excuse whatsoever for not knowing God.
(ROMANS 1:20, NLT)

Probably all of us have had occasions when we're looking for something we can't find, yet it's right before our eyes. 'It's there! Just look!' someone said. 'Oh yes!' was our humbled reply. Well, says the Bible, that's how it is with God. Just look! Open your eyes, look, and see. There before you, in creation, is ample evidence of his existence and ample provocation to thank him.

In Psalm 8 David describes how he looked at the skies and was overwhelmed with the beauty of God's creation. 'O LORD, our Lord, how majestic is your name in all the earth!' (Psalm 8:1, 9) he breathlessly exclaims at both the beginning and the end of the Psalm. But this psalm isn't in praise of 'nature' (an unbiblical concept at the best of times!); it is in praise of God. *He* is the one who brought all this into being. It didn't just 'happen'; *he* created it!

Sadly, so many of us have forgotten how to do what David did: to stop and marvel. Our technological age has robbed us of the joy of wonder. We are both old enough to remember the days of typewriters, carbon paper and duplicators. When computers came along we felt, 'Wow! This is amazing!' But nowadays we don't even pause to think about these wonderful machines without which we couldn't do our writing. Familiarity has caused us to lose a sense of wonder. And familiarity with God's creation can do the same. Because we feel we now understand so much about *how* it works, we forget to think about *why* it works or why it's there.

So, why not take some time today to do what David did: to 'just look'; to look at familiar surroundings and praise God for them; to pick up a leaf, to feel the breeze, to touch your skin, to look at the stars. God made them all! Don't let technology or familiarity rob you of the sense of wonder that leads to praise.

He is the Maker of all things.
(JEREMIAH 10:16)

Inclusive friendship

And you also were included in Christ when you heard the word
of truth, the gospel of your salvation.
(EPHESIANS 1:13)

Some human friendships can be so exclusive that they are unhealthy. They become 'cliques' that no one else can break into, 'inner circles' that have their little ways and secrets, 'groups' that care only for themselves, while others are left on the outside. Sadly, it's not just in society at large that this happens; we can even find it sometimes in the church – the very last place it should be.

God has always demonstrated his big, inclusive heart for people and has always told his people to do the same. Even in the Old Testament, where God had called a particular people, Israel, to be his 'treasured possession' (e.g. Exodus 19:5), their relationship with him was never meant to be exclusive; they were simply meant to be the vehicle of taking his inclusive friendship to others. So, while they were to maintain their distinctiveness as a people, provision was made within the Law, for example, for foreigners among them to enjoy the Sabbath rest and to participate in their festivals.

Jesus, not surprisingly, demonstrated the same sort of inclusive attitude. His heart is so big, and his kingdom is so big, that he made clear there is room for all. The Gospels show him welcoming men and women, Jew and Gentile, young and old, religious and 'sinner'. None was excluded! All were welcomed, all could find a place; and in the security of his friendship, they could start to discover God for themselves.

As friends of God, we too have the promise of being included. None is left on the outside of the circle; none is left on the fringe; none is not part of the group. In Christ, we are his friends, his children, part of his flock, part of his family – a family that stretches across heaven and earth, and through time and space, cutting through every barrier, whether geographical, racial or social. Today we can know we are included, just as he promised.

For there is no difference between Jew and Gentile–the same Lord is Lord of
all and richly blesses all who call on him.
(ROMANS 10:12)

Record transfer fee!

*For He rescued us from the domain of darkness, and transferred
us to the kingdom of His beloved Son, in whom we have
redemption, the forgiveness of sins.*
(COLOSSIANS 1:13–14, NASB)

Hardly a season goes by without another record transfer fee being paid for a soccer player. Sometimes it is because the player has shown great skill and is poached by a rival team for an offer that can't be refused; sometimes, it is because his manager feels he is performing at less than his best and wants to get rid of him; sometimes it is because a club is in financial difficulties and needs to raise some cash quickly. Whatever the reason, the sums paid to transfer soccer players these days can be quite astronomical – sums that (to people who aren't fans) can seem quite crazy. 'How can he be worth thirty million?' we may be left wondering.

Well, here is an amazing fact: God has paid a transfer fee for you that is far higher than the highest transfer fee ever paid! The Bible tells us that, when we put our trust in Christ, we were transferred – out of the old kingdom that we used to belong to (the kingdom of darkness) and into a new kingdom (the kingdom of Jesus). And the transfer fee that God paid to bring this about was quite unbelievable: it cost him the death of his own Son! It is 'in him' – in Jesus – that we have redemption, Paul says; it is Jesus who is our 'transfer fee'. The price has been paid – and we have been transferred. We belong to a new team and have a new manager.

And here is the good news: no one can ever transfer us back again! For there is no greater price to be paid than the one that has already been paid. What an assurance this gives us! We have changed teams – for ever! And if God has paid such a price to get us on his team, how could we possibly think that he would ever change his mind or ever let us go? Remember: if he's given us Jesus, he'll certainly give us everything else we need!

*He who did not spare his own Son, but gave him up for us all – how will
he not also, along with him, graciously give us all things?*
(ROMANS 8:32)

AUGUST 26

Worship and us

'Worship only me, the LORD your God! I will bless you with plenty of food and water and keep you strong.'
(EXODUS 23:25, CEV)

While worship is primarily something that we offer to God, the amazing thing is that it has so many 'spill-over' blessings to us as well! Let's look at just some of the things that the Bible says happens when we give ourselves to worship.

First, worship helps us to experience *God's presence*. When Solomon prayed and dedicated the temple in the context of worship, we read that 'the glory of the LORD filled the temple' (2 Chronicles 7:1). When John had his vision, he was suddenly aware of 'a door standing open in heaven' (Revelation 4:1) drawing him into God's presence and the worship of angels.

Second, worship helps us experience *God's transformation*. When Moses came down from Mount Sinai 'he was not aware that his face was radiant because he had spoken with the LORD' (Exodus 34:29). He didn't know it; but he'd been changed. It really is quite impossible to meet with God and come out the same (if we do come out the same, then we haven't worshipped!).

Third, worship brings us *God's blessing*. God promises that if we will worship and serve only him, then this will lead to blessing in our lives, as our opening verse promises; but if we direct our worship to other gods or other things, we will only bring a curse upon ourselves: 'If you worship other gods, the LORD will become angry and keep the rain from falling' (Deuteronomy 11:16–17, CEV).

Fourth, worship *increases our faith*. The more we focus on God, the more we see how big he is; and the more we see how big he is, the more we grasp how he is able to answer our prayers; and the more we see how he is able to answer our prayers, the more faith we have! As Jehoshaphat put it, 'Have faith in the LORD your God and you will be upheld' (2 Chronicles 20:20).

But remember: these things come to us, not because we search for *them*, but because we search for *God*. May God help us so to focus on him as we worship and pray that all these things become part of our growing experience!

'Seek me and live.'
(AMOS 5:4)

Walking on two legs

Dear friends, if our hearts do not condemn us, we have confidence before God and receive from him anything we ask, because we obey his commands and do what pleases him.
(1 JOHN 3:21–22)

Herbert Lockyer once said, 'Faith and obedience are the two legs a Christian walks with.' That's a rather good summary of how to enjoy our relationship with God. For if we want to see his promises become reality, then the Bible tells us that, not only will we have *faith* in God, but we will *obey* him too.

Of course, this doesn't mean that God is like a parent trying to bribe or encourage his children. 'If you're good, I'll give you a bike for Christmas' (though some Christians live as though they think that's how God operates). Rather, this is God saying, 'If you have grasped who has made these promises to you, then you will want to live rightly before me and you will end up getting the reward that inevitably comes to those who do so.'

Now, while the Bible is clear that obedience cannot save us (only Christ's death on the cross can do that), it does link obedience to God with coming into the enjoyment of his promises. God says things like, 'If you are willing and obedient, you will eat the best from the land' (Isaiah 1:19) and 'Walk in all the ways I command you, that it may go well with you' (Jeremiah 7:23). Obedience and disobedience are what contrast the saved and the unsaved. Christians are 'obedient children' (1 Peter 1:14), while the unsaved are 'disobedient' (Ephesians 2:2). So let's be what we were designed to be! If there are areas of life where we are holding out against God, if God is telling us to do something or not to do something and we are ignoring him, then it shouldn't surprise us if God's promise to us isn't happening yet. We can't expect to be disobedient and still receive the promise (though in his amazing grace, God still sometimes blesses us despite our disobedience!).

Seek to walk on the two legs of faith and obedience today. As you do so, you are lining yourself up with the God of the promises.

All these blessings will come upon you and accompany you
if you obey the LORD your God.
(DEUTERONOMY 28:2)

AUGUST 28

All eyes on God!

'We have no power to face this vast army that is attacking us.
We do not know what to do, but our eyes are upon you.'
(2 CHRONICLES 20:12)

Imagine how you would feel if you were suddenly faced with a coalition of three hostile nations marching against you. This was what faced Jehoshaphat, king of Judah. It would have been so easy for him in that situation to fix his eyes on the 'vast army' (2 Chronicles 20:2) of Moabites, Ammonites and Meunites coming against him. But instead, he called for 'all eyes on God'.

He quickly set the tone of what was needed at such a time, and the people followed his example. 'Alarmed, Jehoshaphat resolved to enquire of the LORD, and he proclaimed a fast for all Judah. The people of Judah came together to seek help from the LORD' (2 Chronicles 20:3–4). The mention of his alarm is realistic; but he didn't get stuck with his alarm. His prayer that follows is utterly focused on God, and not on the circumstances. He remembers the greatness of God; he remembers how he rules over all the nations of the earth; he remembers what God has done for his people in the past; and then he throws himself on God in the words of our opening verse for today. And then, an amazing thing happens!

'Jehoshaphat appointed men to sing to the LORD and to praise him for the splendour of his holiness as they went out at the head of the army, saying: "Give thanks to the LORD, for his love endures for ever." As they began to sing and praise, the LORD set ambushes against the men of Ammon and Moab and Mount Seir who were invading Judah, and they were defeated' (2 Chronicles 20:21–22). What an amazing victory – brought about simply through praise!

Jehoshaphat understood the importance of praising God, even in difficult circumstances. He knew that praise kept them focused on God; and in keeping focused on him, they were focusing on the one thing that could change their situation. Let's seek to do the same ourselves today.

'O LORD, God of our fathers, are you not the God who is in heaven? You
rule over all the kingdoms of the nations. Power and might are in your
hand, and no-one can withstand you.'
(2 CHRONICLES 20:6)

AUGUST 29

Twenty-twenty vision

Where there is no vision, the people perish.
(PROVERBS 29:18, KJV)

'Twenty-twenty vision' is the expression used for 'perfect sight'. As we have got older, our natural eyesight isn't as good as it used to be, and spectacles are much needed! However, while the natural eyesight of God's people may not always be clear, there is absolutely no need for their spiritual vision to be so; for God has promised to give vision to us, and has warned us of the danger of living without it.

Our promise today is translated variously in different English versions; but the heart of it is the same: where people do not get clear direction, they are prone to 'do their own thing'. But God has a vision for each one of us that brings peace and direction; and he wants each of us to get hold of that for ourselves.

One reason we can be so sure that God has vision for our lives is, quite simply, that we are *his*! 'Fear not, for I have redeemed you; I have summoned you by name; *you are mine*,' he says (Isaiah 43:1). In fact, he knew us from before our conception! 'Before I formed you in the womb I knew you, before you were born I set you apart', he told Jeremiah (Jeremiah 1:5). David recognized that God's plan for his life began even before he was born: 'For you created my inmost being; you knit me together in my mother's womb . . . All the days ordained for me were written in your book before one of them came to be' (Psalm 139:13, 16). If God has taken such care in his preparation of us, how can he not have a vision and purpose for us?

If, then, God promises that he has vision for us, the least we can do is to ask him to reveal it to us and to help us to be obedient in walking in it. Perhaps this is something that you have never done; perhaps it is something that you have let go of, because of pressures or circumstances. If so, today is as good a day as any to take hold of God's promise, as you recognize that without his vision you will perish, but that with it you will truly live!

'I was not disobedient to the vision from heaven.'
(ACTS 26:19)

AUGUST 30

A grammar lesson

For God did not send his Son into the world to condemn the world, but to save the world through him.
(JOHN 3:17)

As part of his work Martin sometimes leads seminars on English grammar. The day is spent working through nouns, verbs, adjectives, etc. (though he tries to make it all very interesting!). Take verbs, for example. Verbs have different tenses, such as past, present and future. We can see these at work in how the Bible talks about salvation.

The Bible tells us that we have been saved (past tense). 'It is by grace *you have been saved*,' Paul wrote (Ephesians 2:5). He was thinking of the time when we turned to Christ and trusted him, when we were sorry for our sin and asked him to cleanse us, committing our lives to him.

But the Bible also speaks of our being saved (present tense). 'For the message of the cross is foolishness to those who are perishing, but to us who *are being saved* it is the power of God,' Paul said (1 Corinthians 1:18). And surely that is something that we need to know each day: Christ's ongoing, daily forgiveness and cleansing.

And the future? 'He who stands firm to the end *will be saved*,' Jesus assures us (Matthew 10:22). We are to keep going, not depending on ourselves but on his inexhaustible riches. We hold on to him in the reality that he is holding on to us, for he *will* complete the work that he has begun in us.

But note something else about all these verbs: they are all 'passive': that is, they are all things 'done' to us or for us. As Paul put it, 'It is by grace you have been saved, through faith – and this not from yourselves, it is the gift of God – not by works, so that no one can boast' (Ephesians 2:8–9). We cannot save ourselves (past, present or future); we can only ask Christ to save us. He alone forgives us, cleanses us, and keeps us. Today, rest in him. Live by faith in him, trusting him and in his limitless promises and resources. Allow all that he is to permeate your dreams, your hopes, your fears. Let him in on your 'to-do' list throughout the day!

Our God is a God who saves.
(PSALM 68:20)

AUGUST 31

The challenge to change

'I promise you this. If you don't change and become like a child,
you will never get into the kingdom of heaven.'
(MATTHEW 18:3, CEV)

Change. You either love it or you hate it. Some of us find change exciting and love constant change in our life. For us, keeping things the same is boring! For others, change is far more challenging, and we prefer the steady certainty that keeps everything in its proper place. For us, keeping things the same is wonderful! But whatever our natural inclinations and character, 'change' is something that God looks for in us all. For 'change' lies at the heart of his call on our lives; he loves us too much to let us stay the same!

This challenge to change was central to Jesus' message. His ministry began with the announcement that God's kingdom was near and that, in the light of that, people needed to 'repent and believe the good news!' (Mark 1:15). The word 'repent' means 'change'. In fact, more specifically, the Greek word used means 'a change of mind or heart that leads to a change of action'. Repentance is not just about saying 'sorry', but then living life the same as before. Such an attitude has more to do with feeling sorry for ourselves, or feeling sorry we were 'caught out', than true repentance. True repentance means *saying* sorry and then *living* sorry; in short, it means a life of *constant change*.

In the light of this, we really shouldn't be surprised if God wants to bring change into our lives – either personally or into our church community that we are a part of. But Christians are sometimes the very worst at accepting change! Many a church has experienced uproar when it has been suggested that we change the pews, or the organ, or the hymns, or the order of service, or the leadership structures, or the way we share communion, or the building . . . the list is endless! What a tragic shame for the people who are supposed to be, above all others, the people of change.

What about you? How have you been responding to challenges to change recently? Remember: your very life in Christ is a life of – *change*!

'Do things that show you have really changed your hearts and lives.'
(LUKE 3:8, NCV)

SEPTEMBER 1

Teach us to pray

One day Jesus was praying in a certain place. When he finished,
one of his disciples said to him, 'Lord, teach us to pray . . .'
(LUKE 11:1)

We often find ourselves encouraged by Jesus' disciples – especially by their mistakes and slowness to understand! We can certainly identify with how they felt when they came to Jesus, having seen him praying, and said, 'Lord, teach us to pray' (Luke 11:1). It wasn't that they hadn't prayed before or didn't know how to; as Jews they would often have prayed. But Jesus seemed to have a completely different way of praying. He made it look so easy, so desirable, so enjoyable! And they wanted that for themselves. Jesus' response to them has become perhaps the most famous prayer in history, commonly called *the Lord's Prayer*, and it's this prayer that we will be looking at over the next few days.

The prayer is found twice in the New Testament (in Matthew and Luke) in slightly different forms, perhaps reflecting different occasions when Jesus taught it. Matthew presents it as *a model to be followed* ('This, then, is *how* you should pray', Matthew 6:9), whereas Luke presents it as more of *a prayer to be repeated* ('When you pray, *say . . .*', Luke 11:2). It seems, therefore, that this prayer was used flexibly in the early church. If we do use it as a prayer in its own right, individually or corporately (as many Christians do), we need to take care that we don't recite it in such a way, or at such a speed, that it becomes little more than a 'mantra', especially since Jesus teaches it in the context of not falling into mindless repetition of prayers (Matthew 6:5–8)! As a pattern for prayer, it can be tremendously helpful, especially when we've got rather 'stuck in a rut' in praying.

If you have been finding prayer difficult recently, don't be discouraged. Rather, see it as an opportunity for Jesus to teach you afresh how to pray and what to pray for. Remember: prayer is a journey, not a destination! Ask him to take you on that journey over these next few days.

God's Spirit is right alongside helping us along. If we don't know how or
what to pray, it doesn't matter. He does our praying in and for us.
(ROMANS 8:26, THE MESSAGE)

SEPTEMBER 2

Our Father in heaven . . .

Our Father in heaven . . .
(MATTHEW 6:9)

Sometimes, it's hard to know where to start things in life, especially when the possibilities seem endless. Where do you start when clearing out the garage, for example, or when searching the web, or choosing a special gift? If such ordinary things in life can at times be a challenge, how much more can prayer be! Where on earth do you start? Easy, said Jesus. Start with God! Start with, 'Our Father in heaven . . .'

We need to start with God, not because he is some kind of divine megalomaniac who constantly needs telling how great he is, nor because he is some sort of divine battery that needs regularly charging up through prayer. Rather, we start with God because it's when we remember what *God* is like that everything else starts to take on its proper perspective. Start with yourself, and you'll get discouraged, for your sin will surely rise up to accuse you. Start with your needs, and you'll get overwhelmed, for they will seem so great and insoluble. But start with God and your eyes will be lifted as you remember what a very big God you have!

And don't just start with 'God' in a general way, Jesus said. Start by remembering that this God is your *Father* - nothing like the worst of human fathers and far superior to the best of human fathers. He is a Father *in heaven* – that is, without any of the limitations or restraints that this world brings. Knowing him as Father is his greatest desire for us. His longing for his people is summed up in these words: 'I thought you would call me "Father" and not turn away from following me' (Jeremiah 3:19).

Without calling on God as Father, prayer will be little more than a religious duty, a calming technique, or an attempt to manipulate God in time of need. But with this, prayer is transformed into an exciting relationship and adventure. God is not 'out there' but 'down here', as my loving Father. Set your heart on him today, and let everything else be seen in the light of that.

He will call out to me, 'You are my Father, my God, the Rock my Saviour.'
(PSALM 89:26)

September 3

Be hallowed!

. . . hallowed be your name . . .
(Matthew 6:9)

In yesterday's reading, we saw the importance of starting with 'God' whenever we pray. But having started with him, what do we now say to him? Well, said, Jesus in the Lord's Prayer, focus on three things: first, the honouring of God's name; second, the coming of God's kingdom; third, the doing of God's will. Let's look at the first one of those today: hallowed be your name. Of course, the word to 'hallow' isn't one that is much used nowadays. That's why some modern translations use different expressions: 'help us to honour your name' (CEV); 'may your name always be kept holy' (NCV); 'may your name be honoured' (NLT).

In Bible times, a name was more than how you distinguished one person from another; a name summed up someone's character or calling. So, Abram ('exalted father') had his name changed by God to Abraham ('father of many', Genesis 17:5) to reflect what God was about to do for him and through him; and his promised son was called Isaac ('he laughs', Genesis 21:3–6) to remind his parents of how they laughed with disbelief when God promised him to them, but then laughed with joy when they finally held him in their arms.

Likewise, God's name tells us about who he is: he is first and foremost, Jesus says in this prayer, a *Father.* So when you come to him, start with that thought, and tell him how much you honour and love him for being exactly that! And then think of some of his other names: names like El Shaddai (God Almighty), El Olam (Eternal God), El Roi (the God who sees), Jehovah-Jireh (the LORD who provides), Jehovah-Nissi (the LORD my banner), Jehovah-Shalom (the LORD is peace), Jehovah-Tsidkenu (the LORD our righteousness), Jehovah-Rophi (the LORD my healer) – and that's just a few from the Bible to get us going!

Take a few moments to tell God how very, very pleased you are that he has revealed himself to you through his names; but above all, as a perfect, loving, heavenly Father. Go on, get excited about it (most young children do with their dads!).

Praise be to the God and Father of our Lord Jesus Christ, who has blessed us in the heavenly realms with every spiritual blessing in Christ.
(Ephesians 1:3)

The coming of God's Kingdom

. . . your kingdom come . . .
(MATTHEW 6:10)

Start your praying by focusing on 'God', Jesus models for us in the Lord's Prayer. Begin with the honouring of his name; but then move on to pray for the coming of his kingdom.

The trouble with the word 'kingdom', at least in English, is that it makes us think of 'a place' (like 'the United Kingdom') - and then we start to wonder where that place is! But the words in Hebrew and Greek (the language of the Bible) for 'kingdom' carry the sense, not of a 'place', but of 'rule' or 'government'. This 'kingdom' of God, this 'rule' of God, was the heart of Jesus' message. It's how he started his ministry as he went out preaching, 'The time has come . . . the kingdom of God is near. Repent and believe the good news!' (Mark 1:15), and this remained the core of his message.

In the Lord's Prayer, Jesus tells us to pray for more of this kingdom, this 'kingly rule'. Why? Because when there is more of the kingdom, things change for the better! Isaiah, prophesying over 700 years earlier, had looked forward to Messiah's coming and spoken of 'the increase of his government and peace' (Isaiah 9:7). In other words, what he was seeing was that the more we let God's kingly rule (his government) come, the more peace there will be around. So, pray for that, Jesus says!

Whenever Mike uses this model of the Lord's prayer and comes to today's phrase, he imagines this prayer going outwards, like ripples from a stone dropped into a pond. So, we can start by praying for more of God's kingly rule in our own life and needs; and then pray the same for our family and friends, our church and leaders, our work and workplace, our society and nation, our world and events. But there's absolutely no point praying about the latter if we aren't prepared to start with our own lives first!

Pray for more of God's kingdom to come in *your* life today, Jesus says. It's a prayer God loves to answer!

Therefore, since we are receiving a kingdom that cannot be shaken, let us be thankful, and so worship God acceptably with reverence and awe, for our 'God is a consuming fire.'
(HEBREWS 12:28–29)

September 5

The doing of God's will

. . . your will be done . . .
(Matthew 6:10)

When you pray, begin with God, Jesus says. Focus on him as your Father; honour him; pray for more of his kingdom; and then, Jesus adds, pray for his will to be done. This prayer is not the 'resigned submission' to the Allah of Islam, where whatever God wills, happens, and all I can do is to receive it, for good or bad (though, sadly, this is the view of prayer that some Christians fall into). Nor is it a sort of 'escape route' to let us avoid praying anything meaningful or specific in challenging circumstances. Christian prayer is far more interactive and dynamic than this.

What Jesus is encouraging us to do here, out of a growing trust and confidence in our heavenly Father, is to pray for his will to be implemented on earth, despite all obstacles and opposition, and to learn how to submit ourselves to that will as he shares his heart with us. This, of course, is exactly what Jesus himself did in Gethsemane when he prayed, 'My Father, if it is possible, may this cup be taken from me. Yet not as I will, but as you will' (Matthew 26:39) and then 'My Father, if it is not possible for this cup to be taken away unless I drink it, may your will be done' (Matthew 26:42). Jesus leads us in this matter, not just by words, but by example: pray for God's will to be done, because it's a good will from a good God and you can trust him!

Jesus then adds a phrase: 'on earth as it is in heaven'. These words probably govern all three prayers: may your name be hallowed on earth as it is in heaven; may your kingly rule come on earth as it is in heaven; may your will be done on earth as it is in heaven. And how are these things done in heaven? Joyfully! Instantly! Powerfully! Focus on some of these things when you talk to God in prayer, Jesus says, and your perspective will change and your prayers be answered!

For this reason, since the day we heard about you, we have not stopped praying for you and asking God to fill you with the knowledge of his will through all spiritual wisdom and understanding.
(Colossians 1:9)

Prayer for present needs

Give us today our daily bread . . .
(MATTHEW 6:11)

Once we have focused on God first of all to get our perspective right, Jesus shows us in the Lord's Prayer, then we can start to turn to our own needs, confident that this wonderful, heavenly Father that we have been thinking about really does want to hear our requests and answer us. And so Jesus now follows up his threefold prayer about God with a threefold prayer about us and our own needs. And what he starts with couldn't get more basic and down-to-earth: a prayer for daily bread.

Bread, in many cultures, is the most basic need for daily living, which is why one modern version translates this as 'give us the food we need for each day' (NCV). What Jesus is saying here is that our relationship with God can be such that even the most basic needs of daily life can be brought to him, whether that be food or any other needs that we might have. Nothing is too small or insignificant! Time and time again we have heard people saying things like, 'Oh, I didn't think I could bother God with *that*', referring to some need of life that they thought the Almighty was far too busy to concern himself with. 'Wrong!' Jesus says! God really wants to hear from you about it!

Paul said that we should bring our every need and concern before God. 'Do not be anxious about *anything*, but in *everything*, by prayer and petition, with thanksgiving, present your requests to God,' he wrote (Philippians 4:6). So, whether our need is material (like financial provision) or physical (like healing) or relational (like some relationship breakdown) or emotional (like some inability to cope in some circumstance); whatever the need is, bring it confidently to God, says Jesus! He really does want to hear it, and he really will listen and answer!

So, what 'daily bread' do you need today? Don't keep it from God; don't think he's too busy to listen; tell him about it! Ask with faith and expectation, knowing that Jesus has promised that your heavenly Father really does care and wants to provide.

Give me neither poverty nor riches, but give me only my daily bread.
(PROVERBS 30:8)

SEPTEMBER 7

Prayer for past sin

Forgive us our debts, as we also have forgiven our debtors.
(MATTHEW 6:12)

We never cease to be amazed at how God does things so differently to us. Nowhere is this seen more starkly than in the way Jesus teaches us to pray. For the confession of our sin, he tells us through the Lord's Prayer, should come not at the beginning of our praying, but at the end of it!

Now, we don't know about you, but we often feel that confessing sin is where we need to start. Surely we need to tell God all our sins and shortcomings first, for how can he listen to us otherwise? (Ever felt like that yourself?) Of course, Jesus teaches us here that there is a very real place for 'coming clean' and confessing the wrong that we have thought, or said, or done; but don't *start* there, Jesus says! For if you do, you'll just dig a deeper hole for yourself and end up in misery (the devil will make certain of that!). So don't start with your sin; start with God, Jesus says!

So, why does he say this, for it instinctively cuts across everything within us? Well, it's because once we have seen how big, how gracious, how loving a Father our God is, then we'll know that he wants to forgive us! There won't be a shadow of a doubt about it in our mind. We will have reminded ourselves once again that he is 'the LORD, the LORD, the compassionate and gracious God, slow to anger, abounding in love and faithfulness, maintaining love to thousands, and forgiving wickedness, rebellion and sin' (Exodus 34:6–7). Once we've understood that this is what he is like, then 'coming clean' about our failings won't seem half so hard!

When you pray, don't start with you, then; start with God! Don't start with what you aren't, but start with what he is. Don't start with what's wrong in you but with what's right in him. Go on: give it a go today!

If we say that we have not sinned, we are fooling ourselves, and the truth isn't in our hearts. But if we confess our sins to God, he can always be trusted to forgive us and take our sins away.
(1 JOHN 1:8–9, CEV)

Prayer for future welfare

And lead us not into temptation, but deliver us from the evil one.
(MATTHEW 6:13)

Today we come to the last part of the Lord's Prayer. Having encouraged us to pray about our present need and our past sin, Jesus now tells us to pray for our future welfare. Why? Because this world can be a dangerous place! Accidents, sickness, unforeseen events, natural disasters – let alone the more direct attacks of the devil. So Jesus tells us to pray for protection, for 'your enemy the devil prowls around like a roaring lion looking for someone to devour' (1 Peter 5:8).

The devil loves to tempt and deceive God's people. Just as he did with Adam and Eve, he tempts people to disobey God by dangling what is forbidden in front of them. In fact, he is even called 'the tempter' in the New Testament (Matthew 4:3; 1 Thessalonians 3:5). He tempts because he loves to exploit human weakness, making sin seem attractive and fooling us into thinking that 'it will be all right' (though experience cries out that it has never been all right when we've done it in the past!)

But while the devil has very real power, it's important we remember that he is not *all*-powerful; only God is! So, commit yourself to your heavenly Father, Jesus says; for he is able to keep you against all the attacks, accusations and temptations of the evil one. We may be weak before the devil – but our heavenly Father isn't! Remember that as you go through today.

And so we come to the end of the Lord's Prayer, a prayer that expresses our dependence on God in every area of life; a prayer that, if we prayed it with all our hearts, would change our lives.

(By the way, if you're wondering about the traditional ending – 'For thine is the kingdom, and the power and the glory, for ever and ever, Amen!' (Matthew 6:13, KJV) – these words aren't found in the oldest Greek manuscripts of the Bible and so aren't included in most modern translations. They were added later in church history as an ending suitable for use in liturgical settings.)

My prayer is not that you take them out of the world
but that you protect them from the evil one.
(JOHN 17:15)

Too busy for relationship?

'Stop and consider God's wonders.'
(JOB 37:14)

Increasingly, 'relationship' goes by the board in our busy world. Some are just too busy at work, too goal-orientated, to be bothered with people and relationships. That takes time; and time is money! Others are just too afraid of relationships, perhaps because of how they have been let down in life. Yet relationship is the very heart of life, the very heart of prayer.

The Lord's Prayer, that we've been looking at together, is about *relationship* from start to finish. That's why Jesus begins the prayer by looking to God as 'Father'. Prayer isn't some religious duty or spiritual exercise; it is honest, heart-to-heart sharing between children and their father – and a perfect, heavenly Father at that. Because prayer is all about relationship, we need to develop that relationship; and that means learning how to slow down, how to close the door to the busyness of life so that we can 'stop and consider God's wonders'.

The story of Martha and Mary brings home the importance of stopping. Jesus and his disciples had been invited home by Martha; but having invited them, she then got 'all of a fluster' as she became increasingly anxious about preparing the meal – while Mary just sat at Jesus' feet listening to him. Martha became so annoyed that she eventually asked, '"Lord, don't you care that my sister has left me to do the work by myself? Tell her to help me!" "Martha, Martha," the Lord answered, "you are worried and upset about many things, but only one thing is needed. Mary has chosen what is better, and it will not be taken away from her"'(Luke 10:40–42). Martha needed to learn that relationship takes time, and that means knowing how to stop. For as we stop (even for a few moments in a busy day), we are giving God an opportunity to refocus our hearts on him as our Father who cares and provides.

What about me? Am I like Mary, who stopped? Or like Martha, who was too busy to stop, too busy for relationship? What is the 'one thing' (v. 42) that governs *my* life?

*I have stilled and quietened my soul; like a weaned child with its mother,
like a weaned child is my soul within me.*
(PSALM 131:2)

Faith in action

Faith without deeds is useless.
(JAMES 2:20)

It's very easy to *say* we believe in God; but sometimes God puts what we say to the test! (Yes, *God*, and not the devil!) So, for example, when Abraham was challenged by God to offer up Isaac, the child that had been promised and awaited so long, it was without doubt the most stretching challenge of his life thus far. But after all those years of walking with God and learning how to trust him and his promises, he was now ready for such a test.

Abraham knew that from a human point of view, sacrificing Isaac would mean giving up all hope of seeing God's promises fulfilled: there would be no great nation, no promised land, no blessing to all the nations, as God had promised him; and ultimately, of course, no coming Saviour. Yet because God had made promises to Abraham – and had stressed that they would come to pass through Isaac, and no one else – Abraham just knew that God would do it somehow, whatever it took. As the writer of Hebrews puts it, 'Abraham reasoned that God could raise the dead, and figuratively speaking, he did receive Isaac back from death' (Hebrews 11:19). His faith was met by God's wonderful provision – a provision that foreshadows the sacrifice of the Son of God himself as the sacrificial lamb for our sins.

Abraham's faith was seen not in mere words, then, but in action. Faith is not real faith until we step out and test the promise of God for ourselves.

Perhaps God has been speaking to you recently, encouraging you to step out in faith in some area of your life. You may truly believe what he has said, or what the Bible promises about this matter. But your faith is not real faith until, like Abraham, you do something with it. Let today be a day for stepping out with God and for putting faith into action. For as you do, just as with Abraham, he will meet with you!

Faith by itself, if it is not accompanied by action, is dead.
(JAMES 2:17)

Praying from events

Blow the trumpet in Zion, declare a holy fast, call a sacred assembly. Gather the people, consecrate the assembly . . . Let the priests, who minister before the LORD, weep between the temple porch and the altar. Let them say, 'Spare your people, O LORD'.
(JOEL 2:15–17)

Sadly, you don't have to look too far in the world to find disasters. Some are 'natural disasters' – though the Bible says that they aren't 'natural' at all, for they are not how God designed this world to be. Others are more obviously 'human disasters', like when terrorists wreak their bloody work or when faulty parts or bad workmanship lead to a disastrous crash. But at the heart of every disaster – 'natural' or 'human' – lies the same old thing: sin. It is sin that causes people to make wrong choices and to cut corners; and it is sin that has worked its way into the fabric of creation that means it is now 'subjected to frustration' (Romans 8:20).

But just because sin lies at the root of everything doesn't mean we should just sit by, holding our hands up and saying, 'But what can we do about it?' Do we honestly think that God sits in heaven dispassionately when such disasters happen? That his heart doesn't ache for the suffering that he sees? We, as his people, can catch hold of his heart at such times and call out to him for his protection when disaster approaches or his help when disaster has struck.

That's what the prophet Joel did, as in our opening verses. Joel lived at a time when Israel had been devastated by locusts and drought. But confronted with this disaster, he didn't just sit back and think, 'Well, that's what they deserve for not obeying God.' Rather, he prayed and called others to prayer, challenging them to see what *God* might be saying through all of this (a notion no more popular in his day than in ours!).

Thanks to TV, newspapers and the internet, we are more informed of world events than any previous generation, and so have less excuse for not praying. So whenever you hear of some disaster, impending or actual, don't just feel sorry; pray about it right there and then. Make it part of your routine. You could even start today!

'I look for your deliverance, O LORD.'
(GENESIS 49:18)

Love the light!

*Blessed are those who have learned to acclaim you, who walk
in the light of your presence, O LORD.*
(PSALM 89:15)

All of us will have seen how, when we pick up a large stone in the garden,
all the little creatures beneath it quickly scurry away, eager to get away
from the light and to find some dark corner again. But some people are
like that too. They hate the 'light' – that is the light of truth, integrity and
righteousness – and prefer the 'darkness' – the darkness of lies, deceit and
deception. But the Bible tells us that such things are contrary to God's
very nature; that he hates them and commands us to hate them too. We,
the children of Truth, should be known for our truthfulness; we, the
children of Light, should be known for our living in the light. And since
God knows everything anyway, how can we think we can hide anything
from him?

Just how seriously God sees things like deception is revealed starkly in
the story of Ananias and Sapphira. Trying to put on a false front of
generosity towards others, when in fact they cared only for themselves,
they dropped dead when challenged by Peter for lying to the Holy Spirit
and for trying to deceive the church. This sober lesson certainly brings
home just how much the Spirit is grieved by any sort of deception and
pretence.

Thankfully, there is a positive side to all of this! For God promises that
if we will 'walk in the light' with him – bringing everything out into the
open rather than hiding it – then we will always find forgiveness, release
and a way forward. What we keep in the darkness, the devil holds power
over; but what we bring into the light can be forgiven and dealt with, as
the Bible shows again and again.

So, if you have been 'keeping something in the dark', resolve to stop
doing so right now! Love the light – and you will find the way out!

*If we claim to have fellowship with him yet walk in the darkness, we lie and
do not live by the truth. But if we walk in the light, as he is in the light, we
have fellowship with one another, and the blood of Jesus, his Son,
purifies us from all sin.*
(1 JOHN 1:6–7)

SEPTEMBER 13

The crown of creation

What are human beings that you are mindful of them, mortals that you care for them? Yet you have made them a little lower than God, and crowned them with glory and honour.
(PSALM 8:4–5, NRSV)

Watch any TV programme these days about the animal kingdom or the human race and the viewpoint will always be the same: people are not different from animals. Wrong! says the Bible. They couldn't be more different!

Whatever your personal understanding might be about exactly *how* God created the world, the Bible maintains that men and women are no 'accident', but rather the distinct and separate creation of God. We are not 'just another animal', even an animal of a very superior kind; we alone are made 'in the image of God' (Genesis 1:27). And historically, whenever we have lost a sense of the dignity and uniqueness of the human race, all sorts of horrors have generally followed.

But not only is humankind made by God in a general way; God is intimately involved in the creation of each individual. Not one of us is the result of mere human procreation; and not one of us is an accident. As David poetically put it: 'For you created my inmost being; you knit me together in my mother's womb. I praise you because I am fearfully and wonderfully made' (Psalm 139:13–14). And having created us, he then sustains us! As Paul put it, quoting from a Greek poet, 'In him we live and move and have our being' (Acts 17:28).

Little wonder, then, that David was filled with awe as he looked at the stars one evening, marvelling at God's creation. But his greatest amazement, as he records in Psalm 8, was that, in the light of the vastness of that universe, that God should care about *people* – people that he has made 'a little lower than God, and crowned them with glory and honour' (Psalm 8:5, NRSV).

Don't lose your sense of wonder at God's creation of the human race and its unique position in God's heart and plan. Be like David and praise God for that today.

Come, let us bow down in worship, let us kneel before the LORD our Maker; for he is our God and we are the people of his pasture, the flock under his care.
(PSALM 95:6–7)

SEPTEMBER 14

Carrying his hallmark

It was in Antioch that the disciples were for the first time called Christians.
(ACTS 11:26, THE MESSAGE)

Every aspect of life has an example that is outstanding in its field and that 'sets the benchmark' for all that follows: Abraham Lincoln in American politics, Elvis Presley in rock music, Henry Ford in car production. In terms of early church life, this 'benchmark' came from an unlikely quarter: not Jerusalem, but Antioch. While the Jerusalem church got stuck within narrow confines, Antioch set the standard for what normal Christian life was all about and cast its influence across the known world.

Situated by the north-eastern corner of the Mediterranean, Antioch had a population of 300,000 and was the third largest city in the Roman Empire – clearly a place with great potential for the church. And it was a potential that was realized. We see in Acts that the church refused to be inward looking; whenever God spoke, they responded positively and constantly pushed back the boundaries, seeing both Jews and Gentiles converted to Christ.

In fact, the church at Antioch was so 'successful' that it was here, for the first time, that 'the disciples were called Christians' (almost certainly a nickname at first – the 'Christ-people'). The Greek word that is used in the text for 'were called' actually means 'to transact business in someone's name'. In other words, everything these disciples did had the hallmark of being done in the name of Jesus! Little wonder they were called after him; and little wonder they grew!

God still wants his people to carry the hallmark of Jesus, so that everything we are and do is seen to be 'in his name' and reflecting his heart. Of course, left to our own resources, we could never do this. But the church at Antioch knew they weren't left to their own resources – they knew that the Holy Spirit was with them, empowering them to be Jesus' representatives both in their own city and in the nations to which he sent them. As we yield our lives to him, God promises that this same Holy Spirit will produce that unmistakable hallmark in us too.

And as the Spirit of the Lord works within us, we become more and more like him and reflect his glory even more.
(2 CORINTHIANS 3:18, NLT)

SEPTEMBER 15

Being fruitful

'You did not choose me, but I chose you and appointed you to go and bear fruit – fruit that will last.'
(JOHN 15:16)

In Mike's garden was a plum tree. They had bought a good-quality one from a reputable garden centre; they had planted it and lovingly cared for it (well, at least his wife had!); but despite all the care and attention, while it produced a reasonable crop the first year, it never produced anything ever again! For several years Mike's wife kept giving it her best attention; but despite everything she did, the plum tree produced nothing but leaves – a dreadful disappointment.

And that's how God's people, Israel, had become over the years – like a tree full of leaves, but without fruit, and therefore useless. Seven hundred years before Jesus, Isaiah had sung his song of the vineyard, lamenting that after generations of care that God had put into the vineyard of his people, God 'looked for a crop of good grapes, but it yielded only bad fruit' (Isaiah 5:2). Jesus preached the same message when he told his parable of the fig tree in Luke 13. In both parables the message is clear: what is more useless than a fruitless people of God?

Thankfully, we do not have to settle for fruitlessness, either in our lives or in our churches! Jesus promised his disciples in John 15 that, if they would abide in him, if they would stay close to him and draw life from him, like a branch drawing life from the vine it is joined to, if they would respond to the pruning of his Father the gardener, then the most natural thing in the world would be for them to produce fruit. It wouldn't be hard work, or an effort, or a penance; it would simply happen!

Jesus promised his disciples that, having chosen them, he had now appointed them to go and bear fruit – fruit that would last. And this is still his promise. So, wherever you go today, expect to be fruitful for him!

Blessed is the man who does not walk in the counsel of the wicked . . . he is like a tree planted by streams of water, which yields its fruit in season and whose leaf does not wither. Whatever he does prospers.
(PSALM 1:1, 3)

Work: the gift of God

Moreover, when God gives any man wealth and possessions,
and enables him to enjoy them, to accept his lot and be happy
in his work – this is a gift of God.
(ECCLESIASTES 5:19)

'I like work; it fascinates me. I could sit and look at it for hours.' So said a poster in an office. Perhaps a sentiment shared by many! But the Bible tells us that work is not a nuisance to be avoided, but rather the gift of God! And as his gift, it carries a promised blessing.

From the very beginning, God designed us to work. He told Adam and Eve to 'be fruitful and increase in number' (Genesis 1:28) – the work involved in family life. He told them to 'fill the earth and subdue it' (Genesis 1:28) – the work involved in ruling nature. He put them in the Garden of Eden with a mandate to 'to work it and take care of it' (Genesis 2:15) – the work involved in taking responsibility for ourselves and others. All of this shouldn't surprise us, for God himself is a God who works, Jesus told us; and since we are made in his image, we too are designed to work just like him.

After the Fall, sin began to spoil everything, of course. But it's at this point that many of us have a faulty memory of what the Bible actually says; for it is not *work* that is now cursed, but *the ground* that we have to work on. In other words, work would now be hard at times, and not always the joy that God meant it to be; but work itself is not under God's curse. Indeed, how can it be when it is his gift? And this is why we can ask him to bless it, and why he promises to do so.

If your work has been getting you down or wearying you recently – and by 'work' we mean the duties of the young mother at home just as much as the labourer on the building site or the executive in the office – then reclaim it as God's gift to you; and with it, his promised blessing on all that you set your hands to.

Then the LORD your God will make you most prosperous
in all the work of your hands . . .
(DEUTERONOMY 30:9)

September 17

Risky giving!

*'Bring the whole tithe into the storehouse, that there may be
food in my house. Test me in this,' says the LORD Almighty,
'and see if I will not throw open the floodgates of heaven
and pour out so much blessing
that you will not have room enough for it.'*
(MALACHI 3:10)

Watch what people do with their money, and it will tell you what they really love in life. For, as Jesus said, 'where your treasure is, there your heart will be also' (Matthew 6:21). Sadly, even some Christians miss this truth, often finding it hard to let their faith touch their pockets. But God wants us to learn the excitement of 'risky giving' and the blessing that flows from it.

Perhaps the most risky expression of giving is 'tithing' – giving one tenth of our income to God. This is indeed risky, for we are giving away a tenth of our money and therefore have less to live on. But this is where God's impossible mathematics comes in; for with God, *nine-tenths goes further than ten-tenths!*

Some Christians dismiss tithing on the grounds that it simply belonged to the Jewish Law; but tithing was practised long before the Law existed, arising instinctively in the hearts of people like Abraham and Jacob long before God commanded it. Even Jesus didn't challenge the practice of tithing, simply the twisted way that some people did it. Sadly, objections to tithing, not because people want to give more, but because they want to give less. The widow's mite is often quoted as a basis for giving little – missing completely the point that Jesus made, that it was 'all she had to live on' (Luke 21:4). Even in the Old Testament, tithing was just the beginning, there being many other opportunities for freewill offerings as well. God wants his people to be as generous-hearted as he himself is. So, by all means do not tithe – as long as your giving exceeds it!

What has your attitude been to tithing and giving? One of keeping (and so missing God's promised blessing) or of releasing (and so finding the promised blessing)? Today could be a day for trying it out and seeing that it really does work!

*Remember this: Whoever sows sparingly will also reap sparingly,
and whoever sows generously will also reap generously.*
(2 CORINTHIANS 9:6)

September 18

The heart above all things

'Even now,' declares the LORD, 'return to me with all your heart, with fasting and weeping and mourning.' Rend your heart and not your garments.
(JOEL 2:12–13)

Imagine London without Big Ben; or Paris without the Eiffel Tower; or Sydney without the Opera House. They just wouldn't be the same, would they? Or imagine a car without its engine, or a cycle without its pedals, or a TV without its screen. There are certain things in life that, if you take some bits away from them, just aren't the same any more. And that's how it is with worship and prayer. Take 'the heart' out of them and what we're left with just isn't worship and prayer.

The heart has such an important place that God tells us to pay particular attention to it when we come to him; for without the heart being right – trusting, tender, open to receive – worship and prayer is a meaningless ritual. That's why, again and again in the Bible, we find God calling his people to examine their hearts. Saul thought Samuel would be pleased that he'd offered a sacrifice; but Samuel challenged the complete lack of 'heart' behind it. 'Does the LORD delight in burnt offerings and sacrifices as much as in obeying the voice of the LORD? To obey is better than sacrifice, and to heed is better than the fat of rams' (1 Samuel 15:22). Saul thought the sacrifice would 'work' just because it was a sacrifice; he had forgotten the most important aspect of it: the heart.

This is why the prophets constantly challenged empty ritual that had no 'heart'. Through Isaiah God's challenge was that, 'These people come near to me with their mouth and honour me with their lips, but their hearts are far from me' (Isaiah 29:13); through Ezekiel that, 'With their mouths they express devotion, but their hearts are greedy for unjust gain' (Ezekiel 33:31); through Malachi that 'you have not set your heart to honour me' (Malachi 2:2).

Still today, God is looking for one thing from us: our heart. The prayer, the worship, the service – all are secondary to this one thing. Will we have the courage to stop and let him have our heart again today?

Look deep into my heart, O God, and find out everything I am thinking.
(PSALM 139:23, CEV)

September 19

Fish swim – God forgives!

*The LORD is compassionate and gracious, slow to anger,
abounding in love. He will not always accuse, nor will he
harbour his anger for ever; he does not treat us as our sins
deserve or repay us according to our iniquities. For as high as
the heavens are above the earth, so great is his love for those
who fear him; as far as the east is from the west,
so far has he removed our transgressions from us.*
(PSALM 103:8–12)

Some things are just too big at times for us to get our minds around. The boundless expanse of outer space; weird-looking creatures in the depths of the ocean; the infinite patterns of snowflakes; the amazing perfection of a baby's fingers. And the willingness of a holy God to forgive our sin! It seems beyond belief that God should be concerned with us, let alone forgive us. So, why should a holy God forgive our sin?

God forgives because it is his very nature to do so. Fish swim; birds fly; people breathe; rain falls; the sun shines – and God forgives! That's the way things happen, because that's the way things are. Again and again in the Bible, people discovered, often at their lowest point and in their deepest failure, the truth – the amazing truth – that God revealed to Moses, that he is indeed 'the LORD, the LORD, the compassionate and gracious God, slow to anger, abounding in love and faithfulness, maintaining love to thousands, and forgiving wickedness, rebellion and sin' (Exodus 34:6–7).

It is this revelation of God himself as one who is, by his very nature, forgiving and who therefore delights to forgive, that is the basis for our confidence. It isn't us being presumptuous or naively optimistic; we are simply taking God at his word, repeated again and again, that this is his very nature. He *is* forgiveness, and therefore he forgives.

So often the devil tries to convince us that God will forgive anyone's sins but ours. That's a lie! Don't believe it. Rather, believe the truth and promises of God's word. Fish swim don't they? The sun shines, doesn't it? And God forgives! That's the way he delights for it to be – including for *you!*

I wipe away your sins because of who I am.
(ISAIAH 43:25, CEV)

In times of anxiety

I said, 'I am falling'; But your constant love, O LORD, held me up. Whenever I am anxious and worried, you comfort me and make me glad.
(PSALM 94:18–19, GNB)

Anxiety – worrying about what might happen – is something that can hit us all at times. Sometimes the anxiety is 'free-floating', without any obvious cause to spark it off; sometimes it has more specific causes. Some that are found in the Bible include: concern about the future (e.g. John 14:1–4), getting under pressure to get things done (e.g. Luke 10:38–42), stressful circumstances (e.g. Luke 2:41–48), worrying about others (e.g. Philippians 2:25–30), worldliness (e.g. Matthew 6:25–34), disobedience to God (e.g. Deuteronomy 28:15, 65–68). Those are quite wide-ranging things: some rooted in events over which we have no control, others over which we do.

Whatever our anxiety's cause, the Bible encourages us to bring it to God. That's certainly what David did. In Psalm 55, for example, he mixes honest expression of anxiety with declarations of trust in God. His anxiety comes out in such phrases as: 'My thoughts trouble me and I am distraught at the voice of the enemy, at the stares of the wicked' (vv. 2–3); 'My heart is in anguish within me' (v. 4). In fact, he is so anxious that he just wants to run: 'Oh, that I had the wings of a dove! I would fly away and be at rest' (v. 6). But then there are the declarations of trust in God: 'But I call to God, and the LORD saves me. Evening, morning and noon I cry out in distress, and he hears my voice' (vv. 16–17); 'But as for me, I trust in you' (v. 23). And of one thing he is utterly sure, despite all his feelings at that moment: 'Cast your cares on the LORD and he will sustain you; he will never let the righteous fall' (v. 22).

Whatever our anxieties may be, the Bible encourages us not to pretend they aren't there, but to bring them to God who has committed himself to being faithful to us and to sustaining us until we come through.

Do not worry about anything, but pray and ask God for everything you need, always giving thanks. And God's peace, which is so great we cannot understand it, will keep your hearts and your minds in Christ Jesus.
(PHILIPPIANS 4:6–7, NCV)

SEPTEMBER 21

Grace maintained

'How can I give you up . . .?'
(HOSEA 11:8)

Ever felt like giving up on something? Perhaps you tried and tried to get it right or to get it to work, and it just wouldn't; so you ended up walking away. Or have you ever felt like giving up on someone? Perhaps you worked at some issue with them, giving it your best efforts, but nothing seemed to change; and so you ended up throwing in the towel in despair. Probably all of us have faced times like these.

It's therefore hard for us to understand that God *never* feels like this about anything – including us! When God starts something, he finishes it. The Bible promises us that 'he who began a good work in you will carry it on to completion until the day of Christ Jesus' (Philippians 1:6). But the reason for this confidence has nothing to do with us; it is all about God, from start to finish. God himself has made a covenant – a binding, unbreakable contract – with us through the death of his Son, Jesus Christ. It is because of this covenant that God remains faithful to us, even when we are unfaithful to him. As Paul put it, 'If we are faithless, he will remain faithful, for he cannot disown himself' (2 Timothy 2:13).

Such grace and faithfulness doesn't mean God is 'soft' however! He is not some weak father who 'lets his children get away with anything' – he loves us far too much for that! That is why, in his grace, he promises to bring tender, fatherly discipline into our lives when it is needed. Such discipline proves that we are truly loved – loved, not hated!

Perhaps you have been experiencing the discipline of God. Don't see this as his lack of love for you, but the proof that he truly loves you and wants the best for you. He has promised he will not give you up. So receive his discipline and respond to it; he still has wonderful purposes for you!

My son, do not despise the LORD's discipline and do not resent his rebuke,
because the LORD disciplines those he loves, as a father the son he delights in.
(PROVERBS 3:11–12)

Quick – give me patience!

I waited patiently for the LORD; he turned to me
and heard my cry.
(PSALM 40:1)

'Lord give me patience – and give it me *now!*' Ever felt like that? We confess we have! Perhaps when the bus or train is late (yet again!) and you're about to miss that appointment; or perhaps when the children just won't be co-operative that day and you feel at the end of your tether; or perhaps when the photocopier in the office won't work properly and you're really in a hurry; or perhaps when we are trying to deal with someone who is quite difficult and they just aren't being co-operative; at such times it is all to easy to become impatient.

When we find we are getting impatient, we need to slow down; to stop and to try to see things from God's perspective. One of the best ways to do that is through prayer; but sometimes very practical things can help too. For example, one of Martin's favourite books is a book of games to do while waiting. In our 'instant' society, waiting doesn't come easily to any of us; so he uses the book to help grow the Spirit's fruit of patience in him. All of us need prayerful and practical ways to let the Spirit do this in us.

The Bible says that it is as we learn to 'wait patiently' before God that we receive his promises and help. That's what Abraham learned (who needed patience if anyone did, waiting for that child of promise); but the Bible says of him that, 'after waiting patiently, Abraham received what was promised' (Hebrews 6:15). And how can we be sure that God will give us patience as we call on him? It is because he himself is patient and loves to share what he is with us. The Bible speaks of 'the riches of his kindness, tolerance and patience' (Romans 2:4) – sufficient riches for us too!

Patience is all about being able to wait for things because we *trust* God. Today, as you turn to him and trust him, rest assured that he will bring you all you need for every situation.

Be still in the presence of the LORD, and wait patiently for him to act.
(PSALM 37:7, NLT)

SEPTEMBER 23

Working for God

Whatever you do, work at it with all your heart, as working for the Lord, not for men, since you know that you will receive an inheritance from the Lord as a reward.
(COLOSSIANS 3:23–24)

It's not unusual in Christian circles to hear people speaking about 'full-time work'. What they mean, of course, is 'working for the church'. But in fact this is a tremendously unhelpful way of speaking, for *all* of us are full-time workers for God. As William Tyndale put it, 'There is no work better than another to please God; to pour water, to wash dishes, to be a cobbler, or an apostle, all is one; to wash dishes or to preach is all one as touching the deed, to please God.'

Whatever our calling in life, the Bible makes plain that we are 'working for the Lord, not men'. This means we should give our work our very best, and not see it as a nuisance, or as a hindrance to 'the real work' at church. In fact, the Bible has a lot to say about how we should work. First, it tells us that God wants us to *work hard,* just like Christ himself did. Second, he wants us to work with *integrity,* for integrity and honesty make a tremendous impact in the workplace. Third, God wants us to work with *sincerity,* for the key issue is never *what* work we do, but *how* we do it. Last, but by no means least, God wants us to work with *a servant attitude,* for this is what Christ himself modelled to us throughout his life. All of us can adopt a servant attitude, whether we are the Chief Executive who sits in the office or the cleaner who comes in later to tidy it up. None of us ever gets beyond being a servant!

Working in these ways recognizes that we are working for God, and not for people or for ourselves. And it's when we work like this, that we enjoy our work and receive God's blessing. So if you've been feeling weary in your work, ask God to help you to see it with this new perspective, and claim his promised blessing on your work today.

We were meant to enjoy our work, and that's the best thing we can do.
(ECCLESIASTES 3:22, CEV)

SEPTEMBER 24

Stones of remembrance

*Then Samuel took a stone and set it up between Mizpah and
Shen. He named it Ebenezer, saying,
'Thus far has the LORD helped us.'*
(1 SAMUEL 7:12)

Probably all of us have had times when we were clearing out some drawers
and came across something from years past that made us think, 'Oh look,
I'd forgotten all about that!' And then, for a few moments, the memories
come flooding back – before the object is stuffed back in the drawer again
to await another clear-out! That's how we can be with God too: forgetful,
with memories 'stuffed in the drawer'. So the Bible encourages us to have
'stones of remembrance'.

Our opening verse is drawn from a time when Samuel provided such
a prompt. God had given Israel a supernatural victory over the Philistines.
So Samuel set up a stone, calling it 'Ebenezer' ('stone of help'), to make
sure that God's people would never forget this great blessing of God.
Every time they walked past it, they were to think, 'Ah yes! God helped
us win that victory! He can do it again!'

We too need ways of putting modern-day 'stones of remembrance' into
our lives, families and churches, so that we don't become forgetful of God's
blessings either – both the 'ordinary' blessings that we so easily take for
granted, and those 'special' blessings that change our lives in some way. It's
actually not very difficult to do. For example, we could set up an
'Ebenezer' at meal times by simply stopping and saying thank you to God
before we eat, to remind ourselves that this is his provision and not ours;
we could write Bible verses that we feel God has promised to us in the front
of our Bible and keep coming back to them; we could keep tangible
mementos of special occasions when we knew the blessing or protection of
God in some way; we could pin up photos of special events or people on
the notice board; we could have special church services each year when we
look back and recite together the goodness of God to us. The list is endless!

What about you? Is there some stone of remembrance that God would
have you set up today to help you remember?

*Praise the LORD, I tell myself, and never forget
the good things he does for me.*
(PSALM 103:2, NLT)

SEPTEMBER 25

Failure does not disqualify me

*For the sake of your name, O LORD, forgive my iniquity,
though it is great.*
(PSALM 25:11)

All across the world there are countless people who feel disqualified from knowing God's blessing or from ever being used by God again. The reason? At some point in their past they 'messed up'. Perhaps they experienced some moral failure, or their family life fell apart, or they made serious errors at work, or they got into trouble with the authorities. Whatever it was, they have lived under the shadow of it ever since, feeling disqualified from being useful to God and walking around as a 'second-rate' Christian.

If this is you, we've got good news for you: *failure does not disqualify me*! If failure disqualified us from God's love and purposes, the Bible would be a much thinner book. But in fact it's a very big book, with lots of stories of people who ought to have been disqualified, but who discovered they weren't. People like King David, who failed on countless occasions, as a husband, father and king. And these failures were big! His failure to deal with his sexual appetites led to deception and conspiracy to murder, while his failure to deal with his sons led to endless family problems and civil war. So why did David find new hope while Saul, whom he replaced, never did?

The answer is simple: Saul blamed others, whereas David took responsibility for his actions and confessed his sin. He was truly a 'man after God's heart' (1 Samuel 13:14) who kept his heart tender towards God. And that's the sort of person who discovers that failure does not disqualify us – *providing* we handle the failure properly.

If you feel disqualified because of something in your past, *today* can be the day that this disqualification can end! Stop believing the lie of the devil, and start believing the truth of God. Remember that with God, your failure need never disqualify you - providing you will 'come clean', face those you need to, and embrace whatever process is appropriate. Do so and, like David, you too will discover that *failure does not disqualify me*.

*Although our sins testify against us, O LORD, do something for the sake of
your name. For our backsliding is great; we have sinned against you.*
(JEREMIAH 14:7)

SEPTEMBER 26

The seed of the word

*'Those who sow in tears will reap with songs of joy. He who
goes out weeping, carrying seed to sow, will return with songs of
joy, carrying sheaves with him.'*
(PSALM 126:5–6)

Seeds are amazing things. Such tiny beginnings, yet with such huge
potential; at first, so dry and arid and lifeless, yet ultimately growing and
exploding with life. The way a seed starts out certainly belies how it ends
up. Which is why the Bible is often described as a seed; for God's word
may start out small and insignificant, but in it lies a destiny and power to
grow phenomenally and to take over everything.

Many of Jesus' parables described the word of God as seed. Perhaps
one of the best known is the parable of the sower, where Jesus tells us that
'the seed is the word of God' (Luke 8:11). Such seed carries within itself
tremendous potential for growth; all that needs to happen is for it to be
sown in good soil. The rest is up to God!

In another parable, he spoke about a man sowing seed which grew
irrespective of what the man did or didn't do. 'Night and day, whether he
sleeps or gets up, the seed sprouts and grows, though he does not know
how. *All by itself* the soil produces corn . . .' (Mark 4:27–28). Note that
little phrase: all by itself. Just as a seed has inherent power within itself, so
does the word of God. Whether we fuss over it or not, it still does its work
– because it is *God's* word, not ours. Our part is simply to sow the seed;
God will watch over its growth.

Perhaps you have been seeking to sow the seed of the word in some
situation, but without seeing much apparent success. The Bible tells us to
simply stick at it, watering the seed with prayer, confident that God will
keep his promise that it *will* grow. Even if your seed sowing has seemed
difficult or hard-going, don't give in; the joy of harvest will surely come!

*'Sow your seed in the morning, and at evening let not your hands be idle,
for you do not know which will succeed, whether this or that, or whether
both will do equally well.'*
(ECCLESIASTES 11:6)

SEPTEMBER 27

Being a team player

*Now all of you together are Christ's body, and each one of you
is a separate and necessary part of it.*
(1 CORINTHIANS 12:27, NLT)

Watch children playing football and it won't take long to see how little
they understand the concept of playing as part of a team. They furiously
speed ahead, steadfastly ignoring calls of, 'Pass it to me! To me!' They
want to do it all themselves – especially scoring the goal and being the
hero of the match! Unfortunately, some Christians are just like that, and
so miss God's promised blessing on 'team'.

One of the 'key players' at Antioch was Barnabas. A man 'full of the
Holy Spirit and faith' (Acts 11:24), he played a key role as a leader; but
he was also aware of his limitations. He knew he couldn't do everything
himself, no matter how gifted he was; so, when he found many
responding to the gospel, he went and found Paul, bringing him back to
help. By Acts 13 we quickly find a *team* of leaders in place, who in turn
released yet another team to do more mission. Here was a church that
clearly understood 'the body', 'the team'.

This sort of plural leadership was characteristic of church life from its
earliest days, and the church was all the more effective because of it –
though no doubt it felt painful at times! At Antioch there were 'prophets
and teachers' (Acts 13:1) – a real combination for tension if ever there was
one! But united by the Spirit as a team, they were able to do far more
together than any of them could have done alone.

It is when we forget the importance of 'team' that we get weary and
discouraged, just like Elijah when he complained, 'I am the only one left'
(1 Kings 19:10) – whereas in fact there were another seven thousand like
him! But in his stoicism and self-pity, he had missed them!

Don't try to be a solo player. God has made us part of a team, and has
promised a blessing when we live as such. So live that out today!

*How good and pleasant it is when brothers live together in unity! . . .
For there the LORD bestows his blessing, even life for evermore.*
(PSALM 133:1, 3)

God likes fruit!

*Blessed is the man who trusts in the LORD, whose confidence is
in him. He will be like a tree planted by the water that sends
out its roots by the stream. It does not fear when heat comes; its
leaves are always green. It has no worries in a year of drought
and never fails to bear fruit.*
(JEREMIAH 17:7–8)

Strange as it may seem, some people don't like fruit. Bananas, apples,
oranges, grapes – offer whatever you like, but they will all be met with
rejection. God, however, loves fruit! In fact, fruitfulness pervades
everything he does and looks for.

From the very beginning, God's purpose was that his creation should
be fruitful. God told the living creatures he had made, 'Be *fruitful* and
increase in number' (Genesis 1:22). He made human beings and said, 'Be
fruitful and increase in number; fill the earth and subdue it' (Genesis
1:28). He promised Abraham, 'I will make you very *fruitful*' (Genesis
17:6). The psalmist knew that the righteous are 'like a tree planted by
streams of water, which yields its *fruit* in season' (Psalm 1:3). Ezekiel saw
a vision of God's kingdom in which trees would grow and 'their leaves
will not wither, nor will their *fruit* fail' (Ezekiel 47:12). Jesus promised his
disciples that they would 'go and bear *fruit*' (John 15:16). Paul told
Christians that it was the most natural thing in the world to bear 'the *fruit*
of the Spirit' (Galatians 5:22). And as the Bible closes its pages, describing
God's new creation, we find 'the tree of life, bearing twelve crops of *fruit*,
yielding its *fruit* every month' (Revelation 22:2).

Got the message? God likes fruit! It runs through his purposes for his
people from start to finish. And if God likes fruit, then it must mean that
bearing fruit for him is not difficult – it is part of his purpose for our lives
and is as natural as anything. So don't believe the enemy's lie that you
can't be fruitful. God likes fruit – and he promises that you too will be
fruitful for him.

*The righteous will flourish like a palm tree, they will grow like a cedar
of Lebanon; planted in the house of the LORD, they will flourish in the
courts of our God. They will still bear fruit in old age,
they will stay fresh and green.*
(PSALM 92:12–14)

Helmets on!

'Take the helmet of salvation . . .'
(EPHESIANS 6:17)

Whenever Mike visits developing nations, he sometimes finds himself having to ride on the back of a motorbike without a crash helmet. Back home, that's something he wouldn't dream of doing (not only because it's illegal, but also because it's dangerous!); but in countries where helmets aren't compulsory, and indeed where their cost is prohibitive, he simply has to 'grin and bear it'.

When it comes to protection in our Christian life, however, we certainly don't have to 'grin and bear it'; for God has provided us with all the protection we need, as Paul lists in the believer's spiritual armour in Ephesians 6. One piece of that armour is 'the helmet of salvation'. Like any soldier, a Roman soldier's head needed special protection, and so he wore a sturdy helmet when going into battle. Without that, a blow to the head would be quickly fatal.

We too need protection for our 'heads' – that is, our minds – Paul tells us. It is here that we remember and recall the greatness of our salvation and the certainty of God's promises to us, so that we 'will not grow weary and lose heart' (Hebrews 12:3). Little wonder, then, that Satan does all he can to attack our minds and what goes on there! That is why Paul tells us to get our helmets on, and to 'be transformed by the renewing of your mind' (Romans 12:2). Don't let your thinking go down well-worn paths; stop your thoughts right there, Paul says! Ask God's Spirit to come and renew and strengthen your thinking. Remind yourself of the promise that you are now saved and that nothing can 'separate us from the love of God that is in Christ Jesus our Lord' (Romans 8:39), no matter what our failings or our circumstances.

Remembering and declaring the promise of our salvation is a powerful weapon. Use it today and be strengthened in all you face.

'Since we belong to the day, let us be self-controlled, putting on faith and love as a breastplate, and the hope of salvation as a helmet. For God did not appoint us to suffer wrath but to receive salvation through our Lord Jesus Christ.'
(1 THESSALONIANS 5:8–9)

SEPTEMBER 30

Forget retirement!

'So here I am today, eighty-five years old! I am still as strong today as the day Moses sent me out; I'm just as vigorous to go out to battle now as I was then. Now give me this hill country that the LORD promised me that day.'
(JOSHUA 14:10–12)

Ask someone who has retired how they fill their time, and the common reply will be, 'Oh, I don't have time to do everything I want to!' We love that sort of answer, especially among God's people; for there is no retirement in God's kingdom. *What* we do or can do may change; but the opportunity to do *something* is always there!

It was Caleb who spoke our text for today. He was eighty-five years old at the time, but he wasn't going to let that stop him! The thought of having been through the wilderness and seen the conquest of the promised land, but now stopping before he had received his own inheritance, was just too much to contemplate. He was determined to take Hebron before he died – and he did.

Another person who wasn't planning on retirement was Anna. We meet her in the temple as Jesus' parents came to dedicate him to God. Anna was a prophetess who had given her life to preparing for the coming of Messiah. Her faithfulness in this ministry over the years had prepared her for 'one last big prophecy' over Jesus. (Faithfulness, even in the small things, is important to God.) Luke describes her as 'very old' (Luke 2:36). In fact, assuming she had married at the usual age of fourteen, had then been married for seven years (v. 36), and had been a widow for eighty-four years (v. 37), she was now around a hundred and five! But she was still serving God with all her heart!

It's good to know that there is no retirement in God's kingdom and that some of the key people God used were well advanced in years. There's no reason why that shouldn't include us too. So, if you are getting older, don't let the passing years discourage you and don't let age disqualify you. Simply offer yourself to God for him to use you today.

[The righteous] will still bear fruit in old age, they will stay fresh and green.
(PSALM 92:14)

OCTOBER 1

The secret of contentment

The fear of the LORD leads to life: Then one rests content,
untouched by trouble.
(PROVERBS 19:23)

Nowadays, so few people seem content. Perhaps one reason for that is that we live in a society where we are constantly bombarded with messages telling us that we need something bigger, better, newer, nicer than what we have already; where we are told that our dresses are too long, our ties are too wide, our colours are too bright . . . until next year of course, when we are told that our dresses are too short, our ties are too narrow, our colours are too dull . . . Sounds familiar? Of course it does! The trouble is, we believe it! Little wonder we do not learn how to be content.

A missionary friend of Mike's was working in war-torn Burundi when she came across an old man in ragged clothing, his only possession in the world (other than the clothes he was wearing) being a tin cup held in his hand. She hardly knew what to say to him; but the old man looked up and said with a kindly smile, 'Madam Missionary, I never knew that Jesus was all I needed until Jesus was all I had.' To such faith and deep contentment in Jesus, Madam Missionary could give no answer.

What about you? Does your response to God's provision for you reflect genuine godly contentment? Or have you got caught up in the 'rat race', always looking for 'more' and forgetting Solomon's wisdom when he said, 'Better one handful with tranquillity than two handfuls with toil and chasing after the wind' (Ecclesiastes 4:6). Always wanting 'more' quickly takes us down the path of covetousness, greed, materialism, avarice and ambition, which so quickly lead to loss of contentment, and so to loss of gratitude, and so to loss of a sense of the closeness of God's presence.

The secret of contentment is not more 'things' or 'money' or 'holidays'; it's more of God. In the light of that, how content are you today?

I have learned to be content whatever the circumstances. I know what it is
to be in need, and I know what it is to have plenty. I have learned the secret
of being content in any and every situation . . . I can do
everything through him who gives me strength.
(PHILIPPIANS 4:11-13)

OCTOBER 2

The man who kept going!

*Against all hope, Abraham in hope believed and so became
the father of many nations . . .*
(ROMANS 4:18)

The fact that the name of Abraham occurs 72 times in 68 separate verses in the New Testament shows us that the first Christians clearly believed this was a man from whom we could learn much. Perhaps the thing that stands out most about Abraham was that he was a man who kept hold of God's promises and just kept going – despite everything seeming to be against him.

Paul looks back to Abraham's example in Romans 4, highlighting the way he trusted God. He says that he believed 'against all hope' (verse 18); that is, he didn't let his faith be shaped by the circumstances, but looked the circumstances squarely in the face and said, 'You can change!' He did this 'without weakening in his faith' (verse 19), for faith recognizes that things don't always happen overnight. But faith isn't about 'burying our heads in the sand'. Paul tells us that Abraham 'faced the fact that his body was as good as dead' (verse 19). Faith doesn't pretend that things aren't as they are; it faces up to the reality of the situation, but sees that God is bigger than all of it. 'He did not waver through unbelief' (verse 20), Paul says; that is, he didn't keep doubting what God had said, but kept hold of it and kept coming back to it. He was 'strengthened in his faith' (verse 20), for all of us need to be strengthened and encouraged along the way. And he didn't take any credit for this for himself, but 'gave glory to God' (verse 20), pointing constantly to God and what *he* was doing. In short, he was 'fully persuaded that God had power to do what he had promised' (verse 21), for he had come to know God and could therefore be completely confident in him.

Today, you too may be facing some challenges. If so, be like Abraham – don't give in! keep hold of God's promises and just keep going! For if God has spoken, then God will do it!

. . . let us run with perseverance the race marked out for us.
(HEBREWS 12:1)

OCTOBER 3

What a Father!

'Our Father in heaven . . .'
(MATTHEW 6:9)

When Jesus encouraged us to see God as 'our Father in heaven', he wasn't giving us God's address! 'Oh, you'll find him up there in heaven; third turning on the left after the Milky Way . . .' He was telling us, not where God could be found, but what God was like.

Two things strike us about this expression. First, it tells us that our God is *a Father without limits.* It brings home, not that he is 'out there', but that his heavenly nature has no limitations. He is in heaven and the highest heavens - not trapped in one place like some territorial 'god'. This means that, when we come to him in prayer, we shouldn't think for one minute that there is any limit on what he can do! As Job put it, 'I know that you can do all things; no plan of yours can be thwarted' (Job 42:2). Or as Mary said, 'Nothing is impossible with God' (Luke 1:37).

The second thing this phrase brings home is that our God is *a Father without equal.* He alone is enthroned in heaven; he has no rival; there really is no one like him! As the psalmist puts it, 'Among the gods there is none like you, O Lord; no deeds can compare with yours' (Psalm 86:8). Or as God himself declares, 'To whom will you compare me? Or who is my equal?' (Isaiah 40:25).

If God is our heavenly Father, then a number of things follow. First, it means we can trust him; we need not fear that there is a 'nasty streak' in him or that he wants to 'catch us out' in some way. If we ask him for bread, he won't give us a stone, Jesus assured us (Matthew 7:9–11). He just isn't like that! Second, it means that we can know his love. As John put it, 'See how very much our heavenly Father loves us, for he allows us to be called his children, and we really are!' (1 John 3:1, NLT). Third, it means that we can be intimate with him. We can bring our most personal desires and needs to him, our loving Father.

What a Father this is that you have!

'When you pray, go into your room, close the door and pray to your Father . . .'
(MATTHEW 6:6)

OCTOBER 4

Depending on God in everything

*'Cursed is the one who trusts in man, who depends on flesh for
his strength and whose heart turns away from the LORD . . .
But blessed is the man who trusts in the LORD,
whose confidence is in him.'*
(JEREMIAH 17:5, 7)

The average Christian doesn't find it too hard to turn to God for help or strength in times of crisis. Where most of us get it wrong is in failing to come to him for these things day by day, in the ordinary (dare we say it? – monotonous!) routine of life, when things just keep ticking along. But even here – especially here! – God wants us to derive our strength from him. For it is in the ordinary things of life that we show God that we are resolved to depend completely on him – which, after all, is what the Christian life is meant to be all about.

In fact, the Bible has some rather strong words for those who call themselves God's people, but who don't depend on God (but rather on themselves) in the reality of everyday life. What a contrast this is to Jesus, for whom *every* aspect of life was lived in absolute dependence on his Father, whether praying for 'our daily bread' (Matthew 6:11) or looking to God for 'the right time' (John 7:6) for his every move.

So, how do we get *God's* strength into our lives? Well, first of all, we have to believe that this is how he wants us to live, and that he has promised his help and strength to those who recognize this and ask him for it. Depending on *him* really does bring a blessing! Second, we need to recognise how easy it is to fall into depending on our own strength, into doing things without even praying about them (perhaps because we think they are too 'ordinary' or because we have done them so many times before). Such an attitude is really quite presumptuous (a heart attitude that the Bible says God hates).

Depending on God in everything is a skill we all have to learn and grow in; it doesn't come naturally. But whenever we put it into practice, the blessing of God rushes in. Try it today and see!

'Blessed are those whose strength is in you . . .'
(PSALM 84:5)

October 5

It's God, not nature!

You take care of the land and water it; you make it very fertile.
The rivers of God are full of water. Grain grows
because you make it grow.
(PSALM 65:9, NCV)

Have you ever heard someone say, 'Isn't nature wonderful?' Perhaps they have been admiring some beautiful landscape or sunset or looking at some of the mysteries of earth or outer space on a TV programme. But whenever we hear people say, 'Isn't nature wonderful?' we always want to cry out, 'No! *God* is wonderful!'

The Bible never speaks about 'nature' – at least in the way that the modern world uses that term (which is a convenient way of talking about creation but leaving God out of it). It is not 'nature' that maintains the world, the Bible says; it is *God*. It is his *creation*, not an impersonal 'nature'.

Nor is God rather like an 'absent landlord', as some have seen him. That is, he made creation and then withdrew, leaving it to get on with running itself, rather like a watchmaker might make a clock, wind it up, set it on the mantelpiece and then leave it (a picture used by the Deists in the 18th century). This couldn't be further from what the Bible tells us! For throughout Scripture *God himself* is shown to be actively involved in the ongoing operation of the world. The psalmist says, '*He* makes springs pour water into the ravines . . . *He* waters the mountains from his upper chambers . . . *He* makes grass grow for the cattle, and plants for man to cultivate' (Psalm 104:10,13,14). Not nature – but 'he'. Jesus himself says: '*He* causes his sun to rise on the evil and the good, and sends rain on the righteous and the unrighteous' (Matthew 5:45). Hebrews tells of God's Son 'whom he appointed heir of all things, and *through whom he made the universe*. The Son is the radiance of God's glory and the exact representation of his being, *sustaining all things* by his powerful word' (Hebrews 1:2–3).

So, don't talk about nature; talk about God! Don't be enthralled with 'nature', but with God!

For by him all things were created: things in heaven and on earth, visible
and invisible, whether thrones or powers or rulers or authorities; all things
were created by him and for him. He is before all things,
and in him all things hold together.
(COLOSSIANS 1:16–17)

OCTOBER 6

Godly contentment

*Godliness with contentment is great gain. For we brought
nothing into the world, and we can take nothing out of it. But
if we have food and clothing, we will be content with that.*
(1 TIMOTHY 6:6–8)

Ever tried clearing out a cupboard or a garage? It's amazing what you find there, isn't it? Priceless treasures too good to throw away; documents about past business; bits and pieces that 'may come in handy one day' – or, to put it another way, a whole load of rubbish! Martin once cleared just one cupboard and threw out four dustbins-full of rubbish; Mike clears his garage each Spring and manages to fill the whole car with rubbish for the refuse dump. What an amazing tendency we all have to clutter our lives – which might just be one of the reasons why we find it so hard to be content.

In the cartoon 'Jungle Book', Balloo the bear sings a delightful song entitled 'The Bare Necessities'. He's an easy-going character who, as long as there is a paw-paw or two to eat, is remarkably content and can't see why people get so in a fuss about things. A lot of Christians could do with being a bit more like him! For many of us get so anxious about 'the bare necessities' of life.

When Jesus' disciples were worrying about such 'bare necessities', he told them not to be anxious about 'what you will eat or drink; or about your body, what you will wear' (Matthew 6:25). He pointed to the birds and flowers, saying that if God cared for these, how much more would he care for his children. So, don't worry, he told them! For it's as we seek first the kingdom that we can trust God for such things and be content.

If you have been feeling far from content about the material aspects of your life, consider what having 'more' would really bring you, when you have a God who has promised that you will have all you need for life. So why be anxious for more? Instead, ask for his promised contentment!

*Give me neither poverty nor riches, but give me only my daily bread.
Otherwise, I may have too much and disown you and say, 'Who is the LORD?'
Or I may become poor and steal, and so dishonour the name of my God.*
(PROVERBS 30:8–9)

God's amazing forgiveness

*There is no God like you. You forgive those who are guilty of
sin; you don't look at the sins of your people who are left alive.
You will not stay angry for ever, because you enjoy being kind.*
(MICAH 7:18, NCV)

Ever felt wronged by someone, and forgiven them when they asked you
to do so, but then found it difficult to 'get things back to normal' quickly?
Perhaps you had to work hard at forgetting the issue; or perhaps your
feelings needed to catch up with your will; or perhaps there was a measure
of reserve in the relationship, just in case they let you down again. But
God is never like that! When God forgives, he forgives!

The Bible tells us, first, that God *forgives freely.* There is no cost and
there are no conditions to receiving the forgiveness; no limits to its extent.
It really is 'the gift of God' (Romans 6:23) – a free gift generously given,
with absolutely nothing more to pay because the price has already been
fully and completely paid by Christ on the cross. All we now need to do
is to believe it and to make it our own in our hearts.

Second, God *forgives fully.* He doesn't keep a little bit of judgment in
reserve, just in case he wants to change his mind about us later. And nor
does he keep a memo of our past sins, just in case he needs it. When he
forgives, he forgives completely. At the cross 'he forgave us *all* our sins'
(Colossians 2:13).

Third, God *forgives quickly.* With him, there is no delay in forgiveness,
no time lapse while he thinks about it or waits to see how we get on first,
no need for penance to 'work it off'. When we truly repent, God's
forgiveness comes immediately, as the thief who was crucified with Jesus
discovered when we was assured, after his repentance, that 'today you will
be with me in paradise' (Luke 23:43).

What an amazing God we have! Make sure you are living in the good
of his amazing forgiveness for yourself today.

*How great is God's love for all who worship him? Greater than the distance
between heaven and earth! How far has the LORD taken our sins from us?
Farther than the distance from the east to the west!*
(PSALM 103:11–12, CEV)

The sword of the Spirit

'Take . . . the sword of the Spirit, which is the word of God.'
(EPHESIANS 6:17)

It is interesting to note that when Paul draws up his list in Ephesians 6 of the various components of the spiritual armour that God provides us with to fight our enemy the devil, only this final one – the sword – is an offensive weapon; all the rest are defensive, things that help us stand firm in the battle (reflecting, surely, that the heart of spiritual warfare is not about our needing to take the attack to the devil, but simply standing in the victory that Christ has already won over him at the cross).

The sword Paul is thinking of here is the Roman soldier's short sword, the one that was used in close hand-to-hand combat. Our sword, Paul says – indeed our only weapon – is the word of God, the Bible; for it is in this divinely inspired book that we see more than anywhere else the wonder of God's character, revelation and promises.

This sword of the word was the weapon that Jesus himself used when he was tempted in the wilderness for forty days by the devil. With every fresh attack of the enemy, Jesus would reply, 'It is written . . .' and would quote from the Old Testament scriptures. Interestingly enough each of his replies was taken from the book of Deuteronomy, the story of God's provision for his people during their time in the wilderness. This alone shows us that the Bible always has something relevant for every situation we face!

The word of God has a powerful effect, whether we use it to face temptation, press our way through in prayer, claim God's promises, or release others from the enemy's grip. Of course, it will only be an effective weapon if we have confidence in it, if we truly believe that it really is the inspired and unfailing word of God and are feeding on it regularly so that we can draw on it in times of need.

God promises us that, mixed with faith and prayer, the word of God is a powerful weapon. Use it today!

'For the word of God is full of living power. It is sharper than the sharpest knife, cutting deep into our innermost thoughts and desires.
It exposes us for what we really are.'
(HEBREWS 4:12, NLT)

OCTOBER 9

A Pharisee! What, me?

As a Pharisee, I strictly obeyed the Law of Moses . . .
But Christ has shown me that what I once thought was
valuable is worthless. Nothing is as wonderful as knowing
Christ Jesus my Lord.
(PHILIPPIANS 3:5,7–8, CEV)

Snake pit. Whitewashed graves. Blind guides. Hypocrites. Not terms for winning friends and influencing people! But these were words that Jesus used, not about the 'bad' people of his day, but about the cream of religious society: the Pharisees. We might at times laugh at their behaviour; but tears, not laughter, are really what are called for. For the Pharisees are a classic example of a revival movement gone wrong.

Their roots go back to the time of the exile in Babylon. While there for the seventy years that Jeremiah prophesied, they began to ask, 'How on earth did we end up here?' And as they reflected on their history, they realized that it was because they had disobeyed God's word. And so it was that, as they eventually returned, they began to give themselves to strictly living by God's word lest anything like that should ever happen again. And somewhere around that time, the forerunners of the Pharisees arose.

So fearful were they of breaking God's Law, even accidentally (and so ending up under judgment again), that they began to create a whole body of 'by-laws', added alongside the Law, to help them avoid getting anywhere near breaking the Law. By the time of Jesus, there were hundreds of these 'by-laws'; and what had started out as a well-intentioned revival movement to ensure obedience to God's word had degenerated into a legalistic bunch of nit-picking bigots who would rather have Jesus obey *their* regulations and interpretations than let him do wrong things like heal people on the Sabbath. The revivalists had gone backwards!

Thankfully, Pharisees can change, as Paul himself discovered. But the Pharisaic, legalistic spirit is hard to root out of our lives, and Christians have sometimes been the very worst at resisting new things that God might want to do. What about you? Any Pharisaism in your heart? Ask Jesus to expose it – and be ready to let it go! After all, only Jesus is worth fighting for!

'Unless your righteousness surpasses that of the Pharisees and the teachers of
the law, you will certainly not enter the kingdom of heaven.'
(MATTHEW 5:20)

Watch out for yeast!

*'Be on your guard against the yeast
of the Pharisees and Sadducees.'*
(MATTHEW 16:6)

Yesterday we looked at the origins of the Pharisees; today, let's look at what characterized them and why Jesus warned us to beware of their attitudes which, like yeast, could spread so quickly. In Matthew 23 he highlights seven features of Pharisaic religion – features that are still a challenge today.

First, Pharisees focus on words not deeds (vv. 1–4), being quick to tell others what to do, but slow to do it themselves or help others to do it. Second, Pharisees focus on externals not internals (vv. 5–7). Their practices were often rooted in Scripture; but they had lost the heart behind them. So, they wore tassels, not to remind *them* that they were God's people, but to remind *others*. It was a way of showing off. Third, Pharisees focus on themselves not others (vv. 6–12). They loved being the focus of attention, claiming the best seats and liking the right titles. Fourth, Pharisees focus on their own cause, not God's kingdom (vv. 13–15). They would do anything to promote Pharisaism and go to any lengths to win converts to their cause. But they had little time for God's kingdom; if they had, they would have gladly welcomed Jesus. Fifth, Pharisees focus on the letter not the spirit (vv. 16–22). They could recite every one of Scripture's 613 laws (248 positive, 365 negative) and all their interpretations and by-laws; but they constantly missed the spirit of it. Sixth, Pharisees focus on the minor not the major (vv. 23–28), assiduously tithing even their herbs, but neglecting justice, mercy and faithfulness. Little wonder Jesus called them 'blind guides' (v. 24). Seventh, Pharisees focus on the past not the present (vv. 29–36). An over-rosy view of the past was the constant focus of their attention (vv. 29–31) which they were so locked up in that they couldn't see what was happening in the present, right before their eyes (vv. 33–36). All of this led them to become hard-hearted and unresponsive to God; and so they missed the new thing that God was doing in Jesus.

Thankfully, Pharisees can change! Both Nicodemus and Paul, one-time Pharisees, met Jesus and they changed. And still today, 'Pharisees' can change!

*But by the grace of God I am what I am, and his grace to me
was not without effect.*
(1 CORINTHIANS 15:10)

OCTOBER 11

Strength through togetherness

*But God, who comforts the downcast, comforted us
by the coming of Titus.*
(2 CORINTHIANS 7:6)

One of the devil's greatest tactics is to try to isolate God's people. Right at the beginning, he tried to isolate Eve from Adam, and both of them from God. Thrilled with his success, he has tried to do the same with God's people ever since: he tempted David when he was alone and his friends were away at battle; he tempted Elijah to think he was on his own in confronting Ahab and the prophets of Baal; he tempted Jeremiah to feel utterly deserted to the point of black despair. Truly, isolation is one of his greatest weapons.

This is why it is so important for God's people to meet together; for when we are alone, we are so much more vulnerable to his accusations and attacks. Yet here is the strange thing: when we feel spiritually 'down', the very last thing we want to do is to meet with God or with other Christians! And, of course, the devil confirms such thoughts. 'You're better off by yourself.' 'No one cares about you anyway.' 'No one understands you.' 'You've got to get through this on your own.' Ever felt those sort of things?

Perhaps it was these sort of thoughts that the writer to the discouraged Hebrew Christians had in mind when he reminded them of the importance of gathering together to share in God's presence and to encourage one another. Even as great a figure as the apostle Paul felt the need of God's people. He wrote to the Corinthians of his struggles in Macedonia, and of how gracious God was in sending his dear friend Titus to him to encourage him in his time of need.

To admit we need our brothers and sisters in Christ is not a mark of weakness, but of strength; weakness is to feel that we do not need them! Today, don't let the devil isolate you; rather enjoy God's promised provision through his people.

*And let us consider how we may spur one another on towards love and good
deeds. Let us not give up meeting together, as some are in the habit of doing,
but let us encourage one another – and all the more
as you see the Day approaching.*
(HEBREWS 10:24–25)

OCTOBER 12

Grateful for a cuppa

Jesus then took the loaves, gave thanks, and distributed to those who were seated as much as they wanted.
(JOHN 6:11)

When Mike first visited Uganda (indeed, first visited a developing nation) over twenty years ago, he was just about to drink the cup of tea he had been offered when his host interjected, 'Shall we give thanks?' Slightly embarrassed, Mike put down his cup and saucer until a heart-felt prayer of gratitude for the provision of God was completed. You see, these people had been through civil war; they genuinely knew what it meant to be grateful for a cup of tea, and they didn't want to forget.

But what about us? Are we grateful for our food? Do we despise saying 'Grace' before a meal or see giving thanks each time as being rather legalistic? Or do we say 'Grace' but almost as a mere ritual? Either way, the Bible encourages us to be genuinely thankful for God's provision of food. But why? After all, is it not our money that buys it? Yes; but who upholds creation from where our food comes? Who orders the seasons and sends the rain? Who ultimately provides the food? Our faithful Father God! As the psalmist says, 'He makes grass grow for the cattle, and plants for man to cultivate – bringing forth food from the earth: wine that gladdens the heart of man, oil to make his face shine, and bread that sustains his heart' (Psalm 104:14–15).

If you are grateful to God for his provision of your food, then here are a couple of ways you could show it. First, you could pray a prayer of thanks before each meal, just as Jesus himself used to do (yes, even in the restaurant or the works canteen!). Second, you could share what you have with others, whether through hospitality or the relief of those in need (both practices being highly commended in the New Testament). As Paul put it, 'Share with God's people who are in need. Practise hospitality' (Romans 12:13).

God wants us to develop an *attitude of gratitude* – even for a cup of tea!

After he said this, [Paul] took some bread and gave thanks to God in front of them all. Then he broke it and began to eat.
(ACTS 27:35)

OCTOBER 13

The Lord who redeems

*'Praise be to the LORD, who this day has not left you without
a kinsman-redeemer.'*
(RUTH 4:14)

In the week that we wrote this, a powerful earthquake hit a town in the
Middle East, causing devastation and tens of thousands of deaths. The
pain and loss at such times can barely be imagined. One scene was
particularly dreadful: a young child who had lost a dozen members of his
family stood crying, now absolutely alone in the world.

This is rather how Naomi must have felt: alone in the world. She, her
husband and two sons had left Bethlehem to avoid famine and had gone
to neighbouring Moab. Disaster followed however. First, her husband
died; then, some time later, her two sons (who had by then taken Moabite
wives, Orpah and Ruth). On hearing that the famine back home was over,
Naomi decided to return, but urged her daughters-in-law to stay in
Moab, as she could offer them no future. Orpah stayed; but Ruth resolved
to go with Naomi, saying, 'Where you go I will go, and where you stay I
will stay. Your people will be my people and your God my God. Where
you die I will die, and there I will be buried' (Ruth 1:16–17).

As they returned, they encountered – quite by 'chance' (but then,
nothing is 'by chance' where God is concerned!) – a man called Boaz, a
kinsman-redeemer; that is, a nearest surviving relative who had a duty to help
them. A delightful 'cliff-hanger' of a love story unfolds, which ends happily
ever after as Boaz marries Ruth. Provision is now made for Ruth and Naomi
at last, and a family line established from which King David would come.

This whole story really looked quite hopeless. But unknown to Naomi
and Ruth, God had already made plans for their redemption – for
redemption is what God does best! For us too, God never leaves us
without a kinsman-redeemer – someone who already has plans to rescue
us from our situation and turn things round for our good. Of course, that
'someone' is Jesus.

No matter what your circumstances might be at this time, no matter
how bleak the outlook, your God is your redeemer and he has a rescue
plan for *you*!

'Rise up and help us; redeem us because of your unfailing love.'
(PSALM 44:26)

OCTOBER 14

Who pays?

*Christ's death was . . . a one-time event, but it was
a sacrifice that took care of sins forever.*
(HEBREWS 9:28, THE MESSAGE)

Have you ever been in a restaurant when both you and your friend have insisted on paying the bill? 'I'll pay!'. . . 'No, this one is on me'. . . 'No, I absolutely insist.' And the one who grabs the bill first wins! But you know, that's how many people are with God. They argue with him over who should pay the bill – the bill of our sin. Of course, it may not be as obvious as that; but while we agree to let Jesus pay, there's something within us that feels that we need to contribute something – if only to leave a tip!

A common way of seeking to do this has been through the practice of 'penance': the saying of prayers, doing of good works or giving of money as a *precondition* or an *addition* to receiving God's forgiveness. This practice is completely unknown in the Bible, but it developed quite early in church history, and by the third century a system of public penance had developed. Penitents would often be separated from the rest of the congregation until the prescribed period of prayer, fasting or good works was completed, and only then could they receive the priest's absolution (the declaration that their sins were forgiven). While such public shows of penance may not be common these days, countless Christians still live under the same unnecessary guilt.

The trouble is, this belief that sin must, at least in part, be paid for by us seems so reasonable, doesn't it? But it is completely unbiblical! In fact, it is wholly at odds with the New Testament's teaching that Jesus' sacrifice on the cross is alone sufficient for *all* our sins and that there is absolutely nothing more that we need to, or can, pay – not even a tip!

If you have been trying to 'do' something to pay off your sin to earn or repay God's forgiveness, then stop it! Understand how complete and sufficient Christ's death is for you, and then see how superfluous is the need for penance in the light of that. He has paid it all! So why would you feel you need to pay again?

He offered a sacrifice once for all, when he gave himself.
(HEBREWS 7:27, CEV)

OCTOBER 15

He confides in us

The LORD confides in those who fear him;
he makes his covenant known to them.
(PSALM 25:14)

Martin sometimes feels, when coming to the end of a prayer time, as if Jesus is tapping him on the shoulder and saying, 'I'm not finished with you yet. I want you to linger longer in my presence.' Such lingering can be hard, can't it? It doesn't always come naturally to us, and we're often all too eager to get on with what we think of as 'the real work' of the day (forgetting that prayer is also a 'real work' in itself).

All of us can find prayer hard at times. That's why Jesus told his disciples the parable of the persistent widow 'to show them that they should always pray and not give up' (Luke 18:1). He knows our weakness, our struggles, our resolutions to get up earlier and spend more time in prayer (which rarely last!); yet he never becomes disillusioned with us, for he never had any illusions about us in the first place! But Jesus doesn't want us to see prayer as something we 'have to do', or to see a lack of it as leading to 'points being knocked off'. He wants us to pray so he can confide in us!

Jesus said to his disciples, 'I no longer call you servants, because a master doesn't confide in his servants. Now you are my friends, since I have told you everything the Father told me' (John 15:15, NLT). That's how he wants us to see prayer! As a time when we don't just go through our 'wish-list', but when we let him confide in us. He wants to reveal what is on the Father's heart, to share his secrets with us, to give us keys for the day from his divine perspective (which is so much more accurate than ours!). He wants the relationship of prayer to be part of our life, not something added on to it.

Today, each of us has this amazing relationship with the Lord in which he wants to confide in us. What a privilege! Let's not take it for granted, but stop and ask what he wants to confide in us today, and then live in the light of it.

The LORD detests a perverse man but takes the upright into his confidence.
(PROVERBS 3:32)

The blessing of unity

'How good and pleasant it is when brothers live together in unity! . . . For there the LORD bestows his blessing, even life for evermore.'
(PSALM 133:1, 3)

People have an amazing way of gathering around things. Think of a football match: thousands of supporters, all cheering on their team, all comrades together, but who, beyond the gates, would have little or nothing to do with one another. Yet a common cause has a powerfully uniting effect. If that can happen for football, how much more can it happen for the church. For what joins us together is not a *cause,* but a *person* – the Lord Jesus Christ, who has actually made us 'members of his body' (Ephesians 5:30). You can't get more united than that!

The trouble is, 'unity' sounds a somewhat uninspiring concept, static and lacking in dynamic purpose. But as we see what the Bible means by unity, and what it promises to those who pursue it, it takes on a completely different dimension. Certainly the psalmist saw it as something exciting. For him, living in unity with God's people was as refreshing as 'precious oil poured on the head,' or 'the dew of Hermon . . .falling on Mount Zion' (Psalm 133:2–3). Unity, he understood, is one of God's promised ways of refreshing us. But it isn't something we have to strive to get; the Bible tells us that, in Christ, we have it already! That's why Paul says, 'Make every effort to *keep* the unity of the Spirit through the bond of peace' (Ephesians 4:3).

This gift of unity shouldn't surprise us, for unity lies at the very centre of our Trinitarian God's being. Unity is therefore a most natural gift from him to his people, to bless them and mark them out as his, and so it should be especially treasured and embraced by us. Equally, unity will always be opposed by the devil for he fears the promised power that it releases.

Today, don't let anything get in the way today of God's promised unity for you, your family, your church and all God's people.

'May the God who gives endurance and encouragement give you a spirit of unity among yourselves as you follow Christ Jesus, so that with one heart and mouth you may glorify the God and Father of our Lord Jesus Christ.'
(ROMANS 15:5–6)

OCTOBER 17

When the questioning is over

You asked why I talk so much when I know so little. I have talked about things that are far beyond my understanding. You told me to listen and answer your questions. I heard about you from others; now I have seen you with my eyes.
(JOB 42:3–5, CEV)

If anyone could understandably question God about his ways, it was perhaps Job. Although Job had lived a godly life, everything had gone wrong for him; so he had a few things he wanted answers to! But when all the questioning was over, he was still no further forward. His friends had tried their best to give him answers, though often they were trite or stock answers that failed to 'scratch where things itched' for Job.

What really changed things for Job was not *questioning* God, but *meeting God.* He had said, 'Let the Almighty answer me' (Job 31:35), and God had answered – but not in the way Job expected. In chapters 38–41 God revealed himself to Job in a powerful way through a storm and started to ask Job some questions of his own: Do you know how creation came into being? Can you tell the morning to come? Do you know where light lives? Do you know where snow is kept? Do you understand the universe? Can you make it rain? Do you understand justice? Can you tame the monsters of the sea?

By the time God had finished, Job felt as small as it is possible to feel. Suddenly, his questioning of God and his ways didn't seem so important any more. He didn't have his answers; but he had met with God, and that had put a whole different perspective on things. And so, with renewed humility, Job prayed the words of our opening verses.

Let us ask our questions of God by all means. But let us also remember that the real answers are ultimately to be found, not in arguments and explanations, but in meeting with him.

If you have been asking lots of questions of God and getting no answers, perhaps it's time to ask to meet him instead.

'O LORD, open his eyes and let him see!'
(2 KINGS 6:17, NLT)

Flesh and blood

Because God's children are human beings – made of flesh and blood – Jesus also became flesh and blood by being born in human form. For only as a human being could he die, and only by dying could he break the power of the Devil, who had the power of death.
(HEBREWS 2:14, NLT)

What a staggering truth the doctrine of the incarnation is! That God should become a man! Not some sort of half-god half-man, nor God somehow playing at being a man; but truly and fully 'made of flesh and blood' just like us.

John, one of Jesus' closest friends, couldn't have made it more plain. His first letter was written to Christians who were having difficulties with the very concept that God could become a man. So he begins the letter by emphasising the reality of Jesus' humanity: 'That which was from the beginning, which we have *heard*, which we have *seen* with our eyes, which we have *looked at* and our hands have touched – this we proclaim concerning the word of life' (1 John 1:1). John chose his words carefully: heard, seen, looked at, touched – he wanted his readers to be in no doubt at all that the Jesus with whom he had spent three years of his life was indeed a real man – and yet that this man was indeed God.

Again and again, the New Testament shows Jesus doing all the things that characterize human beings: getting tired, being thirsty, feeling hungry, sleeping, experiencing emotions, enjoying children, relaxing with people over a meal, grieving over the death of a friend, suffering, and (the ultimate human experience) dying.

It is this fact of Jesus being truly 'flesh and blood' that means he can understand us and can keep his promise to help us in every situation; because, whatever we face, he has faced it first. Above all, it means he could die in our place, giving his life 'as a ransom for many', just as he promised (Mark 10:45).

For this reason he had to be made like his brothers in every way, in order that he might become a merciful and faithful high priest in service to God, and that he might make atonement for the sins of the people. Because he himself suffered when he was tempted, he is able to help those who are being tempted.
(HEBREWS 2:17–18)

OCTOBER 19

Waiting patiently for the promises

And so after waiting patiently,
Abraham received what was promised.
(HEBREWS 6:15)

What characterizes a good book or film for you? Perhaps it's a good storyline or a gripping ending. Whatever it is, there will be certain things that mark it out as 'different'. And that's how it is with those who are serious about God's promises. They are somehow 'different'. There are certain things that characterize their life and the way they approach the promises which ensures that, ultimately, they are never disappointed.

One such character was Simeon. Simeon was looking for the coming of God's kingdom; but he hadn't sat around idly waiting for it. He had given himself to what he could do, while waiting patiently for what he couldn't do anything about. We are told he was 'righteous and devout . . . and the Holy Spirit was upon him' (Luke 2:25). 'Righteous' means that he had been obedient to God's commands, while 'devout' means that he had been careful in all his religious duties and the outworking of his faith. Whether in relationship to God or his fellow human beings, Simeon had sought to live in a godly way, with the help of the Holy Spirit; and such living pleases our Father and prepares the way for him to act.

But not only was Simeon righteous, he was also patient. We're told that 'he was waiting for the consolation of Israel' (v. 25). Promises by their very nature demand patience (something none of us find easy!). Promises are God's assurance that something *will* happen, even though it isn't happening yet; and that means – waiting! We don't know how long Simeon had been waiting, for we aren't told whether he was old or young; but, whether young or old, he had been giving himself to prayerfully watching and waiting. That's all you can do with promises at times!

If some of God's promises to you have not yet been fulfilled, don't give up on them. Ask God to make you like Simeon, patient and prayerful, until the promise of God is right there in your hands. Remember: with God, a promise is a promise!

So do not throw away your confidence; it will be richly rewarded. You need
to persevere so that when you have done the will of God,
you will receive what he has promised.
(HEBREWS 10:35–36)

'Who is the LORD . . .?'

Who is like the LORD our God,
the One who sits enthroned on high?
(PSALM 113:5)

'Who is the LORD, that I should obey him?' (Exodus 5:2) asked Pharaoh when Moses demanded, in God's name, that he should free the Israelite slaves. In many ways, Pharaoh's question was an excellent one. Egypt had many gods; why should he obey this one, about whom he knew nothing?

But in contrast to Pharaoh, Moses had had a life-changing encounter with this God. He now knew him, and he'd never be the same again. His first encounter had been at the burning bush in the desert, where he discovered *who God was*. It was here that God revealed his personal name – 'the LORD' – to him. This expression 'the LORD' does not at all convey the sense of the original Hebrew, which carries something of a play on words. God had said his name was 'I AM WHO I AM' (Exodus 3:14) or 'I AM' for short; but he then tells Moses, 'You can call me "Yahweh" ("the LORD")' which means 'HE IS'. God is saying more than 'I exist'; he's saying, 'I am always "I AM". Whether in the past, present or future, "I AM". There is no time and place where I am not, where I do not reign. Therefore look to me and declare "HE IS"!' Here was no mere territorial or national god, then, but the God of the whole earth who is always there; who always has been, and always will be.

Moses would have a second, significant encounter with the LORD at Mount Sinai on the journey through the wilderness, where he discovered *what God was like.* For in response to his request to see God's glory, God came down and revealed himself as 'The LORD, the LORD, the compassionate and gracious God, slow to anger, abounding in love and faithfulness, maintaining love to thousands, and forgiving wickedness, rebellion and sin' (Exodus 34:6–7). What a revelation!

Little wonder then that before this God – LORD over everything yet compassionately caring for his people – Pharaoh's might had to bend. And whatever is facing *you* today, if you will come at it in the name of the LORD, it too will have to give way to him.

'The LORD is a warrior; the LORD is his name.'
(EXODUS 15:3)

Go-getter, or sit-backer?

*I, Daniel, understood from the Scriptures, according to the
word of the LORD given to Jeremiah the prophet, that the
desolation of Jerusalem would last seventy years. So I turned to
the Lord God and pleaded with him in prayer and petition,
in fasting, and in sackcloth and ashes.*
(DANIEL 9:2–3)

There are two kinds of people in life: go-getters and sit-backers. Go-getters see the possibilities and do everything they can to make something happen; sit-backers feel that if something is going to happen, it will happen, and there's nothing they can do about it. In the Bible, there's no doubt that those God blesses are the go-getters; those who understand his promises and who 'go for it'.

Daniel was a go-getter. He was so confident about God's promise that Israel would return to their land, that he prayed it into being. He didn't say, 'God has promised it, so it will happen whether I do anything or not,' but rather, 'God has promised it; *therefore* I will pray it into being.' God's promise was the reason for prayer, not the excuse for inactivity; the reason for activism, not the excuse for fatalism. Within just a few months of that prayer, King Darius of Babylon was gone, and Cyrus sent the Jews back home, just as Jeremiah had prophesied. God had promised it; Daniel prayed for it; and it happened!

Discovering God's promises is part of what it means to pray 'according to his will'. This phrase is not a let-out for unanswered or unbelieving prayers; it is about finding out God's promise from the Scriptures and then confidently praying for it, sure that our prayers are bang on target and therefore *will* be answered! God's unfailing promises are given as both the stimulus and the basis for our prayers. We can confidently ask for whatever is promised and, like the persistent widow in Jesus' parable, stick at it in prayer until the fulfilment of the promise is with us.

Don't let go of what God has promised you. Don't be a sit-backer; be a go-getter!

*This is the confidence we have in approaching God: that if we ask anything
according to his will, he hears us. And if we know that he hears us –
whatever we ask – we know that we have what we asked of him.*
(1 JOHN 5:14–15)

OCTOBER 22

Being ourselves

Trust God, my friends, and always tell him each one of your concerns. God is our place of safety.
(PSALM 62:8, CEV)

Some years ago we each had the privilege of meeting Prince Charles. For months afterwards Mike was kicking himself for the rather inane replies he gave to the Prince's questions. He was rather overwhelmed by the occasion, and so (for once in his life) he was lost for words. Martin, on the other hand, (surprisingly for him) was rather more confident. But when we don't know someone very well, it's quite hard to 'be ourselves', isn't it? Once we've got to know them, it's so much easier. And that's how it is with God. The more we get to know him, the more we can be ourselves and express what's in our hearts – questions, complaints and all.

God is neither embarrassed nor angered by our questions. He is big enough to take them all on board, and he doesn't want us to feel awkward in bringing them to him. Some of the prayers recorded in the Bible may sound quite shocking; but none of them shocked God! God wants the sort of relationship with us where we feel free to bring these sorts of questions – and where we are ready to listen to his answers.

The psalms in particular are full of the whole range of human emotions. Their inclusion in the Bible is God's assurance that we can be ourselves and be free in what we bring to him. God knows everything we're thinking anyway; so why try to hide things from him? Some of the varied emotions expressed in the psalms include feelings of: abandonment (Psalm 31), anger (Psalm 109), depression (Psalm 42), desertion by God (Psalm 22), discouragement (Psalm 55), distress (Psalm 102), doubt (Psalm 10), facing old age (Psalm 71), fear (Psalm 27), gratitude (Psalm 116), impatience (Psalm 13), loneliness (Psalm 3), opposition (Psalm 35), persecution (Psalm 7), sadness (Psalm 43), sickness (Psalm 6), sorrow over sin (Psalm 51), stress (Psalm 142), weariness (Psalm 69). There really is a psalm for all seasons!

So, whatever is in your heart today, be yourself and be real with God. Share it with him, exactly like you feel it. And then, be ready to listen to his answer.

I pour out my complaint before him; before him I tell my trouble.
(PSALM 142:2)

OCTOBER 23

Just trusting

LORD, I have heard of your fame; I stand in awe of your deeds, O LORD. Renew them in our day, in our time make them known; in wrath remember mercy.
(HABAKKUK 3:2)

Have you ever had times when you know God has spoken to you or promised something, but it seems to be taking ages for it to happen? If so, you'll feel at home with Habakkuk, a contemporary of Jeremiah. Habakkuk lived in the days leading up to the Babylonian invasion of Jerusalem. His short recorded writings express his inner struggles that, not only did God's ways seem unfathomable, they seemed downright unjust. To paraphrase his prayer dialogue with God, the conversation went like this:

Habakkuk: 'God, why aren't you answering our prayers? And why does evil prevail?' (1:2). God: 'I'm about to do something you couldn't believe – and I'm going to do it through the Babylonians!' (1:5–11). Habakkuk: 'Wait a minute! How can a holy God like you do that? (1:13–17). Come on, God; give me an answer; I'm waiting!' (2:1). God: 'You'll just have to wait and see! It's not time to tell yet! But believe me: it *will* happen (2:3); Babylon *will* be destroyed (2:4–17); and 'the earth *will* be filled with the knowledge of the glory of the LORD, as the waters cover the sea' (Habakkuk 2:14); and you, Habakkuk, are just going to have to trust me!'

We wonder how you would have responded at that point? A cry perhaps of 'Oh no, not again! Not more waiting!'? It would have been very understandable if that was what Habakkuk had said; but rather, his response was one of praise to God in the face of difficulties, followed by an amazing declaration of trust (see today's closing verses).

Here was a man who had not had all his questions answered; but he had met with God in prayer, and that had changed everything. He was ready to go on trusting – for as long as it took. What about you?

Though the fig-tree does not bud and there are no grapes on the vines, though the olive crop fails and the fields produce no food, though there are no sheep in the pen and no cattle in the stalls, yet I will rejoice in the LORD, I will be joyful in God my Saviour.
(HABAKKUK 3:17–18)

OCTOBER 24

Complain to God!

Hear me, O God, as I voice my complaint.
(PSALM 64:1)

The British aren't very good at complaining – or at least, complaining in the right way. Our complaints generally are *about* people rather than *to* people. In fact, our traditional way of complaining is to go to the pub, find some listening ears, and 'get it off our chest'. The trouble is, that's how we can be with God (whatever our nationality!). We complain *about* him, but not *to* him. God hates the former, but welcomes the latter!

For many, the idea of complaining to God seems inappropriate, even blasphemous. After all, doesn't the Bible tell us of some who complained and were judged, like the Israelites in the wilderness who 'complained about their hardships in the hearing of the LORD, and when he heard them his anger was aroused' (Numbers 11:1). This makes complaining look rather dangerous, doesn't it? And yet, the Bible contains many prayers of complaint: complaints about *what God does*, like when Jonah complained at how Nineveh was spared; complaints about *how God works*, like when Moses complained to God that his being sent to Pharaoh was just making things worse for the slaves; complaints about *what God allows*, like when Habakkuk complained that God was allowing evil to go unpunished in the nation. So, how was it that these people complained and got away with it, while others were punished? What made the difference?

The difference was *how* they complained. In the wilderness, the Israelites complained, blaming Moses for their circumstances; but actually, they were complaining against God. Our complaints shouldn't be *about* God, but *to* God. That's what makes the difference. Don't tell others - tell God! When we complain to others, we're really saying, 'God, *you* don't know what you are doing!' But when we complain to *God*, we're saying, 'God, *I* don't know what you are doing; but I really would like to!'

If you have any complaints about anything, bring them to *God* today! And as you do, listen for him explaining things from his point of view.

'For my thoughts are not your thoughts, neither are your ways my ways,'
declares the LORD. 'As the heavens are higher than the earth, so are my ways
higher than your ways and my thoughts than your thoughts.'
(ISAIAH 55:8–9)

OCTOBER 25

Increasing years

*Even to your old age and grey hairs I am he, I am he who will
sustain you. I have made you and I will carry you;
I will sustain you and I will rescue you.*
(ISAIAH 46:4)

The day Mike hit fifty he woke up and shouted, 'Yes!' What he meant was
that there was lots more life in him yet! While we often think of the
younger men and women that God used in the Bible (like David, Esther,
and Timothy), there are also significant middle-aged and older people in
the list of those God used; people like Caleb, who was sent to explore
Canaan at the age of 40 and who was still serving the Lord with vigour at
85; Moses, who was 40 years old when he fled from Egypt and 80 when
he returned there to lead God's people for the next 40 years (that's 120
years of walking with God!); Anna, who was still serving God in her 80s
and who had the privilege of prophesying over the infant Jesus.

Some of you who are reading this today are from that older generation
(and others of you will be one day!), and today we want to encourage you
in particular with the promises of God. God himself honours those who
are older in years and calls us to do the same – something lacking in
Western society today where old age is generally seen as something bad
and where older people are 'has-beens', to be ignored or forgotten. But the
Bible promises that old age is still a time when we can know both the
friendship and fruitfulness of God.

Whether our days are many or few, God promises us that 'our
strength will equal our days' (Deuteronomy 33:25), for he himself will
continue to uphold us and provide for us through all the changing scenes
of life. Not only will he sustain us, but he will continue to help us bear
fruit for him, even if it takes a different form to when we were younger.
As the psalmist puts it, '(the righteous) will still bear fruit in old age, they
will stay fresh and green' (Psalm 92:14). Don't settle for anything less!

He will renew your life and sustain you in your old age.
(RUTH 4:15)

Questioning God's calling

'Ah, Sovereign Lord,' I said, 'I do not know how to speak; I am only a child.' But the LORD said to me, 'Do not say, "I am only a child." You must go to everyone I send you to and say whatever I command you.'
(JEREMIAH 1:6–7)

'What, me God? Why me?' That's probably how most of us feel when God calls us to do something. So we might find it encouraging to know it's how some in the Bible felt too when God called them.

Jeremiah was very significant in God's purposes; but he was also very reluctant about God's call. His ministry began as God said, 'Before I formed you in the womb I knew you, before you were born I set you apart; I appointed you as a prophet to the nations' (Jeremiah 1:5) – though, as our opening verses show, Jeremiah was quick with his excuses. But four things that God had said to him are still as relevant today for those who question his calling on their lives.

First, 'I formed you.' Our Creator has the right to do with us as he wills, just like a potter with his clay. So who are we to argue or prevaricate? Second, 'I knew you.' Even before he was conceived, God 'knew' him; that is, had committed himself to a relationship with him. When God's choice of us is so personal, it should cause us to respond with grateful hearts and willing dedication. Third, 'I set you apart.' The Hebrew means being set apart from ordinary uses for God's special use. As Paul would put it, 'You are not your own; you were bought at a price. Therefore honour God with your body' (1 Corinthians 6:19–20). If we're set apart for God's sole use, how can we complain when he uses us? Fourth, 'I appointed you.' Jeremiah's call was specific: to go, not just to Judah, but to the nations. God is God of the whole earth, so can send us where he will.

Jeremiah often struggled with his ministry, and frequently felt inadequate. But God doesn't make mistakes and he doesn't change his mind. Question him by all means; but then do what he says! He has called you, and he will enable you. Remember that today!

The one who calls you is faithful and he will do it.
(1 THESSALONIANS 5:24)

OCTOBER 27

Why wait for heaven?

'The kingdom of God is within you.'
(LUKE 17:21)

Look at rock faces, and you will see how the different strata are often clearly visible and how, sometimes, one layer of rock has pushed hard against another, sliding over the top of it and overlapping it. That's how it is with God's kingdom, Jesus said. In him, God's future age has 'pushed hard' into the present age and 'overlapped it'. As his followers, we now live 'in the overlap'. Our life is rooted in the present; and yet the future has overlapped our present and broken through into it so that we can begin to experience the life of the age to come right now. In short, we don't have to wait for heaven to start experiencing it!

Jesus taught that God's kingdom has two aspects. First, he said that the kingdom is here, right now. He described it as 'near' (Matthew 4:17), 'within you' (Luke 17:21), 'upon you' (Matthew 12:28). All this is the language of immediacy and closeness, not of waiting for something yet to come. But while the kingdom was undeniably present (witness his healings, miracles and deliverances), he also taught that there was an aspect of the kingdom still to come. Many parables underline this future aspect, like the parables of the weeds and the net (Matthew 13), the workers in the vineyard (Matthew 20), the wedding banquet (Matthew 22), and the ten virgins, the talents, and the sheep and the goats (Matthew 25). So, the kingdom is *here and now*, but it is also *there and then*.

In other words, we really can experience some of the kingdom now, though we don't have all of it yet! But although we don't have all of it yet, it doesn't mean we can't experience any of it now! The overlapping kingdom is certainly here to be experienced and enjoyed, but it is limited by its co-existence with this present world. But at Jesus' return, this world will be wrapped up and all that will remain will be the kingdom – which is why it makes such sense to invest in it now!

Don't just wait for heaven as your future; for with Jesus, the future starts now! Ask God to reveal and release more of the dynamic of this kingdom into your life and situation today.

'Your kingdom come'
(MATTHEW 6:10)

OCTOBER 28

The goodness of God

You are good, and what you do is good.
(PSALM 119:68)

Calling someone a 'do-gooder' is almost the worst insult you could make about them in today's Western, self-orientated society. 'Do-gooders' are almost always despised - normally, of course, by those who feel guilty for not having done the good themselves. But as the well-known Christian singer Cliff Richard once said in a television interview, 'I'd rather be known as a do-gooder than a do-badder!' And for Christians, that sums it up nicely.

The truth is, God wants us all to do good! But the reason for that is not that this is how we get to know him or win his favour or work our way to heaven (that happens by believing in Jesus alone); the reason God wants us to do good is, quite simply, because he himself *is* good; and because he *is* good, all that he *does* is good; and because all that he does is good, all that he *promises* can be trusted to bring about good too. This was why Joshua, towards the end of his life, could say to God's people that 'not one of all the good promises the LORD your God gave you has failed. Every promise has been fulfilled; not one has failed' (Joshua 23:14). He knew this faithful fulfilling of the promises had been quite simply an expression of God's goodness to them

It is because God has been so good to each one of us, just as he promised, that he invites us to reflect that by sharing his goodness with others – and not just with our friends, but also with those who set themselves up as our enemies. For goodness demonstrated in our lives can begin to open up people to an understanding of our good God and what he is really like.

Don't be afraid of being a 'do-gooder'; rather, reflect the 'family likeness' by enjoying more of God's promised goodness yourself, and then sharing that goodness with others.

Do what is right and good in the LORD's sight,
so that it may go well
with you . . .
(DEUTERONOMY 6:18)

OCTOBER 29

Shielded together

'Take up the shield of faith, with which you can extinguish all the flaming arrows of the evil one.'
(EPHESIANS 6:16)

Faith, in Western culture, has become a very individualized matter, perhaps stemming from the time of the Reformers with their stress that it wasn't 'the church' that saved us but our individual faith in Christ. While this is quite true, it sadly led to something being lost: that while faith must be *personal*, it can never be *private*; for, from the beginning, God has not just been looking to save individuals, but to build a family. Today's text brings home this corporate dimension; for while Paul promises that the shield of faith will overcome the enemy's attacks, it is not a personal, but a corporate, shield he has in mind.

Roman soldiers had two kinds of shields: one that was small and round, ideal for hand to hand combat, and another that was like modern riot shields, full body-length and curved to protect the holder. It is the word for this second type that Paul uses here. Such shields, when held together, formed a solid wall or roof that stopped every missile. Soldiers alone were vulnerable; but in a group, with their shields together, they had a tremendous defence. And so it is with us in the battles that we face.

One thing we cannot see in our English translations of Paul's instructions about spiritual warfare in Ephesians 6:10–20 is that they are all in the plural. He is saying that these are all things we need to do, not alone, but *together*. Although there will be constant individual skirmishes, it is *together* that we stand against the devil's schemes; it is *together* that we are to be strong in the Lord; it is *together* that our faith is strong (which is why good relationships amongst God's people are so important and why Satan tries to spoil those relationships); it is *together* that we can lift our shields of faith and see the enemy's arrows extinguished

Individually, we may be weak in faith; but together, the Bible promises that our shields will overcome every attack of the enemy. Don't stay isolated in *your* battle; share your needs and circumstances with God's people. *Together* you will overcome!

'This is the victory that has overcome the world, even our faith.'
(1 JOHN 5:4)

OCTOBER 30

Your work isn't wasted

Always give yourselves fully to the work of the Lord, because you know that your labour in the Lord is not in vain.
(1 CORINTHIANS 15:58)

Many of the sermons we hear at church, many of the books we read, many of the messages we listen to or watch on satellite television seem to always exhort us to do more, work harder, pray more, read the Bible more, witness more . . . It really does get quite exhausting, doesn't it! So here's some good news for you: today's reading isn't another one of those! Rather, it promises us that our devotion to the Lord – the hard work we put in for him and his kingdom – are never in vain!

Martin confesses that he sometimes has that 'Oh, not more!' feeling when going out to yet another evening meeting that he secretly wonders whether it is worth while and when he'd much rather stay in and settle down to some television therapy. (Of course, none of our readers will ever have felt like that!) The truth is, sometimes we go to our meetings and really do glimpse the eternal perspective of what we are part of; but sometimes we don't glimpse that eternal perspective at all. In fact, we may even feel worse when we get back home than when we left! Well, today's verse encourages us to forget the struggle for a moment. Relax! God is still building his kingdom; and what you do for him will not be wasted.

So, for a few moments, put aside your 'to-do' list or your busy schedule. Realize afresh that you are a child of God. Be confident in *him*. Apply the promises of today's verse to your own life. Your hard work *will* 'pay off', if we may use a secular expression. Your prayers *will* be answered. Your gifts *will* be put to good use. Your hard work *will* bear fruit. Why? Because God's kingdom is not about you, but about him. His kingdom *is* growing, the harvest is coming, and you will hear his voice saying, 'Well done, good and faithful servant!' (Matthew 25:23).

> *Let us not become weary in doing good, for at the proper time*
> *we will reap a harvest if we do not give up.*
> (GALATIANS 6:9)

OCTOBER 31

The power of one

*'Holy Father, protect them by the power of your name – the
name you gave me – so that they may be one as we are one.'*
(JOHN 17:11)

The atmosphere in the Upper Room is hard to imagine. Jesus has shared
the Passover with his disciples; he has washed their feet and spoken of his
departure; he has taught about the coming Holy Spirit; he has warned
them of opposition to come. And now, as their time together comes to its
end, he does the most important thing he can: he prays. And what was
most on his heart – even knowing what was about to happen – was not
himself, but them; and not just them, but also 'those who will believe in
me through their message' (John 17:20). His longing at that moment
seems strange in such circumstances: not for strength for himself, but for
unity for them.

Such unity is not about structures or organizations, he said, but about
heart-felt love based on truth. Both are indispensable foundations to this
unity. Little will be achieved by love if it is not on the basis of biblical
truth; but equally, little is achieved if we are strong on biblical truth but
cannot love, or at least cannot love those followers of Jesus who do some
things differently. Paul said that we were not to pass judgement on other
believers over 'disputable matters' (Romans 14:1). Other versions
translate this verse as: 'Don't criticize them for having beliefs that are
different to yours' (CEV); 'Don't argue with them about what they think
is right or wrong' (NLT); 'Do not argue about opinions' (NCV); 'Don't
jump all over them every time they do or say something you don't agree
with' (The Message). There are some secondary matters on which
Christians have validly different viewpoints, and there must be room to
accept these. As someone has said, 'In necessary things, unity; in doubtful
things, liberty; in all things, charity.'

In the light of Jesus' prayer, will such a heart to be 'one' with fellow
Christians be our passion today, with the powerful results that this can
bring?

*'May they be brought to complete unity to let the world know that
you sent me and have loved them even as you have loved me.'*
(JOHN 17:23)

NOVEMBER 1

Questioning God

'Do you still want to argue with the Almighty? You are
God's critic, but do you have the answers?'
(JOB 40:2, NLT)

Let's face it: God's ways aren't always easy to understand. Why he does some things but not others, is often hard to grasp; and this sometimes causes us to question him.

Abraham was someone who did just that. God had told him that Sodom and Gomorrah were about to be judged. Since his nephew, Lot, had settled in that area, Abraham was quick to challenge God about it. 'Far be it from you to do such a thing – to kill the righteous with the wicked, treating the righteous and the wicked alike. Far be it from you! Will not the Judge of all the earth do right?' (Genesis 18:25). Abraham was struggling with how a moral God could do what, to his eyes, seemed such an 'immoral' thing. Surely God had to do what was right? Of course he did; but the problem was, Abraham didn't know the whole story as God did; and so his assessment of what was 'right' differed from God's.

When the angels came to investigate the cities, they were appalled at the rampant immorality there. The next morning they struggled to overcome the reluctance of Lot and his family to leave, and barely got Lot, his wife and two daughters out of the danger area before burning sulphur engulfed the cities. Sadly, the disobedient hesitation of Lot's wife, perhaps looking back on the destruction of their worldly possessions, caused her death.

Abraham had thought that God was less righteous than he should be, but discovered God was far more righteous than he himself was. God could ultimately find only four righteous people (and one of those didn't make it); but they were spared, no matter what number Abraham had set earlier in his bargaining with God. God was far more concerned for others than Abraham could ever be.

When you are tempted to question God, don't be embarrassed to ask him about it. But as you do so, be ready to discover that God always knows 'one fact more'; and when that comes into play, God is truly seen to be the Judge of all the earth, who always does what is right.

He never does wrong. God can always be trusted to bring justice.
(DEUTERONOMY 32:4, CEV)

Forgiving Father, forgiving children

*Forgive us our sins, for we also forgive
everyone who sins against us.*
(LUKE 11:4)

While we've never quite been able to grasp how people 'see' the father or mother in a one-day-old baby, there's no doubt that family likeness develops as children get older. And the same is true in the Christian life. When we are born again, we take on something of 'the family likeness'. Different ones of us reflect different aspects of our heavenly Father's character; but there are certain features that he looks for in us all. And high on the list is that our forgiving Father expects to see forgiving children.

The Bible makes clear that forgiveness is part of God's very nature. As such, he looks for his children to reflect this quality. The importance of forgiveness is seen in the fact that Jesus teaches about it often and includes it in the Lord's Prayer, as we see in our opening verse.

However, it is important we understand that God's forgiving of us is not conditional on our forgiving of others, though some older English translations, such as the King James Version (and therefore the traditional Lord's Prayer that many of us have learned), almost make it sound that way. In the King James translation of Matthew's version, the prayer reads, 'Forgive us our debts, *as* we forgive our debtors' (Matthew 6:12, KJV), making it sound as though the first action were conditional on the second. But this is not the sense of the Greek, as modern translations make plain.

Rather, what Jesus is saying is this: 'Father, we're asking you to forgive us our sins, because we – sinners as we are – have forgiven (Matthew), or are forgiving right now (Luke), others who have sinned against us. If we have done that, Father, how much more will you do the same for us!' That's why it is so important to deal with unforgiveness in our heart; for as long as it remains there, it undermines our assurance that our forgiving Father has truly forgiven us.

Reflect the family likeness today. Resolve that your forgiving Father will be seen in you, his forgiven and forgiving child.

*Do not repay evil with evil or insult with insult, but with blessing,
because to this you were called so that you may inherit a blessing.*
(1 PETER 3:9)

NOVEMBER 3

A time to . . . think

There is a time for everything, and a season for every activity under heaven: a time to be born and a time to die . . .
(ECCLESIASTES 3:1–2)

Two days before writing this, Mike was sitting on plane heading for India, when conversation opened up with the passenger next to him, whom he discovered was a psychiatrist. The conversation covered all sorts of things, but eventually turned to the meaning of life, which gave Mike a great opportunity to share the gospel, and to throw out a gentle challenge. 'You're a doctor; you must have faced death many times.' 'Many' he replied. 'But what about your own death?' Mike asked. 'Do you think you've faced up to that?' The doctor confessed that he hadn't and that he knew he kept putting off even thinking about it. And that sums up so many people today – which, considering the certainty of death for all of us, is amazingly naïve.

No matter what advances might be made in medical science; no matter how long we might feel we can put off 'the fateful day', or even thinking about the fateful day, we will all face the certainty of 'a time to die' (Ecclesiastes 3:2). For death is not simply a biological fact; it is also a theological certainty, the result of Adam's sin on the human race. And while there are sometimes appointments in life that we can't always keep, our appointment with death is one that none of us will miss or be late for.

That's why it's so important to stop and to take 'a time to think'; time to think about our future destiny. Now, this could sound a dreary thought for the day; but for those who love Jesus, the Bible is packed with promises about our future hope and the wonderful assurance that death is not the end, but only the beginning. This means that we need never be fearful of death, either for ourselves or our loved ones. For as Paul put it, 'He died for us so that, whether we are awake or asleep, we may live together with him' (1 Thessalonians 5:10). And that's certainly a promise worth taking time to think about!

But I trust in you, O LORD; I say, 'You are my God.'
My times are in your hands.
(PSALM 31:14–15)

NOVEMBER 4

Not slaves, but sons

So you are no longer a slave, but a son; and since you are a son,
God has made you also an heir.
(GALATIANS 4:7)

In Bible times a slave was a mere piece of property, something owned by someone else, to be used as they saw fit. While some owners were kind (as Joseph discovered under Potiphar), many were harsh (as Israel discovered under Pharaoh). But whether your master was good or bad, you were still, quite simply, in complete bondage to someone else.

Imagine, therefore, the joy of getting your freedom! No longer would you be at the beck and call of another, having to do what you didn't want to do. You would be free – free to choose! But such freedom was costly; either a price was involved (one that, for most slaves, would be unattainable) or unbelievable kindness from the master was required.

And that, says the New Testament, is exactly what has happened for us. For we were all slaves – in slavery to things like sin, impurity, wickedness, lust, greed, fear, to name just some of the things the Bible mentions; or, as Peter put it, 'A man is a slave to whatever has mastered him' (2 Peter 2:19). But when we put our trust in Christ, we were freed from that slavery! Christ himself paid the price – his life given on the cross – buying us out of all that enslaved us. This in itself is wonderful; but there is even better news! For God did not simply 'free us', sending us now on our way; he made us part of his family, adopting us as his 'sons' (though remember that this does not exclude daughters! It is simply that, in Bible times, it was the son who *received the inheritance*, and this is what the Bible wants to stress.)

Today, don't live as a slave – because, if you are a Christian, you aren't one! Don't say 'yes' to the old things that used to order you around! You have a new master now – listen for *his* voice, the voice of a loving Father to his child; for in responding to that voice, there is both freedom and inheritance.

It is for freedom that Christ has set us free. Stand firm, then,
and do not let yourselves be burdened again by a yoke of slavery.
(GALATIANS 5:1)

NOVEMBER 5

Danger: dynamite!

*When Jesus had called the Twelve together, he gave them power
and authority to drive out all demons and to cure diseases, and he
sent them out to preach the kingdom of God and to heal the sick.*
(LUKE 9:1–2)

What strange people we Christians can be. We say we believe in a
supernatural God who has broken into this world in a supernatural way
(through Jesus) – and yet, when it comes to the supernatural in our own
lives, we can get quite nervous. Even churches that claim to believe in the
Spirit's power can get locked in to him having to do things in the same
way as he did them fifty years ago, so that if he does anything different or
unusual now, it can't possibly be the Spirit. How the church has lost the
truth that the Spirit is God's dynamite!

   Our word *dynamite* comes from the Greek word used for the 'power'
of the Holy Spirit. This power is not about 'adding a little extra
something' to our human abilities; it is something quite supernatural that
lifts people beyond what they themselves could do, so that the glory goes
to God alone. Throughout the Old Testament, God's people often called
on his power to show that he alone was the true God. In the New
Testament we continue to see the Spirit's power. Jesus was anointed with
that power at his baptism and then went out 'in the power of the Spirit'
(Luke 4:14), constantly drawing on it to demonstrate the presence of the
Kingdom and the Father's love. In fact, he frequently challenged those
who were well-versed in the Scriptures, but had no understanding of the
power of God. In Acts the same power continued in the life of the church
as believers were empowered by the 'dynamite' of the Holy Spirit,
resulting in powerful prayer, bold witnessing, and many miracles and
healings.

   God's heart and promise is still for his people to know his 'dynamite'
and not to keep him in the boxes of our humanistic thinking. Ask to
know more of his power today.

*Now to him who is able to do immeasurably more than all we ask or
imagine, according to his power that is at work within us, to him be glory
in the church and in Christ Jesus throughout all generations,
for ever and ever! Amen.*
(EPHESIANS 3:20–21)

NOVEMBER 6

Send the fire!

Oh, that you would rend the heavens and come down, that the
mountains would tremble before you! As when fire sets twigs
ablaze and causes water to boil, come down to make your name
known to your enemies and cause the nations to quake before you!
(ISAIAH 64:1–2)

Ever felt like Isaiah did? Perhaps you've faced some desperate situation
and prayed, like him, 'Oh God – you've got to do something!' We can
almost touch the desperation in his heart. Many of us feel like that about
our own nation at this time. 'Oh God, our nation is in a mess – please do
something! Please send your fire!' Actually, God loves prayers like that;
but when we pray them, we need to be ready; for God always begins to
answer such prayers in the life of the one who prayed it.

So how does this fire of God's power become ours? Many of us have
been to conference after conference and learned new methods and
programmes; yet we still lack the power to put them into practice. What
we need are not more conferences, but more power! With Isaiah, we need
to cry: 'Send the fire – and start with me!'

We can start, first, by telling God we are desperate and can't do it on
our own. If our attitude is, 'I can do it!', we will never be in a place where
the Spirit can bring his fire. Second, we need to believe that God keeps
his promises in this area as much as in any other. Third, we need to put
right anything God shows us is wrong in our lives, for how can we ask a
holy God to work through us if we cling on to things that are unholy?
Finally, we need to 'give away' whatever power God gives us, for it is in
giving that there is growing. It is hard to understand Christians who claim
to have power but do nothing with it. They are rather like a rocket that is
ready for lift-off but which stays on the launch-pad with a never-ending
countdown!

Be desperate today: ask God to send his fire – and be ready for it to
start in you!

When Solomon finished praying, fire came down from heaven and
consumed the burnt offering and the sacrifices,
and the glory of the LORD filled the temple.
(2 CHRONICLES 7:1)

Deal with it!

'Therefore, if you are offering your gift at the altar and there remember that your brother has something against you, leave your gift there in front of the altar. First go and be reconciled to your brother; then come and offer your gift.'
(MATTHEW 5:23–24)

How many times have you sat through a service, or tried to struggle through your own prayer time, with unresolved issues filling your mind? 'What did she mean?' 'Why did he say that?' 'Didn't he know that was hurtful?' On and on our thoughts go. And what do we discover by the end of it all? That we might as well not have bothered to worship or pray, for all the good it did! That's why Jesus stressed the importance of dealing with issues first, before we come to worship or pray.

The trouble is, when we don't deal with issues properly, they are left to fester, to the harm of both us and others. Think of how David failed to deal with things when his son Amnon raped Tamar, his half-sister. We read that 'when King David heard all this, he was furious. Absalom never said a word to Amnon, either good or bad; he hated Amnon because he had disgraced his sister Tamar' (2 Samuel 13:21–22). In other words, rather than dealing it, David just 'swept under the carpet' – and everyone ended up stumbling over the hidden heap! Everybody was mad, but nobody did anything about it. Nobody brought the issues out into the open so that they could be dealt with. And because nobody did anything about it, the whole thing got worse and worse and ultimately led to Absalom's murder of Amnon, which in turn (because this issue too was not dealt with) led to Absalom's rebellion against David and civil war.

What we leave in the darkness, Satan always has power over; but when we bring things 'into the light', Jesus' forgiveness, healing and release can break in. If you recognize that you have left things in the darkness or swept them under the carpet, don't leave them there any longer. Deal with it! Your worship, prayer and relationship with God will then be so much more enjoyable, so much more fruitful.

Whoever loves his brother lives in the light, and there is nothing in him to make him stumble.
(1 JOHN 2:10)

NOVEMBER 8

Here comes trouble!

The LORD is good, a refuge in times of trouble.
He cares for those who trust in him.
(NAHUM 1:7)

Rather like buses, troubles seem to have a way of coming all at once. You know how it is: having just missed one bus, you wait for the next which (the timetable says) should be along in ten minutes. Ten minutes go by; then fifteen; twenty; twenty-five; thirty. Then, all of a sudden, three buses come racing down the road one behind the other. And trouble can be a bit like that, can't it? Life has been going swimmingly, when – suddenly – a whole batch of troubles seems to come all at once: someone in the family gets sick; there are problems at work; the children are struggling at school; the car breaks down; an unexpected bill arrives. At times like that, we really need to know who to turn to!

The prophet Nahum lived in a time of real trouble. The brutal Assyrian empire had been ruthlessly expanding its territory. Samaria, to Judah's immediate north, had already fallen to its tyrannical grip some years back; and now Judah itself looked like it was about to go the same way. But in the midst of all this trouble, Nahum declares in faith that Assyria was about to experience God's judgment for all its cruelty (and indeed this happened shortly afterwards when Babylon overthrew it). And in the meantime, declared Nahum (whose very name means 'the LORD comforts'), God assures his people of his comfort in the midst of trouble. God is still good, Nahum said; he still cares, and we can still find a refuge in him.

Whenever we are facing trouble, God doesn't want us to pretend everything is all right; and nor does he want us to run around as headless chickens panicking and looking for a solution. Rather, he invites us to honestly bring the trouble to him and to make him our refuge. Maybe you are feeling, 'Here comes trouble!' Perhaps so; but here comes the Lord too!

For in the day of trouble he will keep me safe in his dwelling; he will hide
me in the shelter of his tabernacle and set me high upon a rock.
(PSALM 27:5)

NOVEMBER 9

The Father's generous love

How great is the love the Father has lavished on us, that we should be called children of God! And that is what we are!
(1 JOHN 3:1)

One of the thoughts that keeps Martin going through the later months of the year is Christmas. He likes to look ahead and to imagine the Christmas table laid in all its glory; the goodies spread out; the excitement and anticipation of enjoying family company mounting; minor differences set aside. All we need to do is eat!

This is how it is with us as Christians. Our generous God calls us to his table where he lavishes his love on us. He is so incredibly kind that he even calls us his sons and daughters! And that is what *we* are right at this moment, whether you're reading this in bed, on a bus, in a plane, or on Mars (for technology advances so quickly these days!). Whether you *feel* you're a child of God or not is irrelevant. After all, do you always feel your particular nationality or your marital status? Of course not. But that is what you are. And likewise, being a child of God is what you are if you have put your trust in Christ.

The Bible says that 'God has poured out his love into our hearts by the Holy Spirit, whom he has given us' (Romans 5:5). So stop a while, and enjoy his love and his gift of the Holy Spirit. Trust him afresh. Allow him to touch you generously at your point of need.

But, marvellous as all that is, it's not the whole story. For look at the verse at the end of today's reading. When Christ returns and is revealed in all his glory, we will see him – completely, directly, and perfectly clearly! – and not only will we see him, we will be changed to become like him – 'in a flash, in the twinkling of an eye' (1 Corinthians 15:52) – when he takes our mortal bodies and transforms them into glorious bodies like his own. What a thought to encourage us today!

Dear friends, now we are children of God, and what we will be has not yet been made known. But we know that when he appears, we shall be like him, for we shall see him as he is.
(1 JOHN 3:2)

When it's hard to forgive

*'Forgive us our sins, just as we have forgiven those who have
sinned against us.'*
(LUKE 11:4, NLT)

'I can never forgive them.' Perhaps all of us have heard (or even said) those words. Of course, they are often understandable – especially in the heat of the moment, or under pressure, or in a crisis. But how sad if we can never let go of them. For not to forgive, Jesus said, is to lock ourselves in a prison that we can't get out of.

Mike well remembers the mother of a child who was murdered in the town where he led his first church. Of course, it was horrific, and we cannot imagine the agony that the family faced, particularly as the body wasn't found. But throughout that lady's life, the one thing that 'kept her going' was bitterness and a desire for revenge. Whenever interviewed by the newspapers or television, the same bitterness would still be there; she was never ever able to let go of it and she died a bitter, twisted, and lonely lady. She had put herself in prison and thrown away the key.

God's heart is that we should experience something better than this, no matter what we might go through or how people might hurt us. Of course, God knows he is asking us to do something difficult in telling us to forgive; but he also knows that it will be more difficult for us if we don't! That's why Jesus taught so often about the need for forgiveness. Peter thought he had finally got the message, and one day came to Jesus saying, 'Lord, how many times shall I forgive my brother when he sins against me? Up to seven times?' (Matthew 18:21). He expected a pat on the back for his generous viewpoint; but instead Jesus told him he hadn't even started to understand the issue! Seventy-seven times – in other words, an endless number – is nearer the mark, Jesus said.

You may be finding it hard to forgive someone; but the promise of God is that if you will make the decision and just do it, you will find yourself freed. Don't stay in your prison – turn the key and come out!

*Bear with each other and forgive whatever grievances you may have against
one another. Forgive as the Lord forgave you.*
(COLOSSIANS 3:13)

A vision for the nations

In the last days the mountain of the LORD's temple will be established as chief among the mountains; it will be raised above the hills, and all nations will stream to it. Many peoples will come and say, 'Come, let us go up to the mountain of the LORD, to the house of the God of Jacob.'
(ISAIAH 2:2–3)

Have you noticed how some people can be so small-minded, thinking only of themselves and their own small circle of interests? How good it is that God isn't like that! God has a big heart and a big vision. So, while he chose Israel as the vehicle for his love, he never intended that love to stop with them. From the earliest days, his heart was shown to be not just for *one* nation, but for *all* the nations, as he made clear to Abraham when he called him. 'All peoples on earth will be blessed through you,' he told him (Genesis 12:3). God has a passion to see *the nations* saved!

This vision would soon be lost by Israel however, as they became completely inward looking and self-focused. They gradually came to believe that God's purposes were only for them and that all that the Gentiles could expect was judgment. However, some of the prophets looked ahead and saw something bigger and better, promising that one day 'the nations' would flock to know God for themselves. Jesus reinforced this promise of God when he quoted Isaiah at his cleansing of the temple, reminding the people that God had said that, 'My house will be called a house of prayer for all nations' (Isaiah 56:7; Mark 11:17).

Neither God's promise nor God's heart has changed. This means that his vision for the nations is something that should be an integral part of our lives as his people – whether through our praying, our giving, or our going. It is quite impossible for us to remain small-minded when God has such a big heart!

God has promised big things concerning the nations. Why not ask him today what part you can play in that?

'I will shake all nations, and the desired of all nations will come, and I will fill this house with glory,' says the LORD Almighty.
(HAGGAI 2:7)

NOVEMBER 12

Our source of strength

The LORD is the strength of his people.
(PSALM 28:8)

These days so many people look to so many things as their source of strength. For some, it's vitamins. Go into their home and there will be bottle after bottle of pills. For others, it's going to the gym for their regular workout. For yet others, it's their annual holiday, as they get away from the demands of work and the pressures of life and laze by the pool or stroll along the hills. Of course, all these things can be useful. But nevertheless, they all pass so quickly. The pill bottles quickly empty or are replaced by the latest 'fad'; the benefits of the workout are lost at the next good meal; the holiday memories soon fade as life's pressures return once again.

For us, however, there is a source of strength that never runs out: the strength that can be found in the Lord our God. David faced many challenges in life, both before and during the time that he was king. But his psalms show how his first refuge in times of need was – *God!* He could have run to so many things for refreshment and strength; but what he chose to run to was his God. He described God as 'my rock, my fortress and my deliverer; my God is my rock, in whom I take refuge. He is my shield and the horn of my salvation, my stronghold' (Psalm 18:2). He encouraged others to 'look to the LORD and his strength; seek his face always' (1 Chronicles 16:11).

This God is still as great a source of strength as ever he was to the saints of old. The trouble is, we know this – yet he is often our 'last resort'. We so easily turn to other things first, leaving God at the end of the queue; and then, if nothing else works, we 'give him a go'. Of course, we would never consciously think in such a way! But that is what our actions portray.

Today, let God be your *first* port of call as you look for help and strength. For, as we seek him and his strength, he will be found by us, just as he promised.

But David found strength in the LORD his God.
(1 SAMUEL 30:6)

How kind!

But when the kindness and love of God our Saviour appeared,
he saved us, not because of righteous things we had done,
but because of his mercy.
(TITUS 3:4–5)

There is often not a lot of kindness in the world today, is there? People are so often so busy with themselves that they rarely stop to think of others. So, when kindness is demonstrated in some way, it is all the more striking. That is why someone like Mother Teresa, who spent her life working with the destitute in the slums of Calcutta in India, seems so unusual. The worlds stops and says, 'My goodness, that's amazing!' – whereas in fact God wants it to be completely normal.

The Bible tells us that God wants us to be kind. Why? Because he himself is kind! In fact, he is especially kind to those who don't deserve it (which is a real challenge to our own sense of 'fairness'). Jesus was the very incarnation of kindness, coming to us with kindness out of the kind heart of the Father. He spent his whole life being kind to others – healing the sick, giving hope to the hopeless, providing for the needy, setting people free from their bondages; in fact, even as wicked men were nailing him to the cross, he was still being kind, thinking of his mother and asking John to now take care of her. All were at the receiving end of his kindness, even those who were ungrateful. When he healed ten lepers and only one came back to thank him, he expressed his surprise – but he didn't take their healing away from them. This is what our gracious God is like – giving his kindness freely, even to those who don't deserve it, even to the ungrateful.

This is why Paul reminds us that 'God's kindness leads you towards repentance' (Romans 2:4). For it is as we understand how very kind God is to us that we will in turn pass that kindness on to others. Kindness is a promised 'fruit of the Spirit' (Galatians 5:22); let's ask him to grow more of that fruit in us today.

Always try to be kind to each other and to everyone else.
(1 THESSALONIANS 5:15)

NOVEMBER 14

Knowing his presence

*'For where two or three are gathered together in my name,
there am I in the midst of them.'*
(MATTHEW 18:20, KJV)

This promise of Jesus has proved precious to countless believers throughout the ages, whether to those hiding from antagonistic authorities, or to the faithful few gathering for prayer. For all Christians, however, it is the heart of what our faith and life should be about: being assured of his promised *presence*.

Throughout the Bible, it was God's *presence* that transformed things – and people! When Moses came down from Mount Sinai, having met with God, the most obvious thing to the people was that he had been in the presence of God; in fact, his face was so radiant that he had to put a veil over it. This presence became so precious to him that he cried out to God, 'If your Presence does not go with us, do not send us up from here' (Exodus 33:15).

But not only does God want us to *know* his presence (for that in itself could be a fearful thing), he wants us to *enjoy* his presence. When we know we are right with him, there is nothing to fear, only everything to enjoy. This is reflected in the account of the seventy elders going up the mountain with Moses to meet with God, where it is said of them, 'they saw God, and they ate and drank' (Exodus 24:11). What a wonderful picture this is of how God wants us to be at ease and truly *enjoy* his presence. We are not being unholy or presumptuous if we find God's presence enjoyable – it is what he promises to us!

'Great!' 'Fantastic!' 'Brilliant!' 'Wow!' are modern words of enjoyment. This is the sort of heart that God wants to find in us as we come into his presence, whether on our own or in our meetings. Today, stop in the midst of your busyness and take time to remember the promise of his presence – and enjoy it!

*After two days he will revive us; on the third day he will restore us, that we
may live in his presence. Let us acknowledge the LORD;
let us press on to acknowledge him.*
(HOSEA 6:2–3)

Praying for the church

*Please help us by praying for us. Then many people will give
thanks for the blessings we received
in answer to all these prayers.*
(2 CORINTHIANS 1:11, CEV)

There are probably times when we all get frustrated with 'the church'. And yet, it is still the major vehicle through which God acts in the world. So praying for it should be a priority. But what can we pray for?

First, we can pray for *its growth*. Jesus wants his church to grow, not so we can simply see our buildings full on Sundays, but out of his heart to see people saved. He told his disciples, 'The harvest is plentiful, but the workers are few. Ask the Lord of the harvest, therefore, to send out workers into his harvest field' (Matthew 9:37–38). This is not prayer for some vague concept of 'church growth', but rather for workers to go and do the job! The harvest is ready; all it needs is people to bring it in. Paul certainly prayed for believers to be 'active in sharing your faith, so that you will have a full understanding of every good thing we have in Christ' (Philemon 6).

Second, we can pray for *its leaders*. The devil knows the truth of the saying, 'Strike the shepherd and the sheep will be scattered' (Zechariah 13:7), and this was the strategy he used at the cross (Matthew 26:31; Mark 14:27). It is still one he uses today. If he can get leaders weary or discouraged, or attack them in some way, then he can significantly weaken the church. This is why church leaders should be the object of our constant prayers rather than our constant criticism.

Third, we can pray for *its unity*, just as Jesus did when he prayed 'that all of them may be one, Father, just as you are in me and I am in you' (John 17:21). We should be eager to express the unity of the Father, Son and Holy Spirit. But let's face it, that doesn't always come easily! So we need to pray for it – both within our own local church, and between the churches in our cities, towns and villages. Such unity attracts the blessing of God, and makes a powerful impact on the world.

Don't just criticize the church – pray for it!

Finally, brothers, pray for us . . .
(2 THESSALONIANS 3:1)

NOVEMBER 16

What price loyalty?

*'O LORD, God of our fathers Abraham, Isaac and Israel, keep
this desire in the hearts of your people for ever,
and keep their hearts loyal to you.'*
(1 CHRONICLES 29:18)

According to a survey carried out in the United Kingdom towards the end of 2003, loyalty seems to be on its way out. The survey showed that loyalty towards politicians, employers, partners and the Church has plummeted over the past 20 years. More than seventy-five per cent of those interviewed said they felt less loyalty to any political party or religion than in the past; and most said that they felt fewer ties of loyalty to their bosses. Sadly, while loyalty was seen as one of the most desirable qualities when choosing a partner, two-thirds of those interviewed thought that loyalty was now less prevalent in relationships.

By contrast to all that, almost fifty per cent of the people surveyed said that their loyalty towards their football team had increased. And thirty-five per cent said that Britain had become much more loyal to their pets! The survey's results showed a strange contrast, then. On the one hand, Britons have become cynical about loyalty; but on the other hand, it's the thing they seem to want more than almost anything else.

Thankfully, as Christians we have someone who always stays utterly loyal to us! This loyal friend is none less than God himself, who has made covenant – that is, a binding, unbreakable commitment – with us. This means that, even though we may fail him or let him down or wander away at times, God has committed himself to staying loyal and faithful to us. He will always stick by us, never walk away from us, never get weary of us or go off looking for someone else. In Christ, it's *you* he loves and is committed to! Of course, the devil tries to get us to doubt it – especially when we've just failed God (which, of course, is the very moment we need to keep hold of his promise!).

How should we respond to such loyalty? With gratitude, confidence, and a heart that longs to be loyal too. The amazing thing is: even when we don't respond like that, God still stays loyal to us. What a friend!

If we are faithless, he will remain faithful, for he cannot disown himself.
(2 TIMOTHY 2:13)

NOVEMBER 17

Becoming like Jesus

*For those God foreknew he also predestined to be conformed to
the likeness of his Son, that he might be
the firstborn among many brothers.*
(ROMANS 8:29)

As children grow up, they often become increasingly like their parents. Certain family characteristics begin to be more obvious: the shape of the nose, the lie of the hair, the way they walk or stand. It isn't too long before people are saying, 'Oh – he's his father's son!' or 'She looks just like her mother!' The family likeness is beginning to show.

The family likeness certainly showed in Jesus. Everything he did, he did with the compassion of the Father; everything he spoke, he spoke with the kindness of the Father. In fact, he was so much 'his Father's son' that he could say to his disciples, 'Anyone who has seen me has seen the Father' (John 14:9).

But this matter of the family likeness does not stop there; for God wants *us* to reflect the family likeness too! Of course, it goes without saying that none of us could ever totally and completely reflect everything that our heavenly Father is. But each of us can reflect something of what he is like, so that – together, as his people – the world can look at us and say, 'Ah! So that's what God is like!'

Of course if this were a task that were simply left to us, we would be lost before we even began! But thankfully, God has not left us to struggle along in our own efforts; rather, he has promised the gift of his Holy Spirit, who comes and fills us and lives within us, working on us from the inside out. It is as we let him do his work that we begin to show more of 'the fruit of the Spirit' (Galatians 5:22) and begin to be transformed increasingly into his likeness.

Today, ask the Spirit to fulfil God's promise that more and more of the family likeness will be seen in you.

*And we, who with unveiled faces all reflect the Lord's glory, are being
transformed into his likeness with ever-increasing glory, which comes from
the Lord, who is the Spirit.*
(2 CORINTHIANS 3:18)

NOVEMBER 18

God will forgive

If you, O LORD, kept a record of sins, O Lord, who could stand? But with you there is forgiveness; therefore you are feared.
(PSALM 130:3–4)

We would be surprised if there were never a time in your life when you had doubted whether God would forgive you or not. Perhaps you felt you had let him down badly, or fallen into some sin you thought you were free of, or sinned in some way that you never imagined you were capable of. At such times, the devil's whispers are never far away; and the whispers are always the same: God will not forgive you now!

How quick we are to believe this lie, especially when the Bible is so full of promises to the contrary. The truth is, no matter how often we fail, God will forgive – not because of you, but because of Jesus. For the effectiveness of his sacrifice on the cross is so great that there is no limit to how far, or how often, or how deep it can reach out to cleanse. The power of his blood to cleanse us is always greater than the power of our sin to stain us!

King David certainly grasped this. Even with all his experience of God, he still failed him in so many ways. But even after his dreadful act of adultery with Bathsheba, he knew there was still a way back, as he cried out to God, 'Cleanse me with hyssop and I shall be clean, wash me, and I shall be whiter than snow' (Psalm 51:7).

The devil may try to convince us that our particular sin is unforgivable or that we have done it once too often; or our conscience may accuse us and tell us that God will never forgive us now. But it is at such times that we need to stand on the sure promises of God's word. It is time to believe God's truth, and not the accuser's lies!

Who is a God like you, who pardons sin and forgives the transgression of the remnant of his inheritance? You do not stay angry for ever but delight to show mercy.
(MICAH 7:18)

Protected by righteousness

*'Stand firm then . . . with the breastplate of righteousness
in place.'*
(EPHESIANS 6:14)

A key part of a Roman soldier's battle gear was his breastplate, which covered the main body area and protected his vital organs. This was obviously an important piece of equipment and, without it, he wouldn't have lasted long. Paul says that we too need our 'breastplate' in place if we are to stand in the battles we face. And that breastplate is righteousness – our most fundamental, promised protection.

Paul is thinking of righteousness in two senses; first, the righteousness that is *given to us* by God. This righteousness can't be earned, and certainly isn't deserved; in fact, it's got nothing to do with us! It is, quite simply, God's gift; something he puts within us at the moment we trust in Christ and what he did at the cross. Like Abraham, all we can do to get it is to believe it. For it was when he believed that God 'credited it to him as righteousness' (Genesis 15:6).

This righteousness is our greatest protection against the devil's attacks. When he accuses us of sin or failure, the answer is: 'That's true! But Christ has forgiven me; *all* my sins are paid for, and in Christ I am now "not guilty".' When God looks at us, he now sees not us, but Christ in us. Declaring this promise – that 'there is now no condemnation for those who are in Christ Jesus' (Romans 8:1) – is therefore one of our greatest weapons – and one that Satan hates!

But Paul is thinking, secondly, not just of the righteousness that is *given to us*, but also of the righteousness that is *lived by us*, through the help of God's Spirit. This righteousness is about living with integrity, honesty and uprightness – not to get us right with God (that's already done!) but because we know that this is what pleases our Father and what allows the devil no 'foothold' for his accusations. That is why Paul aimed 'always to keep my conscience clear before God and man' (Acts 24:16).

If you have put your trust in Christ, then *you* are righteous. Believe it; live it; speak it out – it's your greatest promised weapon!

*'For surely, O LORD, you bless the righteous; you surround them
with your favour as with a shield.'*
(PSALM 5:12)

NOVEMBER 20

Real, not virtual

The reality, however, is found in Christ.
(COLOSSIANS 2:17)

'Virtual reality' has become increasingly common in our modern world. Through powerful computer technology, 'virtual' (what we used to call 'pretend'!) worlds can be created, allowing a whole range of created realities – whether for the airline pilot handling emergencies in a flight simulator, or for the games enthusiast, combating some imaginary foe on a home computer. It is all to do with the illusion of participation in a created world. What you see and do *looks* and *feels* real; but in reality it is only a computer simulation; there is nothing real about it at all.

This, however, is *not* how the Christian life is meant to be! There is nothing 'virtual' about it, either in terms of our experience of Jesus, or of the impact God intends us to have in the world. God doesn't want us to live in some religious, make-believe world, cut off from reality, playing with a faith that doesn't engage with life; he wants us to live, and grow, in reality. And his Holy Spirit is his provision for ensuring that this happens. It is he who keeps our relationship with Jesus both real and fresh each day so that we can know him with intimacy and then go and serve him with power – out there in the real world. This means we need to be open to the Spirit day by day, taking care not to shut him out.

The trouble is, we so often get distracted by all our 'religious clutter', just like the Colossian church did. They had become so caught up with religious rituals and traditions that they had lost touch with reality; and so Paul called them to focus on Jesus again, the one true reality.

It is as we focus on Jesus today that he will send his Holy Spirit to us, just as he promised. And as the Spirit comes and fills us, he will bring his anointing – anointing for life in the real world.

As his anointing teaches you about all things and as that anointing is real,
not counterfeit – just as it has taught you, remain in him.
(1 JOHN 2:27)

November 21

Listening changes things

'Speak, LORD. I am your servant and I am listening.'
(1 SAMUEL 3:9, NCV)

The story of Samuel is a remarkable example of how listening can change things. A 'miracle baby' born to a barren mother, Samuel was dedicated to God's service even before his conception, and around the age of three was entrusted to the priest Eli at the sanctuary in Shiloh. In contrast to Eli's wicked sons, Samuel was a godly boy who 'continued to grow in stature and in favour with the LORD and with men' (1 Samuel 2:26). As yet, however, he had still had no personal encounter with God; 'the word of the LORD had not yet been revealed to him' (1 Samuel 3:7). But all that was about to change – and all because he listened.

At a time when 'the LORD hardly ever spoke directly to people, and he did not appear to them in dreams very often' (1 Samuel 3:1, CEV), Samuel suddenly found himself hearing the voice of God at the age (according to Jewish tradition) of just twelve. Hearing a voice calling him during the night, he naturally thought it was Eli, in need of something. We can perhaps imagine Eli's irritation on being needlessly awakened! But by the third time it had happened, even Eli – as unspiritual as he had become – realized that something was going on, and that it must be God who was calling. So he told Samuel that if he heard the voice again he should simply say, 'Speak, LORD, for your servant is listening' (1 Samuel 3:9).

And so began a long and distinguished career as the prophet whose 'word came to all Israel' (1 Samuel 4:1), who would steer Israel out of the dark days of the period of the Judges, and who would see Israel through the failure of the kingship of Saul and prepare the way for the success of the kingship of David. A wonderfully successful ministry – but it all began with *listening*.

Who knows what God's purposes for *your* life may be! He wants to tell you, so you can know and begin to pursue your calling. But knowing starts with listening; and listening starts with stopping. Today is as good a day as any to do it.

'Come here and listen to the words of the LORD your God.'
(JOSHUA 3:9)

Why do I want it?

You want what you don't have, so you scheme and kill to get it.
You are jealous for what others have, and you can't possess it, so
you fight and quarrel to take it away from them. And yet the
reason you don't have what you want is that you don't ask
God for it. And even when you do ask, you don't get it because
your whole motive is wrong – you want
only what will give you pleasure.
(JAMES 4:2–3, NLT)

Sometimes, if particular prayers that I have been praying don't seem to have been answered, it's good to stop and ask myself, 'Why do I want this?' Have I been praying for it because it's something I truly believe God put on my heart? Or because it would be such a blessing to others? Or because it's something that is clearly promised in his word? . . . Or have I been praying for this simply for my own sake and because it would bring what 'I' want in life? At such times we need to remember that the Bible tells us that wrong motives profoundly hinder our prayers.

Our passage for today shows that James seems to have had this problem in some of his churches. He described the root of this as 'the desires that battle within you' (James 4:1). The word he uses for 'desires' is the root word from which we get the English word *hedonism* – the belief that *our* pleasure is life's highest goal and good. Sometimes our prayers can be very hedonistic! They can be so 'me'-centred, so focused on what I want or feel I need, that we are little different from the child who sits on Santa's knee in the grotto, telling him what we would like this Christmas.

If you have been praying for something for some time and it's not happened, why not stop and ask God to examine your heart, and to show you if you have been asking for it for the wrong motives. Once our motives are cleared up and sorted out, it wonderfully releases our prayers!

Beloved, if our hearts do not condemn us, we have boldness before God;
and we receive from him whatever we ask, because we obey his
commandments and do what pleases him.
(1 JOHN 3:21–22, NRSV)

NOVEMBER 23

The 'H' word

*For by the grace given me I say to every one of you: Do not
think of yourself more highly than you ought, but rather think
of yourself with sober judgment, in accordance with the
measure of faith God has given you.*
(ROMANS 12:3)

How do you react to the 'H' word? That is, 'humility'. For many folk, humility means letting yourself be trampled over (when everyone knows you have to fight for your rights!); or 'creeping' to get what you want (though you don't mean a word you say), like Charles Dickens' character, Uriah Heap. But true humility has nothing to do with either of these. True humility is about knowing who we really are, and living in the light of that.

Jesus said, 'Unless you change and become like little children, you will never enter the kingdom of heaven' (Matthew 18:3). Many things characterize young children; but one of the main ones is that they are wonderfully 'real'. What you see is what you get! And true humility is about being 'real' – real with ourselves, real before God, real towards others – so that what they see is what they get: someone who is neither too 'full of themselves', nor too dismissive of themselves.

What does such humility involve? First of all, it's about knowing our limitations, and not pushing ourselves forward or making claims beyond that. Paul summed this up when he said, 'Our goal is to stay within the boundaries of God's plan for us' (2 Corinthians 10:13, NLT). Second, true humility is about asking for help when we need it. For many of us, this is often the last thing we would think of doing, thinking it shows weakness or inadequacy (and sadly, some of us are like that even in the church!). Third, true humility is about being ready to take advice, for, as Proverbs puts it, 'The way of a fool seems right to him, but a wise man listens to advice' (Proverbs 12:15).

So, how are you doing with the 'H' word, and with Paul's encouragement to 'think of yourself with sober judgment' (Romans 12:3). This is the sort of childlike, humble heart that our Father is looking for and blesses. Will he find such a heart in us?

*Humble yourselves, therefore, under God's mighty hand,
that he may lift you up in due time.*
(1 PETER 5:6)

The unchanging God of forgiveness

You are forgiving and good, O Lord,
abounding in love to all who call to you.
(PSALM 86:5)

In our fast-moving world, things change so rapidly that you are sometimes not sure where you are. In the week he wrote this, Mike couldn't work out why he couldn't get in through the automatic door of his local D-I-Y store – until someone said, 'It's this side mate!' Since his previous visit, they had completely revamped the store and had made the 'out' door the 'in' door and the 'in' door the 'out' door! Little wonder he didn't know whether he was coming or going! But sometimes the whole of life can feel like that, can't it? Places, people, buildings, things, organizations – all can change so rapidly that you hardly know where you are any more.

In an ever-changing world it is therefore good to remember that there is one who never changes. 'I the LORD do not change' God reminded his discouraged people through his prophet (Malachi 3:6). Many of them were wondering, after their return from exile, whether God had truly forgiven them and was still with them. Of course he is, Malachi said. He made a promise to be your God and to keep you as his people; so how could he – a covenant-keeping, unchanging God – go back on his word?

It is because God does not change that he is as ready to forgive sin today as ever he was. In fact, forgiveness isn't simply something God *gives*; it is something he *is*. For remember how he revealed himself to Moses as 'The LORD, the LORD, the compassionate and gracious God, slow to anger, abounding in love and faithfulness, maintaining love to thousands, and forgiving wickedness, rebellion and sin' (Exodus 34:6–7).

There is no counselling or psychotherapist in the world that can deal with *sin*; only God can. Today, this unchanging God of forgiveness holds that forgiveness out to all who need it. Take it for yourself – and then take it to others!

'I, even I, am he who blots out your transgressions, for my own sake,
and remembers your sins no more.'
(ISAIAH 43:25)

Like clay in God's hand

'O house of Israel, can I not do with you as this potter does?'
declares the LORD. 'Like clay in the hand of the potter,
so are you in my hand, O house of Israel.'
(JEREMIAH 18:6)

Martin's wife, Yusandra, is a potter in her spare time – a 'ceramic sculptor' is their description. She makes decorative figures out of clay. To put it very simply, she coils clay, moulds it, fires it and decorates it. Which is rather how God lovingly deals with us!

God wants to mould us into his people. He wants to fashion our character and our lives. However, we sometimes fight back and don't want to respond to his work in our lives; we resist him when he tries to remove the blemishes or shape things in a way with which we aren't quite as comfortable. We think we know best. But the clay can't talk back to the hand! And our heavenly Father has the right to shape the clay of our lives according to his perfect will.

So today's question is: how receptive and sensitive are we to what God wants to make us? How teachable are we? How open to reason are we? One test is to see how we respond to the situations that God puts us in. Do we resist him – or rest in him? Are we willing to submit to others, or do we always rigidly want our own way? Another test is to see how we respond in conversations. Do we truly listen to other people, or are we just waiting for them to finish so we can give our point of view?

Of course, this doesn't mean that we are to be weak or spiritless, or that we are to have no strong convictions; but we are first and foremost to be given to God and to letting his will prevail. We need to ask him to make us malleable, knocking off those sharp edges of our character, and giving us the strength to keep looking to him when he is disciplining us. May he help us today to truly be like clay in his hands.

Yet, O LORD, you are our Father. We are the clay, you are the potter;
we are all the work of your hand.
(ISAIAH 64:8)

Born with a silver spoon

*His divine power has given us everything we need for life and
godliness through our knowledge of him who called us
by his own glory and goodness.*
(2 PETER 1:3)

There is an old expression that speaks of people being 'born with a silver
spoon in their mouth'. What it means is that they were born with every
conceivable advantage; that everything they could possibly need in life
was there for them, without any effort on their part. All they have to do
is to take what lies before them. Such people would normally be described
as 'very lucky'.

But there is a birth and a silver spoon that has nothing to do with
'luck'! For, in many ways, when you were 'born again' as a Christian, you
too were 'born with a silver spoon in your mouth'. That wasn't luck – it
was the gift of God as you responded to his invitation to come. From that
moment on, every help and advantage is there for you – all you have to
do is to take it! For once we start our new life with God, a whole number
of promises follow. Here are just some of them mentioned in the New
Testament: Jesus is now always with us; God's Spirit is now living within
us; our sins are completely forgiven; we have been put right with God
('justified'); we have been made friends with God ('reconciled'); we have
the gift of eternal life; we have free access into God's presence; we are no
longer under the dominating control of sin; we are secure for ever. The
list could go on and on – but we hope that's enough to remind you of 'the
silver spoon in your mouth'.

These promises are not something to be embarrassed about, as though
it were somehow not 'fair' that we should have them, but not others. They
are God's free gift to all who will come to him through Christ. And they
are his free gift, promised to you for you to experience afresh today.

*Praise be to the God and Father of our Lord Jesus Christ! In his great mercy
he has given us new birth into a living hope through the resurrection of Jesus
Christ from the dead, and into an inheritance that can never perish,
spoil or fade–kept in heaven for you.*
(1 PETER 1:3–4)

Daddy!

Because you are sons, God sent the Spirit of his Son into our hearts, the Spirit who calls out, 'Abba, Father.'
(GALATIANS 4:6)

One of the delightful scenes in life is to see a young child rushing into its father's presence (no matter what important people might be around!) and calling out 'Daddy' as they throw themselves into his arms. Martin still remembers the big smile of his daughter aged two or three as she called out 'Daddy' when they come together after they had been apart for a little while. The amazing thing is: Jesus said we can relate to God in exactly the same way!

Calling God 'Father' was a normal part of Jesus' life and teaching; but he took it one step further.Not only did he call God 'Father', he called him 'Abba' – the word in Aramaic (the everyday language that he spoke) for 'daddy'. That this most intimate and trusting word should be found on his lips at the very moment when he could reasonably have had cause for doubting his Father – in the Garden of Gethsemane – is staggering indeed. 'Abba, Father . . . not what I will, but what you will' (Mark 14:36). This, surely, is the heart of prayer: knowing God in a personal and intimate way, and trusting in his fatherly care for us, even when things don't look good.

But Jesus wasn't content with keeping this word 'Abba' to himself; he extended this privilege to us! And the word clearly made a profound impression on his disciples and the first Christians, for they preserved this Aramaic word as part of their prayer language, as we see reflected in the letters at several points.

The early church understood that calling God 'Father', 'Abba', meant that all Christians are truly his children, adopted into his family through faith in Jesus, with all the privileges this brings. It is this intimate word 'daddy' that reminds us that God is not a cold, formal Father, like the fathers of Victorian times. He is *fatherly* in everything he does and in his intimate knowledge of us and care for us. Enjoy that today!

Those who are led by the Spirit of God are sons of God. For you did not receive a spirit that makes you a slave again to fear, but you received the Spirit of sonship. And by him we cry, 'Abba, Father'.
(ROMANS 8:14–15)

Always be prepared!

'Stand firm then . . . with your feet fitted with the readiness that comes from the gospel of peace.'
(EPHESIANS 6:14–15)

Having the right footwear for the right occasion is obviously important. We wouldn't give Wellington boots to a soccer player, or spiked running shoes to a ballet dancer. Having the right shoes is 'half the battle'; wearing the wrong shoes will almost certainly mean we will lose that battle. The Roman army certainly understood this principle. While their soldiers might wear sandals for normal everyday use, they wore 'half-boots' with studded soles to give a good grip when marching or in battle. Firmness and mobility were essential requirements for such occasions.

We too, as Christ's soldiers, need our boots on, Paul says, so we are ready to 'stand firm' or to 'go' or to share our faith at any moment. The gospel sets us at peace, so we can be at peace in our readiness to share it with others. This isn't something we need to be fearful about or that we have to 'wind ourselves up for'; it should be as natural as anything. After all, we have the good news that everyone needs; and as Isaiah put it, 'How beautiful on the mountains are the feet of those who bring good news, who proclaim peace, who bring good tidings, who proclaim salvation' (Isaiah 52:7).

Probably all of us have experienced times when we did feel timid about speaking up in some situation or about sharing our faith. When we did, however, wasn't it great? Remember: we are here today trusting in Christ because someone dared to speak to us; so how can we rob others of that? As we do speak up, God has promised that he will strengthen us, encourage us, and use us. Who knows what the outcome might be today if we do!

'Get yourself ready! Stand up and say to them whatever I command you. Do not be terrified by them . . . Today I have made you a fortified city, an iron pillar and a bronze wall to stand against the whole land . . . They will fight against you but will not overcome you, for I am with you and will rescue you,' declares the LORD.
(JEREMIAH 1:17–19)

Bad news . . . and good news

'I saw Satan fall like lightning from heaven.'
(LUKE 10:18)

First, the bad news: we have an enemy! Satan, originally one of God's highest angels, but who wanted to be like God himself and so was cast out of heaven, now opposes not only God, but also all God's children. He has many names, reflecting different aspects of his wicked work: the devil ['slanderer'], the evil one, the father of lies, the god of this age, the prince of this world, Satan ['adversary'], the serpent, the tempter. Like his names, his tactics are also many: accusation, affliction, blinding minds, cunning, deception, disguising himself as an angel of light, lies, setting traps, temptation. And to help him in his work he has myriads of servants – angels that were seduced by him and that were expelled from heaven along with him, who now do his business. Even a quick reading of the Gospels shows us that Jesus took the presence and activity of these demons seriously.

But now comes the good news! For while the devil is powerful, he is not *all*-powerful. Only God is! The devil is only a created being and will therefore always be less than God. Some Christians forget that and almost have a worldview of two equal and opposing powers, struggling against one another (like in the *Star Wars* or *Lord of the Rings* movies). But this is not how it is! The Bible promises us that at the cross Jesus completely stripped Satan and his demons of their power, 'triumphing over them' (Colossians 2:15). The picture used here is of a Roman 'Triumph': a procession by a general returning after some great victory, leading his troops through the city with the conquered enemy on display in chains, completely defeated and powerless. *This* is what Jesus did to the devil at the cross! He may still be thrashing around for a while; but his end is absolutely assured, as we see in the book of Revelation – and all because of the cross!

Don't be fearful of the devil; don't focus on him (no matter what pressures might be upon you); focus instead on Jesus, our conquering king who has completely defeated him!

God stripped the spiritual rulers and powers of their authority. With the cross, he won the victory and showed the world that they were powerless.
(COLOSSIANS 2:15, NCV)

NOVEMBER 30

Challenge and opportunity

Who may ascend the hill of the LORD? Who may stand in his holy place? He who has clean hands and a pure heart.
(PSALM 24:3–4)

While some Christians get all 'hot under the collar' about this or that outward form of worship or prayer, it seems clear from the Bible that God cares very little about externals. What matters to him is the heart. And it's this that provides us with both a challenge and an opportunity. The challenge is to ensure that, whatever externals we may use, the essential feature must always be the heart; the opportunity is that, because it is a matter of the heart and not about externals, we have a tremendous breadth for expressing ourselves to God.

This is backed up in the Bible, where we find a wide range of expressions of prayer and worship. In truth, most of us find this challenging, for we all become stuck in our patterns (or are they ruts?) and we are quick to judge others who do things differently. But just look at some of the *expressions* of prayer and worship that God deems acceptable to him: *singing* (e.g. Psalm 33:1–3; Acts 16:25; Ephesians 5:18–20), *speaking* (e.g. Nehemiah 1:4–11; Matthew 26:36–46; Acts 4:23–31), *shouting* (e.g. Ezra 3:11–13; Mark 11:8–10; Revelation 19:1–8), *silence* (e.g. Psalm 4:4; Habakkuk 2:20; Revelation 8:1), *dancing* (e.g. 2 Samuel 6:12–16; Psalm 149:2–3; Luke 15:25), *using music and instruments* (1 Chronicles 6:31–32; Psalm 98:4–6; Ephesians 5:19).

And think about the wide variety of *posture* in worship and prayer. These include: *sitting* (e.g. 1 Kings 19:3–4; Nehemiah 1:4; Luke 10:13), *standing* (e.g.1 Samuel 1:26; 1 Kings 8:22; Mark 11:25), kneeling (e.g. Daniel 6:10; Acts 9:40; Ephesians 3:14–19), *bowing* (e.g. Exodus 34:8–9; Psalm 95:6; Matthew 2:11), *prostrating oneself* (e.g. Genesis 17:3; Joshua 5:13–14; Luke 17:15–16), *lifting hands* (e.g. Exodus 17:11–16; Psalm 28:2; 1 Timothy 2:8).

With such variety given us, don't get stuck in your ruts; try something different! For 'Who may ascend the hill of the Lord?' Anyone – not who knows the right postures or ways – but who has a good heart. Wherever there is such a heart, God will hear us.

Take words with you and return to the LORD. Say to him: 'Forgive all our sins and receive us graciously, that we may offer the fruit of our lips.'
(HOSEA 14:2)

DECEMBER 1

The promise keeper

*For no matter how many promises God has made,
they are 'Yes' in Christ.*
(2 CORINTHIANS 1:20)

'I promise I'll come!' We wonder if you have ever said those words, but then found later that you couldn't keep the promise you made. Something happened – an unforeseen visitor, a crisis at work or in the family, the car broke down, time just flew by – and you felt dreadful as you realized that you just wouldn't be able to keep the promise after all. Thankfully, God is *never* like that. He says what he means, and he does what he says. Nothing can ever occur that takes him by surprise, upsets his plans or keeps him from his promise.

Right at the beginning of human history, after the fall of Adam and Eve, God promised that he would send someone to deal with the mess that they had made; someone who could deal with humanity's most basic problem – sin. That someone would be no less a person than his own dear Son. It took many, many years of preparation before the time was right; but throughout the Old Testament period, God kept reinforcing his promise again and again: 'He's coming! He's coming!' In fact, there are over 300 prophecies in the Old Testament that we see fulfilled in the New Testament in the Lord Jesus Christ, covering many different aspects of who he is and what he came to do.

The fact that God kept this promise should be a tremendous encouragement to us to believe that God is truly 'the promise keeper'. Whatever promises he has made in his word, he is prepared to stand by them. Our part is simply to claim what he has promised; to remind him of what he has said and to say that we have 'come to cash the cheque'; to claim his 'yes!' as we come in the name of Jesus.

Let today be a day for reminding God of some of his promises over your life.

*God is not a man, that he should lie, nor a son of man,
that he should change his mind.*
(NUMBERS 23:19)

The joy of the Lord

'This day is sacred to our Lord. Do not grieve,
for the joy of the LORD is your strength.'
(NEHEMIAH 8:10)

Wherever Jesus went, he brought joy – gladness, happiness, to use more ordinary words. He himself knew how to be 'full of joy through the Holy Spirit' (Luke 10:21) and wanted his joy to be in his disciples so that 'your joy may be complete' (John 15:11). He said that his Father's kingdom was all about 'righteousness, peace and joy in the Holy Spirit' (Romans 14:17). In fact, words like 'joy', 'joyful' and 'rejoice' occur over 400 times in the Bible! So 'miserable religion' has no place in the Christian faith (though, sadly, the church has often made it seem like it does!).

Joy is a theme that runs through Luke's Gospel from start to finish. It begins with joy characterizing Elizabeth and Mary in their pregnancies; it runs through the joy that the disciples experienced in engaging in their ministry; it ends with their joy after the ascension as they returned to Jerusalem in eager expectation of what was yet to come.

But joy is not restricted to just happy feelings (though we are quite sure that God prefers us to be happy than sad!); joy is about a deep confidence in God, no matter what happens. That is why Nehemiah could tell God's people that, 'The joy of the LORD is your strength.' After all their efforts to rebuild the walls of Jerusalem, they suddenly felt overwhelmed with failure as Ezra read God's law to them and they realized how much they had failed him. What they needed at the moment, as Nehemiah understood, was not to be weighed down with guilt, but to be lifted up through joy – the joy of knowing that God had not abandoned them and that he was still with them despite everything.

So today, don't settle for miserable religion. No matter what your circumstances, the Bible promises that God wants you to know his joy, and through that joy to know his strength.

It was a time of happiness, joy, gladness and honour for the Jewish people.
(ESTHER 8:16, NCV)

DECEMBER 3

Who never sins?

If we say we have no sin, we are only fooling ourselves and refusing to accept the truth. But if we confess our sins to him, he is faithful and just to forgive us and to cleanse us from every wrong.
(1 JOHN 1:8–9, NLT)

'Since I've become a Christian, I never sin any more.' We might think that someone who spoke like that lived on a different planet! It certainly isn't the experience of most of us! But, strange as it may seem, there were people in New Testament times who thought just like that; and this was one reason why John wrote his first letter.

John's heart for God's people was most definitely that they *should not* sin, as he makes plain throughout the letter; but John was also realistic enough to know that we aren't perfect yet and that we still *do* sin – and sometimes, dreadfully. So, anyone claiming to be without sin was simply fooling themselves, he said; it just lacks reality. But anyone who owned up to their sin could be sure that Jesus would forgive them, he stressed.

Throughout church history there have been those who have claimed 'sinless perfection'; but only by a strange re-definition of what sin is, or by deceitfulness of heart, can we claim to be sinless – at least, on this side of heaven! Only when Jesus returns, when he will 'transform our lowly bodies so that they will be like his glorious body' (Philippians 3:21), will we finally be free of sin and be like him at last.

So, here is both a challenge and a promise: *the challenge is – don't sin!* You know it doesn't do you any good! While the temptation might seem pleasant, you know it always turns out to be a trap of the Devil; the moment you have done it, you feel bad, not good! But *the promise is: when you do sin, Jesus will forgive you.* Today, let's aim for both the challenge and the promise! In this way, a double defeat will be inflicted on our enemy!

When they sin against you – for there is no-one who does not sin . . . then from heaven, your dwelling-place, hear their prayer and their plea, and uphold their cause.
(1 KINGS 8:46, 49)

DECEMBER 4

The eternal word

'Your word, O LORD, is eternal; it stands firm in the heavens.'
(PSALM 119:89)

Best sold, least read, worst understood. That, sadly, sums up the Bible. To many it is a book for buying for christenings or weddings, but one that is just full of genealogies and 'thou shalt not's'. Such thinking couldn't be further from the truth! For this book is nothing less than the eternal Word of God, relevant in very generation.

This is why it's good to read the Bible – not so we become walking encyclopaedias of Bible facts, but so that we can know God, his ways and his promises. For the Bible is not like any other book; it is the 'God-breathed' word (2 Timothy 3:16). That is, it is not people's attempts to describe God or recount their experiences of him; it is the very 'breath' of God, breathed into the writers by God's Spirit, so that what they wrote was exactly what God wanted written. And this is why it can be trusted and is still so relevant for today.

The writer of Psalm 119 was certainly a believer in God's word. The psalm is beautifully constructed, each stanza beginning with the successive letters of the Hebrew alphabet. But not only is it beautifully written, it is passionately written. This writer was passionate about Scripture! This is reflected in the wide range of terms he uses to describe it: *law* (used 45 times), *statutes* (23 times), *precepts* (21 times), *decrees* (22 times), *commands* (22 times), *word(s)* (30 times), *promise(s)* (13 times). Clearly he loved God's word! But it was not a love of it for its own sake; he had experienced how it revealed God's heart to him and how transforming it was as he applied it in everyday life.

The Bible is not a book for meditation by recluses or analysis by academics; it is God's eternal word, given to reveal him and to change us. Set your heart to let it do its work in *your* life today.

For you have been born again, not of perishable seed, but of imperishable, through the living and enduring word of God. For, "All men are like grass, and all their glory is like the flowers of the field; the grass withers and the flowers fall, but the word of the Lord stands for ever."
(1 PETER 1:23–25)

DECEMBER 5

The word that penetrates

*'His word can cut through our spirits and souls and through
our joints and marrow, until it discovers
the desires and thoughts of our hearts.'*
(HEBREWS 4:12, CEV)

Some years ago there was a series of well-known TV adverts for a brand of lager. Whatever the scenario, it always ended up with someone being refreshed by a glass of their lager; and the punch line was always the same: '[X] refreshes the parts other beers cannot reach'. Well, if you will forgive the analogy, God's word does exactly the same – but in a rather more substantial way!

The Bible reaches parts that no other book can reach. Other great works of literature can certainly stimulate us, move us, challenge us, or even stir us to action. The Bible does all of this; but then it does far more. For the Bible doesn't just reach into our minds or our emotions; it cuts right through to the deepest parts of our being, discerning our heart and motivations and revealing things that even we ourselves have missed. It reveals what is going on deep down inside, beneath the veneer we put on for others, discovers what is going on down there, and then passes judgment on 'what makes us tick' (sometimes leaving us very uncomfortable as it does so!)

Such judgment, however, is not designed to leave us in condemnation, but rather to bring us to the God who loves us. He reveals what is wrong, only so we can bring it to him, who alone can put it right. He shows us what we are, only so that we will come to him, who alone can make us what we should be.

But for this to happen, we need to let the Bible be what it is: the word of God. We need to remember that it is there to judge us, not the other way round. This means that we cannot lay aside the bits we don't like, or rationalize certain parts as relevant only for a bygone age, or 'theologize' away God's truth. This book is God's eternal word, expressing his unchanging truth for each changing generation. Let it do whatever work God wants it to do in your life today. Let it refresh the parts no other book can reach.

'Humbly accept the word planted in you, which can save you.'
(JAMES 1:21)

The water of the word

'As the rain and the snow come down from heaven, and do not return to it without watering the earth and making it bud and flourish, so that it yields seed for the sower and bread for the eater, so is my word that goes out from my mouth: It will not return to me empty, but will accomplish what I desire and achieve the purpose for which I sent it.'
(ISAIAH 55:10–11)

In Bible times Israel was wholly dependent on rain for its fertility. While Egypt and Mesopotamia could irrigate from their great rivers, Israel could not, since its only major river (the Jordan) lay well below sea level. The Israelites were therefore entirely dependent upon God sending rain. Because of this, they sometimes became enticed by the Baal worship of the surrounding peoples. This was a form of fertility worship, with debased sexual practices which sought to provoke the gods to send the rains and release fertility on the land. But again and again the prophets drew them away from this, focusing them on the living God alone as the one who sends the rain.

But the prophets also said that, as surely as God sent literal rain on the land, so he brings 'spiritual rain' to feed and refresh his people through his word. When such rain comes, they promised, the word and promise of God would surely be brought to pass.

One of the strange things about a drought is that we tend not to notice it until it is too late. We enjoy the pleasant summer and basking in the sunshine; but then, suddenly, it is announced that we are short of water. Hosepipe bans are enforced; we can't water the garden or wash the car. We suddenly need water and recognize how much we have missed it. Isn't that exactly how it often is in our Christian lives? We are going along happily, thinking we are doing OK, when – suddenly – we feel there is a desperate shortage of 'spiritual water' in our lives.

Perhaps you feel like that today. If so, Isaiah has the answer. Ask God to fulfil his promise of breaking up your hardness and renewing you and your circumstances through his Spirit-inspired word.

'You gave abundant showers, O God; you refreshed your weary inheritance.'
(PSALM 68:9)

DECEMBER 7

A lamp to my feet

'Your word is a lamp to my feet and a light for my path.'
(PSALM 119:105)

Mike lives in the ancient city of Oxford. With its narrow medieval streets, and the consequent traffic congestion that this brings, cycling has for many years been the favoured means of transport. Particularly in university term time, the streets are often packed with cyclists – and that's where the nightmare for drivers begins! For not only do Oxford cyclists operate according to a Highway Code completely of their own making, they frequently ride at night without any lights on – not good for being seen by others (and not good for avoiding potholes!). A lamp is really a quite essential basic need.

And that's what the Bible is like – a lamp; a lamp that shines into the darkness of this world and which brings things into the light. As Paul puts it, 'But everything exposed by the light becomes visible, for it is light that makes everything visible' (Ephesians 5:13–14). The Bible is one of God's main ways of bringing his light into situations. The light the Bible brings, first, dispels the darkness and helps us distinguish right from wrong. It shows up the dirt – in our own lives as much as anywhere else! But when it does so, it is important for us to remember that God's intention is only to help us clear up the rubbish, not to catch us out. We can't clean up what we don't know is there! Second, like the cyclist's lamp, the Bible helps us see the way ahead. It lights up the path for us, both helping us to see obstacles and to know which way to take. Brought alive by the Spirit, the Bible truly is one of God's main ways of guiding us, both individually and corporately.

As writers, we have countless testimonies of how God has used the Bible to speak to us and guide us over the years. Again and again, he has brought just the right passage to us at just the right time with just the right word that we needed. The Bible truly is a lamp. Ask God to keep his promise and bring his light into your situation through his word today.

'The unfolding of your words gives light.'
(PSALM 119:130)

DECEMBER 8

Strong God, strong people

*'The people that do know their God shall be strong,
and do exploits.'*
(DANIEL 11:32, KJV)

Amongst the nations of Bible times, it was believed that a god's strength was reflected in the strength of his people. So if one nation defeated another, it was clear to all that the conqueror's god was obviously greater. This was why, for example, the Philistines put the ark of the covenant they had captured after their victory over Israel into the temple of their gods to show who was the greatest (though events that followed soon led them to think again!).

Our God too wants his people to be strong, so that through this others might recognize that he alone is the one true God. He wants it known that no situation, no obstacle, no crisis has strength that is greater than his strength. Note that important little word, however: *his* strength. This is all about *his* strength, not *our* strength. It is as we are strong in him that we can 'do exploits' (KJV) or 'take action' (NRSV).

This is what Israel discovered when faced with the impenetrable barrier of the Red Sea ahead of them and the invincible might of Pharaoh's army behind them, and when Moses simply said, 'Do not be afraid. Stand firm and you will see the deliverance the LORD will bring you today . . . The LORD will fight for you; you need only be still' (Exodus 14:13–14). It's what they discovered many centuries later on returning from exile, wondering how on earth they would ever be able to rebuild the temple in the light of all the difficulties and opposition they faced. But Zechariah reminded them that it would happen 'not by might nor by power, but by my Spirit' (Zechariah 4:6).

God's promise is that as we know him and trust in him, we shall be strong and we shall do great things. Knowing this promise should prompt us to action, for these are days when we need Christians who will 'do exploits' for God – out of *his* strength, not *ours*. Claim the promise for yourself today and see what 'exploit' God would have you do for him today, that people might see how great our God is.

'You then, my son, be strong in the grace that is in Christ Jesus.'
(2 TIMOTHY 2:1)

Dangers of not listening

Today, if you hear his voice, do not harden your hearts.
(PSALM 95:7–8)

When our children were little we would often warn them of something that would happen if they continued doing what they were doing. Of course, they always 'knew better' and carried on – until experience proved that we knew better after all! Little by little, through the mini-disasters of life, children learn (we hope!) the danger of not listening. But as God's children, we too need to learn the same lesson. For there are consequences in not listening to him.

First, God is disappointed when we don't listen. God can expect unbelievers not to listen; but when his own people don't listen, that breaks his heart, as he said through Isaiah: 'I reared children and brought them up, but they have rebelled against me. The ox knows his master, the donkey his owner's manger, but Israel does not know, my people do not understand' (Isaiah 1:2–3).

Second, not listening to God brings its own natural consequences. When we do listen, we reap the consequent blessings; but when we don't, it will always be to our harm. In Proverbs there are many calls to listen to God's wisdom and to enjoy the benefits of doing so. In fact, wisdom itself calls out and says, 'Whoever finds me finds life and receives favour from the LORD. But whoever fails to find me harms himself; all who hate me love death' (Proverbs 8:35–36).

But the third thing that happens when we stop listening to God is that – eventually – God stops speaking. This is a solemn thought, but it's what the Bible says. Thankfully, God's nature is always to be patient and forgiving and to hold his arms out to us. But a point does come when he says, 'Enough!' and has nothing more to say to wilfully deaf people and declares '"When I called, they did not listen; so when they called, I would not listen," says the LORD Almighty' (Zechariah 7:13).

Don't be unwise by not listening to God. And if you feel there are matters where you haven't been listening, then stop turning a deaf ear and start listening again today. Ask him for forgiveness – he will be quick to give it!

Now then, my sons, listen to me; blessed are those who keep my ways.
(PROVERBS 8:32).

DECEMBER 10

The bad news . . . and the good news!

*All men will hate you because of me, but he who stands firm
to the end will be saved.*
(MATTHEW 10:22)

'Do you want the bad news, or the good news first?' So begins a whole series of jokes. But there is one event in life that has both 'bad news' and 'good news' that is by no means a joke: the return to this earth of the Lord Jesus; for both aspects are true of the time leading to his coming again.

First, the bad news. Many of the things that will characterize life before Jesus returns have been characteristic of every age, ebbing and flowing over the centuries; but their intensity will increase as the end draws closer. Clear hallmarks include: first, the growth of apostasy and false religion when 'many will turn away from the faith and will betray and hate each other, and many false prophets will appear and deceive many people' (Matthew 24:10–11); second, an increase in general godlessness when 'people will be lovers of themselves, lovers of money . . . lovers of pleasure rather than lovers of God – having a form of godliness but denying its power' (2 Timothy 3:2,4–5); third, an increase in catastrophes and strife, when 'nation will rise against nation, and kingdom against kingdom, [and] there will be famines and earthquakes in various places' (Matthew 24:7); fourth, the persecution of believers, who will be 'handed over to be persecuted and put to death, and . . . be hated by all nations because of me' (Matthew 24:9); until finally, 'the man of lawlessness' (2 Thessalonians 2:3) or antichrist appears, opposing Christ and all he stands for.

So far, it's all been bad news. But now for the good news! For Jesus promised that, despite all of this, the gospel *will* spread, the church *will* grow, and the kingdom *will* be extended. The idea of a faithful few believers 'holding the fort until Jesus comes' does not tie in with New Testament teaching. Things *will* get worse, yes; but things *will* also get better!

So, yes, there is bad news; but let's rejoice today in the promised certainty of the good news that overcomes it!

*He will keep you strong to the end, so that you will be blameless
on the day of our Lord Jesus Christ.*
(1 CORINTHIANS 1:8)

Ready, steady, go!

*'So you also must be ready, because the Son of Man will come
at an hour when you do not expect him.'*
(MATTHEW 24:44)

Timetables can be strange things: sometimes incomprehensible; often unreliable; frequently ignored. But unlike such timetables, God has a timetable that is extremely accurate: the timetable for the return of Jesus; a timetable known only to himself. Indeed, Jesus said, 'No one knows about that day or hour, not even the angels in heaven, nor the Son, but only the Father' (Matthew 24:36).

It shouldn't surprise us therefore to discover that whenever Christians have tried to work out this timetable, they have always got it wrong. All we get in the Bible are general indicators – and even some of these will probably happen in ways that will surprise us. But the Bible's emphasis is not theoretical or speculative, but practical. Teaching on Christ's return is always designed to provoke us to ask: Are we ready? Are we living daily in the light of his return, 'making the most of every opportunity, because the days are evil' (Ephesians 5:16)?

And when he returns, what a glorious event that will be! 'For the Lord himself will come down from heaven, with a loud command, with the voice of the archangel and with the trumpet call of God, and the dead in Christ will rise first. After that, we who are still alive and are left will be caught up together with them in the clouds to meet the Lord in the air. And so we will be with the Lord for ever' (1 Thessalonians 4:16–17). What a message of hope this is! God says: the world is going somewhere, and it's going somewhere purposeful. History will come to a close; the problem of evil will be resolved; and, as the final curtain falls at the end of time, the author of the drama of life will walk on to the world's stage and everyone will see him, whether in judgment or in joy.

While his coming may seem slow, it isn't late. Don't give up believing in it simply because our Father is more patient than we are! Rather, keep alert and be ready!

*'Therefore keep watch, because you do not know on what day
your Lord will come.'*
(MATTHEW 24:42)

DECEMBER 12

God's agenda

*'For my thoughts are not your thoughts, neither are your ways
my ways,' declares the LORD.*
(ISAIAH 55:8)

A little while ago, Martin was having a difficult day. Too much work,
stress . . . you know the kind of thing? He thought, 'All I want to do is
get through my work!' But then the thought occurred to him, 'No, God's
agenda is different. God wants you to get your work done, but he doesn't
want you to trample all over other people in the process. God also wants
you to be a loving husband, a devoted father, a kind friend, a good boss.'
God's thoughts were very different from Martin's!

We might want to take short cuts in our work (the old word was
'being sloppy'!), but that isn't good enough for God; he wants us to work
hard for him, because it is not a human master or some faceless
corporation we are serving but, as Paul put it, 'it is the Lord Christ you
are serving' (Colossians 3:24). We may desperately want a close friend or
spouse to be saved and may be working hard to 'make it happen'; but God
says that the only way is through Christ, not by any other way. We may
have planned our whole lives out before us – married by 30, a partner in
the firm by 35 – but in doing so, we take away the Lord as our primary
focus.

How are you doing at putting Christ and his agenda first? Are you
trying to fit him into your plans, rather than making him the priority in
your life? Putting him first is risky at times, but that is how we were
designed to live. God wants us to walk closely with him and his agenda,
and putting him first is the way to know the fulfilment of his promises.

Martin finds it helpful in this area to begin where he is (which is often
not where God wants him to be!). He constantly re-assesses his priorities
and asks God's forgiveness when he sees that he has not been following
his agenda. Today, if you sense that you have been drifting from God's
agenda for your life, come back into line with it and submit once again to
his will.

'Who was I to think that I could oppose God?'
(ACTS 11:17)

What gets in the way

*With what shall I come before the LORD and bow down before
the exalted God? . . . He has showed you, O man, what is good.
And what does the LORD require of you? To act justly and to
love mercy and to walk humbly with your God.*
(MICAH 6:6,8)

The amazing thing about the gospel is that Jesus makes it so easy to come
into God's presence! No special rituals are needed; no special places or
methods or times; we can simply come 'just as we are'! There is only one
thing God requires: that we come with right attitudes. For the Christian
faith is not some magic cult where the very act of worship or prayer in
itself brings benefit; worship and prayer derive their value from our heart.
And this priority of the heart is reflected in the fact that the Bible tells us
that worship and prayer can be hindered, especially through wrong
relationships.

First, the Bible says that *wrong relationships with God* hinder prayer
and worship. That's why David said, 'If I had cherished sin in my heart,
the Lord would not have listened; but God has surely listened and heard
my voice in prayer' (Psalm 66:18–19). David certainly knew what it was
to let things get in the way of his relationship with God at times; but he
also discovered the importance of dealing with things quickly.

But second, the Bible says that *wrong relationships with others* hinder
prayer and worship too. That's why Jesus said, 'Therefore, if you are
offering your gift at the altar and there remember that your brother has
something against you, leave your gift there in front of the altar. First go
and be reconciled to your brother; then come and offer your gift'
(Matthew 5:23–24). With the same thought in mind, Peter encouraged
husbands to treat their wives properly 'so that nothing will hinder your
prayers' (1 Peter 3:7).

Acting justly (relationships towards others) and walking humbly
(relationships towards God) are keys to making sure there are no obstacles
to our worship and prayers. If you're aware of any such obstacles in your
life, why not deal with them right now?

*The LORD searches every heart and understands every motive
behind the thoughts. If you seek him, he will be found by you.*
(1 CHRONICLES 28:9)

DECEMBER 14

Don't stand on ceremony!

I, the LORD, invite you to come and talk it over.
(ISAIAH 1:18, CEV)

Young children have little sense of the 'right' or 'appropriate' moments to do certain things. If they want you, they rush into your presence no matter how inconvenient it is; if they blurt out their questions, they do it no matter what 'important' visitor is there; if they 'tell things as they really are', they do it even if the whole world is listening. Why? Because you are their parent, and that's what parents are for. Young children don't stand on ceremony; they simply come in. And that, said Jesus, is exactly how we can be with God.

Jesus stressed that prayer is not about 'getting it right' – getting the right words or form or time or place – but simply about a spontaneous relationship with our Father God. Many people get in such a muddle when it comes to praying. 'Where should I do it? What should I say? Should I stand or sit or kneel? What direction should I face? When should I do it?' To all of these questions Jesus said: it simply doesn't matter! It's not about where or when or how you pray; what matters is *the heart.*

The priority of the heart comes out clearly in Jesus' conversation with the Samaritan woman, for whom the externals of prayer and worship seemed so important. He told her, 'Believe me, the time is coming when it will no longer matter whether you worship the Father here or in Jerusalem ... But the time is coming and is already here when true worshippers will worship the Father in spirit and in truth. The Father is looking for anyone who will worship him that way. For God is Spirit, so those who worship him must worship in spirit and in truth' (John 4:21, 23-24, NLT). It's the inside, not the outside, that matters.

Prayer is not about doing it in the right place or at the right time or in the right way. As long as we are sincere, God will hear us. So don't feel you have to stand on ceremony today. Go on, walk right in, and talk to your Father!

'That's the kind of people the Father is out looking for: those who are simply and honestly themselves before him . . .'
(JOHN 4:23, THE MESSAGE)

DECEMBER 15

Reverence and relationship

But I, by your great mercy, will come into your house; in reverence will I bow down towards your holy temple.
(PSALM 5:7)

How people speak to God can so easily fall into one of two extremes: either so formal as to have no intimacy, or so casual as to reduce almighty God to the level of a 'mate'. The Bible, however, encourages us to pray with both reverence and relationship.

The trouble is, reverence means different things to different people. For some English-speaking Christians, the only appropriate way to address God is by 'Thee' and 'Thou', seeing this as more respectful. But is this 'biblical'? (strange question though this may seem!). There are two things to remember here. First, there is no such distinction in the original languages of the Bible. The same words are used of speaking to God as to men and women. So to add 'reverence' to our prayers by using 'Thee' and 'Thou' is to add something that the Bible never intended. Second, this isn't how the words 'Thee' and 'Thou' were originally used in English. In the period when The King James (or Authorized) Version was written, 'thee' and 'thou' were simply common words of friendship and intimacy, such as a man and wife would use with one another or with their children, or a friend would use with a friend. The words in no way carried a sense of 'respect' or 'esteem for someone higher'. Sadly, as the English language changed its usage, this original meaning was lost, and we were left with a tradition that thought God needed special vocabulary if he is to be addressed 'properly'. Richness of language is no substitute for reality of relationship, however.

But equally, while people in the Bible saw God as their friend, they didn't see him as their 'mate'. There was intimacy, but respect; friendship, but an acknowledgment of his lordship.

So, what about the language that I use in prayer? Does it genuinely help me to know God better and talk to him more? Does it help me to know him as my Father and my friend, my companion and my God? Today let reverence and relationship be marks of all your conversations with him.

'My Father, my friend from my youth.'
(JEREMIAH 3:4)

DECEMBER 16

Like a little child

Jesus said, 'Let the little children come to me, and do not hinder them, for the kingdom of heaven belongs to such as these.'
(MATTHEW 19:14)

As we look back to the time when our children were little, we never cease to be amazed at how they trusted us. They would leap from high walls into our arms, never for one moment thinking that we might miss them! They would run to us after a fall, never for one moment considering that a kiss on the knee might not 'make it better'! One of Martin's children expected her dad to fly like Superman to fetch the balloon that was rising quickly into the sky!

There is something wonderfully trusting about young children – something we lose as we grow up. Of course, we rationalize it: the world is a hard place; people trample on you if you trust them; things go wrong in life and you get hurt. Or to put it another way, we get hardhearted. But, said Jesus, if you really want to know the Father's heart, then you'll become like those little children again.

So what are some of those childlike qualities that God is looking for in us? The first must surely be trust, for trust is foundational to any good relationship. In fact, without trust, there *is* no relationship; and without trust, the relationship will never grow. So, God our Father wants us to trust him. Whenever you find that hard, turn to the psalms (like Psalms 23, 46 or 91), for they are packed with declarations of trust to help you.

Another characteristic of young children is weakness. There are things they cannot do. As we get older, few of us like acknowledging there are things we can't do on our own. But if we truly trust someone, we let them in on the areas where we're weak, and not just the areas where we're strong. True childlike trust says, 'This is what I'm really like!' and invites God to come and help.

Jesus doesn't ask us to be childish; but he certainly asks us to be childlike, trusting him and acknowledging our weakness and need of him. With such people, God can do anything!

Those who know your name will trust in you, for you, LORD, have never forsaken those who seek you.
(PSALM 9:10)

358

DECEMBER 17

Waiting for the whispers

Be still before the LORD and wait patiently for him.
(PSALM 37:7)

One of the things that probably most of us find hard to do is to *wait*. Waiting is not easy at the best of times; but after a time of great activity or excitement, it can almost be unbearable. That's how Elijah felt after the exciting demonstrations of God's power in the contest with the prophets of Baal on Mount Carmel. He was now completely exhausted – so exhausted that when Queen Jezebel merely threatened him, he simply ran. What he needed to experience right now was not God's power, but God's presence.

In fact, that's exactly what God brought him. As Elijah stood on the mountain, a great wind came, followed by an earthquake and fire. These were all traditional ways in which God had manifested his power; but, no doubt to his surprise, God appeared in none of them, but rather in 'the sound of a gentle whisper' (1 Kings 19:12, NLT). What Elijah needed to do was to simply *stop* and *listen*; and as he did so, he heard God's whisper.

The Bible invites all of us to be still before the Lord – not because stillness is somehow more holy than noise (in fact, the Bible has far more to say about vibrant, expressive worship than silent worship!); but because being still gives us the opportunity to experience what we might otherwise miss. Being still allows us to 'know that I am God' (Psalm 46:10) and to hear God speak, like Elijah did that day. Being still is a challenge to us westerners with our busy lifestyles; but being still and waiting carries a promise with it, that 'they that wait upon the LORD shall renew their strength; they shall mount up with wings as eagles; they shall run, and not be weary; and they shall walk, and not faint' (Isaiah 40:31, KJV).

If you have been busy recently, running through life at full pelt, God invites you to stop today, to wait for his whispers, and to be ready to hear his voice, just as he promised.

But as for me, I will look to the LORD, I will wait for
the God of my salvation; my God will hear me.
(MICAH 7:7, NRSV)

DECEMBER 18

At work behind the scenes

'It was not you who sent me here, but God.'
(GENESIS 45:8)

Sometimes God's intervention in our lives or in events is fairly obvious. But for most of the time, his intervention generally remains unseen by us until much later. Think, for example, of how you became a Christian; the process probably started long before you ever thought it did. One character in the Bible who certainly came to understand the intervention of God is Joseph – but it was a long and tortuous journey that God took him on to show him this.

Throughout Joseph's story there are constant glimpses of God's intervention 'behind the scenes'. Sometimes it is in the amazing timing of events, like when his brothers, weary of his arrogance, had just thrown him down a well and were contemplating killing him, when Ishmaelite slave traders just happened to pass by at that very moment. At other times it is in the significance of what happened, like when the slave traders just happened to be going down to Egypt, the very place God would use to provide for his people during years of famine. Sometimes it is in the way that he constantly seems to win the favour of those he is put with (like the jailer, Potiphar, and Pharaoh himself). At other times it is in the people he just 'happened to meet' (like Pharaoh's cupbearer and baker while in jail). Through it all, there is the usefulness of the gift of interpretation of dreams that God had given him. A lot of 'coincidences', don't you think?

But it is not until Joseph eventually reveals his true identity to his brothers (and remember, twenty years had passed since they had last seen him and he had only been a teenager at the time, so it is little wonder they didn't recognize him!) that we see that at last 'the penny has dropped', as we see in our opening verse for today.

Be reassured that God is at work in your life too, even if you can't quite see how at this moment. And even when we have made a mess of things, he can gloriously redeem the mess, if only we will 'come clean' with him.

We know that in all things God works for the good of those who love him,
who have been called according to his purpose.
(ROMANS 8:28)

DECEMBER 19

Thankful for answers

LORD, I thank you for answering me.
(PSALM 118:21, NCV)

How do you feel when you've given someone a present and they don't even say, 'Thank you'? Or when you've done someone a favour and it isn't even appreciated? You probably feel disappointed. It's not that you wanted an accolade of gratitude; it's simply that, well, saying thanks is just so appropriate. But if gratitude to one another is appropriate, how much more so when it is due to God, especially when he has answered our prayers. While thankfulness doesn't always come easily, we can train ourselves in it. Here are three simple things that can help.

First, being thankful in everyday life. Thankfulness is a mind-set, and we won't be thankful to God unless it's part of our ordinary, everyday living. Start saying 'Thank you!' much more each day: to the shopkeeper, the bus driver, your child's teacher, the canteen workers, the refuse collectors, the postman. Learn to say thank you for the little things in life, and to the people who normally never get thanked.

Second, keeping a list of answered prayers. Sometimes we aren't thankful to God simply because we just don't think about the answers he has already given. It's almost as if we take his blessings and run! We can remember all sorts of trivia, but do not recall his answers to prayer – even the 'big ones'. One simple way of 'not forgetting' is to write down the things God says and the answers God gives, along with the date that they happened. Because the more we remember, the more we will thank; and the more we thank, the more we will see of God's fresh resources released from heaven.

Third, telling others what God has done for you. Why keep good things to yourself? If God has answered your prayer in some way, tell others about it too. Not only does that glorify God, it will encourage others (if they are Christians) or stir them to think (if they aren't). Telling what God has done for us strengthens the gratitude of our heart.

Which of these three things could you do today to help you become more thankful?

Let them give thanks to the LORD for his unfailing love
and his wonderful deeds for men.
(PSALM 107:8)

DECEMBER 20

Time to trust

I am the LORD, your God, who takes hold of your right hand and says to you, Do not fear; I will help you.
(ISAIAH 41:13)

Not many of us will recognize the name of Jean-Francois Gravelet. But perhaps we are more familiar with his stage name: Blondin. A nineteenth century tightrope-walker, Blondin became famous by crossing the Niagara Falls on a tightrope 1,100 feet long, suspended 160 feet above the rushing waters. In fact, he made the crossing several times, with increasing levels of difficulty: in a sack, with a wheelbarrow, on stilts, sitting down halfway across to cook an omelette. But perhaps his best known crossing was when he asked a bystander if he believed he could do it. 'Absolutely!' the man replied. 'I've got every faith in you.' 'Then why don't you come and sit on my shoulders and cross it with me?' asked Blondin. No doubt the man's face turned pale; but he climbed on Blondin's shoulders and risked it – and, yes, they made it safely across to the other side. Now, that's faith!

And that's rather how it's meant to be with God and us. God invites us to, as it were, 'climb on his shoulders' and to trust him, rather than to stand on the sidelines with our comments, questions or advice thrown safely from a distance. Faith isn't really faith until we step out and risk it. And the time we really risk it is when we can't see the outcome or when the challenges are great; when our own resources are at an end; when we're 'sunk' unless God steps in. But that's what the Christian life is all about: trusting God and not ourselves. The trouble is, we go through so much of life depending on our own strength, resources and gifting (with a prayer for God to add his blessing!), that when it's time to really have to step out in faith it comes as a shock. We start to wonder, 'Where is God?' But he's where he has always been: on the tightrope, waiting for us to climb on his shoulders.

Don't trust in yourself – there's no faith in that. Whatever is facing you today, climb on God's shoulders and trust him. He will not let you down.

Blessed is the man who makes the LORD his trust.
(PSALM 40:4)

DECEMBER 21

God our Saviour

Praise be to the Lord, to God our Saviour, who daily bears our burdens. Our God is a God who saves.
(PSALM 68:19–20)

Mike and his wife were on a boating holiday with friends when they suddenly became aware of people on the opposite riverbank shouting and waving in their direction. Unable to hear what they were saying, they simply gave a cheery wave in return. But when the crowd started frantically pointing downwards, raising their voices still more, they looked over the side of the boat and there, being swept downstream with the strong current, was a young boy, unable to swim. Without a moment's hesitation, Mike's friend leapt into the river to get him out, while Mike hung over the railing to pull him on board. The youngster was saved and was returned to his parents. Of course, we would all have done the same. So, why should it surprise us to discover that God, in whose image we are made, is a God who 'leaps in' to come and help us, a God who is 'our Saviour'?

The word 'salvation' isn't often used these days, even by Christians. Perhaps we think it sounds rather old-fashioned and carries connotations of miserable Christians with big black Bibles. But 'salvation' is a very strong concept in the Bible, where God is constantly described as 'our Saviour'. Throughout the Old Testament God was often acknowledged as his people's Saviour, rescuing them from all sorts of situations. And it was remembering this that provided a strong basis for praise and thanksgiving, a strong motivation to prayer, and a strong encouragement to stand firm in the face of difficulties. As David summed it up: 'You are God my Saviour, and my hope is in you all day long' (Psalm 25:5). In the New Testament the theme becomes even stronger as the Son of God himself became a man, showing the lengths to which God will go to save us.

It is this sure confidence that God himself is our Saviour – not because of anything we have done, but solely because of Christ – that inspires confidence and removes fears so that, with David, we can pray, 'The Lord is my light and my salvation – whom shall I fear?' (Psalm 27:1).

The LORD lives! Praise be to my Rock! Exalted be God,
the Rock, my Saviour!
(2 SAMUEL 22:47)

DECEMBER 22

Born to give us second birth

'I tell you the truth, no-one can see the kingdom of God
unless he is born again.'
(JOHN 3:3)

We both love Christmas carols. They're so much a part of Christmas. In fact, Martin still gets a tingle down his spine in singing 'Yea, Lord we greet Thee, born this happy morning' each Christmas Day. While we perhaps see fewer carol singers in Britain than we once used to, thankfully some still continue, whether for community fund raising, or advertising Christmas services, or for collecting a few coins by youngsters who hardly know the words! Whenever we hear them, there's always something quite moving – like when we hear young children singing 'Away in a manger' or a soloist singing 'Silent night'.

Martin in particular really loves carols. But, while he sometimes leads worship at his local church, he's never yet had the courage to choose a carol for the congregation to sing outside the Christmas period! However, he did once break up a Bible study with a quiz which had a 'carol' question. The study was on 'being born again', focusing on the discussion between Jesus and Nicodemus in John 3. Nicodemus was one of the 'leading lights' of his day as far as religion went; but he still needed to be reborn spiritually – radically changed inside by God's Spirit – in order to see the kingdom of God. Martin's question was this: 'Which Christmas carol mentions the new birth?' No one could think of the answer – well, at least until he told them! It was Charles Wesley's carol, 'Hark! the herald-angels sing', in which the last line of one verse is 'Born to give them second birth'.

Christmas reminds us, not just of Christ's birth, but also of our own need to be 'born again'. So, as carols start to ring in the air once again, now is a good time to stop and ask: have I responded to Jesus' challenge that I need to be born again? If I have, am I living in the good of that? And if I haven't, then what is there to stop me?

He chose to give us birth through the word of truth, that we might be
a kind of firstfruits of all he created.
(JAMES 1:18)

DECEMBER 23

He's come!

When the time had fully come, God sent his Son, born of a woman, born under law, to redeem those under law, that we might receive the full rights of sons.
(GALATIANS 4:4–5)

Waiting, waiting, waiting. The years had ticked by so slowly. And still they were waiting. God had said the Messiah would come; but still they waited. Of course, many became weary and gave up, or adopted their own agendas. Some became revolutionaries (like the Zealots), seeking to bring God's kingdom by force; others pursued legalistic righteousness (like the Pharisees), trying to pave the way. But for the handful of truly faithful, the waiting was at last over. 'The time had fully come'; God's plan of salvation was about to burst onto the scene. Except the plan was not a plan; the plan was a person.

But as the promised Messiah arrived, it was not how people expected. For him, no glorious palace and luxurious cradle; but rather, a humble (and no doubt smelly) stable with a feeding trough from which the animals had just been shooed away. And yet, through the Spirit, some just knew who this was: the Saviour!

Shepherds – working-class men of the time – were the first to hear of his arrival and to join in with the angelic thanksgiving. At the other end of the social scale were the Persian astrologers, wealthy intellectuals of their day, who also came to acknowledge the arrival of the King of Kings with their worship and their gifts. When Jesus was six weeks old and was taken by his parents to the temple, two others added their testimony. Simeon, stirred by the Spirit, went there just as they arrived. Seeing Jesus, he just knew that this was the one they had been expecting for so long. He took him in his arms and thanked God that 'my eyes have seen your salvation' (Luke 2:30). And then a godly prophetess, Anna, came and 'gave thanks to God and spoke about the child to all who were looking forward to the redemption of Jerusalem' (Luke 2:38). At last, the Saviour was here!

As we approach Christmas, let's not lose sight of the very heart of this festival: he's come! May our preparations and celebrations focus on this amazing fact.

The Father has sent his Son to be the Saviour of the world.
(1 JOHN 4:14)

The mystery of the virgin birth

'How will this be,' Mary asked the angel, 'since I am a virgin?'
The angel answered, 'The Holy Spirit will come upon you, and
the power of the Most High will overshadow you. So the holy
one to be born will be called the Son of God.'
(LUKE 1:34–35)

Talk about the virgin birth and the average person in the street will tell you it just couldn't have happened. After all, we know too much about biology these days to believe in that sort of thing, don't we? Surely it was just some story created by the church to show that Jesus was somehow 'special'.

But let's stop and think for a moment: if God *were* to come into this world, why would he have to do so in a way no different to us? Is he so limited, so powerless that he can do no better than we ourselves can do? If that were the case, what a poor God he would be! No, what we have here is a divine miracle, just as promised.

Perhaps the most telling proof of the virgin birth is that neither Mary nor Joseph believed it themselves at first! When Mary was promised that she was about to bear God's Son, she asked, 'How will this be . . . since I am a virgin?' (Luke 1:34). She knew enough of the facts of life to know it was impossible! Joseph too didn't believe it, thinking his wife-to-be had been unfaithful. Only the appearance of another angel convinced him that 'what is conceived in her is from the Holy Spirit' (Matthew 1:20).

The promise of the virgin birth brings home that here was no ordinary child; for this Jesus was the one who had laid aside his divine glory in order to take upon himself a brand new, unspoiled human nature, created by the Holy Spirit for him within Mary's womb, in order that, as a sinless human being, he could pay the price for our sin. What we need to remember is: no virgin birth, no forgiveness!

True, the 'incarnation' was nothing less than a miracle. But then, who wants a God who cannot do miracles?!

Therefore the LORD himself will give you a sign: The virgin will be
with child and will give birth to a son, and will call him Immanuel.
(ISAIAH 7:14)

DECEMBER 25

God with us!

'The virgin will be with child and will give birth to a son, and they will call him Immanuel' – which means, 'God with us.'
(MATTHEW 1:23)

The birth of a baby is always a special event. Think of the joy of parents at their new arrival; of the smiles of family and friends; of flowers and cards that crowd the home or the hospital bedside. What a special time it is! What a cause for celebration!

But the birth of Jesus was a birth like none other before or since, and a cause for celebration like no other. For the New Testament tells us that Jesus was not like any other human being; nor was he simply a 'chosen one', called to be an enlightened prophet or guru that God would one day use; rather, he was the very Son of God, the one who had been with the Father right from the beginning, but who had now come into this world – not as God pretending to be a man, nor as some sort of a half-god half-man – but as a real human being, as fully human as us.

Probably no verse sums up this miracle more succinctly than when John says: 'The word became flesh and made his dwelling among us' (John 1:14). The Greek word John used for 'flesh' is quite a stark one; it is rather like our expression 'flesh and blood'. It is almost as if John is saying: 'Go on – pinch yourself – feel your body – because that's the stuff that Jesus became!'

The conviction of the early church was that when you were looking at Jesus you were looking at no one less than God himself!

At this season of Christmas, we remember once again that the one who has come to us is no mere prophet or holy man; he is none less than God incarnate – *God* with us! – just as God promised long ago through the prophets. Let's thank him today that such was his love for us that he did not send another, but came himself.

For in Christ all the fulness of the Deity lives in bodily form.
(COLOSSIANS 2:9)

I shall return!

But the day of the Lord will come . . .
(2 PETER 3:10)

'I shall return' are words often found of the lips of thwarted villains in films, eager to 'have another go' at their dastardly plan. Sometimes they return, sometimes they don't. But there is a promised return that is absolutely certain: that of Jesus – a promise that he will surely keep, for it is a promise he made often. In fact, there are over 250 references to his return in the New Testament.

But what will this return be like? It's impossible to describe! For it will be the climactic event of life as we know it, transcending everything we have ever known and therefore can describe. In the light of this, we cannot possibly hope to work out all the details (though many try!); and even if we could, the Lord would no doubt have some surprises up his sleeve!

Because there is no systematic teaching about Christ's return in the Bible, Christians come up with different scenarios of what will happen, or in what order things will happen. But nevertheless, some things are promised very clearly and are the ground of our hope.

First, we are told that Christ's return will be *physical*, that is, it really will be him who comes, in person, and not in some vague spiritual way, for he 'will come back in the same way you have seen him go into heaven' (Acts 1:11). Second, his return will be *public*, for there will be nothing hidden or obscure about it, but rather 'as lightning that comes from the east is visible even in the west, so will be the coming of the Son of Man' (Matthew 24:27). Third, it will be *sudden*, for 'the Son of Man will come at an hour when you do not expect him' (Luke 12:40). Fourth, it will be *glorious*, as we see 'the Son of Man coming on the clouds of the sky, with power and great glory' (Matthew 24:30).

The promised return of Jesus at the end of the age is not a doctrine for speculation, but for provocation. Let it provoke us to live in the light of that return today.

The Lord himself will come down from heaven, with a loud command, with the voice of the archangel and with the trumpet call of God.
(1 THESSALONIANS 4:16)

Eyes of faith

*'Sovereign Lord, as you have promised, you now dismiss your
servant in peace. For my eyes have seen your salvation, which
you have prepared in the sight of all people, a light for
revelation to the Gentiles and for glory to your people Israel.'*
(LUKE 2:29–32)

Simeon's song of praise (often known as the 'Nunc Dimittis', from its
first two words in the Latin Bible) has been used by many churches down
the ages. When you think about it, it really took some faith! After all,
what could Simeon see? Just a six-week-old baby, and nothing more. Yet
in faith he spoke out what the Spirit had put in his heart, seeing beyond
what his natural eyes could see. He had only seen a baby; and yet he had
seen enough, for the Sprit had opened his eyes to see in faith and therefore
to speak in faith. And so he gave thanks to God for what this child Jesus
would mean, both to him personally and to the whole world. And now,
having 'seen', he was happy to die in peace.

We can only speak what we can 'see'. That's why it's so important to
take seriously God's promise that he really does want us to see, in order
that, having seen, we might speak out in faith and release the resources
and purposes of heaven onto the earth. The Bible is full of people who
'saw' and 'spoke'. People like Abraham and his wife who were childless;
but Abraham 'saw' the big family that God had promised him and so 'he
did not waver through unbelief regarding the promise of God, but was
strengthened in his faith and gave glory to God, being fully persuaded
that God had power to do what he had promised' (Romans 4:20–21).
People like Elisha who 'saw' the angelic armies of God that were just
waiting for God's signal to move against the Arameans that were
threatening Israel, and which enabled him to speak out boldly God's
promised protection and power.

What does God want you to 'see' today? Ask God to open your eyes
so that you may 'see'; and having 'seen', step out into the promises of
God.

And the LORD asked me, 'What do you see?'
(AMOS 7:8)

DECEMBER 28

The best departure of all!

Now we know that if the earthly tent we live in is destroyed, we have a building from God, an eternal house in heaven, not built by human hands.
(2 CORINTHIANS 5:1)

There's nothing like an exciting departure; like when you've just checked in at the airport for a flight to somewhere new. But the Bible promises that, for those who trust in Christ, there is a departure far more exciting than that: it is the departure that takes us from this life and into the next!

Of course, many people these days are sceptical about an afterlife. 'When you're dead, you're dead' is the most common attitude. 'Wrong!' the Bible says. When you die, you go somewhere, as surely as when entering that airport departure lounge. In fact, the Bible describes death as a 'departure'. When Moses and Elijah appeared at Jesus' transfiguration 'they spoke about his departure, which he was about to bring to fulfilment at Jerusalem' (Luke 9:31); Paul said, 'I desire to depart and be with Christ, which is better by far' (Philippians 1:23). Both were looking forward to their 'departure', to leaving this life and going to somewhere better. But where does the departure take us?

When we die the '*soul*' (that which makes you 'you') and the '*spirit*' (that which relates to God) separate from the body (which is why onlookers often say, 'He's gone!'). The body, which we no longer need, now begins to decay. But for Christians, the Bible promises that this is not the end of the story! For as we slip away from our body and this life, we immediately pass into heaven – and what a wonderful place it is! The Bible describes heaven in many ways: a place of seeing God, serving God, and receiving God's reward; a place of joy, rest, and freedom from all troubles; a place of real fellowship, with Jesus at the centre of everything. But even this is not the end! Heaven itself is but a glorious waiting room for the next departure – God's creation at the End of his 'new heaven and a new earth' (Revelation 21:1).

Be encouraged today about the sure promise of this departure and its destination; and look to share its good news with someone else.

'. . . *with Christ, which is better by far*'.
(PHILIPPIANS 1:23)

When we have failed

*Forgetting what is behind and straining towards what is ahead,
I press on towards the goal to win the prize for which God has
called me heavenwards in Christ Jesus.*
(PHILIPPIANS 3:13–14)

If you are anything like us, there will be times when you fail, times when
you let God down, times when you feel you are going backwards in your
Christian life rather than forwards. There we are, trying to be like Jesus,
trying to love him and follow him – when suddenly, we stumble. And
what is worse: we even do it deliberately at times! So, why does this
happen? The Bible says that it is because sin – forgiven though it is – is
still at work within us. There's a war going on inside: a war between the
still-surviving desires of our old sinful nature and the growing desires of
the new nature that Christ has given us. So sometimes we don't do the
good that we really *want* to do; and sometimes the bad thing we *don't*
want to do is exactly what we end up doing! Ever felt like that? Paul
certainly did, as he describes in Romans 7.

At the moment our lives are rather like a building site: the old ways
are in the process of being demolished, and new ways are starting to
replace them as Jesus the builder, through his Spirit, builds according to
the plans of the Father. Right now, our lives often look like a 'disaster
area' with so many changes going on; but one day the construction work
will result in something beautiful and complete.

So, when we fail, what do we do? Give in? Accept that's just how
things are? That we will have to 'live with it' until we get to heaven? No!
Paul said that we shouldn't get bogged down in the past, in what has
been; rather, we should keep pressing on towards the goal that Jesus has
secured for us.

If you have failed, don't give in! Rather, trust God's promise that he
is still at work in your life and that he *will* bring that work to completion.

*Therefore, since we are surrounded by such a great cloud of witnesses, let us
throw off everything that hinders and the sin that so easily entangles,
and let us run with perseverance the race marked out for us.*
(HEBREWS 12:1)

DECEMBER 30

Partners with the Spirit!

May the grace of the Lord Jesus Christ, and the love of God,
and the fellowship of the Holy Spirit be with you all.
(2 CORINTHIANS 13:14)

Today's prayer is one that most of us will have used often. In many Christian traditions these words of blessing – often called 'the benediction' or 'the grace' – are the final words of a service or meeting. But the final phrase of that prayer – 'the fellowship of the Holy Spirit' – is more staggering than most of us realize, encompassing a powerful promise of God: a promise about *us* being partners with *him*!

The word *fellowship* in Greek means 'participation in something together'. One of its common uses in New Testament times was of a 'business partnership'. Now – apply that to us and what we see is this: the Holy Spirit is saying, 'I want *us* to be business partners! You and me! And all these others that I've brought to the Father. I want us to be partners in the Father's business!' And this 'partnership' is the Spirit's gift to us as much as *grace* is the gift of Jesus and *love* is the gift of the Father.

This 'fellowship of the Holy Spirit' is not some warm glow or cosy spiritual feeling to make us feel good as we leave a meeting; rather, it is the assurance of the Spirit's presence as we go out into the world to make a difference, and the assurance of the Spirit's uniting us with other members of the Body of Christ so that we know we are not alone. Fellowship with the Spirit will *always* be demonstrated in fellowship with one another - and if it doesn't, then there is something terribly wrong.

Today, remember that you are not left alone to 'struggle through' life. If you have put your trust in Christ, then *you* too are a business partner with the Spirit of God himself – and with all God's people! What an encouragement that should be to each one of us!

If you have any encouragement from being united with Christ, if any
comfort from his love, if any fellowship with the Spirit, if any tenderness
and compassion, then make my joy complete by being like-minded,
having the same love, being one in spirit and purpose.
(PHILIPPIANS 2:1–2)

DECEMBER 31

Blessing for the future

Jabez cried out to the God of Israel, 'Oh, that you would bless me and enlarge my territory! Let your hand be with me, and keep me from harm so that I will be free from pain.' And God granted his request.
(1 CHRONICLES 4:10)

Well, here we are: the end of another year; a time to look back and look forward. What lies behind? Probably a mixture of good and bad. What lies ahead? None of us knows. We are like the Israelites on the edge of Canaan when Joshua told them, 'You have never been this way before' (Joshua 3:4). But while he didn't know the way, he knew that God would lead them, and symbolized that by having them follow the ark. For us too, God will move ahead of us this year; all we need to do is to follow.

Having looked at so many of the Bibles' prayers and promises over this past year, it's hard to know where to finish on New Year's Eve. But we want to commend to you the prayer of Jabez (today's opening verse). This most unexpected prayer is tucked away in those endless lists of genealogies in 1 Chronicles. So, why is it there?

At first sight it looks rather selfish, doesn't' it? 'Me . . . me . . . me' seems to be its only focus. Yet God granted his request! Why? The answer lies in the purpose of Chronicles. Written after the return from exile, God's people desperately needed to know that God was still with them. One way the Chronicler showed this was by recording the continuity of God's promises and people, and that's why we have the long list of names and ancestors. But in the midst of the lists, one man stands out as symbolizing what was needed at such a time: someone who would dare to cry out to God to bless him in order that, through him, the whole people of God might be blessed too. His prayer for blessing and expansion was what he had needed – and was exactly what God's people at that time needed too.

We believe that this is exactly what we too need at this time: a blessing, in order to be a blessing. Be bold in asking for it – and giving it – in the coming year!

May your blessing be on your people.
(PSALM 3:8)

Index

This index lists the main Bible verses used in the
opening and closing verses of each day's reading.
However, a wide range of further verses is also
quoted and referred to within the text itself.

Book	Reference	Date
Genesis	1:1-2	Jun 4
	11:6	Jun 22
	13:4	Jan 25
	28:16-17	Jul 5
	32:24-25	Aug 9
	45:8	Dec 18
	49:18	Sep 11
Exodus	3:13-14	Jan 25
	8:1	Mar 15
	14:13-14	Jun 28
	15:3	Oct 20
	15:11	Jan 17
	15:13	Jun 30
	15:26	Jun 24
	20:2-3	Mar 1
	23:25	Aug 26
	33:18	Jan 19
	34:6-7	Jan 28
Leviticus	20:7-8	Jun 15
	20:8	Mar 2
Numbers	6:24-26	Feb 14
	11:14-15	Jun 27
	23:19	Dec 1
Deuteronomy	1:11	Feb 17
	4:7	Feb 21
	6:18	Oct 28
	7:21	Feb 4
	10:21	Jul 7
	15:7, 10	Jul 16
	28:2	Aug 27
	30:9	Sep 16
	31:8	Aug 12
	32:4	Feb 13, Nov 1
	33:25	Feb 19
	33:27	Jan 3, Apr 30
Joshua	1:5	Aug 14
	1:8	Jan 5
	3:9	Nov 21
	14:10-12	Sep 30
Judges	6:17	Apr 27
Ruth	4:14	Oct 13
	4:15	Oct 25
1 Samuel	3:9	Nov 21
	7:12	Sep 24
	17:45-47	Apr 29
	23:16	Jun 13
	30:6	Nov 12
2 Samuel	12:13	Mar 11, Jul 14
	22:4	Apr 12
	22:33	Feb 19
	22:47	Dec 21
1 Kings	6:13	May 24
	8:46, 49	Dec 3
	19:4-5	Jul 31
2 Kings	6:16-17	May 3
	6:17	May 7, Oct 17
1 Chronicles	4:10	Dec 31
	5:20	Jul 2
	28:9	Dec 13
	29:18	Nov 16
	29:22	Jul 18
2 Chronicles	7:1	Nov 6
	15:15	Jun 12
	20:6	Aug 28
	20:12	Aug 28
	30:9	Feb 6
	36:22	Jul 17
Ezra	8:21, 23	Feb 8
	8:23	Feb 9
Nehemiah	8:10	Dec 2
	9:6	Jun 7
Esther	4:16	Jun 18
	8:16	Dec 2

Book	Reference	Date
Job	1:21	Aug 17
	5:2	May 9
	5:17-18	Mar 8
	10:1	Jul 19
	23:10	Aug 19
	26:13-14	Jun 7
	33:13-14	Jul 28
	33:14	May 6
	37:14	Sep 9
	40:2	Nov 1
	42:3-5	Oct 17
	42:5	Mar 18, Aug 15
Psalms	1:1, 3	Sep 15
	3:1-3	Jul 9
	3:7	Jul 19
	3:8	Dec 31
	5:7	Dec 15
	5:12	Nov 19
	8:1	Aug 7
	8:4-5	Sep 13
	9:10	Dec 16
	17:6	Feb 27
	19:14	Jan 5
	22:1	Apr 6
	23:4	Jan 8
	24:3-4	Nov 30
	24:9-10	Feb 12
	25:11	Sep 25
	25:14	Oct 15
	27:1	Jul 3
	27:4	Apr 16
	27:5	Nov 8
	27:13	Jul 15
	28:8	Nov 12
	31:14-15	Apr 30, Nov 3
	32:5	Jul 4, Aug 18
	32:7	Jul 13
	32:8	Jan 24
	33:18	Aug 10
	34:1	Mar 21
	37:7	Sep 22, Dec 17
	38:18	Jul 4, Aug 6
	39:7	Mar 22
	40:1	Sep 22
	40:1-2	Jul 26
	40:4	Dec 20
	42:5	Mar 22
	42:11	Aug 13
	44:26	Oct 13
	46:1	Jul 9
	46:10	Jun 28
	46:11	Feb 12
	47:2	Jan 17
	48:14	May 1
	50:15	Aug 5
	50:23	Jul 7
	51:17	Mar 19
	55:17	Feb 2
	55:22	Aug 3
	55:23	Jul 28
	62:8	Feb 3, Oct 22
	63:1	Jul 26
	64:1	Oct 24
	65:9	Oct 5
	66:18-19	Aug 18
	68:9	Dec 6
	68:19-20	Dec 21
	68:20	Aug 30
	68:35	Mar 7
	75:1	Feb 21
	84:5	Oct 4
	85:6	Jan 12
	85:8	Jan 2
	86:5	Nov 24

Book	Reference	Date
	86:11	May 4
	89:15	Sep 12
	89:26	Sep 2
	91:1-2	Aug 5
	92:12-14	Sep 28
	92:14	Sep 30
	94:18-19	Sep 20
	95:6-7	Sep 13
	95:7-8	Dec 9
	103:2	Sep 24
	103:8-12	Sep 19
	103:11-12	Oct 7
	107:8	Dec 19
	112:1	Jul 22
	113:5	Oct 20
	115:1	Aug 11
	116:7	Jul 15
	116:16	Apr 2
	118:13-14	Jun 27
	118:21	Dec 19
	119:68	Oct 28
	119:71	Jul 27
	119:89	Dec 4
	119:105	Dec 7
	119:130	Dec 7
	121:8	Jun 30
	126:5-6	Sep 26
	130:3-4	Nov 18
	131:2	Sep 9
	133:1, 3	Sep 27, Oct 16
	136:26	Aug 21
	139:10	Jul 20
	139:23	Jul 29, Sep 18
	139:23-24	Jun 19
	142:2	Oct 22
	149:6	Apr 12
Proverbs	3:5-6	Jan 24
	3:11-12	Sep 21
	3:32	Oct 15
	4:6-8	Mar 5
	4:23	Jun 19
	8:17	Jan 16
	8:32	Dec 9
	8:34	Jun 29
	10:9	Jun 20
	14:30	Jun 10
	18:24	Aug 14
	19:23	Oct 1
	21:1	Jul 17
	22:11	Jul 1
	23:17-18	Aug 10
	24:32	Mar 30
	28:13	Jan 27
	28:27	Jul 16
	29:18	Aug 29
	30:8	Sep 6
	30:8-9	Oct 6
Ecclesiastes	3:1-2	Nov 3
	3:22	Sep 23
	4:9-10	Mar 12
	5:2	Feb 3
	5:19	Sep 16
	11:6	Sep 26
Song of Songs	2:3-4	Aug 20
	5:16	Aug 20
Isaiah	1:17	May 13
	1:18	Mar 31, May 6, Dec 14
	2:2-3	Nov 11
	2:3	Apr 17
	6:1	Feb 20
	6:3	Mar 2
	6:5	Jun 15
	7:14	Dec 24
	8:17	Apr 6
	9:2	Mar 14

Book	Reference	Date
	12:2	Mar 13
	26:13	Mar 1
	30:19	Aug 4
	30:21	May 1
	32:1-3	May 7
	37:14	Jun 18
	40:9-10	Feb 4
	40:29	Jan 13
	40:29-31	Mar 7
	41:10	Aug 12
	41:13	Dec 20
	42:16	Apr 27
	43:25	Sep 19, Nov 24
	44:21	Feb 10
	45:22	Mar 28
	46:4	Oct 25
	49:6	May 14
	49:15-16	Feb 10
	52:2-3	Apr 2
	55:1	May 26
	55:2-3	Jun 29
	55:6-7	May 10
	55:8	Dec 12
	55:8-9	Oct 24
	55:10-11	Dec 6
	56:6-7	Jul 11
	58:9	Feb 27
	59:16	Jul 23
	61:3	Jul 31
	64:1-2	Nov 6
	64:4	Jul 23
	64:8	Nov 25
	65:1	Jul 5
	66:1	Feb 1
	66:13	Feb 22
	66:14	Jul 20
Jeremiah	1:6-7	Oct 26
	1:17-19	Nov 28
	2:35	Jun 21
	3:4	Dec 15
	3:12-13	Jul 24
	3:19	Feb 26
	3:22	Feb 23
	10:16	Aug 23
	14:7	Sep 25
	14:20	Jul 24
	15:18	Aug 13
	15:19	Aug 2
	17:5, 7	Oct 4
	17:7-8	Sep 28
	18:6	Nov 25
	18:7-8	Aug 1
	20:7	Aug 2
	23:24	Feb 28
	23:29	Jan 22
	29:7	Mar 20
	29:13-14	Jan 16
	31:13	Jan 21
	31:33	Feb 16
	32:39	Jun 1
	33:3	May 3, Jul 11
Lamentations	2:19	Feb 5, Jul 18
	3:23	Feb 13
Ezekiel	3:3	Jul 22
	11:19	Jun 1
	22:30	Aug 1
	34:11	May 2
	34:16	Mar 29
	36:26-27	May 25
	37:6	May 19
	37:23	Feb 23
Daniel	9:2-3	Oct 21
	10:12-13	Jul 30
	11:32	Dec 8

Book	Ref	Date
Hosea	6:2-3	Nov 14
	6:3	Apr 17
	11:8	Sep 21
	12:3-5	Aug 9
	14:2	Nov 30
Joel	2:12-13	Sep 18
	2:13	Jan 30
	2:15-17	Sep 11
	2:28	May 15
Amos	5:4	Aug 26
	7:8	Dec 27
	8:2	May 8
Obadiah	15	Apr 8
Jonah	4:2-3	Jul 25
Micah	4:2	Apr 26
	6:6, 8	Dec 13
	7:7	Dec 17
	7:18	Oct 7, Nov 18
Nahum	1:7	Nov 8
Habakkuk	2:18-20	Jan 2
	3:2	Jan 12, Oct 23
	3:17-18	Oct 23
	3:19	Mar 13
Zephaniah	3:9	Mar 6
	3:17	Mar 28
Haggai	2:7	Nov 11
Zechariah	4:6	May 22
	8:20-21	Apr 26
	12:10	Feb 18
Malachi	3:10	Sep 17
Matthew	1:23	Dec 25
	5:20	Oct 9
	5:23-24	Nov 7
	6:6	Oct 3
	6:7-8	Feb 11
	6:9	Sep 2, Sep 3, Oct 3
	6:10	Sep 4, Sep 5, Oct 27
	6:11	Sep 6
	6:12	Sep 7
	6:13	Sep 8
	6:14	Mar 16
	6:16	Feb 9
	6:33	Jan 18, Apr 1
	7:11	Apr 22
	10:22	Dec 10
	11:28-30	Jan 13, Aug 16
	13:11	Jun 17
	16:6	Oct 10
	16:18	Feb 7
	16:24-26	Aug 11
	17:20	Jun 16
	18:3	May 25, Aug 31
	18:14	May 2
	18:20	Nov 14
	19:14	Dec 16
	19:21	Jan 9
	19:29	Jan 31
	20:15	May 9
	24:42	Dec 11
	24:44	Dec 11
	26:24	Apr 9
	27:46	Apr 13
	28:18, 20	May 14
	28:20	Jul 21
Mark	1:17	Apr 19
	2:17	Feb 15
	3:28-29	Feb 15
	10:16	Feb 25
	11:25	Mar 16
	13:11	Jun 17
Luke	1:34-35	Dec 24
	1:68	Apr 21
	2:29-32	Dec 27
	3:8	Aug 31
	3:16	May 29
	4:8	Mar 14
	4:18-19	May 28
	7:16	Apr 21
	9:1	Jun 22
	9:1-2	Nov 5
	9:23-24	Jan 31
	10:18	Nov 29
	11:1	Sep 1
	11:2	Feb 26
	11:4	Nov 2, Nov 10
	11:9-10	Jun 26
	12:34	Apr 1
	15:18-19	Jul 14
	17:6	Apr 28
	17:21	Oct 27
	18:13	Aug 6
	18:13-14	Mar 19
	19:9-10	Jan 9
	19:10	Mar 29
	22:31-32	Feb 24, Mar 30, May 13
	22:42	Jun 8
	24:27	Mar 27
	24:32	Apr 16
John	1:45	Mar 27
	3:3	Dec 22
	3:8	May 19
	3:17	Aug 30
	4:13-14	May 26
	4:23	Dec 14
	4:35	May 8
	4:42	Mar 18
	6:11	Oct 12
	6:37	Jun 26
	6:39	Jan 23
	7:37-39	May 23
	8:12	Mar 14
	10:11	Apr 4
	10:27-28	Jan 23
	11:11	Aug 8
	12:21	Jan 7
	14:6	Aug 22
	14:13-14	May 5
	14:16	May 31
	14:17	May 21, Jun 2
	14:18	May 24
	15:5	May 20
	15:13-14	Mar 3
	15:15	Mar 3, Aug 8
	15:16	May 18, Sep 15
	16:7	May 31
	16:13	Jun 5
	16:14	May 17
	16:23	May 5
	17:11	Oct 31
	17:15	Sep 8
	17:21	Nov 15
	17:23	Oct 31
Acts	1:4-5	May 27
	1:5	May 29
	1:8	May 21
	2:31-32	Apr 13
	2:33	May 15
	2:39	May 27
	3:19	Jan 27
	4:12	Aug 22
	4:24	Aug 7
	11:17	Dec 12
	11:21	Jun 17
	11:26	Sep 14
	15:33	Feb 25
	16:25-26	Jul 13
	17:6	Aug 16
	17:30-31	Apr 8
	18:9-10	Jul 21

	19:2, 6	May 23
	20:28	Feb 7
	23:11	Jan 8
	26:19	Aug 29
	27:35	Oct 12
Romans	1:20	Aug 23
	2:4	May 10
	3:4	Jul 6
	3:22-24	Apr 14
	4:18	Oct 2
	4:20-21	May 16
	5:1	Apr 11
	5:8	Mar 25
	5:10	Apr 4
	7:24-25	Mar 11
	8:1	Apr 8
	8:1-2	Apr 14
	8:9	Jun 4
	8:14-15	Nov 27
	8:15	May 11
	8:23	Apr 10
	8:26	Feb 18, Jun 3, Sep 1
	8:28	Jan 20, Dec 18
	8:29	Nov 17
	8:32	Aug 25
	10:12	Aug 24
	10:13	Apr 25
	12:3	Nov 23
	12:4-5	Jun 9
	12:14	Mar 4
	12:17-19	Apr 3
	15:5-6	Oct 16
	15:30	May 12
1 Corinthians	1:8	Dec 10
	1:23-24	Apr 15
	1:25	Apr 29
	3:9	Jun 14
	10:13	Jul 10
	11:23-25	Mar 24
	12:12	Jun 9
	12:13	Jun 6
	12:27	Jan 14, Sep 27
	13:5	Apr 3
	14:1	Jun 12
	15:3	Apr 9
	15:9-10	Mar 31, Apr 19
	15:10	Oct 10
	15:42-43	Apr 10
	15:58	Oct 30
2 Corinthians	1:3-4	Feb 22
	1:4	Jun 13
	1:11	Nov 15
	1:20	Jan 4, Dec 1
	3:18	Sep 14, Nov 17
	5:1	Dec 28
	5:17	Jan 1
	6:16	Mar 6
	7:6	Oct 11
	7:10	Jan 21
	9:6	Sep 17
	12:7-9	Aug 15
	12:8-9	Jul 29
	12:9	Jun 3
	13:14	Dec 30
Galatians	3:9	Apr 28
	3:26-28	Jul 8
	4:4-5	Dec 23
	4:6	Nov 27
	4:6-7	May 11
	4:7	Nov 4
	5:1	Nov 4
	5:22-23	May 20
	6:3-5	Jun 10
	6:9	Oct 30

Ephesians	1:3	Sep 3
	1:4-5	Apr 23
	1:7-8	Apr 22
	1:11-12	Jan 20
	1:13	Aug 24
	1:18-19	Jan 26
	1:22-23	Jan 14
	2:4	Mar 26
	2:19	Apr 24
	3:4-5	May 17
	3:6	Mar 23
	3:14-15	Apr 24
	3:20-21	Nov 5
	4:3-6	Jun 6
	4:30	Jun 2
	5:25	Apr 20
	6:11	Jun 11
	6:13	Mar 9
	6:14	Jun 20, Nov 19
	6:14-15	Nov 28
	6:16	Oct 29
	6:17	Jan 11, Sep 29, Oct 8
	6:18	May 30
Philippians	1:14	Feb 5
	1:23	Dec 28
	2:1-2	Dec 30
	2:12-13	Feb 17
	3:5, 7-8	Oct 9
	3:8	Jan 7, May 4
	3:10	Jan 19, May 22
	3:12	Apr 23
	3:13-14	Dec 29
	4:4	Jan 15
	4:6	Jan 29
	4:6-7	Sep 20
	4:7	Mar 26
	4:11-13	Oct 1
	4:19	Jan 18
	4:20	Apr 18
Colossians	1:9	Sep 5
	1:13-14	Aug 25
	1:16-17	Oct 5
	1:20	Apr 11
	2:2-3	Jul 8
	2:9	Dec 25
	2:15	Nov 29
	2:17	Nov 20
	3:13	Nov 10
	3:15	Jun 25
	3:23-24	Sep 23
1 Thessalonians	2:13	Jan 22
	4:16	Dec 26
	5:8-9	Sep 29
	5:15	Nov 13
	5:16-18	Feb 2, Jun 25
	5:18	Aug 21
	5:24	Oct 26
	5:25	May 12
2 Thessalonians	2:13	May 18
	3:1	Nov 15
	3:2-3	Feb 8
1 Timothy	1:17	Jan 3
	2:1-2	Mar 20
	2:8	Feb 1
	4:10	Apr 25
	6:6-8	Oct 6
2 Timothy	1:1	Mar 23
	1:9	Apr 20
	1:9-10	Apr 15
	2:1	Dec 8
	2:8	Mar 24
	2:13	Nov 16
	3:16-17	Jan 11
Titus	3:4-5	Nov 13

Book	Reference	Date
Philemon	3	Jul 25
	22	Jul 2
Hebrews	2:14	Oct 18
	2:17-18	Oct 18
	2:18	Mar 10
	3:15	Feb 6
	4:12	Oct 8, Dec 5
	4:13	Feb 28
	4:15-16	Mar 10
	6:15	Oct 19
	6:17-18	Jan 10
	7:24-25	Feb 24
	7:27	Oct 14
	9:28	Oct 14
	10:23	Jan 4
	10:24-25	Oct 11
	10:35-36	Oct 19
	11:1	Jun 23
	11:6	Jun 16
	11:11	Jun 23
	12:1	Oct 2, Dec 29
	12:5-6	Mar 8
	12:7	Jul 27
	12:28	Mar 17
	12:28-29	Sep 4
	13:6	Jul 3
	13:8	Jan 10
	13:15	Jan 15, Mar 21
James	1:2-4	Jul 10
	1:5	Mar 5
	1:17	Jul 6
	1:18	Dec 22
	1:21	Dec 5
	1:22	Jul 12
	1:23-25	Jul 12
	2:17	Sep 10
	2:20	Sep 10
	2:23	Jul 1
	4:2	Jan 29
	4:2-3	Nov 22
	4:6	Jan 6
	4:7	Jun 11, Jul 30
	4:14-15	Aug 17
	5:11	Jan 30
	5:14-15	Jun 24
1 Peter	1:3-4	Nov 26
	1:18-19	Mar 25
	1:23-25	Dec 4
	2:5	Jun 14
	2:9	Jan 26
	2:10	Feb 16
	2:24	Apr 7
	3:9	Nov 2
	3:18	Apr 7
	4:7	Jan 6
	5:6	Nov 23
	5:7	Aug 3
	5:8-9	Mar 9
	5:10	Jan 28
2 Peter	1:3	Nov 26
	2:9	Aug 19
	3:10	Dec 26
1 John	1:6-7	Sep 12
	1:8-9	Sep 7, Dec 3
	1:9	Jun 21
	2:10	Nov 7
	2:27	May 28, Nov 20
	3:1	Nov 9
	3:2	Nov 9
	3:21-22	Aug 27, Nov 22
	4:11	Mar 12
	4:14	Dec 23
	5:4	Oct 29
	5:6	Jun 5

Book	Reference	Date
	5:14	Jun 8, Aug 4
	5:14-15	Oct 21
2 John	3	Feb 14
3 John	2	Feb 18
Jude	20	May 16, May 30
	24-25	Apr 18
Revelation	4:2	Feb 20
	11:15	Mar 17
	19:1	Apr 5
	19:6	Apr 5
	21:5	Jan 1

THE EAGLE BIBLE REFERENCE LIBRARY

THE EAGLE HANDBOOK OF BIBLE PRAYERS

Compiled by
Martin Manser & Mike Beaumont

How should I pray? - When should I pray? - Who should I pray to? - What should I pray about? - Why pray at all? - Does God answer prayer? - What about prayers that aren't answered?

You will find the answers to these questions and many more in this book. **The Eagle Handbook of Bible Prayers** covers every single prayer in the Bible. It groups them in such a way as to make them relevant to your daily life and to provide an overview of the Bible's teaching on prayer. Prayers of joy and sorrow, thanks and pain; long prayers and short prayers; famous prayers and obscure prayers - you will find them all here. Over 2500 verses and more than 2500 additional references have been carefully selected from most books of the Old and New Testaments and also includes prayers drawn from throughout Church history.

The Eagle Handbook of Bible Prayers is divided into six sections: Prayers that say:

'FATHER' - examining our relationship with a God who reveals himself as our Father and who encourages us to get to know him.

'AMAZING' - learning to praise God from our hearts because of who he is.

'THANKS' - thanking God for who he is, what he has done in creation and salvation, and in our own lives.

'SORRY' - the blessings of confession, repentance, restitution.

'WHY?' - being honest in prayer and praying when perplexed or angry.

'PLEASE' - praying about the needs of others (whether individuals or nations) and ourselves.

ISBN 0 86347 442 X   320pp HB £16.99

THE EAGLE BIBLE REFERENCE LIBRARY

THE EAGLE HANDBOOK OF BIBLE PROMISES

Compiled by
Martin Manser & Mike Beaumont

Are God's promises still relevant today?
If so, what assurances does God give for this life
and the hereafter?
What part do we play in seeing God's promises to us fulfilled?

Discover not only **the promises of God** but also **the God of the promises** as you are personally encouraged and challenged throughout this book.

The Eagle Handbook of Bible Promises covers all the promises in the Bible and orders them thematically as they apply to daily life. It contains over 2,000 verses, carefully selected from every book in the Bible as well as over 3,500 additional references for further study.

Section headings:

KNOWING GOD – understanding and claiming the mystery of a great and loving God

TRUSTING JESUS – making the promises of the Saviour our own

GROWING IN THE SPIRIT – harnessing the power of the Spirit

BELONGING TO THE CHURCH – becoming an effective part of Christ's body on earth

LIVING IN THE WORLD – promises to help us live victoriously in the real world

GETTING READY FOR THE FUTURE – waiting on the promises of future glory

ISBN : 0 86347 586 8 320pp HB £16.99

THE BIBLE APPLICATION HANDBOOK
By
J.I. Packer and Derek Williams

The Bible Application Handbook brings home book-by-book and chapter-by-chapter the message of the Bible today.

- Helps you understand what the text is really saying
- Suggests how each passage can be applied to your daily attitudes, actions, beliefs and behaviour
- Is based on the New International Version of the Bible
- Is arranged alphabetically for easy access - no long searches for Amos or Zephaniah!
- Contains articles related to - and illustrated by - everyday experiences and current issues
- Explains each book of the Bible chapter - chapter
- Contains the following book-by-book features:

AT A GLANCE: An overall summary and a chapter-by-chapter listing.

FOR TODAY: Sums up key application in each book for further thought and action.

FAST FACTS: Quick guides to the historical, religious and literary background, setting each book in its context.

WHERE AM I?: Locates each book in its chronological and biblical place, so that you know where you are in the story.

HARD QUESTION: Tackles head-on the hard questions of practice and belief raised by the text so as to encourage faith.

KEY QUOTE: Highlights a key verse for each book as a focus for its theme and message.

ISBN : 0 86347 482 9 432pp HB £16.99